Intellectual Property Law in France

Intellectual Property Law in France

Third Edition

Nicolas Bouche

This book was originally published as a monograph in the International Encyclopaedia of Laws/Intellectual Property Law.

Founding Editor: Roger Blanpain
General Editor: Frank Hendrickx
Volume Editor: Hendrik Vanhees

Wolters Kluwer

Published by:
Kluwer Law International B.V.
PO Box 316
2400 AH Alphen aan den Rijn
The Netherlands
Website: www.wolterskluwerlr.com

Sold and distributed in North, Central and South America by:
Wolters Kluwer Legal & Regulatory U.S.
7201 McKinney Circle
Frederick, MD 21704
United States of America
Email: customer.service@wolterskluwer.com

Sold and distributed in all other countries by:
Quadrant
Rockwood House
Haywards Heath
West Sussex
RH16 3DH
United Kingdom
Email: international-customerservice@wolterskluwer.com

ISBN 978-90-411-9054-3

e-Book: ISBN 978-90-411-9060-4
web-PDF: ISBN 978-90-411-9066-6

This title is available on www.kluwerlawonline.com

The Author

Nicolas Bouche is Doctor of Law and Senior Lecturer (*Maître de Conférences*) at the University Jean Moulin – Lyon 3 where he teaches Civil Law, International Private Law, and Intellectual Property Law. He studied at the University of Dijon (Burgundy). During the preparation of his thesis about the principle of territoriality in intellectual property, he made a research stay in the Max-Planck Institute for Foreign and International Patent, Copyright and Competition Law (Munich), with a student's grant of the Max-Planck Society. He received his doctoral degree in 1999 and his thesis was published in 2002 ('Le principe de territorialité de la propriété intellectuelle', Paris, Budapest, Torino, L'Harmattan, Coll. Logiques juridiques, 2002). He is director of the Graduate Master Degree on Intellectual Property Law (*Master 2 Droit de la propriété intellectuelle*) at the University Jean Moulin – Lyon 3, and a contributor to the French law review 'Propriété industrielle'.

The Author

Table of Contents

The Author 3

List of Abbreviations 21

General Introduction 23

Chapter 1. General Background 23

§1. Geography 23

§2. Political System 23

I. The Legislative Power 23
II. The Executive Power 24
III. The Judicial Power 24

§3. Sources of French Law 25

I. Written Sources 25
II. Unwritten Sources 26

§4. Structure of the French Law 28

I. Private Law 28
II. Public Law 29

Chapter 2. Introduction to Intellectual Property Law 30

Part I. Copyright and Neighbouring Rights 33

Chapter 1. Sources: Legislation 33

Chapter 2. Subject Matter of Protection 34

§1. Different Categories of Protected Works 34

I. Literary Works 34
A. Written Works 34

B. Oral Works 34
II. Musical Works 35
III. Art Works 36
A. Architecture Works 36
B. Copies of Art Works 36
C. Photographs 36
D. Designs and Models 37
E. Fashion Creations 37
IV. Audiovisual Works 37

§2. Works Excluded of Protection 37

§3. Special Categories of Works 38

I. Computer Software 38
A. Conditions of Protection 38
B. Ownership 38
C. Scope of Protection 39
1. Exploitation Right 39
2. Moral Right 40
D. Infringement and Remedies 40
II. Databases 41
A. Protection by Copyright 41
1. Databases as Derived Works 41
2. Exceptions to Copyright Protection 42
3. Evidence of Infringement 42
B. Sui Generis Protection 42
1. Subject Matter of Protection 43
2. Beneficiaries of Protection 43
3. Scope of the Protection 43
4. Provisional Measures (Article L. 343-2) 45
5. Sanctions 46
6. Criminal Sanctions 46
7. Civil Sanctions 47
8. Evidence of Infringement 47
III. Others 48

Chapter 3. Conditions of Protection 49

§1. Formal Requirements 49

§2. Substantive Requirements 49

I. Work of the Mind 50
II. Requirement of Originality 50
III. No Other Requirements 51

A. The Type and Form of the Work Are Meaningless 51
B. The Merit of the Work Is Meaningless 52
C. The Purpose of the Work Is Meaningless 52

Chapter 4. Ownership 53

§1. The Author (Initial Authorship) 53

§2. Joint Works/Works Created by Several Persons 54

I. Joint Works 54
II. Composite (or Derived) Works 56
III. Collective Works 57

§3. Works Made for Hire 57

Chapter 5. Transfer 59

§1. Formal Requirements 59

I. Evidence 59
II. Listing of Transferred Rights 59

§2. Substantive Requirements 60

I. Prohibition of Global Assignment 60
II. Author's Remuneration 61

§3. Collective Management of Rights 62

Chapter 6. Scope of Exclusive Rights 65

§1. Moral Right (Droit Moral) 65

I. The Components of the Moral Right 65
II. The Characteristics of the Moral Right 69
III. Moral Right on Works Created by Several Persons 71
A. Moral Right on Joint Works 71
B. Moral Right on Composite Works 72
C. Moral Right on Collective Works 72

§2. Exploitation Rights 73

I. Reproduction Right 73
II. Performing Right 74
III. Adaptation and Translation Rights 75

IV. Other Rights 75
A. 'Droit de suite' or Resale Right 75
B. Right of Destination 77
C. Public Lending Right 77

Chapter 7. Limitations to the Scope of Copyright Protection 79

§1. Exceptions to Reproduction Right 79

I. Private Copies 79
II. Exceptions for Public Use 81
III. Technical Copies 83
IV. Safeguard Copies 83

§2. Exceptions to Performing Right 83

§3. Exceptions to Both Reproduction Right and Performing Right 84

I. For Purpose of Illustration for Teaching or Scientific Research 84
II. For the Benefit of People with a Disability 84
III. For Purpose of News Reporting 84

Chapter 8. Duration of Protection 85

Chapter 9. Neighbouring Rights 87

§1. Common Provisions 87

§2. Rights of Performing Artists 89

I. Exploitation Rights 89
II. Moral Rights 91
III. Transfer of Rights 91
A. General Rules 92
B. Rules Specific to the Contract for Production of an Audiovisual Work 92

§3. Rights of Producers of Phonograms and Videograms 93

I. Definitions 93
A. Definition of Producers of Phonograms 93
B. Definition of Producers of Videograms 93
II. Content of Rights 93
A. Principles 93

B. The Legal Licence Relating to Phonograms Published for Commerce 94
III. Transfer of Rights 95

§4. Rights of Audiovisual Communication Firms 96

Chapter 10. Infringement, Procedure, and Remedies 97

§1. Infringement 97

I. Violation of the Reproduction Right 97
II. Violation of the Performing Right 98
III. Violation of the 'Droit de Suite' 98
IV. Violation of Moral Right 98
V. Offer to the Public, Export and Import 99
VI. Violation of the Neighbouring Rights 99

§2. Procedure 100

§3. Remedies 105

I. Criminal Sanctions 105
A. Principal Remedies 105
B. Supplementary Sanctions 106
C. Criminal Protection of Technological Measures and Rights-Management Information 107
II. Civil Remedies 108

Chapter 11. Relation to Other Intellectual Property Rights 110

§1. Copyright and Registered Designs and Models 110

§2. Copyright and Trademarks 110

§3. Copyright and Patents 110

Part II. Patents 111

Chapter 1. Sources: Legislation 112

Chapter 2. Patentable Subject Matter 113

§1. Creations Not Deemed as Inventions 113

I. Discoveries, Scientific Theories, and Mathematical Methods 113

II. Aesthetic Creations 113
III. Plans, Principles, and Methods as Well as Presentation of Information 113
IV. Computer Software 114
V. Presentation of Information 114

§2. Inventions Contrary to Public Order or Good Morals 114

§3. Medicine 114

§4. Biotechnologies 115

§5. The Second Therapeutic Application 116

§6. Inventions Made or Used in Outer Space 117

Chapter 3. Conditions of Patentability 118

§1. Novelty 118

I. The Invention Must Be Compared to the State of the Art 118
A. Abusive Disclosure 119
B. Disclosure at a Public Exhibition (Article L. 611-13, b) 119
C. Disclosure Covered by a Priority Right 120
II. The Invention Must Be External to the State of the Art 121

§2. Inventive Step (Non-obviousness) 121

I. The Invention Must Be Compared to the State of the Art 121
II. The Invention Must Not Be Obvious as Compared to the State of the Art 122

§3. Industrial Application 123

Chapter 4. Formalities 124

§1. Filing of a French Patent Application 124

I. The Applicant 124
II. The Place of the Application 124
III. The Content of the Application 125
A. General Rules 125
B. The Request 125
C. The Description 126
1. The Physical Requirements 126
2. Characters of the Description 127

D. The Claims 127
1. Formal Requirements (Article L. 612-6) 127
2. Substantive Requirements 128
3. Adaptation of the Claims 128
E. The Drawings 129
F. The Abstract 129
G. Justification of Payment of Fees 129

§2. Processing of a French Patent Application 130

I. Examination 130
A. Examination by the Ministry of Defence 130
B. Examination by the INPI 130
II. Documentary Search 131
III. Publication of the Application 132
IV. Grant of the Patent 132

Chapter 5. Scope of Exclusive Rights 134

§1. Renunciation to or Limitation of a Patent Claim 134

§2. Acts Prohibited Without Condition of the Infringer's Bad Faith 135

§3. Acts Prohibited under Condition of the Infringer's Bad Faith 136

Chapter 6. Ownership and Transfer 138

§1. Ownership 138

I. General Rules 138
II. Joint Ownership 138
III. Ownership in Employees' Inventions 139
A. Classification of Employees' Inventions 139
1. Criterias of Classification 139
2. Procedure of Classification 140
B. Dispute Resolution 140
IV. Ownership in Officials' or Public Servants' Inventions 141

§2. Transfers 141

I. Assignment of a French Patent 142
A. Conditions of the Assignment 142
1. Formal Conditions 142
2. Substantive Conditions 142

B. Effects of the Assignment 143
1. Transfer of Rights 143
2. Parties' Obligations 143
a. The Transferor's Obligations 143
b. The Transferee's Obligations 144
II. French Patent Licence 144
A. Conditions of the Patent Licence 145
1. Formal Conditions 145
2. Substantive Conditions 145
a. Conditions Relating to the Parties 145
b. Conditions Relating to the Object 145
B. Effects of the Patent Licence 146
1. The Licensor's Obligations 146
a. Delivery 146
b. Warranty 146
c. Other Obligations 147
2. The Licensee's Obligations 148
a. Obligation to Pay the Price 148
b. Obligation to Exploit the Patent 148
c. Other Obligations 149

Chapter 7. Limitations and Exceptions: Compulsory Licences 150

§1. Limitations and Exceptions to the Scope of Patent Protection 150

§2. Compulsory Licences 151

I. Expropriation 151
II. Compulsory Licences 151
A. Compulsory Licences of Judicial Origin 151
1. Compulsory Licence for Lack of Exploitation (Article L. 613-11–L. 613-14) 151
2. Compulsory Licence for Dependency (Article L. 613-15) 152
B. Compulsory Licences of Administrative Origin 153
1. Automatic Licence in the Interest of Public Health (Article L. 613-16 and L. 613-17-1) 153
2. Automatic Licence in the Interest of Economic Development (Article L. 613-18) 154
3. Automatic Licence in the Interest of National Defence (Article L. 613-19) 154
4. Automatic or Compulsory Licence in the Interest of Competition 155

Chapter 8. Duration of Protection 156

§1. Date of Coming into Force of Patent Rights 156

§2. Date of Termination of Patent Rights 156

I. Total Termination of Rights 156
II. Partial Termination of Rights (Exhaustion) 157

Chapter 9. Infringement and Remedies 159

§1. Action for Declaration of Non-infringement 159

§2. Action for Infringement 159

I. The Starting of the Action 159
II. The Development of the Action 160
A. The Plaintiff's Arguments 160
1. Determination of the Protected Technique 160
2. Determination of the Infringing Technique 161
3. Comparisons Between the Protected and the Infringing Techniques 162
B. The Defendant's Arguments 162
III. The Outcome of the Action 163
A. Temporary Injunction (Article L. 615-3) 164
B. Dismissal of the Action 164
C. Success of the Action 165
1. Civil Sanctions 165
2. Criminal Sanctions 166

Chapter 10. Relation to Other Intellectual Property Rights 168

Part III. Utility Models 169

Chapter 1. Sources and Legislation Relating to 'Certificates of Utility' 170

§1. Substantive Conditions of Protection 170

§2. Formal Conditions of Protection 170

Chapter 2. The Protection of Utility Models 171

Part IV. Trademarks 173

Chapter 1. Sources: Legislation 174

Chapter 2. Subject Matter of Protection 175

Table of Contents

§1. Signs Which May Not Serve as Trademarks 175

§2. Signs Which May Serve as Trademarks 176

I. Denominations 176
A. Current Words 176
B. Fantasy Words 177
C. Letters, Numerals, Acronyms 177
D. Surnames and Pseudonyms 177
1. The Trademark Owner's Name 177
2. A Third Person's Name 178
E. Geographical Names 178
II. Audible Signs 178
III. Figurative Signs 178

§3. Collective Trademarks 179

I. 'Ordinary Collective Trademarks' 179
II. 'Collective Trademarks of Certification' 179

Chapter 3. Conditions of Protection of Trademarks 181

§1. The Sign Must Be Distinguishing 181

I. Criteria of the Distinguishing Character 181
A. The Sign Must Not Consist of the Common Designation of the Object 181
1. Generic or Necessary Signs 181
2. Usual Signs 182
B. The Sign Must Not Consist of the Necessary or Essential Shape of the Product 182
II. Date of Evaluation of the Distinguishing Character 183

§2. The Sign Must Be Vacant 183

I. Conflict with an Earlier Trademark (Article L. 711-4 a) 183
II. Conflict with the Name or Style of a Company (Article L. 711-4 b) 184
III. Conflict with a Geographical Name (Article L. 711-4 d) 185
IV. Conflict with Trade Names or Shop Signs (Article L. 711-4 c) 185
V. Conflict with a Right on a Design or Model (Article L. 711-4, f) 186
VI. Conflict with Copyright (Article L. 711-4, e) 186
VII. Conflict with Personal Rights (Article L. 711-4, g and h) 186

Chapter 4. Formalities 188

§1. Filing of Applications 188

§2. Processing of Applications 189

I. Examination 189
II. Publication 189
III. Observations and Oppositions by Third Parties 190
A. Observations 190
B. Oppositions 190
IV. Registration 191

Chapter 5. Scope of Exclusive Rights 192

§1. Infringement Without Likelihood of Confusion 192

I. Reproduction 192
II. Use 194
III. Affixing 196
IV. Suppression or Modification 196

§2. Infringement with Likelihood of Confusion 196

I. Use for Similar Goods or Services 196
II. Use of an Imitated Trademark 197
III. Condition of Likelihood of Confusion 197
IV. Protection of Well-Known Trademarks 198

Chapter 6. Ownership and Transfer 199

§1. Ownership 199

§2. Transfer 199

I. Assignment of Trademark 199
A. Conditions of Assignment 200
1. Substantial Conditions 200
2. Formal Conditions 201
B. Effects of the Assignment 201
II. Licence 201
A. Conditions of the Licence 202
1. Substantial Conditions 202
2. Formal Conditions 202
B. Effects of the Licence 202
1. The Licensor's Obligations 203

a. Warranty of Hidden Defects 203
b. Warranty of Eviction (or of Peaceful Enjoyment) 203
c. Other Obligations 203
2. The Licensee's Obligations 204

Chapter 7. Exceptions and Limitations 205

§1. The Use by the Owner of an Earlier Right 205

§2. The Use as a Necessary Reference 205

§3. The Use as a Geographical Indication 205

§4. The Use in 'Comparative Advertising' 205

Chapter 8. Use Requirements 207

Chapter 9. Duration of Protection 208

§1. Date of Entry into Force 208

§2. Date of Extinguishment 208

I. Normal Date of Extinguishment 208
II. Anticipated Date of Extinguishment 208

Chapter 10. Infringement and Remedies 211

§1. Preliminary Proceedings 211

§2. The Starting of the Action for Infringement 212

§3. The Development of the Action for Infringement 213

I. The Plaintiff's Arguments 213
II. The Defendant's Arguments 214

§4. The Outcome of the Action for Infringement 215

I. Temporary Measures 216
II. Definitive Measures 217
A. Civil Sanctions of Infringement 217
1. Injunction 217
2. Recall, Removal, Confiscation, Destruction, or Publicity Measures 217
3. Damages 218

B. Criminal Sanctions of Infringement 219
C. Customs Sanctions of Infringement 219

Chapter 11. Relation to Other Intellectual Property Rights 221

§1. Trademarks and Patents 221

§2. Trademarks, Designs, and Models and Copyright 221

§3. Trademarks and Trade Names 221

§4. Trademarks and Geographical Names 222

Part V. Trade Names 225

Chapter 1. Sources: Legislation 226

Chapter 2. The Protection of Trade Names 227

§1. Acquisition 227

§2. Transfer 227

§3. Protection 227

Part VI. Industrial Designs 229

Chapter 1. Sources: Legislation 230

Chapter 2. Conditions of Protection 231

§1. The Shape Should Be Independent from Its Function 231

§2. The Shape Should Be Visible 232

§3. The Shape Should Be New 232

§4. The Shape Should Be Individual 234

Chapter 3. Formalities 235

§1. The Ordinary Registration 235

§2. The Simplified Registration (Article L. 512-2) 236

Chapter 4. Ownership and Transfer 237

Table of Contents

§1. Ownership 237

§2. Transfer 237

Chapter 5. Scope of Exclusive Rights 239

§1. General Rules 239

§2. The Exclusive Right to Use 239

§3. The Exclusive Right to Offer to Sell 240

§4. The Exclusive Right to Import 240

Chapter 6. Limitation of the Scope of Protection 241

Chapter 7. Duration of Protection 242

Chapter 8. Infringement and Remedies 243

§1. Starting of the Action for Infringement 243

§2. Development of the Action for Infringement 244

I. The Plaintiff's Arguments 244
II. The Defendant's Arguments 246

§3. Outcome of the Action for Infringement 247

I. Dismissal of the Action 247
II. Success of the Action 247
A. Success of the Criminal Action 247
B. Success of the Civil Action 248

Chapter 9. Relation to Other Intellectual Property Rights 250

§1. Relations with Patents 250

§2. Relations with Copyright 251

§3. Relations with Trademarks 251

Part VII. Plant Variety Protection 253

Chapter 1. Sources: Legislation 253

Chapter 2. Subject Matter of Protection 254

Chapter 3. Conditions of Protection 255

§1. Novelty 255

§2. Distinctness 256

§3. Uniformity 257

§4. Stability 258

Chapter 4. Formalities 259

Chapter 5. Scope of Exclusive Rights 264

Chapter 6. Ownership and Transfer 265

§1. Contractual Transfers 265

§2. Authoritative Transfers 265

Chapter 7. Limitations of the Scope of Protection 268

Chapter 8. Duration of Protection 270

Chapter 9. Infringement and Remedies 271

Chapter 10. Relation to Other Intellectual Property Rights 275

§1. Relations to Patents 275

§2. Relations to Trademarks 276

Part VIII. Chip Protection 277

Chapter 1. Sources: Legislation 277

Chapter 2. Subject Matter of Protection 278

Chapter 3. Conditions of Protection 279

Chapter 4. Formalities 280

Chapter 5. Ownership and Transfer 281

Table of Contents

§1. Ownership 281

§2. Transfer 281

Chapter 6. Scope of Exclusive Rights 282

Chapter 7. Limitations of the Scope of Protection 283

Chapter 8. Duration of Protection 284

Chapter 9. Infringement and Remedies 285

Chapter 10. Relation to Other Intellectual Property Rights 289

Part IX. Trade Secrets/Confidential Information 291

Chapter 1. Sources: Legislation 291

Chapter 2. The Protection 293

§1. Criminal Liability for Usurpation of Know-How 293

§2. Civil Liability for Disclosure of Know-How 294

§3. Liability in Contracts 294

Selected Bibliography 297

Index 317

List of Abbreviations

Ann. propr. Ind.	*Annales de la propriété industrielle*
Art.	Article
Bull. civ.	*Bulletin des arrêts de la Cour de cassation, chambres civiles*
Bull. crim.	*Bulletin des arrêts de la Cour de cassation, chambre criminelle*
Cass. civ. 1	*Cour de cassation, Première chambre civile*
Cass. civ. 2	*Cour de cassation, Deuxième chambre civile*
Cass. civ. 3	*Cour de cassation, Troisième chambre civile*
Cass. com.	*Cour de cassation, Chambre commerciale*
Cass. Ass. plén.	*Cour de cassation, Assemblée plénière*
CCE	*Communication, commerce électronique*
CFI	Court of First Instance of the European Communities
Chron.	Chronique
Coll.	Collection
comm.	Commentaire
concl.	Conclusions
D.	*Recueil Dalloz-Sirey*
D. Aff.	*Recueil Dalloz, Cahier Droit des affaires*
doct.	Doctrine
EC	European Community
ECJ	European Court of Justice
ed.	Edition
EEC	European Economic Community
EEA	European Economic Area
EU	European Union
Gaz. Pal.	*Gazette du Palais*
I.R.	Informations rapides
JCP	*La semaine juridique (édition générale)*

JCP ed. E.	*La semaine juridique (édition entreprise)*
JCP ed. CI	*La semaine juridique (édition commerce et industrie)*
JORF	*Journal Officiel de la République française*
jur.	Jurisprudence
LPA	*Les petites affiches*
No.	Number
obs.	Observation
OJEC L	Official Journal of the European Community (legislation)
OJEC C	Official Journal of the European Community (communication)
p.	Page
pan.	Panorama
PIBD	*Propriété industrielle, Bulletin documentaire de l'Institut National de la Propriété Industrielle*
Propr. ind.	*Propriété industrielle* (WIPO, Geneva)
Propr. industr.	*Propriété industrielle*
Propr. intell.	*Propriétés intellectuelles*
RDPI	*Revue du droit de la propriété intellectuelle*
Rev. crit. DIP	*Revue critique de droit international privé*
Rev. dr. Aff. Int.	*Revue de droit des affaires internationales*
Rev. dr. propr. Ind	*Revue du droit de la propriété industrielle*
RIDA	*Revue internationale du droit d'auteur*
RIDC	*Revue internationale de droit comparé*
RIPIA	*Revue internationale de la propriété industrielle et artistique*
RTD civ.	*Revue trimestrielle de droit civil*
RTD com.	*Revue trimestrielle de droit commercial*
S.	*Sirey (revue)*
et seq.	and following
som.	*sommaire or sommaires commentés*
T. civ.	Tribunal civil
T. com.	*Tribunal de commerce*
T. corr.	*Tribunal correctionnel*
TGI	*Tribunal de grande instance*

General Introduction

Chapter 1. General Background

§1. Geography

1. France (officially called the French Republic – *République française*) is located in the western part of Europe; from the West to the East and from the North to the South it is boarded by the North Sea, the English Channel, Atlantic Ocean, Spain, the Mediterranean Sea, Italy, Switzerland, Germany, Luxembourg, and Belgium. It covers an area of about 551,000 sq km and has the approximate shape of a hexagon. According to census results, the population of France is 65 million inhabitants.[1]

§2. Political System

2. The Constitution, basis of the Fifth Republic, was promulgated on 4 October 1958. The French Republic is a unitary (non-federal) State; it is a founding member of the European Union (EU) since the Treaty of Rome (1957). The administrative areas into which France is divided for central administrative purposes are: communes (36,700), departments (101), and regions (13). The territory of the Republic also comprises overseas communes (112), departments and regions (5 'DROM', for 'Départements et Régions d'Outre-Mer'), communities (5 'COM', for 'Collectivités d'Outre-Mer'), and territories.

3. The general structure of the state is based on the principle of separation of powers between the legislative, executive, and judicial.

I. The Legislative Power

4. Since the Constitution of 1958, the legislative function is shared between the Parliament and the Government. The French bicameral Parliament consists of the National Assembly (Assemblée Nationale) whose members are elected by direct universal suffrage for five years and the Senate (Sénat) whose members are elected

1. Decree No. 2015-1851 of 29 Dec. 2015 (JORF, 31 December) which authenticates the results of the 2013 census.

by indirect suffrage for six years. In order to be enacted, a statute must be voted by each of the Chambers. In exceptional cases, the Constitution allows a referendum.

5. The Government may also enact so-called autonomous regulations in matters which are not exclusively assigned by the Constitution to the Parliament.

II. The Executive Power

6. The executive functions are exercised by the President of the Republic (elected for five years by direct universal suffrage) and the Government, headed by a Prime Minister appointed by the President of the Republic. The Government's political responsibility may be brought into play either on the initiative of the National Assembly, using the motion of censure against the Government, or by the Prime Minister who may engage the responsibility of his Government before the National Assembly. He may do so either on the Government's programme, or on a general policy declaration, or on the vote of a statute by the National Assembly. If a motion of censure is passed, the Government must resign.

III. The Judicial Power

7. The judicial function is divided between two systems of courts: judicial and administrative, as a consequence of the French interpretation of the principle of separation of powers (it is thought that this principle would be violated if the judiciary could intervene in the administrative process). Therefore, the court structure in France includes two different and distinct hierarchies: the judicial and the administrative.

8. The judicial system consists of 164 regular courts ('*Tribunaux de grande instance*') and a series of specialized courts (commercial courts, criminal courts, labour law courts, social security courts, etc.); appeals are brought in one of the thirty-seven courts of appeal ('Cours d'appel'). The hierarchy is headed by the '*Cour de cassation*', Supreme Court for civil and criminal matters. The public interest is carried on by a specialized body of agents called the '*Ministère Public*' (public attorneys), who have the status of magistrates.

9. The administrative system consists of forty-two administrative courts ('*Tribunaux administratifs*') and eight appellate administrative courts ('*Cours administratives d'appel*'); the hierarchy is headed by the '*Conseil d'Etat*' (Council of State). Conflicts of jurisdiction between judicial and administrative courts are solved by the '*Tribunal des conflits*' (Tribunal of Conflicts), which consists of an equal number of judges from the '*Cour de cassation*' and from the '*Conseil d'Etat*'.

10. It must be stressed that none of these courts is competent in constitutional and electoral matters. Those questions are entrusted to a specialized organ created in 1958: the Constitutional Council ('*Conseil constitutionnel*'). The Council consists of nine members, appointed for nine years. Three are designated by the President of the Republic, three by the President of the National Assembly, and three by the President of the Senate; former Presidents of the Republic are members as of right. For a long time, the Council may decide on the constitutionality of statutes only prior to the date of their promulgation and on the initiative of the President of the Republic, the Prime Minister, the President of either of the Chambers of the Parliament, or sixty deputies or senators. Since the revision of the Constitution on 23 July 2008, the Council may also decide *a posteriori* on the constitutionality of statutes. A new Article 61-1 provides that any citizen may claim in an action pending before an administrative or judicial court that an applicable statute violates the constitutional rights and liberties ('*Question prioritaire de constitutionnalité*', 'Priority question on constitutionality'). The '*Conseil d'Etat*' or the '*Cour de cassation*' may then seize the '*Conseil constitutionnel*' of such a claim.

§3. Sources of French Law

11. French law belongs to the Civil Law family, theoretically characterized by the pre-eminence of enacted law.

I. Written Sources

12. The written sources of law are placed within a hierarchy, where the texts of a lower level may not contradict those of a higher degree.

13. Constitution is to be found at the summit of this pyramid. The international treaties ratified by the French Parliament may not go against the Constitution, but are superior to ordinary French statutes. In particular, the Treaty of Rome of 1957, instituting the EU has an authority superior to this of the French statutes, even enacted later. On the third level are placed ordinary laws enacted by the Parliament and 'autonomous' regulations taken by the Government. Other decrees and regulations which are designed to implement existing statutes are dependent on those statutes and may not contradict them.

14. Many statutes and regulations are incorporated into codes, which present the rules of law in a logical and coherent order. The great movement of codification was initiated at the beginning of the nineteenth century with the five so-called Napoleonic Codes. The most famous is the Civil Code (1804) which influenced numerous legal systems in the world. It was followed by the Code of Civil Procedure (1806), the Code of Commerce (1808), the Code of Criminal Procedure (1811), and the Penal Code (1811). All five have been frequently amended and the Code of Criminal Procedure was superseded by the Code of Penal Procedure in 1959. A new Code of Civil Procedure entered into force in 1976 and a new Penal Code in 1994. Although frequently amended, the old codes have survived and contain the basic principles and rules of ordinary law. It must be noted that the inclusion of a rule into a Code does not confer upon it any superior authority: those rules may be modified or abrogated as any other ones.

15. New collections of texts have been published since the Second World War in social and economic matters: the Labour Code, the Customs Code, the General Tax Code, the Rural Code, the Insurance Code, the Intellectual Property Code, the Consumer Code, etc. Those 'Codes' lack the principled and thoughtful presentation of basic rules characteristic of the Napoleonic Codes. As a consequence, they do not have the moral authority of the old Codes, and are mainly considered as 'consolidations' of pre-existing statutory material making legal rules easier to consult for practitioners.

16. The development of state interventionism brought about a dramatic increase in the volume of enacted law, which makes the effective knowledge of the rule of law difficult. All French statutes, regulations, and governmental decisions are published in the Official Journal of the French Republic (Journal Officiel de la République française (JORF)). The texts which have a wide scope may be found in private compilations such as the Bulletin Législatif Dalloz (1918–1982), or in the section 'Législation' in the main legal periodicals (*see infra* paragraph 23). Practitioners make frequent use of private editions of the Codes (Codes Dalloz; Codes LexisNexis, etc.), which are brought up to date each year and contain not only the text of the Code itself, but also related provisions, together with summaries of decided cases.

II. Unwritten Sources

17. Although important, the enacted rules are not the exclusive source of French law. Judges frequently give authority to unwritten rules which have the same binding force as the written ones. Those rules have their origin in the so-called general principles of law, in the custom, and in the decided cases.

18. For the solution of a case, French courts sometimes apply unwritten general rules, which express superior requirements inspiring the legal order. Those principles are often expressed in the form of a Latin maxim as they have been elaborated at a time when the legal language was Latin (e.g., '*fraus omnia corrumpit*' – fraud sets aside any rules; '*Nemo jus ignorare censetur*' – no one is supposed to ignore the law). French judges consider they are the depositors of the legal tradition embodying such principles, even if they were not expressed by the legislator: there is a general agreement in the legal world about such reasoning.

19. Custom is defined as a general and constant usage which is thought to be compulsory. Prior to the Revolution of 1789, French law was mainly based on custom. All those customary rules have been set aside upon the enactment of the Civil Code in 1804. Thus the place of custom is nowadays limited and its authority uncertain. When custom is referred to by a statute, it is said to have a delegated authority. Such is the case, for instance, with Articles 1194, 1163, and 1166 of the Civil Code, which state that contracts have to be interpreted according to usages. The reference to custom is considered to be implicit when the legislator uses general concepts without precisely defining them (e.g., 'fault', 'public order', 'good morals', etc.). Lacking a statutory reference, custom is used to fill legislative gaps. Such is the case mainly in the area of commercial contracts. On the contrary, a custom may never abrogate a mandatory statutory rule.[2]

20. According to the principle of separation of powers, the judges may not exercise a legislative function. Article 5 of the Civil Code expressly forbids the judges to make a general and regulatory decision. Each court's decision only aims at solving the case in dispute, and no judge is bound by a former judgment. Consequently, the decisions of the superior courts only illustrate the law, but are not law themselves. It

2. Cass. Chambres réunies, 10 Mar. 1960: JCP 1960 II 11569*bis*, note Vivez.

is not the practice for the courts to cite individual precedents in their decisions. Moreover, a judgment of a lower court explicitly based on an earlier judgment would be quashed by the Cour de cassation for lack of legal basis. Thus, the importance of enacted law in the French system is revealed by the duty of the judge to rely on *ratio legis*, whatever interpretation he gives to the rule he is using. Legal writing is an important source of inspiration for the French judges.

21. A final decision may be appealed to the Cour de cassation or the Conseil d'Etat only on the ground that the legal rule has been misinterpreted or misapplied or some other rule has been neglected; those courts judge the law, not the facts. Both Supreme Courts which crown the judicial and the administrative hierarchies enforce a uniform interpretation of the legal rule on the whole French territory and thus play a capital role in the formation of lines of cases. This role has been extended by a statute authorizing lower courts (except criminal courts) to ask the Cour de cassation for advice on the meaning of a legal rule, when 'a new legal question is raised, offering a serious difficulty and concerning numerous cases'.[3] Such an advice is not binding upon the court, which requested it, but inevitably previews the interpretation of the Cour de cassation in a real future case.

22. Thus, constitutional principles do not entirely reflect the real function of the decided cases in the French legal system. Practical observation of the judicial position on a given problem shows that lower courts spontaneously adapt to the point of view expressed by the Supreme Courts. This is not to be explained by the binding authority of those decisions, or a judicial respect of hierarchy, but by the desire to provide the citizens with legal security, by the convincing reasoning of the Supreme Court's decisions and by the moral authority of the magistrates of the Supreme Court. As a consequence, from a practical point of view, a steady line of cases ('jurisprudence constante') adopted by the Cour de cassation or the Conseil d'Etat has an authority as strong as the one of a statutory rule. The legal profession pays great attention to the evolution of the case law ('jurisprudence') and the decisions of the courts are cited in oral and written arguments as well as in textbooks.

23. The decided cases may be found in a series of collections. The only official reports of court decisions are those for the Cour de cassation: a '*Bulletin des Arrêts de la Cour de cassation rendus en matière civile*' (cited as Bull. civ.) from 1792 (for civil matters), and a '*Bulletin des Arrêts de la Cour de cassation rendus en matière criminelle*' (cited as Bull. crim.) from 1798 (for criminal matters). The decisions of the Conseil d'Etat are collected since 1821 in '*Recueil des arrêts du Conseil d'Etat*' (often cited as Recueil Lebon). Private compilations most frequently used are Juris-Classeur périodique, Recueil Dalloz-Sirey, Gazette du Palais, etc. It must be noted that not all the judicial decisions are published (even those of the Supreme Courts). Numerous decisions are also accessible through computerized databases (LexisNexis, Lexbase, etc.) and especially through 'Legifrance' (www.legifrance.gouv.fr), which provides a free and very large access to decisions of the 'Cour de cassation', 'Conseil d'Etat', 'Conseil constitutionnel', and 'Tribunal des conflits' as well as a selection of decisions of inferior courts.

3. Act No. 91-491 of 15 May 1991 and Decree No. 92-228 of 12 Mar. 1992.

§4. Structure of the French Law

24. As in any legal system of the Romano-Germanic family, the French legal science has developed on the basis of Roman *ius civile* taught in the European Universities in the Middle Ages. Consequently, mainly for historical reasons, the law has evolved as an essentially private law, which aims at regulating private relationships between individual citizens. Thus, the principles of 'private law' remain the main branch of the French legal system and legal reasoning. Public law, regulating relations with public persons (State, cities, departments, etc.) developed later and less perfectly. The legal approach in matters of public interest is still different from those of purely private law. The division between private and public law is essential in the French legal reasoning and is materialized by the existence of two separate hierarchies of courts (*see supra* paragraph 7).

I. Private Law

25. Private law is dominated by the Napoleonic Codes (*see supra* paragraph 14). For that reason, the inside classifications of the private law coincide with the domain of the various nineteenth century Codes: civil law, commercial law, criminal law and criminal procedure, and civil procedure.

26. Civil law ('droit civil') incorporated in the Civil Code is the basis of private law: it is considered as '*droit commun*', in the sense that it must be referred to whenever there is no more specific legal rule relating to the problem at stake. Thus, the Civil Code is to be applied even to other parts of private law. For instance, the rules of the Civil Code apply to business contracts in the situations where no specific commercial rules exist. The civil law covers a very wide area: family relations (marriage, divorce, matrimonial property regimes, affiliation, protection of incapables, successions), contracts, torts, and property.

27. Commercial law ('droit commercial') – nowadays called business law – encompasses the rules applicable to merchants and commercial activities. The autonomy of this branch is to be linked to the existence of commercial courts ('Tribunaux de commerce') staffed with elected merchants.

28. Some substantive differences separate civil and commercial law: oral evidence is admissible in many situations where civil law requires a written proof; commercial debtors are presumed to be joint and several; the procedures of 'bankruptcy' are applicable to juristic persons and individual merchants, but not to civil individuals (subject to a special procedure for handling over indebtedness). However, business law keeps close relations with civil law, not only because it is considered as a system derogatory to the civil law, but also because appeals from the commercial courts are brought in the Courts of Appeal.

29. Other branches are considered as part of civil law, because they deal mainly with private interests: labour and social security law, construction law, insurance law, intellectual property law, private international law, etc. These distinctions are more or less artificial: they are due to the necessity of dividing subjects for pedagogical and practical specialization purposes. In all those branches, the fundamental reasoning is that of the civil law. Criminal law and procedure as well as civil procedure are also classified as part of the civil law, although with more hesitation, given the importance of the public interests at stake.

30. No such distinction as that between rights in equity and rights at law is to be found in French civil law. This is due to the fact that the French legal system never needed to invent an extraordinary remedial jurisdiction comparable to the one of the Chancellor's in England. Roman and Canonic law provided rules elaborated enough to treat new problems. One of the consequences is that a French judge may not base his decision solely on 'équité', and must look for some enacted or customary rules.

II. Public Law

31. To the sphere of public law belong all the rules relating to a situation where the State or a public person is a party. Although older than private law, it is less elaborated and has never been codified (unless the Constitution is considered as a codification). These rules are applied by the administrative courts (*see supra* paragraph 9), where procedure and enforcement of the decisions are different from those used by civil courts.

32. Public law is subdivided into constitutional, administrative, financial, and public international laws. The legal reasoning in those matters takes into account the notions of public interest and public service.

Chapter 2. Introduction to Intellectual Property Law

33. Intellectual property rights are temporary exclusive rights on various immaterial goods which can be aesthetical creations (literary and artistic works, designs, and models), technical innovations (inventions, plant varieties, chips), or distinctive signs (trademarks, trade names, geographical names). The function of such rights is to promote economic, cultural, or technological development, by giving to some persons an advantage in competition. Unlike the tangible goods, immaterial goods are not able to be materially appropriated. Their value, related to their rarity, will therefore be lost as soon as they become intellectually accessible to others. Rarity may be kept either by maintaining such goods secret, or by organizing a legal system of appropriation. Intellectual property law answers these needs by conferring to the creators or possessors of immaterial goods an exclusive right limited in time, even after their disclosure.

34. Although they both belong to the intellectual property law, literary and artistic property and industrial property constitute two distinct branches, each of them having a specific logic.

35. Literary and artistic property gathers the copyright, neighbouring rights, and the sui generis right of the producer of databases. Copyright is based on the statement that a work of art expresses its author's personality, is the result of his talents and efforts, can be of great cultural or economic value, whereas its reproduction by third persons does not require any effort of reverse engineering. The legal protection of such works solves this problem by conferring to the author an exclusive right based on the act of creation, without any administrative procedure designed to evaluate its originality or merit. This exclusive right first includes the so-called economic rights or exploitation rights, which are the right of reproduction, the right of performance, and the *'droit de suite'* (a resale royalty right). However, copyright is not only an instrument of economic reward of the creation; it also aims at protecting the author's personality, in allowing him to control the use of his work even after the assignment of the economic attributes, by enforcing his 'moral right'. The neighbouring rights reward performing artists, producers, and audiovisual communication enterprises which are precious auxiliary of the artistic creation in that they participate in the diffusion of the works. They confer to these beneficiaries an exclusive right on their respective creation (the performance, the phonogram or videogram, the audiovisual programme). This exclusive right is only based on the act of creation, without any administrative procedure, and it is only an 'economic right' (with the exception of a very limited 'moral right' conferred to the performing artists). The sui generis protection rewards the producer who takes the initiative and the risk of the substantial investments necessary for the constitution, the verification, or the presentation of the content of a database. It does not depend on an administrative procedure and it only confers an 'economic right' to the producer.

36. Unlike literary and artistic property rights, industrial property rights are not attached to the act of creation: the exclusive right is granted by a decision of a public authority upon a request by the interested person.

37. In consideration of their object, industrial property rights belong to one of the following categories:

- Rights on industrial creations: patents and related rights protect useful industrial creations. The exclusive right aims here at encouraging not only the making of technological inventions interesting the society, but also their public disclosure in a patent application, in order to allow further research. Designs and models protect ornamental industrial creations. They cover the ornamental design for an object having practical utility.
- Rights on distinctive signs: registration protects signs or shapes designed to distinguish products or services from the competing ones (trade and service marks, trade names, and geographical names). Exclusive rights on this category of creations do not aim at encouraging technical progress, but only to ensure order in relations between competitors as well as consumer information, by permitting the economic operators to identify their goods or services.

38. Sources of the French intellectual property law are to be found in the rules of national, international, and European origin.

39. All the French legal and regulatory rules relating to intellectual property were abrogated by the law No. 92-597 of 1 July 1992,[4] in order to be included without material changes in the new Intellectual Property Code enacted by this statute. The Code consists of a Part One, on Literary and Artistic Property (Articles L. 111-1–L. 343-7 and Articles R. 111-1–R. 343-1), and a Part Two, on Industrial Property (Articles L. 411-1–L. 731-4 and Articles R. 411-1–R. 722-7).[5] The subdivisions of each Part are ordered in a hierarchical order: Book ('Livre'), Title ('Titre'), Chapter ('Chapitre'), Section ('Section'), Paragraph ('Paragraphe'), and finally Articles. The existing texts have been classified in a systematic order and given new modernized numbers.[6] It should be noted that some rules are still left outside of the Code, such as the ministerial decrees ('arrêtés'), or various rules of labour law, tax law, consumer protection, etc., applicable in some instances. Several private editions of the Code are published, presenting all the texts useful in intellectual property matters and even comments and reference to case law.[7]

40. The oldest international source is the Paris Convention on the Protection of Industrial Property of 1883, which has been ratified by France in all its modifications (last is the Stockholm version of 1967)[8] and arrangements. A more recent international treaty is the Marrakesh Convention, of 15 April 1994, creating the World Trade Organization which includes as its Annex 1c the Agreement on Trade Related Aspects

---

4. JORF, 3 Jul. 1992, p. 8801. The regulatory part of the Code was enacted by a Decree No. 95-385 of 10 Apr. 1995 (JORF, 13 Apr.).
5. A Part Three (Art. L. 811-1 and L. 811-4; Art. R. 811-1–R. 811-3) is devoted to the application of the Code in the Overseas territories and Mayotte.
6. Articles of statutory origin are preceded by the letter L (for Legislative Part); those from regulatory origin by the letter R (for Regulatory Part). *See* : V.-L. Benabou and V. Varet, La codification de la propriété intellectuelle, Paris, La Documentation française, 1998.
7. The official text of the Code is published by Direction des Journaux Officiels (26, rue Desaix, F 75015 Paris) in 'Les éditions des Journaux Officiels'. The private publications include: Code Dalloz (annotated by Prof. P. Sirinelli, S. Durrande, A. Latreille & N. Maximin); Code LexisNexis (annotated by Prof. M. Vivant & J.-L. Navarro).
8. The Stockholm text is in force since 12 Aug. 1975.

of Industrial Property rights (TRIPs Agreement).[9] France is also member to most of other specific international treaties in the field of intellectual property (*see infra*).

41. The European sources consist of the Rome treaty (nowadays called 'Treaty on the Functioning of the European Union') creating the EU and its derived rules, which apply to the exercise of French intellectual property rights,[10] harmonize French and other Member States' intellectual property law (through directives) and create new European intellectual property rights (through regulations: EU trademark, Community design right, Community plant variety right, Community designations of origin or geographical indications). Directives harmonizing various aspects of intellectual property law are regularly implemented into French law. Regulations providing for substantive rules in this area are directly applicable in France.

9. The Act No. 94-1137 of 27 Dec. 1994 authorized the ratification of the TRIPS Agreement. The Act No. 96-1106 of 18 Dec. 1996 introduced the necessary adaptations into the IP Code (JORF, 19 Dec. 1996, p. 18687). *See* : L. Masson, La transposition en droit interne de l'Accord relatif aux aspects des droits de propriété intellectuelle touchant au commerce (Accord ADPIC), Gaz. Pal. 1997, 2, doct., p. 979.
10. Articles 34–36 of the Treaty on the Functioning of the European Union as for free circulation of goods; Arts 101 and 102 as for free competition.

Part I. Copyright and Neighbouring Rights

Chapter 1. Sources: Legislation

42. Today, the sources of French copyright law are contained in the Intellectual Property Code, enacted by the statute of 1 July 1992. At the time of the enactment of the Code, copyright was ruled by the Act of 11 March 1957, modified by the Act of 3 July 1985. The Code did not modify the prior statutes and decrees, but only gathered them under a systematic numbering. Copyright is the object of the Part One of the Code, devoted to Literary and Artistic Property ('Propriété Littéraire et Artistique'). This Part is divided into three Books: Book One deals with Copyright ('Droit d'auteur': Articles L. 111-1–L. 135-7); Book Two with the Neighbouring Rights ('Droits voisins': Articles L. 211-1–L. 217-3), and Book Three contains some General Provisions relative to copyright, to neighbouring rights, and to the rights of database producers ('Dispositions générales relatives au droit d'auteur, aux droits voisins et droits des producteurs de bases de données': Articles L. 311-1–L. 343-7). However, it is sometimes necessary to refer to sources outside the Code: ministerial decisions ('arrêtés') are not codified. Moreover, some rules regarding intellectual property law are to be found in other sources, such as the Labour Code, Penal Code, tax laws, competitions laws, etc.

43. To the French national sources should be added the EU sources, as well as the international multilateral Conventions ratified by France.[11] Moreover, several bilateral conventions were signed between France and another State.

11. Berne Convention of 9 Sep. 1886 for the protection of literary and artistic works, as last revised in Paris on 24 Jul. 1971, entered into force in France on 15 Dec. 1972 as for Arts 22 and 38 and on 10 Jul. 1974 as for Arts 1–21. Universal Geneva Convention of 6 Sep. 1952 on author's rights, as revised in Paris on 24 Jul. 1971, entered into force in France on 10 Jul. 1974. Rome Convention of 26 Oct. 1961 on the protection of performing artists, producers of phonograms, and broadcasting organizations, entered into force on 3 Jul. 1987 (JORF 24 Dec. 1986). Geneva Convention of 29 Oct. 1971 for the protection of producers of phonograms against unauthorized duplication of their phonograms, entered into force on 12 Sep. 1972. TRIPS Agreement of 15 Apr. 1994, entered into force on 1 Jan. 1995. WIPO Copyright Treaty of 20 Dec. 1996, entered into force on 14 Mar. 2010. WIPO Performances and Phonograms Treaty of 20 Dec. 1996, entered into force on 14 Mar. 2010.

Chapter 2. Subject Matter of Protection

§1. Different Categories of Protected Works

44. The different categories of protected works are viewed in Chapter 2 of the Book One of the IP Code (Article L. 112-1–L. 112-4). In a general way, Article L. 112-1 states: 'The dispositions of the present Code protect author's rights on any work of mind, whatever its kind, form of expression, merit, or destination.'

45. Article L. 112-2 lists in a sampling way, the protectable works. In this list of fourteen examples, it is possible to see four main categories of works: literary works, musical works, art works, and audiovisual works.

I. Literary Works

46. Literary works may appear either in a written or in an oral form.

A. Written Works

47. Article L. 112-2, 1° cites as protectable works 'books, brochures and other literary, artistic and scientific writings'. This implies that any (original) written work may be protected, no matter its cultural level or object: catalogues, dictionaries, guides, formulas, slogans, press articles, missive letters, etc. This list is in no way exhaustive.

48. Moreover, not only the initial works are protected, but also derived works based thereupon, such as anthologies, translations, adaptations, commentaries, updatings, databases (Article L. 112-3). Such works are original in their composition or expression, but borrow formal elements from an already existing protected work.

49. Article L. 112-4 deals specifically with the case of titles: 'The title of a work of mind, when having an original character, is protected as the work itself.' As a consequence, no one may use the same title to designate a work of the same kind in conditions likely to create confusion.[12] The title is protected even when its author is not the one of the work itself.[13]

B. Oral Works

50. Article L. 112-2, 2° cites 'Conferences, speeches, sermons, pleadings and other works of the same nature'. Already before this statutory statement, French courts have protected oral (original) works.[14]

---

12. Paris, 14 Apr. 1960: D. 1991, jur., p. 535, note Desbois, the title of the novel 'Liaisons dangereuses' may not be used without authorization for a film.
13. Paris, 27 Jan. 1984: D. 1984, I.R., p. 285, obs. Colombet.
14. Lyon, 17 Jul. 1845: D. 1845, 2, 128, Lacordaire's sermons; T. civ. Seine, 9 Dec. 1893, DP. 1894, 2, 262, as for the lectures of a professor.

51. Conferences and speeches are protected, whether made by a private person or a politician.[15] As for 'other works of the same nature', professors' classes are copyrightable works; professors are bound to teach only in front of their audiences and their courses may not be reproduced without the author's authorization.[16] However, the protection of some of the oral works is temporarily suspended for the purpose of public information under Article L. 122-5, which states: 'When the work has been disclosed, the author may not forbid (...) 3) the publication, even in full, by the means of press or telediffusion as news information, of public speeches made in political, administrative, judiciary or academic assemblies, public political meetings and official ceremonies.' Public interest justifies such an exception to copyright. But as soon as the work has lost its topicality, it is no more published as 'news information' and the copyright may be opposed.

II. Musical Works

52. Article L. 112-2 cites 'dramatic and drama-musical works' as well as 'musical compositions with or without words'. The originality of such a musical work may consist of its melody, harmony, or rhythm.[17] A song which was already a part of the folklore is not protectable[18] unless the author brings an original contribution.[19] Musical arrangements consisting of adaptations of a work written for an instrument to another one, or of the orchestration of a work, are a kind of musical translation and are protected as such if original.[20] Musical variations imply more independence than arrangements, since the composer adds new elements or modifies rhythm or harmony. If the initial work may be recognized, the variation is protected as a derived work (*see infra* paragraph 139).

53. Article L.112-2, 4° also cites 'choreographic works, circus acts and feats, pantomimes, the acting form of which is set down in writing or in other manner'. This implies that such works need to be fixed in a material support (writing, film, phonogram, etc.). However, such fixation is not a condition of the copyright's protection. It is not considered as an exception to the principles of protection without formality and of indifference towards the form of expression. It is considered as a rule on the taking of evidence; otherwise, it would be almost impossible to evidence the existence and content of such works.

15. TGI Paris, 6 Jul. 1972: D. 1972, jur., p. 628, note Pactet, De Gaulle's speeches are protected; TGI Paris, 25 Oct. 1995, RIDA, January 1996, p. 294 and p. 203, obs. Kérever, Mitterrand's speeches are protected.
16. TGI Paris, 11 Dec. 1985: D. 1987, I.R. p. 155, obs. Colombet, Jacques Lacan's seminars are protected.
17. T. civ. Seine, 31 Oct. 1950, D. 1950, jur., p. 763; Cass. civ. 1, 11 Oct. 1989, RIDA, July 1990, p. 325.
18. Cass. civ. 1, 23 Oct. 1962: Bull. civ. I, p. 440.
19. Cass. civ. 1, 1 Jul. 1970: D. 1971, jur., p. 734, note Edelman; RTD civ. 1971, 706, obs. Desbois, airs of guitar improvised by Manitas de Plata.
20. Paris, 10 Mar. 1970: RIDA, 1970, p. 139; RTD civ. 1971, 91, obs. Desbois, orchestration by Ravel of the work 'Paintings of an Exhibition' by Stravinski.

III. Art Works

54. Article L. 112-2 cites as examples of protectable art works: works of drawing, painting, architecture, sculpture, engraving and lithography, photographic works, and works made through analogous techniques, graphical and typographical works, works of applied art, illustrations, geographical maps, plans, sketches, and plastic art works relative to geography, topography, architecture, and science. Moreover, French case law recognizes as art works: stagings;[21] various artistic productions, such as a haircut,[22] a bouquet of flowers,[23] etc.

55. Some explanations are necessary as for certain art works cited by the Code.

A. Architecture Works

56. As for architecture, are protectable not only the drawings and models, but also the buildings themselves (through their volumes, colours, or fitting-out), which may not be reproduced without the architect's authorization.[24]

B. Copies of Art Works

57. A specific problem is raised concerning copies of art works. Most manual copies are themselves art works, because the personality of the copier cannot totally disappear. Nevertheless a copy is only relatively original, since it is inspired by the model; the copy is thus treated as a derived work.[25] The copy is not a protected work if it is purely mechanical and leaves no room for expression of the copier's personality. Moreover, an author may only forbid copies of his specific works, and not a simple imitation of his ideas, styles, or processes (*see infra* paragraph 63).

C. Photographs

58. The status of photographs has been uncertain for a long time. The Act of 1957 protected only 'artistic or documentary' photographs. These criterions were so difficult to apply, that the law of 3 July 1985 suppressed them. Article L. 112-2, 9° now cites photographs as such, without any further qualification; as any other works, they are protectable if original.[26]

---

21. TGI Seine, 2 Nov. 1965, JCP 1966 II 14577, note Boursigot; Paris, 8 Jul. 1971: RIDA, January 1973, p. 134; RTD com. 1973, 100, obs. Desbois; TGI Paris, 6 Jul. 1990, RIDA, January 1991, p. 348.
22. T. corr. Paris, 12 Jul. 1977: Gaz. Pal. 1978, 1, jur., p. 41.
23. Paris, 10 Apr. 1995: RIDA, October 1995, p. 241, obs. Kéréver.
24. Paris, 19 Jun. 1979: RIDA, 1981, 208; D. 1981, I.R., p. 83, obs. Colombet.
25. Cass. civ. 1, 9 Nov. 1993: D. 1994, som., p. 91, obs. Colombet.
26. Cass. civ. 1, 17 Dec. 1991: Bull. civ. I, No. 360; JCP 1992 IV 68; RDPI 1993, 49.

D. Designs and Models

59. Designs and models are copyrightable works of art, but may under some conditions be protectable under Book Five of the Code, as registered designs and models or under Book Seven of the Code, by patents (*see infra* paragraphs 879 et seq.).

E. Fashion Creations

60. The last paragraph of Article L. 112-2 cites 'creations of the seasonal industries of clothing and adorning'. This deals with the industries of fashion which have to renew their models frequently. Formerly, a statute of 1952 provided for specific rules for such creations: they are now under the ordinary rules of copyright law.

IV. Audiovisual Works

61. Article L.112-2, 6° cites 'Cinematographic works and other works consisting of animated sequences of images added or not with sound effects, together referred to as audiovisual works.' Such works may consist of films, television series, and video games.[27]

§2. Works Excluded of Protection

62. Given the general statement of Article L. 112-1 (*see supra*, paragraph 44), no works are excluded per se. Any creation of mind is copyrightable, if only it fulfils the unique substantive condition of protection which is originality (*see infra* paragraphs 119 et seq.).

63. A 'work' is a creation embodied in a formal expression: ideas are not copyrightable as such, whatever their originality or interest. Creation would be exceedingly hampered if the ideas could be reserved under an exclusive right: thus, only the form is protected, not the idea on which it is based.[28] A general style of work is also not protectable.[29] It was held that the person who brings an idea may be considered as the co-author of the final work, if he participates in its formal realization.[30]

64. It may be sometimes difficult to distinguish the idea from the form. For instance, the idea of 'wrapping' the trees on the Champs Elysées in Paris, without any formal realization, is not protectable,[31] whereas the actual 'wrapping' of the Pont-Neuf

27. Cass. Ass. plén., 7 Mar. 1986: JCP ed. E, 1986 II 14713 and 14737*bis*, note Mousseron, Teyssié and Vivant; JCP ed. E, 1986 I 15791, No. 1, obs. Vivant and Lucas; D. 1986, jur., p. 405, concl. Cabannes and note Edelman.
28. Cass. com., 29 Nov. 1960: Bull. civ. III, No. 389; Ann. propr. Ind. 1961, 309, note Bleustein, a teaching method is not copyrightable.
29. Paris, 9 Mar. 1967: D. 1967, jur., p. 664, note Greffe.
30. Cass. civ., 18 Dec. 1978: D. 1980, jur., p. 49, note Colombet.
31. TGI Paris, 26 May 1987: D. 1988, som., p. 201, note Colombet.

bridge in Paris by Christo was an original creation expressed in a form and thus copyrightable.[32]

65. However, in French law, a person may be liable for using an unprotected idea if there is a likelihood of confusion,[33] or if the user intended to take advantage of the plaintiff's notoriety.[34] Such behaviours would be sanctioned under the unfair competition ('concurrence déloyale') or 'parasitism' theories.

§3. Special Categories of Works

I. Computer Software

66. Computer programs were introduced into the list of copyrightable works by the statute of 3 July 1985.[35] Already before that statute, French courts applied copyright to original software.[36] Although the substantive conditions of protection are in principle the same for software as for any other works, the scope of rights is more limited.

A. Conditions of Protection

67. As any other copyrightable work, computer software is subject to the only condition of originality (*see infra* paragraphs 119 et seq.). Nevertheless, a more objective definition of originality was given here by the Supreme Court: software is original if it bears the marks of the *author's intellectual contribution,*[37] or of his *personal contribution.*[38] However, the innovative character of the solutions adopted by a computer program is not a sufficient evidence of its originality.[39]

B. Ownership

68. The legislation brought here an important exception to the principle according to which copyright on a work always belongs to its creator (*see infra* paragraphs 127 et seq.). Borrowing from the patent law, a specific system applies to software created by employees 'in the exercise of their functions' or 'following the instructions given by their employer'. Unless otherwise provided by statutory provision or stipulation,

32. Paris, 13 Mar. 1986: D. 1987, som., p.150, obs. Colombet.
33. Paris, 17 Nov. 1992: JCP ed. E, 1993 II 418, note Greffe.
34. Cass. com., 19 Oct. 1966: Bull. civ. III, No. 401.
35. Such is also the solution of the EEC Directive No. 91/250 of 14 May 1991 on the protection of computer programs: OJEC, 17 May 1991, replaced by EC Dir. No. 2009/24 of 23 Apr. 2009 on the legal protection of computer programs (codified version), OJEC No. L. 111, of 5 May 2009, p. 16–22.
36. Paris, 2 Nov. 1982: RIDA, 1983, 148. – Cass. Ass. plén., 7 Mar. 1986, two decisions, *supra,* n. 25, §61.
37. Cass. Ass. plén., 7 Mar. 1986, *supra,* note 1, §61.
38. Cass. civ. 1, 16 Apr. 1991: Bull. civ. I, No. 139.
39. Paris, 5 Apr. 1993: JCP ed. E, 1994 I 357, obs. Vivant and Le Stanc.

the economic rights in such creations belong 'exclusively' to the employer (Article L. 113-9). This implies that the sole existence of a contract for employment entails the application of the legal rule, without it being necessary to evidence an assignment of the economic rights on the computer software created by the employee. Article L. 113-9 shall also apply to servants of the State, of local authorities and of public establishments of an administrative nature.

69. It was decided that computer software may be a collective work within the meaning of Article L.113-2, §3 (*see infra* paragraph 141 et seq.).[40]

C. Scope of Protection

70. Whereas most of the ordinary rules apply to the exploitation right on computer software, the author's moral right is much more restricted.

1. Exploitation Right

71. Computer software may be the object of the usual contracts: assignment or licence of copyright, as well as of a collateral ruled by Article L. 132-34 ('nantissement'). Whereas the price paid to the author for his assignment of copyright consists, in principle, of a royalty assessed on the proceeds of the exploitation (Article L. 131-4, §1; *see infra* paragraph 156), this rule is set aside as for computer software. Assignment of rights may here be made in exchange for a lump sum (*ibid.*, §5). However, as in any such case, the author may seek 'rescision pour lésion' (rescission because of an important economical imbalance of the contract) (*see infra* paragraph 158).

72. As for the exceptions to the scope of copyright protection, a specific provision deals with copies of computer software. Whereas under the ordinary rules, private copy is authorized by law (under some conditions; *see infra* paragraph 227 et seq.), such copies are illegal as for software. Article L. 122-6-1 only allows the person authorized to use the software to make one *safeguard copy*.[41] Since the aim of this rule is to ensure the safeguard of the program, the user has no longer the right to make a copy, when he received from the seller one extra copy of the software (same decision). It is unlawful to offer a software which makes possible copies of a protected program (same decision). This prohibition was confirmed by the Act of 10 May 1994, introducing the EEC Directive No. 91/250 of 14 May 1991 on computer software[42] (new Article L. 122-6-2).

73. Moreover, the person authorized to use the software may complete any act 'necessary' for the software exploitation (in practice, its analysis/reverse engineering in view of its interoperability with another software), under the only – and vague – reservation of the software's conformity to its destination.

74. No exception for educational or research purposes is admitted.

---

40. Cass. civ. 1, 3 Jul. 1996: D. 1997, jur., p. 328, note Françon.
41. Cass. com., 22 May 1991: Bull. civ. IV, No. 172; JCP 1992 II 21792, note Huet; JCP ed. E, 1992 I 141, obs. Vivant and Lucas; only one copy is authorized.
42. EEC Directive No. 91/250 of 14 May 1991 on the protection of computer programs: OJEC, 17 May 1991, replaced by EC Dir. No. 2009/24 of 23 Apr. 2009 on the legal protection of computer programs (codified version), OJEC No. L. 111, of 5 May 2009, pp. 16–22.

75. Exhaustion of right applies to software[43] once it was sold with the rightholder's consent on the territory of a Member State of the European Economic Area.[44] The owner may no longer control the sale of the software, but still may forbid its public lending, according to the ordinary rules.

2. Moral Right

76. The ordinary components of the moral right (*see infra* paragraphs 165 et seq.) are seriously restricted as for software under Article L. 121-7.

77. The right to withdraw or to reconsider is excluded, and the right to oppose alterations is strictly limited: its author may oppose a modification of the software by the assignee of copyright only when such a modification damages his honour or reputation. Finally, the author enjoys only his right to disclose his work and his right to be mentioned as such on the copies of the software (right to paternity).

D. Infringement and Remedies

78. Any unauthorized use of a computer software – copy except the first backup copy, read or reproduce on screen or hard disc, adaptation,[45] etc – is an infringement (Article L. 335-3, §2). The ordinary sanctions apply (*see infra* paragraph 334 et seq.).

79. As for jurisdiction, Article L. 113-9, §2 ascribes the disputes between employer and employee concerning the attribution of the copyright to the Tribunal de Grande Instance. Otherwise, for all the other actions concerning computer software, the ordinary rules of jurisdiction shall be applied.[46]

80. Finally, a specific procedure of counterfeit seizure is organized under Article L. 332-4,. Any person with authority to bring an action for infringement shall be entitled, on the order issued upon request by the competent civil court (the President of the Tribunal de Grande Instance), to direct any bailiff, accompanied by experts appointed by the claimant, to proceed in any place with either the detailed description, with or without taking samples, or the effective seizure of the allegedly infringing software as well as any related document. The President shall order, for the same evidential purposes, the detailed description or the effective seizure of equipment and tools used to manufacture or distribute the allegedly infringing software as well as any related document. The order shall authorize the effective seizure of any document relating to these software, equipment and tools, even in the absence of the latter. The President may also condition the implementation of the measures it ordered to the furnishing by the claimant of security to ensure, if necessary, the defendant's compensation if the infringement action is subsequently held unfounded or the seizure is lifted. The

43. T. com. Créteil, 12 Nov. 1996, RIDA, April 1997, p. 310.
44. CFI, 3rd Ch., 16 Dec. 1999, RIDA, 2000, No. 185, p. 377,CCE 2000, comm. No. 18, note Caron; there is no exhaustion when it was sold in Canada; no international exhaustion.
45. Cass. crim., 25 May 1992: Bull. crim., No. 206. – Cass. com., 9 Nov. 1993: RTD civ. 1994, 373, obs. Gautier, a firm may enforce its right against a client who has its software adapted by a competitor.
46. Paris, 5 Apr. 1990, JCP ed. E, 1990 II 15920, No. 2, obs. Vivant and Lucas.

'description-seizure' ('saisie-description') which is less dangerous as the effective seizure and may be done by the way of a copy.

81. The seizure is void (may not be used as evidence of infringement) if the plaintiff does not sue within a period of time set by regulation (Article L. 332-4, §3): the time limit granted to the claimant for the institution of proceedings on the merits shall be twenty working days or thirty-one civil days if this time limit is longer, as from the day on which the counterfeit-seizure is realized (Article R. 332-4).

II. Databases

82. Protection of databases is organized by the Act No. 98-536 of 1 July 1998, introducing the EC Directive No. 96/9 of the European Parliament and the Council of 11 March 1996 on the legal protection of databases.[47] A definition of the database is introduced into Article L. 112-3, §2: 'A database is a collection of works, data or other independent materials, arranged in a systematic or methodical way, and individually accessible by electronic means or any other means.'

83. Previously, original databases were recognized as copyrightable works by the French courts.[48] Under the new law, two independent systems are available: traditional copyright and/or a sui generis protection (*See* Article L. 341-1, §2, 'This protection is independent and applies without prejudice to the protection of copyright or any other right over the database or one of its component elements').

A. Protection by Copyright

84. The databases are subject to the ordinary rules of copyright law, where some changes of detail were introduced by the new statute.

1. Databases as Derived Works

85. Databases were introduced into Article L. 112-3, §1, relating to the protection of derived works, which now state: 'The authors of translations, adaptations, transformations or arrangements of works of the mind shall enjoy the protection afforded by the present Code, without prejudice to the author's rights on the original work. The same shall apply to the authors of anthologies or collections of works or various data, such as databases, which, by reason of the selection or the arrangement of their contents, constitute intellectual creations.'

---

47. EC Directive No. 96/9 of the European Parliament and of the Council of 11 Mar. 1996 on the legal protection of databases, OJEC, No. L. 77, 27 Mar. 1996, pp. 20–28.
48. Cass. Ass. plén., 30 Oct. 1987, *Le Monde v. Microfor: JCP* 1988 II 20932, rapport Nicot and note Huet; JCP ed. E, 1988 II 15093, No. 4, obs. Vivant and Lucas; RTD com. 1988, 57, obs. Françon.

2. Exceptions to Copyright Protection

86. Specific exceptions to copyright protection are listed into Article L. 122-5. This article was modified by the Act of 1 July 1998 to take the specificity of databases into account. On the one hand, Article L. 122-5, 2° expressly excludes 'copies or reproductions of an electronic database' from the benefit of the exception of 'Private Copies' (according to which third parties are allowed to make copies or reproductions of a protected work, on condition they are made from a lawful source and 'strictly reserved for the copyist's private use and not intended for any collective use' *see infra* paragraph 227).

87. On the other hand, a new specific exception to copyright protection was added to the list of Article L. 122-5; under the new paragraph 5, are authorized by law 'The acts necessary to access the content of an electronic database for the purposes and within the limits of the use provided by contract.'

3. Evidence of Infringement

88. Article L. 332-4 relating to the procedure of 'counterfeit-seizure' in the area of copyright includes also the databases. The procedure here is the same as for software seizure: a prior authorization by president of the Tribunal de Grande Instance is needed (Article L. 332-4, §1; *see supra* paragraph 80).

89. Any person with authority to bring an action for infringement shall be entitled, on the order issued upon request by the competent civil court (the President of the Tribunal de Grande Instance), to direct any bailiff, accompanied by experts appointed by the claimant, to proceed in any place with either the detailed description, with or without taking samples, or the effective seizure of the allegedly infringing database as well as any related document. The President shall order, for the same evidential purposes, the detailed description or the effective seizure of equipment and tools used to manufacture or distribute the allegedly infringing database as well as any related document. The order shall authorize the effective seizure of any document relating to these database, equipment, and tools, even in the absence of the latter. The President may also condition the implementation of the measures it ordered to the furnishing by the claimant of security to ensure, if necessary, the defendant's compensation if the infringement action is subsequently held unfounded or the seizure is lifted. The 'description-seizure' ('saisie-description') which is less dangerous as the effective seizure and may be done by the way of a copy.

B. Sui Generis Protection

90. Producers of databases are granted a specific protection organized by the new Title 4 of the Book Three of the Intellectual Property Code (new Articles L. 341-1–L. 343-7). These provisions define the subject matter, the beneficiaries of the sui generis protection, its scope, duration, and sanctions.

1. Subject Matter of Protection

91. A database may be the subject matter of the sui generis protection when the constitution, the verification, or the presentation of its content evidences a substantial financial, material, or human investment (Article L. 341-1, §1). This allows a sui generis protection even on databases which are not original, but which imply a substantial investment within the meaning of the statute.

2. Beneficiaries of Protection

92. The producer is defined as the person who takes the initiative and the risk of the necessary investments.[49] Since the statute does not make any distinctions between natural and juristic persons,[50] both may qualify as producers.[51]

93. Such producers may claim protection according to French law when:

- they are citizens or permanent residents of a Member State of the EU or of the European Economic Area;
- they are companies or enterprises formed in accordance with the legislation of a Member States of the EU and having their registered office, central administration, or main branch within the Union or a State party to the Agreement on the European Economic Area. However, where such a company or enterprise has only its registered office in the territory of such State, its activities must be genuinely linked on an ongoing basis with the economy of one of such States.

Producers of databases who do not fulfil the above conditions may benefit of the sui generis protection when a special agreement has been concluded by the EU Council with the State of their citizenship.

3. Scope of the Protection

94. The producer has the right to forbid:

- The extraction, by permanent or temporary transfer, of the totality or of a substantial part of the content of a database to another medium, by any means and in any form (Article L. 342-1, 1°).
- The re-use, by making available to the public all or a substantial part of the content of a database, in any form (Article L. 342-1, 2°).
- The public lending is not considered as an act of extraction or re-use of the database.
- The repeated and systematic extraction or re-use of non-substantial parts of the content of a database, when such operations obviously go beyond the normal conditions of use of the database (Article L. 342-2).

---

49. Cass. com., 23 Mar. 2010: Propr. industr. 2010, comm. 43, p. 40, note Bouche.
50. *See* Art. L. 341-2, 2°, which mentions 'companies and enterprises' as possible producers.
51. T. com. Paris, 7 May 1999.

95. The substantial character of a part of a database is to be evaluated either in quantity[52] or in quality.[53]

96. Under the same provision, the producer has the right to authorize third parties to exploit its database, either under a transfer of rights, or a licence.

97. The producer's exclusive rights are effective as from the date of the completion of the database; they expire fifteen years after the first day of the calendar year following that of completion. When a database has been made available to the public before the expiry of the above period, the rights expire fifteen years after the first day of the calendar year following the date when the database was first made available to the public. When a database is the object of a new substantial investment, its protection expires fifteen years after the first day of the calendar year following that in which this new investment was made (Article L. 342-5).

98. The producer's sui generis rights are protected by the IP Code as from 1 January 1998. This protection is available for databases completed after 1 January 1983 and which, at the date of publication of the Act of 1 July 1998 comply with the conditions of the sui generis protection. In this case, the duration of the protection is fifteen years from 1 January 1998. The sui generis system does not apply to Acts and agreements entered into prior to the date of entry into force of the Act of 1 July 1998 (Article 8).

99. The rightholder may not forbid, after the database is made available to the public (Article L. 342-3):

- The extraction or re-use of a non-substantial part, evaluated qualitatively or quantitatively, of the content of the database by the person having lawful access. Any contrary clause is void.
- The extraction for private use of a qualitatively or quantitatively substantial part of the content of a non-electronic database, subject to compliance with the copyrights or neighbouring rights over the works or materials incorporated into the database.
- The extraction or re-use of a database by establishments open to the public which activity consists in conceiving, manufacturing and distributing media to the benefit of certain handicapped persons (Article L. 342-3 3° and Article L. 122-5, 7°, §§1-2).
- The extraction or re-use of a substantial part, evaluated qualitatively or quantitatively, of the content of the database, with the exception of pedagogical databases or databases intended for digital edition of writings, for certain non-profit pedagogical or research purposes (Article L. 342-3 4°).
- Copies or digital reproductions of the database made, by a person having lawful access, for studies of texts and of datas included or associated with the scientific literature for a research purpose, excluding any commercial purpose (Article L. 342-3 5°).

---

52. Paris, 12 Sep. 2001, CCE 2001, comm. No. 121, obs. Caron; JCP 2002 II 10000, note Pollaud-Dulian.
53. TGI Paris, 5 Sep. 2001, CCE 2002, comm. No. 16, obs. Caron.

However, all those exceptions shall satisfy the so-called three-steps test which requires that any such exception must neither go beyond 'normal exploitation of the database' nor 'unreasonably prejudice the legitimate interests of the database's producer (Article L. 342-3 §3).

100. The rightholder may not control the resale of a material copy of a database after he consented to its first sale in a Member State of the EU or of the European Economic Area (EEA) (Article L. 342-4); such a first sale exhausts the producer's right within the usual meaning of this notion as applied to the intellectual property rights (*see infra*). However, the producer's right to control the resale of a material copy of the database or a part of it is not exhausted in case of transmission online.

101. Under the new Article L. 331-4, 'The rights mentioned in the first part of this Code may not prevail over any acts necessary for the accomplishment of a parliamentary control, a judiciary or an administrative procedure provided by law, or undertaken for public safety reasons.' In other words, the holder of rights on a database may not prohibit the access to this base in such cases.

4. Provisional Measures (Article L. 343-2)

102. Any person with authority to bring an action for infringement may, in preliminary proceedings, request the competent civil court to order, under a penalty of a daily fine if necessary, against the alleged infringer or intermediaries whose services it uses, any measure aimed at preventing an infringement about to be committed against the producer's sui generis right or aimed at stopping any further allegedly infringing act. The competent civil court may also order ex parte urgent measures when the circumstances require that such measures should not be taken in the presence of both parties, in particular when any delay would be likely to cause an irreparable damage to the claimant. The court, in preliminary or ex parte proceedings, may order the requested measures only if evidence, reasonably accessible to the claimant, makes it likely that its rights are infringed or that such infringement is about to be committed.

The court may enjoin the carrying out of the allegedly infringing acts, condition it on the furnishing of security to ensure, if necessary, the claimant's compensation or may order the seizure or the remittance to a third person of the products allegedly infringing the rights conferred by the title, to prevent their introduction or circulation in the channels of commerce.

The court may also award an advance payment to the claimant when the damage suffered cannot be seriously disputed.

The court, in preliminary or ex parte proceedings, may condition the implementation of the measures it has ordered on the furnishing of security by the claimant to ensure, if necessary, the claimant's compensation if the infringement proceedings are subsequently held unfounded or if the measures are void.

When the measures taken to stop the infringement of rights are ordered before the commencement of proceedings on the merits, the claimant shall institute legal proceedings, either by civil action or criminal action, or by filing a complaint with the Public Prosecutor, within a period of time set by regulation (twenty working days or thirty-one civil days if this time limit is longer, as from the day on which the order is given, Article R. 343-1). Failing that, upon the defendant's request and without its having to justify its application, the measures ordered are void, without prejudice to the damages which may be claimed.

5. Sanctions

103. The Article L. 343-4–L. 343-7 provides for criminal sanctions of infringements of the producers' rights such as defined in Article L. 342-1; moreover, these infringements, as well as infringements of the rights listed under the Article L. 342-2, are subject to civil sanctions.

6. Criminal Sanctions

104. An infringement of the producer's rights listed in Article L. 342-4 and committed by a natural person shall be punishable by a term of three years' imprisonment and a fine of EUR 300,000. The infringement is punished by a term of seven years' imprisonment and a fine of EUR 750,000 where it is committed by an organized gang (L. 343-4).

105. Natural persons penally liable may be further obliged, at their own costs, to remove from the channels of commerce the goods found to be infringing and all things which were used or intended to infringe the producer's right. The courts may also order the destruction, at the expense of the infringer, or the delivery up to the injured party of the goods removed from the channels of commerce or seized, without prejudice to the damages which may be claimed. The courts may also order the dissemination of the information concerning the decision, including displaying and publishing, at the expense of the infringer (Article L. 343-5).

106. Juristic persons may be declared penally liable in accordance with Article 121-2 of the Penal Code. According to Article L. 343-6 IPC, the infringement committed by a juristic person shall be punishable by a fine whose maximum amount shall be EUR 1,500,000 (Article 131-38: 'The maximum amount of a fine applicable to legal persons is five times that which is applicable to natural persons by the law sanctioning the offence') and the penalties listed in Article 131-39 of the Penal Code: (1) dissolution, where the legal person was created to commit a felony, or where it was diverted from its objects in order to commit it; (2) prohibition to exercise, directly or indirectly the activity at the origin of the infringement, either permanently or for a maximum period of five years; (3) placement under judicial supervision for a maximum period of five years; (4) permanent closure or closure for up to five years of the establishment, or one or more of the establishments, of the enterprise that was used to commit the offences in question; (5) disqualification from public tenders, either permanently or for a maximum period of five years; (6) prohibition, either permanently or for a maximum period of five years, to make a public appeal for funds; (7) prohibition to draw cheques, except those allowing the withdrawal of funds by the drawer from the drawee or certified cheques, and the prohibition to use payment cards, for a maximum period of five years; (8) confiscation of the thing which was used or intended for the commission of the offence, or of the thing which is the product of it; (9) posting a public notice of the decision or disseminating the decision in the written press or using any form of communication to the public by electronic means. The penalties under 1°

and 3° above do not apply to those public bodies which may incur criminal liability. Nor do they apply to political parties or associations, or to unions. The penalty under 1° does not apply to institutions representing workers.

The courts may also order the destruction, at the expense of the infringer, or the delivery up to the injured party of the goods removed from the channels of commerce or seized, without prejudice to the damages which may be claimed.

107. In the event of a repetition of the offences, or if the offender has been contractually bound to the aggrieved party by a contract, the penalties involved shall be doubled. Moreover, the offenders may be deprived for a period not exceeding five years of the right to elect and to be elected in professional elections (Article L. 343-7, commercial courts, chambers of commerce and industry, professional chambers, and labour dispute conciliation boards).

108. The technological measures of protection and rights-management information relating to a database (Article L. 342-3-1 and L. 342-3-2) are protected against circumvention by the criminal sanctions provided for by Article L. 335-4-1 and L. 335-4-2 (concerning neighbouring rights).

7. Civil Sanctions

109. Although the IP Code does not expressly mention any civil sanctions of the infringement of the producer's rights, such sanctions do apply, either as a supplement to criminal sanctions, or independently (according to the procedure chosen by the plaintiff). The infringement of an exclusive right always amounts to a civil wrongdoing and entails the obligation to compensate the damage it caused to the rightholder. This compensation is to be evaluated according to the ordinary rules of liability in torts, in the same way as for violations of the intellectual property rights (*see infra*).

8. Evidence of Infringement

110. According to Article L. 343-3, the proof of the existence of the infringements may be provided by the statements of sworn agents designated by professional organizations of producers; such agents must be approved by the Minister responsible for culture.

111. The Act No. 2007-1544 of 27 October 2007 has finally created a specific procedure of counterfeit seizure to take evidence of the infringement of the producer's sui generis right (Article L. 343-1). Any person with authority to bring an action for infringement shall be entitled, on the order issued upon request by the competent civil court (the President of the Tribunal de Grande Instance), to direct any bailiff, accompanied by experts appointed by the claimant, to proceed in any place with either the detailed description, with or without taking samples, or the effective seizure of the allegedly infringing media or articles as well as any related document. The President shall order, for the same evidential purposes, the detailed description or the effective seizure of equipment and tools used to manufacture or distribute the allegedly infringing media or articles as well as any related document. The order shall authorize the effective seizure of any document relating to these media, articles, equipment, and tools, even in the absence of the latter. The President may also condition the implementation of the measures it ordered to the furnishing by the claimant of security to ensure, if necessary, the defendant's compensation if the infringement action is subsequently held unfounded or the seizure is lifted.

112. The distrainee or the garnishee may ask the President of the 'Tribunal de grande instance' to lift the seizure or to limit its effects (Articles L. 343-1 §6 and L. 332-2). Such a claim must be submitted to the President within twenty working days or thirty-one civil days if this time limit is longer, as from the day on which the seizure is realized (Article R. 332-2). In such a case, if the President allows the request of the distrainee or garnishee, he may order the petitioner to deposit a sum as a guarantee for any damages to which the producer might be entitled (Article L. 332-2, §2). The seizure is void if the distrainer does not file a complaint with the Public Prosecutor or does not submit the matter to the criminal or civil competent court within twenty working days or thirty-one civil days if this time limit is longer, as from the day on which the seizure is realized (Articles L. 343-1 §6, L. 332-3 and R. 332-3).

III. Others

113. Since the list of Article L. 112-2 is illustrative and not limitative, the courts accepted the protection of other original works: characters of cartoons;[54] characters of television series;[55] and a character created by a mime artist.[56] Other cases of protectable works were the 'wrapping' of the Pont-Neuf bridge in Paris,[57] a son et lumière display,[58] the text of a patent,[59] and even a button.[60]

---

54. Chambéry, 10 Dec. 1951: Gaz. Pal. 1951, 1, jur., p. 116, the character of *Professor Nimbus*. Paris, 15 Oct. 1964: Ann. propr. Ind. 1965, 213, *Donald Duck*.
55. TGI Paris, 23 Sep. 1992: RIDA, 1993, p. 257.
56. Versailles, 9 Jul. 1992: RIDA, 1993, 208.
57. Paris, 13 Mar. 1986: D. 1987, som., p. 150, obs. Colombet.
58. Cass. civ. 1, 3 Mar. 1992: D. 1993, jur., p. 358, note Edelman.
59. Trib. corr. Paris, 17 Jan. 1968: Gaz. Pal. 1968, 1, jur., p. 197; RTD com. 1968, 1037, obs. Chavanne.
60. Cass. civ. 1, 11 Feb. 1997 (1st decision): JCP 1997 II 22973, note Daverat.

Chapter 3. Conditions of Protection

§1. Formal Requirements

114. Article L. 111-1 states 'The author of a work of mind enjoys on that work, by the mere fact of creation, an exclusive right of intangible property effective against anyone.' This implies that copyright follows creation and does not require any formalities.

115. Such formalities did exist in the French system since the statute of 19 January 1793 and until the statute of 19 May 1925. The action for infringement was subjected to the deposit of two copies of the work.

116. The Act of 19 May 1925 removed the deposit of the works from the conditions of the copyright protection; nevertheless it instituted the obligation for publishers, importers, producers, and printers to make a deposit ('dépôt légal') of the works they publish, import, or print. The Act of 20 June 1992 (now replaced by Article L. 131-1–L. 133-1 of the Patrimony Code, 'Code du patrimoine') extended the obligation to all printed, engraved, photographic, sound, audiovisual, multimedia documents, whatever the technical process of production, edition, or publication may be. Computer programs and databases are subject to the deposit whenever they are published in a material support. This deposit is designed to allow the collection and conservation of works which are available to the public, as well as the constitution and diffusion of national bibliographies and the public consultation of the works. The deposit may be made with the following institutions: the National Library, the National Cinematographic Centre, the National Institute for Audiovisual Works, and the Department of Legal Deposit of the Ministry of Home Affairs. A penal fine of a maximum amount of EUR 75,000 (Article L. 133-1 of the Patrimony Code) is foreseen against those who do not respect their obligation to make the deposit. But the deposit is not a condition of protection of the works and the violation of such obligation do not affect the copyright on the work.

§2. Substantive Requirements

117. Surprisingly, French statutory law does not provide for a definition of the substantive conditions of protection of copyrightable works. Article L. 111-1 states that the copyright shall benefit to 'the author of a work of the mind', but it gives no definition of such a 'work of the mind'. In a negative way, Article L. 112-1 states 'Provisions of the present Code protect authors' rights upon any work of mind, regardless of their type, form of expression, merit or destination.' And the following Article L. 112-2 only provides for an open list of protectable works (*see supra* paragraph 113). The legislator considered that a general definition would exceedingly hamper the judicial power of appreciation and preferred to provide only some examples. Nevertheless, the courts read a general rule into Article L. 112-2: since the type, form, merit or destination are meaningless, thus the only condition of protection is the originality of the work, which is necessarily associated with the notion of creation of a work of the mind (originality is expressly required only as for protection of the titles of works, by Article L. 112-4).

I. Work of the Mind

118. A work can be defined as a creation of form, because the idea must be clearly distinguished from its expression. In French law, the protection of the copyright is excluded as for ideas, concepts, principles, discoveries, informations, hard facts... Only the form created by the author (it is then an 'original' form because it has its origin in the author) to express such an idea can be reserved by copyright.[61]

II. Requirement of Originality

119. The originality of the work of mind is a positive requirement of the copyright's protection: the French Supreme Court requires that the lower courts verify the originality of copyrightable works[62] and explain why a given work is original.[63]

120. Case law ('jurisprudence') and learned writers ('doctrine') define originality as the mark of the author's personality.[64] The notion may be illustrated by the decision of the Cour de cassation refusing protection for a collection of books, because it does not bear the mark of the collector's personality.[65] Purely functional forms, that is to say forms which are only dictated by the function of their material support, are also not copyrightable[66] because they are not original creations of an author. More generally, a work of mere compilation of information is not original.[67] However, choices may, under circumstances, be original:[68] this condition applies to databases under the Act of 1998 (*see supra* paragraph 82 et seq.).

121. A written work is original in its composition or expression (the ideas not being copyrightable). The personal execution is meaningless: the author may have handwritten his work, typed or dictated it. In a musical work, composition and expression consist of the melody, rhythm, and harmony. Originality may thus appear in any of these elements. Here again, personal execution of a musical composition is meaningless as for its originality. As for plastic art works, the composition may be incorporated into a preparatory work (sketches, drawings, etc.), which is in itself protectable, independently from the definitive work. The latter's originality is to be sought in its

61. Cass. Civ. 1, 25 May 1992, RIDA, October 1992, p. 156; D. 1993, jur., p. 184.
62. Cass. civ. 1, 6 Mar. 1979: Bull. civ. I, No. 82; RTD com. 1979, 462, obs. Françon.
63. Cass. com., 11 Mar. 1986: Gaz. Pal. 1986, 2, pan., p. 123.
64. Cass. civ., 27 May 1942: S. 1942, 1, 124.
65. Cass. com., 27 Feb. 1990: RIDA, 1990, p. 319; JCP 1990 II 21545, note Pollaud-Dulian; RTD com. 1990, 208, obs. Françon. Also: Paris, 25 May 1988: D. 1988, jur., p. 542, note Edelman, refusing protection to a collection of cars.
66. Cass. com., 23 Jun. 1987: Bull. civ. IV, p. 156. Paris, 20 Sep. 1993: PIBD 1993, III, 713.
67. Cass. civ. 1, 2 May 1989: JCP 1990 II 21392, note Lucas; D. 1990, som., p. 49, obs. Colombet.
68. Paris, 14 Oct. 1993: RIDA, 1994, 240, selection of postcards presented in an original way.

composition and expression. Unlike the other categories of works, the plastic art work has to be executed personally by the artist (painter, sculptor). This rule must, however, be qualified as for certain joint works (*see infra*).

122. The decision on originality may be a difficult one, especially when a work borrows from a pre-existent one (adaptations, arrangements, anthologies). Originality does not imply novelty:[69] a work may not be objectively new (it rests on a prior work), but may be original (it bears the mark of its author's personality). If only the idea has been borrowed, then the work is absolutely original and its author does not owe anything to the first one. If, on the contrary, not only the idea, but also the composition or the expression has been partially taken from the pre-existent work, then the second one is a derived work, only relatively original (it must nevertheless bear the mark of its author's personality, otherwise it would be a mere counterfeit). Its author needs the authorization of the author of the initial work (*see infra*).

III. No Other Requirements

123. According to Article L. 112-1, the type, form of expression, merit, or purpose of a work is meaningless as for its protection. Consequently, originality is the sole condition of copyright.

A. The Type and Form of the Work Are Meaningless

124. The copyrightable work may belong to one of the classical types: literary works, dramatic works, musical works, pictorial, graphic and sculptural works, pantomimes and choregraphic works, motion pictures, and audiovisual works. But it may also be a work of a new type or form of expression, such as perfumes[70] or multimedia works.[71] It should be noted that the protection of perfumes by copyright is controversial. The Cour de cassation refused such protection to perfumes on the ground that 'the fragrance of a perfume, which proceeds of the simple implementation of a know-how, does not constitute the creation of a form of expression being able to profit from the copyright's protection of works of mind'.[72] However, some inferior courts do not share this view, tend to 'resist' and give copyright's protection to perfumes.[73]

69. Cass.civ. 1, 11 Feb. 1997: JCP ed. E, 1998, pan. 342, No. 14.
70. Paris, 3 Jul. 1975: D. 1976, som., p. 19.
71. TGI Paris, 13 Feb. 2001, Propr. intell. October 2001, p. 66, obs. Sirinelli; about the home page of a website.
72. Cass. civ. 1, 13 Jun. 2006, RJDA October 2006, p. 919, obs. Bouche; and again Cass. com., 1 Jul. 2008, Bull. civ. IV, No. 136; Cass. civ. 1, 22 Jan. 2009, No. 08-11404.
73. TGI Bobigny, 28 Nov. 2006; Paris, 14 Feb. 2007, RG 06/9813; TGI Nancy, 6 Apr. 2009; TGI Lille, 22 Oct. 2009.

B. The Merit of the Work Is Meaningless

125. It is a classical principle of the French copyright law, today expressed in Article L. 112-1: the protection may not stay on an evaluation of the aesthetic, technical, cultural, merits, or qualities of the original work of mind. The copyright's protection does not depend on the legislator's or judge's tastes and preferences.[74] It may not either, depend on moral considerations, which vary from one country to another and change with time.[75]

C. The Purpose of the Work Is Meaningless

126. As a consequence of the theory of the 'unity of art', introduced in the nineteenth century by the French author Eugène Pouillet, a work is protected regardless of its purpose. It may be a purely aesthetic work of art, or a work with a utilitarian aim. Consequently, works of applied arts are copyrightable under the same conditions as any others.[76] It should be noted that a work having a utilitarian purpose may be cumulatively protected by copyright and as a registered design or model if it fulfils the conditions of such a protection (*see infra*).

---

74. Cass. crim. 13 Feb. 1969: D. 1969, jur., p. 323, cartoons; -Cass. crim., 9 Oct. 1974: D. 1974, I.R., p. 228, bottle opener. -Cass. Ass. Plén., 7 Mar. 1986, *supra,* videogames.
75. Cass. crim., 6 May 1986: RIDA, 1986, 149; D. 1987, som., p. 151, obs. Colombet, pornographic films may be protected.
76. Cass. crim., 30 Oct. 1963: D. 1964, jur., p. 678, note Françon, a salad container is copyrightable. Cass. com., 18 Mar. 1970: Bull. civ. IV, p. 108, a wallpaper is copyrightable.

Chapter 4. Ownership

§1. The Author (Initial Authorship)

127. The author is the person who imprinted the mark of his personality on the work; it is neither enough to bring the idea or the theme underlying the work,[77] nor to manufacture the object following the artist's instructions.[78] Since juristic persons are artificial persons created by law and not human beings, they have not their own creative personality and are not able, properly speaking, to create works of mind and to imprint a mark of their own personality on that work. Consequently a juristic person on principle may not be the author[79] (initial authorship, i.e., *see* Article L. 113-7, §1 and Article L. 113-8, §1). However, exceptionally, an artificial person may be the author, in case of a collective work,[80] or as the creator's employer in case of computer software (*see supra* paragraph 68). Authors of pseudonymous and anonymous works enjoy copyright on these works (Article L. 113-6, §1). They are represented in the exercise of their rights by the original editor or publisher until such time as they reveal their true identity and prove their authorship. The 'orphan work' is a disclosed and protected work whose rights holder cannot be identified or found, despite diligent, proven, and serious searches. When a work has more than one copyright owner and one of the owners has been identified and located, it is not considered as an orphan work (Article L. 113-10). Implementing the Directive UE No. 2012/28, the Act No. 2015-195 of 20 February 2015 has introduced in the French Intellectual Property Code a new chapter (also applicable to neighbouring rights, Article L. 211-7) relating to certain uses of orphan works (Article L. 135-1–L. 135-7). Publicly accessible libraries, educational establishments and museums, as well as archives, film or audio heritage institutions (as for books, journals, newspapers and magazines, or other writings), and public-service broadcasting organizations (as for audiovisual works and phonograms produced by public-service broadcasting organizations up to and including 31 December 2002 and contained in their archives, Article L. 135-1) are authorized to make available to the public and to reproduce for the purposes of digitization, making available, indexing, cataloguing, preservation, or restoration (Article L. 135-2), the orphan works contained in their collections, provided that such use fulfils their public interest missions. These organizations may generate revenues in the course of such uses, for the exclusive purpose of covering their costs of digitizing orphan works and making them available to the public (Article L. 135-2). The Decree of 6 May 2015, adopted for the application of the Act No. 2015-195 of 20 February 2015, lays down detailed rules for the application of the new provisions on certain uses of orphan works, in particular the appropriate sources of information to be consulted, for each category of works, for diligent, proven,

77. Cass. civ. 1, 8 Nov. 1983: Bull. civ. I, No. 260.
78. Paris, 26 Apr. 1982: Gaz. Pal. 1983, 1, som., p. 132; Poitiers, 7 Dec. 1999: JCP ed. E, 2000, p. 1375, obs. Brochard.
79. Cass. com., 5 Nov. 1985: Bull. civ. IV, No. 261, RIDA, October 1986, p. 140.
80. Cass. civ. 1, 8 Dec. 1993: RIDA, October 1994, p. 469.

and serious searches and the manner in which a right holder in a work declared orphaned may manifest himself so that its use ceases and fair compensation is paid to him (Article R. 135-1–R. 135-4).

128. Under Article L. 113-1, authorship is presumed to belong to the person or persons under whose name the work has been disclosed. The legal presumption of authorship exempts the one under whose name the work was disclosed to bring evidence of his authorship.[81] The presumption is rebuttable: the interested persons may bring evidence by any means of proof that the author (or authors) is not the one under whose name the work has been disclosed.[82]

129. A foreign author whose work was first disclosed out of France may benefit of the French copyright on condition that it exists reciprocity: Article L. 111-4 states that when it is ascertained, after consultation with the Minister for Foreign Affairs, that a State does not afford to works disclosed for the first time in France, in any form whatsoever, protection that is adequate and effective, the French copyright protection may be refused to the foreign author whose work was first disclosed in that State. However, in such a case, two components of the moral right are preserved (the right to paternity and the right to the respect of the work) and the due royalties are paid to general interest bodies designated by decree. Article L. 111-4 expressly reserves the effect of international conventions, whose basic principle is the 'national treatment'[83] so that in practice foreign authors often benefit of the French copyright protection regardless of reciprocity.[84]

§2. Joint Works/Works Created by Several Persons

130. Article L. 113-2 lists three categories of works created by several authors: joint works ('œuvres de collaboration'), composite works ('œuvres composites' or 'œuvres dérivées'), and collective works ('œuvres collectives').

I. Joint Works

131. A joint work is created by the participation of several persons (Article L. 113-2, §1). Such a work may associate only natural persons.[85] A personal and original contribution in the creation of the work's form, and not only an advice or inspiration, is required from each of these natural persons to be a co-author. And this association of personal contributions must have been first concerted: a concerted common creative

81. Cass. civ. 1, 3 Jul. 1990: Bull. civ. I, p. 189; RTD com. 1991, 48, obs. Françon, as for the co-author.
82. Cass. civ. 1, 24 Nov. 1993: RIDA, April 1994, p. 216.
83. As for copyright: Art. 5 of the Berne Convention, Art. 2 of the Universal Geneva Convention, Art. 3 of the TRIPS Agreement. As for neighbouring rights: Art. 2 of the Rome Convention of 26 Oct. 1961 on the protection of performing artists, producers of phonograms, and broadcasting organizations, Art. 3 of the TRIPS Agreement.
84. Paris, 28 Apr. 1998: RIDA, October 1998, p. 264.
85. Paris, 10 Mar. 1988: RDPI 1988, 109; D. 1990, som., p. 187, obs. Burst.

work is required.[86] In the dispute between the sculptors Renoir and Guino, a specific situation appeared: late Renoir could no longer sculpt himself and gave detailed instructions to Guino who executed them in the presence and under Renoir's control. It has been decided that the sculptures were joint works: Renoir oral compositions were original works, and Guino brought the mark of his personality into their expression.[87]

132. Other examples of joint works: an engraving made after a design; a geographical atlas; an interview when the interviewer has a large choice of questions and the interviewed person reserved himself the right to give a personal mark to the expression of his thought; the weaver of a tapestry working after a design, a composer and the librettist or the choreograph, etc.

133. A specific provision deals with the designation of the co-authors of an audiovisual work. Under Article L. 113-7 the authors of such a work are the natural persons who realized its intellectual creation. The article then provides for a list of persons who are presumed (rebuttable presumption) to be co-authors: the author of the scenario, the author of the adaptation, the author of the script, the author of the musical compositions (with or without words) especially made for the audiovisual work, and the director. Finally, when the audiovisual work is based on a pre-existent work still protected, the authors of the latter are treated as authors of the new work. The courts accept that other persons claim authorship if they bring evidence of their original contribution to the audiovisual work. For instance, the author of a first scenario which has been incorporated into the final one is co-author of the film.[88] On the contrary, the photographer, who is a mere technical assistant following the director's orders,[89] or the author of the poster advertising for the film[90] are not considered as co-authors of the film.

134. It should be noted that the producer is not cited in the legal list of presumed co-authors of an audiovisual work. A juristic person being a producer may never be a co-author (*see supra* paragraph 131). A natural person may be co-author if he evidences his original contribution in the creation of the work; a mere financial contribution is not sufficient.

135. Another specific provision is devoted to the definition of authors of a radio work. Under Article L. 113-8, the natural persons who participate in the intellectual creation of a radio work are co-authors of this work. The legislator did not provide here for a list of presumed authors. The text sends back to Article L. 113-7 in the case when the radio work is based on a pre-existent work (*see supra* paragraph 133).

136. The legal rules applicable to the exploitation of a joint work are provided under Article L. 113-3: the authors are joint owners of such a work. Thus, the co-authors must exercise their rights by common consent. Consequently, the publication (or any other form of exploitation) of the work without the authorization of one of the co-authors is illegal. In case of disagreement, the civil courts may supply a co-author's opposition and authorize the others to exploit the work. The court will in such cases also dispatch the proceeds of the exploitation between the co-authors.

---

86. Cass. civ. 1, 2 Dec. 1997: Bull. civ. I, No. 348; D. 1998, jur., p. 507, note Edelman.
87. Cass. civ. 1, 13 Nov. 1973: D. 1974, jur., p. 533, note Colombet.
88. Cass. civ. 1, 24 Nov. 1993: RIDA, 1994, 216.
89. Paris, 2 Nov. 1981: D. 1983, som., p. 91, obs. Colombet.
90. Paris, 18 Mar. 1987: D. 1988, som., p. 209, obs. Colombet.

137. When a co-author brings an action in courts, he must call the others, under the sanction of refusal of the action.[91] Each co-author may, however, act alone for the defence of his moral right. Similarly, when a third person brings an action for infringement, he must call all the co-authors.

138. Article L. 113-3, §4 states that when the contributions are of different types (e.g., music and words), each of the co-authors, unless otherwise agreed, may exploit alone his personal contribution, however, without prejudicing to the exploitation of the common work. For instance, the author of the text of a song may publish it separately, or read it as a poem, etc., whereas the composer of the music may have it played without the words. However, such a separate exploitation would be illegal if it damages the joint work; for instance, the author of the words may sue the composer for damages if the latter sold his composition for a film, when this hampered the sales of the recorded song.[92]

II. Composite (or Derived) Works

139. According to Article L. 113-2, §2, a composite work is a new work in which is incorporated a pre-existent work without the collaboration of the latter's author. In other words, the author uses an existent work in order to create another work. The composite work is characterized by the lack of participation of the first author.[93] The classical examples are translations and adaptations, variations, musical transcriptions, etc. However, composite works do not always consist of an adaptation or transformation of a prior work; they may also result from a mere superposition or integration of two works: such is more and more often the case for works created with modern technologies (e.g., videoclips or multimedia works). The Act of 18 December 1996 added into Article L. 112-3 the case of 'collection of data' (databases; *see supra* paragraph 82). It was decided that a work may be at the same time composite and joint work, for instance, when the author dies before finishing his work which is then completed by several of his followers.[94]

140. The composite work belongs to the author who created it, but he must take into account the prior author's rights, as long as the pre-existent work is protected by copyright (on the ground of the exploitation rights as of the moral right) (Articles L. 112-3 and L. 113-4). Consequently, both authors have concurrent rights on such a work; however, the first author's situation is preeminent.[95] The first author's authorization

91. Cass. civ. 1, 4 Oct. 1988: RIDA, July 1989, p. 251. -10 May 1995: RIDA, October 1995, p. 285; RTD com. 1996, p. 57, obs. Françon.
92. *See also*: Cass. civ. 1, 6 May 1997: D. 1998, jur., p. 80, note Edelman; JCP ed. E,1998, chr., p. 1252, No. 3, obs. Laporte-Legeais, for cartoons.
93. Cass. civ. 1, 26 Jan. 1994: Bull. civ. I, No. 35; D. 1994, I.R., p. 55; transformation of caricature drawings into puppets for television.
94. Cass. civ. 1, 14 Nov. 1973: Bull. civ. I, No. 390; RIDA, April 1974, p. 66, obs. Desbois; RTD com. 1974, 514, obs. Desbois, the opera 'Prince Igor' started by Borodine and finished by Rimsky-Korsakow and Glazounov is a composite and a joint work.
95. Cass. civ. 1, 9 Feb. 1994: RIDA, July 1994, 335, note Gautier; D. 1994, jur., p. 405, 2nd case, note Edelman; the author of the novel 'Gens de Mogador' may exercise her right to oppose the use of the derived work after the expiry of the contract for authorization.

is required for any exploitation of the derived work, so that the latter will often share its revenues with the former. For instance, the publication of the translation of a novel must be authorized by its author; although the translator has a copyright on his own (derived) work, he must often share the royalties with the author of the novel (on a contractual basis). The author of the initial work keeps the right to continue or to begin its exploitation as such.

III. Collective Works

141. According to Article L. 113-2, §3, a collective work is created at the initiative of a natural or artificial person, who edits it, publishes it, and discloses it under its direction and name; the personal contribution of the various authors is merged in the whole, without it being possible to attribute to each of them a separate right on the ensemble. The classical examples are dictionaries, newspapers, or encyclopaedias, but the courts also qualified as collective works: elements of a car body,[96] a computer program,[97] a poster,[98] a guide of administrative formalities,[99] etc.

142. In the collective work, it is impossible to specify the individual role of each of the contributors even if their names are known. Consequently, the work is published under the entrepreneur's name, and belongs to him (Article L. 113-5). This is one of the rare cases in French law where a juristic person may be the initial owner of a work, without having to evidence an assignment of copyright.[100]

§3. Works Made for Hire

143. Works made under a contract ('works made for hire') are dealt with only indirectly under Article L. 111-1, §3, which states that 'The existence or conclusion of a contract of employment or for services by the author of a work of the mind does not imply any exception to the rights recognized to him under §1 [author's right], subject to the exceptions contained in the present code.'

144. Consequently, a work created by an employee during his contract of employment belongs to him and not to his employer (*see supra* paragraph 68, the exception of computer software made by an employee). The latter may exploit the work only under an assignment of copyright by the employee-author. Although some lower courts accepted an implicit assignment of copyright in a labour contract,[101] the

96. Cass. crim. 6 Jun. 1991: D. 1993, som. p. 86, obs. Colombet.
97. Cass. civ. 1, 3 Jul. 1996, JCP 1996 IV 2008; D. 1997, jur., p. 328, note Françon.
98. Cass. civ. 1, 8 Dec. 1993: Bull. civ. I, No. 361.
99. Cass. civ. 1, 2 Dec. 1997: JCP ed. E, 1998, pan., p. 155.
100. Cass. civ. 1, 17 Mar. 1982: D. 1982, jur., p. 71, note Greffe; RTD com. 1982, 428, obs. Françon. Cass. civ. 1, 24 Mar. 1993, 1st case: JCP 1993 II 22085, note Greffe; the juristic person which exploits a work under its own name is presumed to own a collective work when several authors contributed to it. Cass. civ. 1, 9 Jan. 1996: RIDA, July 1996, 342; RTD com. 1997, 95, obs. Françon.
101. Paris, 17 May 1969: D. 1969, jur., p. 702, note J.-F.P.

French Supreme Court decided that such a transfer is subject to the ordinary rules of assignment: it must be done in writing, and specified the assigned rights as to their scope, duration, and purpose.[102]

145. The same solution applies as for works created under a contract for services by an independent creator: he owns the copyright on his work, unless he assigns it to his client.[103] An exception is provided under Article L. 132-31 as for works made for advertisement: such contracts between a creator and an advertising agency imply a presumption of assignment to the firm, on condition the contract provides with precision for the author's remuneration for each type of exploitation of the work, considering the geographical area, the duration and the importance of the exploitation, and the nature of the support. Another exception deals with contracts for audiovisual production (Article L. 132-24), where the rights are presumed to be assigned to the producer.

146. As for works created by civil servants, the Act No. 2006-961 of 1 August 2006 has introduced a new provision in Article L. 111-1 to expressly affirm the same principle: the owner of the copyright is the work's creator and not his public employer. However, if the work was created by certain civil servants[104] either during the performance of their functions, or according to the instructions provided by their public employer, the economic rights are automatically transferred, as from the creation and only to the extent of what is necessary in view of the implementation of a mission of public service, to the public employer (Article L. 131-3-1 and L. 131-3-2). For the commercial exploitation of the work, the public employer enjoys only a priority, except if the research activities result from a contract concluded with a private juristic person. Furthermore, the moral right of these civil servants is strongly limited by Article L. 121-7-1: the exercise of their right to disclose the work must respect the specific rules attached to their function and to the organization, functioning, and activity of their public employer; they cannot oppose a modification of their work, when such a modification is decided by their hierarchy in the interest of the service and does not damage their honour or reputation; they cannot exercise their right to reconsider or to withdraw the work without the consent of their hierarchy.

147. Finally, the sale of the material support incorporating a work of art does not entail assignment of copyright on this work (Article L. 111-3).

---

102. Cass. civ. 1, 16 Dec. 1992: JCP ed. E, 1993 I 246, No. 4, obs. Vivant and Lucas; RIDA, 1993, p. 193, obs. Kéréver. -Cass. civ. 1, 21 Oct. 1997: JCP ed. E, 1998, jur., p. 1047, note J.M. Mousseron.

103. Paris, 4 Jul. 1865: DP 1865 2, 201. – Cass. civ., 14 Mar. 1900: DP 1900, 1, 497, report Rau, concl. Desjardins, note Planiol.

104. Agents of the French State, a territorial entity, a public establishment of an administrative nature, an independent public service authority with legal personality or of the 'Banque de France'.

Chapter 5. Transfer

148. The French law does not make the distinction between assignment and licence of copyright and deals only with assignment (Article L. 131-1–L. 131-8). French authors acknowledge that the distinction is only a question of degree in transfer of copyright.[105] Assignment may take place within a contract for publication, for performance, for production of an audiovisual work, or an order for advertisement. Each of these contracts is subject to a specific regulation.[106] Only the general rules common to all transfers of copyright will be exposed here.

§1. Formal Requirements

I. Evidence

149. According to Article L. 131-2, contracts for performance, publication, and audiovisual production and, since the Act No. 2016-925 of 7 July 2016, all contracts transferring author's rights, shall be in writing. In all other cases, the provisions of Articles 1359–1362 of the Civil Code apply. The courts limit the scope of the rule to the agreements listed in the legal provision. For instance, it was held that the rule does not apply to contracts for translation or adaptation.[107]

II. Listing of Transferred Rights

150. Article L. 131-3, §1 requires that the contract lists separately each of the rights to be assigned and defines the scope and purpose of the authorized exploitation, as for its duration and place. Consequently, the scope of the assignment must be precisely defined by the parties, under the sanction of nullity. For instance, was declared invalid a clause 'all rights included' ('tous droits compris'), as being too general.[108] However, the Supreme Court limits the application of the rule to transfers made by the author himself and excludes it as for contracts made by the assignee of copyright.[109] The legislation provides for a presumption of transfer in some contracts, such as audiovisual production, for the benefit of the producer (Article L. 132-24), or for

105. Colombet, Droit de la propriété littéraire et artistique, 9th ed., 1999, No. 290.
106. Contract for publication, *see* Art. L.132-1–L. 132-17-8 of the IP Code; contract for performance, *see* Art. L. 132-18–L. 132-22; contract for production of an audiovisual work, *see* Art. L. 132-23–L. 132-30; order contract for advertisement, *see* Art. L. 132-31; contract to use the exploitation right on a computer software as a collateral, *see* Art. L. 132-34; contract on works of a journalist, Art. L. 132-35–L. 132-45.
107. Paris, 10 May 1973: D. 1973, jur., p. 548, concl. Cabannes.
108. Cass. civ. 1, 9 Oct. 1991: RIDA, Jan. 1992, No. 151, p. 292.
109. Cass. civ. 1, 13 Oct. 1993: D. 1994, jur., p. 166, note Gautier; RTD com. 1994, 272, obs. Françon, for a contract between an advertising agent and his client.

advertisement (Article L. 132-31). The conclusion of a contract of employment does not entail such a presumption as for works created by the employee (*see supra* paragraph 143).

151. As a corollary to the requirement of a formal list of the transferred rights, Article L. 122-7, §4 provides for a rule of interpretation: when a contract includes the transfer either of the reproduction right or of the performing right, the scope of assignment is limited to the modes of exploitation expressly provided. The courts apply this rule of interpretation to all the mentions required under Article L. 131-3, §1 (scope, destination, place, duration of the transfer whatever its object): the transfer is thus limited to what was expressly agreed upon. Conflicts often arise in relation to advertising, mainly when the transferor sues the transferee for infringement because the work was used out of the limits set by contract. For instance, assignment of the reproduction right for advertising does not include the performing right also for advertising of the same design.[110] In another case, it was held that the assignment of the reproduction right of a design in a newspaper does not allow reproduction on tee-shirts, etc.[111]

§2. Substantive Requirements

I. Prohibition of Global Assignment

152. Article L. 131-1 of the Code states that: 'The global assignment of future works is void'. This rule is an exception to the principle asserted under the Civil Code (Article 1163), whereby future things may be the object of an obligation. The aim is to protect the author against the temptation to sell in advance the copyrights on all his future works, whatever their nature and quality.

153. The law foresaw two exceptions to the prohibition of global assignment of future copyrights. The first exception relates to the preference clause which is authorized in contracts for publication (Article L. 132-4). Under such a clause, the author may agree to grant to his publisher a preference for the publication of five of his future works, or for creations made during the next five years, on condition that the type of these works is clearly determined. For instance, a preference clause mentioning works in 'human sciences', which is too vague, is void;[112] but a clause granting a preference for 'essays' is valid, when the author's specialty allows to determine the nature of such essays.[113]

154. The second exception is provided under Article L. 132-18, §1, which authorizes the 'general performance contract'. A 'general performance contract' means a contract under which a professional body of authors grants to an entertainment promoter the right to perform, for the duration of the contract, the existing or future

110. Cass. civ. 1, 18 Dec. 1979: JCP 1980 II 19307, concl. Gulphe.
111. Paris, 21 Nov. 1991: Juris-Data, No. 24330.
112. Cass. civ. 1, 5 Feb. 1980: D. 1980, I.R., p. 272.
113. TGI Paris, 23 Apr. 1971: RTD com. 1971, 1017, obs. Desbois.

works constituting the repertoire of such body under the conditions stipulated by the author or his successors in title.

155. Outside these two exceptions, the transfer of copyright (one, some, or all of the economic rights) on a plurality (two or more) of future works is void (only the author may sue for avoidance). However, the courts tend to interpret this provision in a rather limited way. For instance, it was held that a transfer of copyright in future works by a painter is valid if limited in time and not including obligations incompatible with the author's moral right,[114] or when it is possible, because of the circumstances, to individualize the assigned future works.[115] Another court pointed out to the usefulness of such contracts, whereby 'Young artists may give themselves up to their art, without material constraints'.[116] And the prohibition only relates to the global assignment of future copyrights. Consequently, it does not apply to the global assignment of a part or of all the future production of an artist (material supports incorporating the works) (*see supra* paragraph 147, Article L. 111-3).

II. Author's Remuneration

156. According to Article L. 131-4, §1, the author's remuneration for transfer of his rights must consist of royalties on the sales or on the exploitation of the work. This rule aims at protecting the author against the risk of a transfer in exchange for a low lump sum. Any other clause is void. The royalties used as a basis for remuneration must be assessed on the list price.[117] The efficacy of this protective rule may be jeopardized by the fact that no minimum percentage of royalty is required by law.

157. Some exceptions to this rule are accepted (Article L. 131-4, §2). The main exception comes into play when the basis for calculating the royalty cannot be practically determined, which may have a very wide scope, since the basis of the royalty can be computed only when the exploitation of the work brings takings likely to be individualized. Such is not the case when the public does not pay to access the work: e.g., the work is used only for advertisement, or is communicated to the public in a hotel, etc. The second exception applies when there are no means to control the enforcement of the royalty (e.g., juke-box); or the cost of such a calculation and control would be out of proportion with the expected results. A further exception excludes the royalty system when it is made impossible given the nature or the conditions of exploitation of the work (e.g., articles in newspapers or accessory works such as musical arrangements). A further exception excludes the royalty system when the transferred rights relate to a software. Finally, other exceptions are provided under Article L. 132-6 of the Code: a lump sum is possible in contracts for publishing for the first edition of certain kinds of books and written documents: 'scientific or technical works', 'prefaces, introductions, annotations, and forewords', 'anthologies and encyclopedias', 'limited de luxe editions',

114. Cass. civ. 1, 19 Jan. 1970: D. 1970, jur., p. 483, RTD com. 1972, 103, obs. Desbois. -Nimes, 4 Jul. 1966: JCP 1967 II 14961, concl. Champeil, RTD com. 1967, 709, obs. Desbois.
115. Cass. civ. 1, 6 Nov. 1979: RIDA, July 1980, p. 167, JCP 1980 IV 25, D. 1980, I.R., p. 207.
116. Aix-en-Provence, 23 Feb. 1965: Gaz. Pal. 1965, 1, jur., p. 316; RTD com. 1965, 849, obs. Desbois.
117. Cass. civ. 1, 9 Oct. 1984: RIDA, July 1985, p. 144.

'prayer books', 'translations', 'cheap popular editions', and 'cheap picture books for children'. A transfer for a lump price may also be agreed when one of the parties is established abroad. In the case of works of the mind published in newspapers and periodicals of any kind and by press agencies, the remuneration of an author bound to the information enterprise by a contract for hire or of service may also be laid down as a lump sum.

158. In all these cases, the lump remuneration requires the author's explicit agreement. Moreover, the supposed dangers of a transfer for a lump price are corrected by the possibility given to the author to demand review of the price conditions under the contract, when he suffers a prejudice of more than seven-twelfth as a result of a burdensome contract or of insufficient advance estimate of the proceeds from the work (Article L. 131-5).

§3. Collective Management of Rights

159. More and more often, the authors are individually unable to control the use of their works. This phenomenon has increased with the new means of communication and reproduction; cable and satellite retransmission, as well as Internet arise new problems for the authors' remuneration, which can be solved only by the way of a collective management of rights through 'collecting societies' (*see* Articles L. 321-1–L. 328-2 IPC which contain the rules relating to these 'collecting societies'[118]).

160. However, this form of administration is not new: the oldest organization of authors is the 'Société des Auteurs et Compositeurs Dramatiques' (SACD), founded in 1829. The 'Société des Gens de Lettres' (SGDL) was created under Balzac's influence in 1838; its repertory is administered since 1981 by the 'Société Civile des Auteurs Multimédia' (SCAM). In 1851 the 'Société des Auteurs, Compositeurs et Editeurs de Musique' (SACEM) was founded, which not only manages authors' rights but also the publishers' interests. In 1935 was created the 'Société pour l'administration du droit de reproduction mécanique des auteurs, compositeurs et éditeurs' (SDRM). In the world of graphic arts, the 'Société des Auteurs dans les Arts Graphiques et Plastiques' (ADAGP) was founded in 1953 and the 'Société des Auteurs des Arts Visuels' (SPADEM), founded in 1954, was existing until its compulsory liquidation in 1996. These are just some examples of the twenty-five existing collecting societies.

161. The relations between the agency and the author are contractual. The author mandates the organization to manage his rights, or assigns his rights, but at the same time becomes member of the organization. The latter collects and dispatches according to its charter, the revenues from the exploitation of its members' rights. The organization may also defend its members' interests, by suing the infringers (Article L. 321-1, §2).

162. As for the relations between the agency and the users of copyrighted works, the former licences the rights to the latter. For obvious practical reasons, the price does

118. These rules have been modified or created by the Order No. 2016-1823 of 22 Dec. 2016, OJ No. 0298 of 23 Dec. 2016, text No. 63, implementing EU Directive 2014/26 of the European Parliament and of the Council of 26 Feb. 2014 on collective management of copyright and related rights and multi-territorial licensing of rights in musical works for online use in the internal market, OJEU No. L 84, 20 Mar. 2014, pp. 72–98.

not consist of royalties on the exploitation of the work by the user, but of a lump sum. Frequently, such prices are collectively negotiated by users' organizations in various sectors. A famous conflict opposed the SACEM and the association of owners of night clubs. The users sued the SACEM for abuse of a dominant position on the French and European Community (EC) markets of copyright management. They showed that the prices asked by the SACEM were far higher than those in force in all other EC Member States. French courts[119] and the Court of Justice of European Communities,[120] stated that such unjustified differences in price might be abusive. Finally, the conflict came to an end by agreement in 1994.

163. Recently, the problem of the non-available books of the twentieth century has also been solved thanks to a system of collective management of rights (*see* Article L. 134-1–L. 134-9 IPC), by the Act No. 2012-287 of 1 March 2012.[121] A non-available book of the twentieth century is a book published in France from 1 January 1901 to 31 December 2000, no longer commercially released by a publisher and not even currently published in a printed or digital form (Article L. 134-1). All these books are first to be listed by the National Library of France ('BNF') in a public database, freely accessible online (Article L. 134-2). As from the date of registration of a book in the database and within six months, its publisher may oppose to this registration provided that he exploits the book within the two following years (Article L. 134-4, II). Its author may also oppose, at any time, to this registration. But if he does later than six months after the registration, he must justify that the reproduction or performance of his book may damage his honour or reputation (Article L. 134-4, I). When a book is registered in that database for six months, without opposition, an agreed collecting society (i.e., SOFIA) may then exercise the right to authorize the digital reproduction and performance of this book (Article L. 134-3). It shall first propose to the book's editor an exclusive authorization for a digital reproduction and performance (for ten years renewable). If the editor does not expressly agree, in a written form within two months, this proposal is deemed to be refused. The authorized editor must exploit the book through digital reproduction or performance within three years after the authorization's notification. If not, he loses the benefit of the authorization. If the editor does not agree with the proposal or loses the benefit of the authorization, the collecting society may deliver to third parties a non-exclusive authorization for digital reproduction and performance (for five years renewable). The royalties collected by the collecting society from the authorized persons shall be equitably shared between the author and the publisher of the book (the author's part shall not be inferior to the editor's part) (Article L. 134-3, III, 5°). If the subject matter of the book is an orphan work, the collecting society must investigate in order to identify its rightholders. If the collecting society does not succeed in identifying the rightholders, ten years after their collect, the royalties shall be used for action to assist creation, for training schemes for writers

119. Cass. com., 5 Nov. 1991: D. 1993, jur., p. 63, note Daverat.
120. ECJ, 13 Jul. 1989: RIDA, October 1989, p. 289.
121. Act No. 2012-287 of 1 Mar. 2012 relating to the digital exploitation of the non-available books of the twentieth century, JORF, No. 53, 2 Mar. 2012, p. 3986, completed by Decree No. 2013-182 of 27 Feb. 2013 implementing Art. L. 134-1–L. 134-9 of the Intellectual Property Code on the digital exploitation of unavailable books of the twentieth century, JORF, No. 51, 1 Mar. 2013, p. 3835.

and for actions to promote the public reading in libraries (Article L. 134-9). Even if exploitation's authorizations have been given by the collecting society, the publisher or the author may withdraw the collecting society's right to authorize the digital reproduction or performance of the book. To that end, the author must justify that he is the holder of the right of digital reproduction or performance. The publisher must exploit the book within the eighteen following months and tolerate, until its term, the digital exploitation already engaged by third parties according to the authorization given to them by the collecting society (Article L. 134-6). However, this system will have to be revised as it has been partially condemned by the Court of Justice of the European Union[122]. The Copyright Directive No. 2001/29 does not preclude the digital exploitation of non-available books of the twentieth century in the cultural interest of consumers and of society, provided that implicit expression of the author's consent is preceded by actual prior information. Every author must actually be informed of the future use of his work by a third party and the means at his disposal to prohibit it if he so wishes. It cannot reasonably be presumed that, without opposition on their part, every author of these 'forgotten' books is in favour of the 'resurrection' of their works, in view of their commercial use in a digital format. The author must be able to put an end to the future exploitation of his work in a digital format, without having to depend on the concurrent will of persons other than those to whom that author had given prior authorisation to proceed with such a digital exploitation and, thus, on the agreement of the publisher holding only the rights of exploitation of that work in a printed format, also without having to submit beforehand to a formality consisting of proving that other persons are not, otherwise, holders of other rights in that work, such as those concerning its exploitation in printed format.

122. ECJ, 3rd ch., 16 November 2016, Case C-301/15.

Chapter 6. Scope of Exclusive Rights

164. French legislation has a dual conception of copyright. According to Article L. 111-1, author's rights include 'moral and intellectual attributes, as well as economic attributes'. Each category of rights is subject to specific rules.

§1. Moral Right (Droit Moral)

165. Although considered as the most important author's right, the moral right has no precise statutory definition. Article L. 121-1 only provides for a list of attributes implied in the moral right: third persons must respect the author's quality, name, and work. Article L. 121-2 adds the author's right to disclose the work. Finally, it is only in Article L. 121-4 that appears the right to reconsider or to withdraw the work, the only one which is regulated in detail. In addition, Article L. 121-1 gives a list of characteristics of the moral right: it is personal, perpetual, transmissible only upon the author's death, its exercise may be entrusted to a third person by a provision of a will.

166. Only the person having the quality of author may prevail himself of the moral right. Following these statutory provisions, it is necessary to explain first the components of the moral right, then its characteristics and finally the specific problems with moral right on works created by several persons.

I. The Components of the Moral Right

167. The author's moral right comprises the right to disclose the work, the right to paternity, the right to the respect of the work, and the right to reconsider or to withdraw the work.

168. The right to disclose is the first and the most remarkable component of the moral right. It means that the author may not be forced to disclose his work. This right is in compliance with the rule set under Article L. 111-2: a work is created irrespective of any disclosure, by the mere fact of its realization, even unfinished, by the author. This means that the moral right applies even to an unpublished work.[123] But as soon as the work has been disclosed, i.e., made available to the public in any way with the consent of the author, the right to disclose is exhausted.

169. The publication by a third person of a work which the author considered as unfinished is illegal.[124] A work restored by a third party after being destroyed by the author,[125] or published in a form not authorized by the author is also infringing.[126]

123. Cass. civ. 1, 25 Feb. 1997: JCP 1997 II 22873, note Ravanas, the partial reading of an unfinished work during a court audience did not violate the moral right.
124. Orléans, 17 Mar. 1965: JCP 1965 II 14156, note Boursigot, Rouault's unfinished paintings.
125. Paris, 6 Mar. 1931: DP 1931, 2, 88, note Nast, Camoin's destroyed paintings. – Cass. crim., 13 Dec. 1995: RIDA, July 1996, p. 516, note Granier de Cassagnac.
126. Paris, 24 Nov. 1992: RIDA, January 1993, p. 191, obs. Kéréver, unlawful publication of Roland Barthes's classes which he wanted to be kept oral.

Consequently, the right to disclose gives to the author also the possibility to refuse to deliver the commissioned (finished or unfinished) work to the other party to the contract: only damages may be ordered, not an injunction.[127] A limitation applies to audiovisual works under Article L. 132-24. As for works not yet published, the right to disclose opposes seizure of the material support of the work, which would lead to the disclosure of the work without the consent of the author. Only the author may decide to publish them or not. And such a seizure would in fact hamper the author's moral right to decide upon publication.

170. Article L. 111-3 solves the conflict between the author's moral right and a third party's right of ownership on the material support of the work. It states that copyright is independent from the ownership of the material object in which the work is incorporated. Consequently, the purchaser of a work does not acquire copyright on it. For example, the author of a painting may forbid its reproduction by the buyer;[128] this right remains with the author (or his successors). The author may not claim from the owner that he puts the material support of the work at his disposal in order to allow the exercise of the author's rights. However, the owner's right may be judicially limited in case of 'manifest abuse', of unjustified resistance preventing the exercise of his rights by the author (Article L. 111-3, §2).

171. The right to paternity first allows the author to require that his work be published under his name. The author may then re-establish the truth in case of usurpation or omission. The author may claim that the publisher mentions his first and last name, as well as his qualities (e.g., distinctions) not only on the different reproductions of the work itself (books, records, etc.), but also on the advertisements.

172. However, the author has no obligation to do so. The right to paternity also permits to the author not to be mentioned in relation with his work. The author may prefer to leave his work anonymous or to publish it under a pseudonym (Article L. 113-6, *see supra* paragraph 127). But he does not lose for all that his author's right which he may exercise through a representative (the editor or a special agent). The representative is liable in torts when he reveals the author's identity against his will. The author may always reveal his identity and then recover the direct exercise of his rights. The consequence is the same if the pseudonym leaves no more doubt as to the true identity of the author (Article L. 113-6, §4).

173. The author may also refuse to be mentioned if he thinks that his work has been altered. And court decisions consider that the right to paternity also allows the author to claim against the work which is wrongly attributed to him.

174. The author may not renounce his right to paternity: consequently, the author may always reveal his identity if he so wishes, even when he undertook a contractual obligation not to do so.[129] It was held that the reproduction of the author's signature on a work fallen into public domain is not a violation of his moral right, when no likelihood of confusion exists with the original work.[130]

127. Cass., 14 Mar. 1900: DP 1900, 1, 497, the French-American painter Whistler lawfully refused to complete the portrait of Lady Eden.
128. Paris, 23 Oct. 1991: Juris-Data, No. 24068; a painter's heirs may sue a museum for unauthorized reproduction of a painting on postcards and catalogues.
129. Paris, 1 Feb. 1989: RIDA, October 1989, p. 301, note Sirinelli.
130. Cass. crim., 11 Jun. 1997: JCP ed. E, 1997, pan. No. 1152.

175. The right to the respect of the work allows the author to oppose any distortion in the work's form or spirit. The author normally does not have to justify his opposition to any distortion of his work. He may prohibit anyone to use his work in a way which distorts it (any deletion, addition, or modification) or even devaluates it. For instance, the presentation of a scholarly study in the middle of advertising messages and local information in a free newspaper is a violation of the author's moral right, whose work is devaluated.[131] The author may enforce his right not only against third parties, but also against the assignee of copyright on his work, and against the buyer of the material support of the work. Consequently, any unauthorized change brought to the work violates the author's moral right, even if it is minor, as long as it is not in itself an original protectable work.

176. Some examples may be taken from an abundant case law: Illegal are unauthorized changes in screen paintings;[132] suppression of an introduction chosen by the author;[133] insertion of a warning into the credit list, which gives a new idea of the work;[134] cutting out into several panels of a refrigerator decorated by a painter;[135] destruction of a work, whatever its content;[136] publication of a condensed version of the work;[137] cuts in a film;[138] and colouring of a film.[139] Even if the work has an illegal content (e.g., violates another person's right of privacy, incites to crime, etc.), the editor who takes the initiative to modify the work (e.g., to reject the racist passages at the end of the book) violates the author's right to the respect of the work.

177. The author may not renounce his right to respect any clauses of a contract whereby the author authorizes the assignee in advance to bring changes to the work are void.[140] Specific statutory provisions enforce this rule as for contracts for publishing (Article L. 132-11) and for performance (Article L. 132-22, *see infra*).

178. Some limitations are brought to the exercise of the author's right to respect of his work.

179. First, in one case it was surprisingly decided that the unauthorized additions do not violate the author's moral right if they do not alter the public's idea of the work (perhaps because the modified costumes were of secondary importance compared to

131. Caen, 6 May 1997: JCP ed. E, 1997, pan., p.1477.
132. Paris, 20 Nov. 1935: DH 1936, 26.
133. Trib. Civ. Seine, 12 Oct. 1957: Gaz. Pal. 1958, 1, jur., p. 24.
134. Cass. civ. 1, 4 Apr. 1991: Bull. civ. I, p. 120.
135. Paris, 30 May 1962: JCP 1963 II 12989, note R. Savatier; D. 1962, jur., p. 570, note Desbois; Cass. civ., 6 Jul. 1965: Gaz. Pal. 1965, 2, jur., p. 126, conflict between the painter Bernard Buffet who had decorated a refrigerator and its buyer, the latter dismantled the work and intended to resell it in six parts.
136. Paris, 25 Nov. 1980: RIDA, April 1981, p. 162.
137. Paris, 6 Jun. 1979: D. 1981, som., p. 85, obs. Colombet.
138. Paris, 14 Jun. 1950: Ann. propr. Ind. 1950, 109.
139. *See* in the famous Huston case: Cass. civ. 1, 28 May 1991: JCP 1991 II 21731, note Françon; JCP ed. E, 1991 II 220, note Sirinelli and Ginsburg; RIDA, July 1991, p. 161, obs. Kéréver; Rev. crit. DIP, 1991, 752, note Gautier.
140. TGI Seine, 27 May 1959: RIDA, July 1959, p. 148.

the lyrical work).[141] The second limitation is linked to the nature of the work. Whereas a publisher may not modify the work in any way, the translator or adaptor enjoys more freedom. The adaptation of a work (e.g., from a novel into a film) necessarily implies modifications of the work; the director must nevertheless remain faithful to the author's text and conception.[142] The translator chooses freely his expressions and words: the initial author may only oppose mistranslations. And finally, the right to the respect of the work does not mean a right to impunity: if the work has an illegal content, courts may forbid its publication; the author cannot forbid the critique of his work, except if the appreciation is offensive or abusive.

180. As for cuts for advertisements made in an audiovisual work, the Act of 30 September 1986 (modified by the Act of 17 January 1989) authorizes only one such cut, in order to protect the work's integrity.

181. The right of ownership allows normally the owner to dispose of his thing or to modify it. To what extent may the author of the work oppose such destruction or modification, by claiming violation of his moral right?

182. The Code does not expressly forbid the destruction of a work of art by its owner. The author's right to the respect of the work can obviously conflict with the property right of the owner of the material support of the work. The owner can destroy his thing. The destruction of the material support (e.g., a building) necessarily entails the destruction of the work (architectural work). French case law is then generally seeking for compromises. The destruction (or alteration) can be approved only if there is in the circumstances of the case a good reason, because of the nature of the work, its state, its site. For instance, a fresco could be destroyed because it was already damaged by humidity.[143] In another case, the Cour de cassation approved an architect who was claiming against an alteration of his work, noting that the city of Lille had not demonstrated the reality of the alleged technical necessities.[144] But a work of architecture may not be intangible, given its utilitarian destination. Thus, the architect may not oppose modifications dictated by economic, legal, or technical imperatives. In another case, an open-air sculpture made out of iron railings and which was rusting was destroyed by its owner (the city of Grenoble) because of the dangers of accident; the court did not hold the owner liable towards the sculptor, because destruction was motivated by needs of public security.[145] If the author is aware of the intention to destroy, he will be able to claim access to his work, for instance to take photographs, in compliance with Article L. 111-3, §2.

183. Courts can also make use of a contract existing between the parties in order to save the work. For instance, in the conflict between Jean Dubuffet and Renault (French car manufacturer), the latter started the construction of a monument after the model made by the former, then decided (a year later) not to complete it and even to

141. Cass. civ., 5 Mar. 1968: D. 1968, jur., p. 382; RTD com. 1969, 492, obs. Desbois, refusing Salvador Dali's claim against a theater for having added accessories to the costumes which he designed.

142. TGI Paris, 27 Nov. 1985: RIDA, July 1986, p. 166, note Françon.

143. Basse-Terre, 30 Sep. 1996: D. 1998, som. p. 58, obs. Robert.

144. Cass. civ. 1, 1 Dec. 1987: RIDA, April 1988, p. 137.

145. Trib. adm. Grenoble, 18 Feb. 1976: RIDA, January 1977, p. 116, obs. Françon; RTD com. 1977, 120, obs. Desbois.

destroy the part already done. The Cour de cassation approved the interpretation of the contract given by the Court of Versailles: as soon as Renault has started the construction, it was engaged to complete the work – in order to respect the moral right of the artist – and naturally not to destroy it. The completion of the work was ordered.[146]

184. The right to reconsider or to withdraw the work is the only aspect of the moral right which is regulated in detail under Article L. 121-4. The law-maker took into account the author's changes of mind and allowed him to reconsider his work, that is to say to modify it, or to withdraw his work, that is to say to put an end to its exploitation, even after the assignment of the economic rights and publication. He may recall his work even after the assignment of copyright and publication. However, the assignee's interests are protected, since the author must, before exercising his right, indemnify him for all the present loss (e.g., reimburse the books already printed and which will not be sold), and also for loss of future profits (e.g., future re-editions already certain). Moreover, if the author later decides to publish again his work, he must first offer the economic rights to the assignee he originally chose and under the conditions originally agreed.

185. The 'doctrine' (legal writers) considers that the right to reconsider or to withdraw is an exception and must be strictly interpreted. It may then concern only the works published under an assignment of copyright – because Article L. 121-4 expressly mentions 'assignee' and the 'assignment' – not the commissioned works or the works on a material support. For instance, a painter could not take back a painting from its owner.

II. The Characteristics of the Moral Right

186. After listing the components of the moral right, Article L. 121-1, §2 states: 'This right is attached to his person (author). It is perpetual, inalienable and indefeasible. It may be transmitted to the author's heirs upon his death. Its enforcement may be entrusted with a third person by a provision of a will.' French courts added to this list that the moral right may not be seized but, however, does not have an arbitrary character.

187. The personal character means that the moral right is linked to the person so that it is excluded from the frame of the marriage settlement and cannot be the object of the 'action oblique' of the author's creditors.[147]

188. The perpetual character is linked to the nature of the work, which is itself perpetual and bears the mark of the author's personality even after his death. Consequently, the moral right survives the termination of the economic rights.[148] After the author's death, the moral right is enforced by his heirs, or any other person entrusted with such a mission. The general rules of succession apply to the different components of the moral right (Article L. 121-1, §4), except for the right to disclose. The latter, according to a special rule (Article L. 121-2, §2) is attributed to the executor or executors appointed by a will of the author. The executor may be a juristic person and is not compelled to

146. Cass. civ. 1, 16 Mar. 1983: Bull. civ. I, p. 101; Versailles, 8 Jul. 1981: D. 1982, som., p. 45, obs. Colombet.
147. *See* Art. 1341-1 of the Civil Code.
148. Versailles, 3 Oct. 1990: RIDA, April 1991, 148, note Gautier.

accept that mission. If there are no executors, or after their death and unless the author has willed otherwise, the right to disclose shall be exercised in the following order: by the descendants; by the spouse against whom there exists no final judgment of separation and who has not remarried; by the heirs other than descendants, who inherit all or part of the estate; by the universal legatees or donees of the totality of the future assets. No one is compelled to accept that mission. Article L. 121-3 states that in the event of manifest abuse in the exercise or non-exercise of the right of disclosure by the deceased author's representatives referred to in Article L. 121-2, the First Instance Court may order any appropriate measure. The same shall apply in the event of a dispute between such representatives, if there is no known successor in title, no heir, or no spouse entitled to inherit. It seems possible to extend such mechanism to the other components of the moral right.[149]

189. Because of the inalienable character of the moral right, the author may not assign or renounce his moral right during his life. For instance are unenforceable the conventions whereby an author renounces his right to paternity and authorizes another person to be mentioned as the author of the work,[150] whereby an author assigns his moral right to the editor[151] or to his employer.[152] Any other form of renunciation is normally void;[153] however, some courts' decisions have tolerated the renunciation made *a posteriori* with full knowledge of the facts, or the renunciation to the right to the respect of the work in the context of the derived works.[154]

190. The moral right is indefeasible. This character is linked to the perpetuity of the moral right. It only means that the moral right may be enforced as long as the work remains in the people's memories, by the author or his successors. It does not mean, however, that actions for the defence of the moral right are not subject to time limitations: as for any civil action, the period of limitation is thirty years from each illicit act.

191. Because of the personal, inalienable, and non-economic character or the moral right, the moral right itself may not be seized.

192. The imperative character of the moral right is applicable to any work the protection of which is claimed in France, even if the assignment of copyright occurred abroad according to a foreign law.[155]

193. In spite of its imperative character, the moral right is not arbitrary; upon action by an interested person, the courts may control its exercise by the author in order to sanction misuse. Although Article L. 121-3 only speaks about the manifest abuse in the exercise or non-exercise of the right to disclose the work (in which case the court may take any appropriate measure), the court's decisions extend the judicial

149. Cass. civ. 1, 28 Feb. 1989: RIDA, July 1989, p. 257, note Françon, the Cour de cassation held that the First Instance Court may order any appropriate measure in case of abuse of the 'representatives of the deceased author'.
150. Cass. civ. 1, 4 Apr. 1991: RIDA, October 1991, p. 125.
151. Paris, 23 Nov. 1977: Ann. propr. Ind. 1979, p. 68.
152. Aix-en-Provence, 21 Oct. 1965: D. 1966, jur., p. 70, note Greffe, JCP 1966 II 14657, RTD com. 1966, p. 68, obs. Desbois.
153. Paris, 20 Jan. 1971: D. 1971, jur., p. 307, concl. Lecourtier.
154. Paris, 23 Nov. 1970: RIDA, July 1971, p. 74.
155. Cass. civ., 28 May 1991, *supra,* Huston case on film colouring.

control upon all the aspects of the moral right. For instance, if an author may always modify, or even destroy his work, he may not do so only with the aim of annoying his spouse.[156] In another case, the Cour de cassation held that the moral right to reconsider or to withdraw was exercised in an abusive way when the problem consisted of the exceedingly low royalty paid to the author by the publisher.[157]

III. Moral Right on Works Created by Several Persons

194. The content and exercise of the moral right raises specific problems when the work is either a joint work, a composite, or a collective work (for the definition of these categories in French law, *see supra* paragraph 130 et seq.).

A. Moral Right on Joint Works

195. As for the joint work, the moral right remains with each co-authors: each of them may defend his right to paternity, the respect due to the work, or exercise his right to disclose the work, to reconsider, or to withdraw the work. But in case of disagreement between co-authors on the exercise of moral right on the joint work, the civil courts shall decide. The civil courts shall then favour the co-author whose position is more reasonable and refuse any misuse of the moral right.[158] As for the contribution of a co-author in the joint work, Article L. 113-3 states: 'Where the contribution of each of the co-authors is of a different kind, each may, unless otherwise agreed, separately exploit his own personal contribution without, however, prejudicing the exploitation of the common work.' This rule may be extended to the exercise of moral right on the co-author's contribution.[159]

196. Article L. 121-6 provides for a specific rule as for audiovisual works: 'If one of the co-authors refuses to complete his contribution to an audiovisual work, or is prevented from completing it by a force majeure, he may not oppose use of his already existing contribution, for the purpose of completing the work. He shall have the quality of author of that contribution and enjoy the ensuing rights.' This provision paralyses the right to reconsider or to withdraw as for joint authors of an audiovisual work, as long as the work is not completed. Each author's partial contribution may be used even against his will and may be completed by another author.

197. Article L. 121-5, §1 brings a useful supplement, in defining the moment when an audiovisual work is deemed completed: 'The audiovisual work is deemed completed when its definitive version has been established by a common agreement between on the one hand the director, or eventually the co-authors, and on the other, the producer.'

198. And as soon as the audiovisual work is completed, the moral right is again effective: 'The individual authors' rights such as defined under Article L. 121-1 (*see*

156. Cass. civ. 1, 14 May 1945: JCP 1945 II 2835, note R.C.; D. 1945, jur., p. 287, note Desbois. – Cass. civ. 1, 4 Dec. 1956: Gaz. Pal. 1957, 1, jur., p. 56.
157. Cass. civ. 1, 14 May 1991: RIDA, January 1992, p. 272, note Sirinelli.
158. Paris, 18 Apr. 1956: D. 1957, jur., p. 108, note Desbois.
159. Bordeaux, 24 May 1984: D. 1986. I.R., p. 181, obs. Colombet.

supra paragraph 165 et seq.) may be enforced only on a completed work' (Article L. 121-5, §5). 'It is forbidden to destroy the matrix of this (definitive) version' (Article L. 121-5, §2). 'Any modification of this version by addition, suppression or modification of any element requires the agreement of the above mentioned persons' (Article L. 121-5, §3). 'Any transfer of an audiovisual work on another type of support in view of another mode of exploitation must be preceded by a consultation of the director' (Article L. 121-5, §4).

B. *Moral Right on Composite Works*

199. A composite work is a new work in which is incorporated a pre-existent work. The author of the composite work naturally enjoys moral right on its work. But the moral right of the author of the pre-existent must also be taken into account: if the composite work seems to have distorted his initial work, he may claim his moral right to respect of the work. It is accepted, however, that given the nature of the composite work, adaptations, translations, variations, necessarily entail some changes in the initial work; e.g., it is not possible to transfer textually a book into a film. In such cases, the author of the initial work may only claim respect to the work's spirit and character.[160]

200. Each of the authors may exercise his right to reconsider or to withdraw as for his part of the work; Article L. 121-4 does not exclude such a right as for composite works.

C. *Moral Right on Collective Works*

201. Although the entrepreneur who legally owns the collective work and is sometimes an artificial person, does not have the quality of author *stricto sensu*, it owns not only the economic rights, but also the moral right on the collective work[161] and may prohibit any distortion of it, etc. However, each co-author keeps his moral right on his individualized contribution to the collective work. He may enforce his right either against third persons,[162] or against the producer if the latter introduces unauthorized changes or cuts in the work.[163]

202. Nevertheless, the specific nature of the collective work sets limits on the contributors' moral right, because of the necessary co-ordination of their contributions. The Cour de cassation decides that the producer may modify the individual contributions, but only to the extent of what is necessary in view of the harmonization of the whole.[164] More generally, the contributors' moral right may be enforced only within the limits set by the fusion of each contribution with the one of the other co-authors.[165]

---

160. Cass. civ. 1, 22 Nov. 1966: Bull. civ. I, p. 518; JCP 1968 II 15331, note Plaisant; D. 1967, jur., p. 485, note Desbois, 'Dialogues des Carmélites'.
161. Cass. civ. 1, 8 Dec. 1993: Bull. civ. I, No. 361; RIDA, July 1994, p. 303.
162. Versailles, 20 May 1988: D. 1989, Som., p. 44, obs. Colombet, the author of individualized photographs included in a catalogue which is a collective work may claim the mention of his name.
163. Cass. civ. 1, 8 Oct. 1980: D. 1981, Som., p. 85, obs. Colombet.
164. Cass. civ. 1, 16 Dec. 1986: RIDA, July 1987, p. 183.
165. Cass. civ. 1, 15 Apr. 1986: Bull. civ. I, No. 89.

§2. Exploitation Rights

203. The so-called economic rights include the right of reproduction, the right of performance, and the *'droit de suite'*.

I. Reproduction Right

204. According to Article L. 122-3, reproduction consists of 'the material fixation of the work, by any process permitting it to be communicated to the public in an indirect way'. The text adds an open list of processes of reproduction, which implies that the nature of the support is unimportant: 'it may be carried out, in particular, by printing, drawing, engraving, photography, casting and all processes of the graphical and plastic arts, mechanical, cinematographic or magnetic recording'. CD-ROM and numerical recordings, multimedia, or fixation on a computer disc may then be considered as reproductions.[166] This is to say that a work may be counterfeit by reproduction on any kind of support.

205. Article L. 122-3, §3 relates more specifically to works of architecture and still illustrates the idea that any change of support is unimportant. It states that the reproduction of a protected plan or standard project may also consist of the construction of a building in accordance with that plan or standard project.

206. The author may forbid even a partial reproduction of his work. Consequently, the author of a secondary work may not stay too close to the initial work: translations and adaptations are considered as specific aspects of the reproduction right and are illicit without authorization by the initial author (also: *see supra,* paragraphs 139 et seq).

207. The main difficulty is to decide to what extent the secondary work only borrows the idea of the initial work, which is allowed since ideas are not protected, or 'reproduces' the initial work, which is illegal. There is no simple answer. The notion of originality is the only general rule which allows to make the distinction between illicit reproduction and tolerated plagiarism. In a work inspired from a prior one, only original elements are copyrightable. In such conflicts, the courts tend to evaluate the degree of originality of the secondary work in relation to the initial one. A well-advertised case may illustrate the difficulties of such an evaluation.

208. The heirs of Margaret Mitchell sued Régine Desforges, French author of 'La bicyclette bleue' ('*The blue bicycle*') for unauthorized reproduction and adaptation of '*Gone with the Wind*'. The Paris Court of Appeals dismissed the claim considering that Régine Desforges created 'a personal and original work', based on a hackneyed theme (theme of a young girl in love with a man who prefers another woman, whereas she is loved by an older man). The French Supreme Court quashed this decision,[167]

166. TGI Paris, ord. Réf., 5 May 1997, case Raymond Queneau: JCP 1997 II 22906, note Olivier; RIDA, October 1997, p. 265: an unauthorized reproduction of a work on *Internet* is a violation of the author's right. However: TGI Paris, 10 Jun. 1997: JCP ed. E, 1998, chr., p. 850, nr. 31, obs. Vivant and Le Stanc, where a reproduction of the work on *Intranet* of an organization is not considered as infringement.

167. Cass. civ. 1, 4 Feb. 1992: D. 1992, jur., p. 182, note Gautier; JCP 1992 II 21930, note Daverat.

and sent it back to the Court of Versailles, requiring that the court verified if similar scenes and dialogues did not involve likeness constituting reproductions or adaptations of the first novel. The Court of Versailles,[168] considered that the characters of each novel had a status and role which were original and specific and linked to historical events. The action for infringement was finally dismissed.

209. As for scientific works, the courts are more demanding to admit illicit reproduction, since such a work necessarily stays on objective facts or findings of the past.

II. Performing Right

210. Article L. 122-2 defines performance as 'the communication of the work to the public by any means'. The 'public' is to be defined by opposition to the 'family circle' mentioned under Article L. 122-5, 1°. An effective communication to the public is not required: a film shown in an empty cinema is nevertheless 'communicated to the public'.

211. The direct performance consists of the execution of the work in presence of the public (e.g., concerts), or by reading of a recording (e.g., diffusion of gramophone records in a discotheque[169]). The Article L. 122-2 gives examples of such direct representation: public recitation, lyrical performance, dramatic performance, public presentation, public projection, or telediffusion in the meaning of distribution by any telecommunication process. The hotels or restaurants managers must request an authorization to diffuse recorded works for their clients.[170] The viewing of the work on the screen of a computer is a performance whenever the work is directly accessible with the producer. It is unimportant whether the work is viewed at the same place and time by the users, since the users are a 'potential public'.

212. Secondary performance implies the retransmission to the public of a signal produced by the initial emission. The statute itself mentions 'the transmission in a public place of a telediffused work' (Article L. 122-2). There, courts had to solve conflicts between authors or producers and hotels or restaurants managers when the latter retransmit simultaneously radio or television programmes to their clients. The latter must request an authorization, for example, as for retransmission in hotel rooms of a television channel by satellite.[171]

213. In practice, the authors do not aim at the prohibition of such a secondary performance, but only at a supplementary remuneration. The Act No. 97-283 of 27 March 1997, implementing the EC Directives of the European Council No. 93/83 of

168. Versailles, 15 Dec. 1993: D. 1994, jur., p. 132, note Gautier.
169. Cass. civ. 1, 1 Mar. 1988, JCP 1988 II 21120, note Françon.
170. Paris, 18 Sep. 1974: D. 1975, som., p. 87; RIDA, January 1975, p. 112.
171. Cass. civ. 1, 6 Apr. 1994: D. 1994, jur., p. 450, note Gautier; JCP 1994 II 22273, note Galloux, quashing Paris, 10 Jan. 1992: RIDA, July 1992, p. 174, note Kéréver, in the case *CNN*.

27 September 1993[172] and No. 93/98 of 29 October 1993,[173] added an Article L. 132-20-1 into the Intellectual Property Code: as from the date of entry into force of the new Act, 'the right to authorize the simultaneous, integral and unchanged cable retransmission, on the national territory, of a work broadcast from a Member State of EC may be exercised only by a royalty collection and distribution society'.

III. Adaptation and Translation Rights

214. Adaptation and translation rights are considered as specific aspects of reproduction right (*see supra* paragraph 204 et seq.).

IV. Other Rights

A. *'Droit de suite' or Resale Right*

215. The *'droit de suite'* is the inalienable right of an artist to divert to his or her own benefit a small part of the resale price (a 'royalty') of the original material support of his or her work, subsequent to the first transfer of the work by the author. The main provision on *'droit de suite'* is Article L. 122-8. This article has been modified by the Act No. 2006-961 of 1 August 2006 implementing the EC Directive No. 2001/84[174] and a decree No. 2007-756 of 9 May 2007 has laid down all necessary details for the implementation of the resale right (Article R. 122-1–R. 122-11).

216. Not all types of works are concerned, but only 'works of graphic or plastic art', such as pictures, collages, paintings, drawings, engravings, prints, lithographs, sculptures, tapestries, ceramics, glassware, photographs, and plastic creations on audiovisual or numerical support (Article R. 122-2 §1). Article L. 122-8 mentions the *'droit de suite'* upon sales of the 'original work', which is the work made by the artist himself but also copies made in limited numbers by the artist himself or under his authority if such copies have been numbered, signed, or otherwise duly authorized by the artist (Article R. 122-2 §2).

217. Not all types of resale acts are concerned. This resale right shall apply to all acts of resale of a minimum amount of EUR 750,[175] involving as sellers, buyers, or intermediaries art market professionals, such as salesrooms, art galleries, and in

---

172. EC Directive No. 93/83 of 27 Sep. 1993 on the coordination of certain rules concerning copyright and rights related to copyright applicable to satellite broadcasting and cable retransmission, OJEC, No. L. 248, 6 Oct. 1993, pp. 15–21.
173. EC Directive No. 93/98 of 29 Oct. 1993 harmonizing the term of protection of copyright and certain related rights, OJEC, No. L. 290, 24 Nov. 1993, pp. 9–13, repealed and replaced by EC Directive 2006/116 of the European Parliament and of the Council of 12 Dec. 2006 on the term of protection of copyright and certain related rights (codified version), OJEC, No. L. 372, 27 Dec. 2006, pp. 12–18.
174. EC Directive 2001/84 of the European Parliament and of the Council of 27 Sep. 2001 on the resale right for the benefit of the author of an original work of art, OJEC, No. L. 272, 13 Oct. 2001, pp. 32–36.
175. EUR 750 is the auction price or the sale price received by the seller, net of tax, Art. R. 122-4.

general, any dealers in works of art. However, it shall not apply to acts of resale where the seller has acquired the work directly from the author less than three years before that resale and where the resale price does not exceed EUR 10,000.[176] The resale act must take place on the French territory or the resale act must be subject to the French value added tax (Article R. 122-1).

218. Not all artists shall enjoy the benefit of the resale right. Citizens of a Member State of the EU or of the EEA may benefit of the resale right. And artists which are neither citizens of a Member State of the EU nor citizens of a Member State of the EEA may benefit of the resale right only if it exists reciprocity: their national law must give protection of the resale right to the artists citizens of a Member State of the EU or of the European Economic Area. This reciprocity is no more required of foreign artists (and of their successors in title) who took part to the life of French Art and had their residence in France for a continuous or discontinuous period of at least five years. The artists or their successors in title shall file an application with the minister responsible for culture who takes his decision upon the advice of a special committee (Article R. 122-3).

219. The royalty shall be set at the following rates (Article R. 122-5): (a) 4% for the portion of the sale price up to EUR 50,000; (b) 3% for the portion of the sale price from EUR 50,000.01–EUR 200,000; (c) 1% for the portion of the sale price from EUR 200,000.01–EUR 350,000; (d) 0.5% for the portion of the sale price from EUR 350,000.01–EUR 500,000; (e) 0.25% for the portion of the sale price exceeding EUR 500,000. However, the total amount of the royalty may not exceed EUR 12,500. The royalty is payable by the seller. The professional involved in the act of resale (the company involved in voluntary sales of chattels by public auction, the court valuer, and auctioneer of chattels, or if the resale act involves several professionals, the professional seller, or by default, the professional who received the payment as intermediary or by default, the professional buyer, Article R. 122-8) shall be liable for payment of the royalty. The art market professionals shall furnish to the artist or to a collecting society (agreed by the minister responsible for culture, Article R. 122-6) in charge of the collective management of the resale right any information that may be necessary in order to secure payment of royalties in respect of the resale, within a period of three years as from the date of the resale act. A penal fine is foreseen against the art market professionals who do not pay the royalty to its beneficiary or do not give the necessary informations to the beneficiary or a collecting society (Article R. 122-11).

220. The beneficiary of the resale right is normally the author himself because this right is said 'inalienable'. The author cannot transfer or forego this right. However, after the death of the author, the resale royalty right shall subsist to the benefit of the legal heirs, and with respect to usufruct laid down in Article L. 123-6, of the spouse for the current calendar year and seventy years thereafter (Article L. 123-7 I). For a long time, the resale royalty right was to benefit exclusively to the family of the deceased author, as Article L. 123-7 explicitly excluded 'all legatees and successors in title'. Since the Act No. 2016-925 of 7 July 2016, new Article L. 123-7 allows the author, subject to the rights of the descendants or of the surviving spouse, to transmit

176. EUR 10,000 is the auction price or the sale price received by the seller, net of tax, Art. R. 122-4.

his resale royalty right by legacies. In the absence of any legal heir or legatee, the resale royalty right shall subsist to the benefit of the universal legatee, or in his absence, to the owner of the moral right. Finally, in the absence of any known successor or in case of escheat of the succession, the Tribunal de Grande Instance shall entrust the resale royalty right to an agreed collecting society.

B. Right of Destination

221. The reproduction right has a broad content, which allows its holder to keep control upon the use and circulation of the copies of the work. Such a 'right of destination' was asserted by the Supreme Court in numerous cases. For instance, when a phonogram has been recorded with the author's consent, the author accepted only the commercial sale of the record; then, if a radio station wishes to broadcast it, it will have to pay a royalty not only for public performance, but also for reproduction, since the reproduction has here a different destination from the first one (commercial sale of the record). When the author authorizes reproduction of his musical work on a record, this is in view of its sale to the consumers but not for a public use such as in a night club. In the case between the SACEM and an organization of night club owners the Court decided that 'the authorization given by the SACEM to extend the exploitation of the reproduction right to a new destination – public use in a night club – justified the payment of a supplementary royalty for mechanical reproduction'.[177] When the author authorizes the reproduction of his work for a film, this does not imply an authorization for videocassettes[178] or television.[179] The translation authorized for a given country does not imply authorization for other countries,[180] etc.

222. The reproduction right is exhausted by the first publication of the work in the form authorized by the rightholder; reproductions in another form are infringements. Such is the case, for instance, for a second reproduction in another magazine.[181]

223. This 'destination right' is based on the interpretation of Article L. 131-3, §1, which requires that the transfers of copyright mention the destination of the exploitation. It is probable however, that the 'destination right' disappears under the influence of EC law, which applies the theory of exhaustion of copyright by the first authorized sale.

C. Public Lending Right

224. An exclusive right to authorize or prohibit the rental and lending of originals and copies of works, on any material support (such as paper or CD) or through numerical transmission on line, is recognized by an EC Directive No. 2006/115 of 12 December

177. Cass. civ. 1, 19 Apr. 1988: JCP 1988 II 21120, 3rd case, note Françon.
178. Cass. civ. 1, 29 Jun. 1982: D. 1983, jur., p. 33, note Edelman; RTD com. 1983, 435, obs. Françon.
179. Cass. civ. 1, 29 Jun. 1994: RIDA, January 1995, 197.
180. TGI Seine, 31 Mar. 1966: D. 1966, som., p. 97, case Ionesco.
181. Cass. civ. 1, 21 Feb. 1989: Bull. civ. I, No. 90.

2006[182] to authors, performers, phonogram producers, and producers of the first fixation of a film. All types of works are concerned with the exception of architectural works and works of applied art. 'Rental' is defined by the directive as 'making available for use, for a limited period of time and for direct or indirect economic or commercial advantage'. 'Lending' is defined by the directive as 'making available for use, for a limited period of time and not for direct or indirect economic or commercial advantage, when it is made through establishments which are accessible to the public'. The rental right can be transferred but the authors or performers shall retain the right to obtain an equitable remuneration for the rental. That right to equitable remuneration cannot be waived and its administration may be entrusted to collecting societies representing authors or performers. Member States may also derogate from the exclusive right in respect of public lending, provided that at least authors obtain remuneration for such lending; and Member States may even exempt certain categories of establishments from the payment of that remuneration. The TRIPs Agreement also provides for such a right (Article 11).

182. Directive No. 92/100 of the Council, 19 Nov. 1992: OJEC, No. L. 346, 27 Nov., pp. 61–66, repealed and replaced by EC Dir. No. 2006/115 of 12 Dec. 2006 on rental right and lending right and on certain rights related to copyright in the field of intellectual property (codified version), OJEC, No. L. 376, 27 Dec. 2006, pp. 28–35.

Chapter 7. Limitations to the Scope of Copyright Protection

225. Article L. 122-5 cites various situations where third parties may use a protected work without its author's authorization. This list of exceptions has been enlarged by the Act No. 2006-961 of 1 August 2006 implementing the EC Directive No. 2001/29.[183] These exceptions may be used only after the work was disclosed.[184] All those exceptions shall satisfy the so-called three-steps test which requires that any such exception must neither go beyond 'normal exploitation of the work' nor 'unreasonably prejudice the legitimate interests of the author'. The legal provisions relate to the reproduction right, as well as, to the performing right.

§1. Exceptions to Reproduction Right

226. The reproduction right suffers four exceptions, whereby an unauthorized reproduction is lawful: private copies, some public use reproductions, technical copies, and safeguard copies.

I. Private Copies

227. Article L. 122-5, 2° exempts from copyright 'copies or reproductions made from a lawful source and strictly reserved for the private use of the copyist and not intended for collective use'. However, that exception does not cover certain specific private copies: 'copies of works of art destined to be used for aims identical to those of the original work' (e.g., the copy of a painting, even destined to take place in the private collection of an art lover); 'copies of software other than backup copies made in accordance with paragraph II of Article L. 122-6-1' (*see supra* paragraph 72); 'as well as copies or reproductions of an electronic database' (*see supra* paragraph 86).

228. More often than not, the 'copyist' is the natural person who makes a copy. However, in a case where the role of a 'photocopy shop' was questioned, the French Supreme Court decided that such a shop may act as copyist since it possesses and exploits the equipment necessary to make copies and keeps it at its clients' disposal. And such copies are not made for private use.[185]

229. As for the meaning of 'private use', it obviously excludes any commercial destination of the copies, i.e., any distribution against payment. However, lack of

183. EC Directive 2001/29 of the European Parliament and of the Council of 22 May 2001 on the harmonization of certain aspects of copyright and related rights in the information society, OJEC, No. L. 167, 22 Jun. 2001, pp. 10–19.

184. Cass. civ. 2, 8 Jul. 1981: Bull. civ. II, No. 151; D. 1982, jur., p. 65, note Lindon.

185. Cass. civ. 1, 7 Mar. 1984: JCP 1985 II 20351, note R. Plaisant. -Paris, 25 Jun. 1997: JCP ed. E, 1997, pan. No. 1348.

remuneration does not necessarily justify the copy: 'private use' also means 'personal use', which excludes any collective use such as inside of an institution or firm.[186]

230. 'Private copy' does not imply a 'single' copy: several copies may be made for private use; however, an important number lets presume a public or at least a collective use.[187] A private copy can also be the copy of a work's part as of the whole.

231. Because of the improvement of the different recording devices and because of the increase of audio, video, or digital recording, private copies necessarily signify an important loss of royalties for authors, performers, producers. The Act of 3 July 1985 (completed by the Act of 7 July 2016) compensated that loss by creating a tax assessed on recording mediums (audio, video, digital recording) that may be used for reproduction of works for private use (Article L. 311-1). Its amount is fixed by a special commission (Article L. 311-5). The tax is to be paid by the manufacturer, the importer, or the person making an intra-Community acquisition of recording mediums that may be used for reproduction of works for private use, at the time these mediums enter into circulation in France, and also (since Act No. 2016-925 of 7 July 2016) by the editor of a radio or television service or its distributor within the meaning of Law No. 86-1067 of 30 September 1986 on freedom of communication, which provides an individual, through remote access, reproduction for private use of works from a programme linearly broadcasted by the editor or its distributor, provided that such reproduction is requested by the individual before the broadcast of the programme or during the broadcast for the remaining part Article L. 311-4). Finally, this tax is paid by the final consumer, through the price of the recording mediums or of the radio or television services. This tax is not due by persons who acquire the recording mediums for business purposes in conditions, which do not allow to assume a use for the purposes of private copying or for their own use or production. This is specifically the case of: audiovisual communication enterprises, phonogram, or videogram producers, persons who carry out the reproduction of phonograms or videograms on behalf of the producers, publishers of works published on digital medium; juristic persons or bodies that use recording mediums for the purpose of assisting persons with sight or hearing disability. The tax is not due either by the persons conducting the export or intra-Community supply of recording mediums entered into circulation in France (Article L. 311-8). The beneficiaries of the tax are the authors and performers of works fixed on phonograms or videograms, the producers of such phonograms or videograms, the authors and publishers of works, fixed on any other medium than on a phonogram or a videogram, reproduced on a digital recording medium. It is collected by COPIE-FRANCE. This collecting society must devote 25% of this tax to support creation, live shows, cultural and artistic education, and artists' training (Article L. 321-9). As for phonograms, the tax benefits for one half the authors, for one quarter the performing artists, and for one quarter the producers (Article L. 311-7, §1). As for videograms, the tax is shared by thirds between the authors, the performing artists, and the producers (Article L. 311-7, §2). As for works, which are fixed on a phonogram or a videogram, and reproduced on a digital recording medium, the tax is shared by halves between the authors and the publishers

186. Paris, 1 Oct. 1990: D. 1990, I.R., p. 235; RIDA, 1991, No. 149, 206, obs. Kéréver. It also excludes a professional use of the copy, even if it is free: Cass. civ. 1, 20 Jan. 1969: Gaz. Pal. 1969, 1, jur., p. 217.

187. Paris, 8 Oct. 1982: RIDA, January 1983, p. 138; RTD com. 1983, 434, obs. Françon.

(Article L. 311-7, §3). The authors entitled to a share of the proceeds of the tax are 'authors within the meaning of the present Code'; this provision is meant to exclude the producers and other participants who are considered as authors in some foreign copyright systems.

232. As for phonograms and videograms, foreign authors, performers, and producers, under reservation of international conventions, are entitled to share the proceeds of the tax only if the phonogram or the videogram (fixation of a sequence of sounds, or fixation of a sequence of images, accompanied of sounds, or fixation of a sequence of images, accompanied by sounds or not, in a material support) was fixed for the first time in a Member State of the EU (Article L. 311-2). Because of the reservation of international conventions, citizens of Member States of the Geneva and Berne Conventions as well as of the World Trade Organization (TRIPs Agreement) may claim the benefit of the national treatment in order to receive a share of the tax (on condition they are considered as authors within the meaning of the French law; *see supra* paragraph 127 et seq.).

233. The non-payment of the tax is sanctioned by a fine of EUR 150,000 (Article L. 335-4 §3).

234. As for works, which are fixed on any other medium than on a phonogram or a videogram and reproduced on a digital recording medium, foreign authors and publishers are entitled to share the proceeds of the tax if they fulfil to the general requirements of Article L. 111-4 (*see supra* paragraph 129).

235. No equivalent remuneration exists for photocopies. A tax of 3.25% does exist on photocopiers manufactured or imported in France, but its proceeds are assigned to the Centre National du Livre for cultural purposes.[188]

II. Exceptions for Public Use

236. Article L. 122-5, §3 allows 'analysis and short citations justified by the critical, polemical, pedagogical, scientific or information character of the work into which they are incorporated' on condition that the name of the author and the source are clearly stated. An 'analysis' cannot be only a digest of the work[189] but must represent a study of the work or at least some contribution to the knowledge of the work. The analysis must not exempt the public from having recourse to the original work.[190] 'Short citations': this exception has been obviously intended to apply to literary works, but case law applies it even to pictorial, graphical, and sculptural works.[191] The expression 'short citations', which could be seen as redundant, means that the borrowing from the quoted work must be necessary and reasonable. Therefore, the Cour de cassation refuses to treat as 'short citations' every complete reproduction (even in a

188. This tax was held to be compatible with Art. 85 of the EC Treaty: ECJ, 3 Feb. 1981: RIDA, July 1981, p. 192.

189. TGI Paris, 25 Apr. 1968: D. 1968, jur., p. 740.

190. Cass. civ. 1, 9 Nov. 1983, JCP 1984 II 20189, note Françon.

191. TGI Paris, 15 May 1991: D. 1992, jur., p. 146, note Debbasch; Versailles, 20 Nov. 1991: D. 1992, jur., p. 402, note Edelman; Cass. Ass. plén., 5 Nov. 1993: D. 1994, jur., p. 481, note Foyard; Cass. civ. 1, 4 Jul. 1995: D. 1996, jur., p. 4, note Edelman.

very small size) of a work[192] and every 'long' citations.[193] If this exception is normally tolerated only if the citation clearly mentions the author's name and source, and if it is incorporated in another work, this latter condition was, however, set aside in the famous case *Le Monde v. Microfor*, where it was decided that a database consisting of an ensemble of short citations of articles is an 'information work' in itself.[194]

237. The fact that a complete reproduction, even in a small size, of a work cannot be admitted as a short citation was embarrassing for the catalogues of the judicial sales which contain such reproductions. An Act of 27 March 1997 has then introduced a new exception for 'complete or partial reproductions of works of graphic or three-dimensional art intended to appear in the catalogue of a judicial sale held in France, in the form of the copies of the said catalogue made available to the public prior to the sale for the sole purpose of describing the works of art offered for sale'. A decree by the 'Conseil d'Etat' shall determine the characteristics of the document and the conditions governing their distribution.

238. Under the same condition of mentioning the author's name and source, Article L. 122-5, 3° exempts 'press reviews'[195] and the publication, even in full, by the means of press or telediffusion as news information,[196] of public speeches made in political, administrative, judiciary, or academic assemblies, public political meetings and official ceremonies from the right of reproduction: such works may be made without the author's authorization.

239. More important is the exception relating to parody. The word 'parody' must be understood in a broad sense, as encompassing also caricature and pastiche, which are mentioned under Article L. 122-5, §4. A work may be freely reproduced under the exception of parody, under condition the reproduction is made in a humorous intention.[197] Excessive distortion of the initial work could, however, be sanctioned.

240. Since the Act No. 2003-517 of 18 June 2003, the author of a work who has concluded a contract in order to publish and diffuse it in book form ('contrat d'édition') cannot oppose his or her exclusive right to the lending of that edition by a public library. But this public lending is compensated by a special remuneration. That remuneration is for one part paid by the French State (and corresponds to a lump sum paid by each user of a public library with the exception of the school libraries) and for the other part assessed on the public sale price paid by the juristic persons which manage public libraries and buy books.

---

192. Cass. civ. 1, 13 Apr. 1988: Bull. civ. I, p. 96; JCP 1989 I 3372, obs. Vivant; Cass. civ., 17 Dec. 1991: Bull. civ. I, No. 360; D. 1993, jur., p. 89, obs. Colombet; Cass. Ass. plén., 5 Nov. 1993: D. 1994, jur., p. 481, note Foyard, JCP 1994 II 22201, obs. Françon.
193. For example, TGI Paris, 25 Apr. 1968: D. 1968, jur., p. 740; TGI Paris, 6 Jul. 1972: D. 1972, jur., p. 628, note Pactet; Paris, 10 May 1973, JCP 1973 II 17475, concl. Cabannes; Paris, 24 Oct. 1984: D. 1985. I.R., p. 312, obs. Colombet.
194. Cass. Ass. plén., 30 Oct. 1987: D. 1988, jur., p. 21, concl. Cabannes.
195. A 'press review' is defined as a comparison between several press articles, completely or partially reproduced, concerning a same theme or event and possibly giving rise to a comment or a controversy: Paris, 5 Jun. 1975: D. 1976, jur., p. 74, note Lindon; Cass. crim., 30 Jan. 1978: D. 1979, jur., p. 583, note Le Calvez.
196. That was not the case of Mitterrand's speeches made in 1981 and reproduced in 1995: TGI Paris, 25 Oct. 1995, RIDA, January 1996, p. 294.
197. Paris, 11 May 1993: RIDA, July 1993, No. 157, p. 340.

III. Technical Copies

241. Article L. 122-5, 6° exempts from copyright temporary acts of reproduction which are transient or incidental and an integral and essential part of a technological process and whose sole purpose is to enable a lawful use of a work or its transmission in a network between third parties by an intermediary. This temporary reproduction can only apply to works other than software or databases and must have no independent economic significance.

IV. Safeguard Copies

242. Article L. 122-5, 8° exempts from copyright acts of reproduction made by publicly accessible libraries, museums, or by archives, which are not for direct or indirect economic or commercial advantage and whose purpose is to preserve the work and its public consultation.

§2. Exceptions to Performing Right

243. Under Article L. 122-5, §1 'performances which are private and free and made exclusively in a family circle' are not covered by copyright. This tolerance is limited to reproductions made 'in the intimacy of a family or friendly circle, consisting of parents, allied, or persons in usual relationship'.[198] Such is not the case for more open meetings: sports clubs inviting foreign players and their families, circle of employees of a firm, playing grounds open to members of a children's home, etc. Moreover, the provisions of Article L. 122-5, §3 providing for an exception to the right of reproduction, can also apply to the performing right (analysis and short citations,[199] broadcasting of official speeches, parody).

244. Certain public performances, even if they do not benefit from an exception to copyright protection are treated with favour: Article L. 132-21, §2 provides for such a limited exception in favour of cities and Societies of Popular Education. These entities are entitled to a reduced royalty to be paid to the SACEM on the occasion of public performances made during local feasts or in the frame of their usual activities.

198. Grenoble, 28 Feb. 1968: RIDA, July 1968, No. 57, p. 166, note Desbois.

199. Cass. Ass. plén., 5 Nov. 1993: D. 1994, jur., p. 481, note Foyard, JCP 1994 II 22201, note Françon. Even if the performance lasts a very short time, Cass. civ. 1, 4 Jul. 1995: D. 1996, jur., p. 4, note Edelman, JCP 1995 II 22486, note Galloux; Cass. civ. 1, 13 Nov. 2003: D. 2004, jur., p. 200, note Bouche.

§3. Exceptions to Both Reproduction Right and Performing Right

245. All those exceptions have been created by the Act No. 2006-961 of 1 August 2006 implementing the EC Directive No. 2001/29.[200]

I. For Purpose of Illustration for Teaching or Scientific Research

246. Article L. 122-5, 3° e) exempts from copyright the reproduction or performance of works' extracts (with the exception of works specially intended for a pedagogical purpose and of sheet music) for the sole purpose of illustration for teaching or scientific research (with the exception of play or playtime activity), as long as this reproduction or performance is intended, in particular by means of a digital workspace, to a public composed mainly of pupils, students, teachers, or researchers directly involved in the act of teaching, training, or research activity, including the preparation and diffusion of examination subjects following the teaching which required that representation or reproduction, provided that there is no publication or distribution to a third party, that the use of this representation and reproduction does not give rise to any commercial exploitation and is compensated by a negotiated remuneration.

II. For the Benefit of People with a Disability

247. Article L. 122-5, 7° exempts from copyright the reproduction or performance of works by moral persons and publicly accessible establishments, such as libraries, archives, documentation centres and multimedia cultural centres, for the benefit of people with a disability, which are directly related to the disability and of a non-commercial nature, to the extent required by the specific disability. The Act No. 2016-925 of 7 July 2016 has removed the details of this exception from Article L. 122-5, 7° to new Article L. 122-5-1. And according to new Article L. 122-5-2, the accessible format copies may also be made available to foreign authorized non-profit entities.

III. For Purpose of News Reporting

248. Article L. 122-5, 9° exempts from copyright the reproduction or performance, complete or partial, of graphic, plastic, or architectural works by the means of press or audiovisual communication or online, for the sole purpose of news reporting as long as the author's name is indicated.

200. EC Directive 2001/29 of the European Parliament and of the Council of 22 May 2001 on the harmonization of certain aspects of copyright and related rights in the information society, OJEC, No. L. 167, 22 Jun. 2001, pp. 10–19.

Chapter 8. Duration of Protection

249. Article L. 123-1 states that the author enjoys protection for his works during his lifetime. Upon his death, the rights are transferred to the heirs, who may exercise them during seventy years. This duration results from the EC Directive No. 93/98 of 29 October 1993[201] implemented into French law by the statute of 27 March 1997.[202] The economic rights are in principle transferred according to the general rules of successions (according to a will or, in its absence, according to the legal rules of succession). By exception, the *'droit de suite'* is transferred only to the legal heirs (not heirs chosen by a will) (Article L. 123-7). However, Article L. 123-6, provides a special usufruct for the surviving spouse: 'the surviving spouse, against whom there is no final decision of separation, shall enjoy the usufruct of any right of exploitation that the author has not assigned, irrespective of the type of marriage arrangements and of the rights of usufruct deriving from Articles 756 to 757-3 and 764 to 766 of the Civil Code with respect to other assets of the estate. However, if the author has left forced heirs, the usufruct shall be reduced to the benefit of the heirs, according to the proportions and distinctions laid down by Article 913 of the Civil Code. Such right shall lapse should the spouse contract a new marriage'. In the event of manifest abuse of the artist's successors in the exercise or non-exercise of the rights of exploitation (right of reproduction, performing right) the First Instance Court (TGI) may order any appropriate measure[203] (Article L. 122-9).

250. The moral right is perpetual. After the author's death, the right to disclose the work is exercised by his successors in the order set by Article L. 121-2 §2: executors, descendants, spouse (on condition there was no separation or divorce, and no remarriage), other heirs who receive all or part of the succession, or legatees receiving all the succession. In the event of manifest abuse in the exercise or non-exercise of the right to disclose the work by the deceased author's successors, Article L. 121-3 provides that the First Instance Court may order any appropriate measure. The other components of the moral right (right to paternity, right to the respect of the work, right to reconsider or to withdraw the work) are transferred according to the general rules of successions.[204]

251. In various cases, the duration of the post mortem protection is longer. Such is the case for the joint works (œuvres de collaboration); their protection starts at the death of the last surviving joint-author (Article L. 123-2, §1). As for audiovisual works, their protection starts at the death of the last survivor of the following joint authors: the author of the scenario, the author of the dialogue, the author of the musical

201. EC Directive No. 93/98 of 29 Oct. 1993 harmonizing the term of protection of copyright and certain related rights, OJEC, No. L. 290, 24 Nov. 1993, pp. 9–13, repealed and replaced by EC Directive 2006/116 of the European Parliament and of the Council of 12 Dec. 2006 on the term of protection of copyright and certain related rights (codified version), OJEC, No. L. 372, 27 Dec. 2006, pp. 12–18.

202. JORF, 3 Jul. 1997, p. 1008; this statute also implements the EC Directive No. 93/83 of 27 Sep. 1993 relating to the broadcasting by satellite and cable.

203. For example, in the famous case Fujita, *see* Cass. civ. 1, 28 Feb. 1989: Bull. civ. I, No. 101; D. 1989, jur., p. 57, note Durrande; Rennes, 16 Nov. 1990, RTD com. 1991, 594, obs. Françon.

204. Paris, 11 Jul. 1990, RIDA, October 1990, p. 299.

compositions with or without words, specially composed for the work and the main director (Article L. 123-2, §2). Pseudonymous, anonymous, and collective works are protected during seventy years computed from 1 January of the calendar year following the first publication, if that publication takes place during the seventy years following the year of their creation. If the pseudonymous, anonymous, or collective work is disclosed after the expiry of that term, its owner, by succession or on another ground, who publishes it or causes it to be published shall enjoy exclusive rights for twenty-five years from 1 January of the calendar year following that of publication (Article L. 123-3).

252. If the work has not been published during the author's life (posthumous work) but during the seventy years following the death of the author, the right of exploitation shall belong to the author's successors in title and shall last seventy years from the date of publication. If the work has been published after the expiry of that term, the right of exploitation shall belong to the owners of the work, whether by succession or for other reason, who publish or have the work published, and shall last twenty-five years from 1 January of the calendar year following that of publication (Article L. 123-4).

253. The normal duration of copyright protection was extended after the First and the Second World War.[205] The interest of these extensions is still actual, in order to determine whether a given work was still protected in France on the date of entry into force of Article L. 123-1.

254. The duration prorogated because of the Second World War (Article L. 123-9) shall be further extended for a term of thirty years if the author, the composer, or the artist has died for France, as recorded in the death certificate. Where the death certificate has neither to be drawn up nor registered in France, the Minister responsible for culture may extend by order to the heirs or other successors in title of the deceased person the benefit of the additional extension of thirty years; such order, issued after obtaining the opinion of the authorities referred to in Article 1 of Ordinance No. 45-2717 of 2 November 1945, may only be issued in those cases where the entry 'died for France' would have appeared on the death certificate if such certificate had been drawn up in France (Article L. 123-10). Where the rights extended under Article L. 123-10 have been assigned for consideration, the assignors or their successors in title may apply, within a period of three years as from 25 September 1951, to the assignee or his successors in title for a review of the conditions of the assignment as compensation for the advantages resulting from the extension.

255. The Berne convention may also have an effect on the copyright's duration. Article L. 123-12 states that 'Where the country of origin of the work, within the meaning of the Paris Act of the Berne Convention, is a country outside the EC and the author is not a national of a Member State of the Community, the term of protection shall be that granted in the country of origin of the work, but may not exceed that provided for in Article L. 123-1.'

205. Respectively Art. L. 123-8: 6 years and 152 days and L. 123-9: eight years and 120 days. Both extensions may be added in the case of works disclosed before 1914. For an example of calculation, *see* : Cass. civ. 1, 21 Jun. 1961: Bull. civ. I, No. 332, case 'Ave Maria' by Gounod. -Paris, 5 Mar. 1974: RIDA, July 1974, 131, case Renoir.

Chapter 9. Neighbouring Rights

256. The Book 2 of the French Intellectual Property Code is called: 'Rights neighbouring to author's right' ('Droits voisins du droit d'auteur'). This title implies that such rights have some likeness with copyright without being identical. The Code creates exclusive rights for three categories of beneficiaries: performing artists, producers, and audiovisual communication enterprises.

257. France has ratified the Rome Convention of 26 October 1961 on the protection of performing artists, producers of phonograms, and broadcasting organizations (in force since 3 July 1987) and also the WIPO Performances and Phonograms Treaty of 20 December 1996 (entered into force on 14 March 2010).

258. All these beneficiaries are auxiliary of the artistic creation in that they participate in the diffusion of the work. Accordingly, Article L. 211-1 states that 'Neighbouring rights shall not prejudice author's rights. Consequently, no provision of the present title shall be interpreted in such a way as to limit the exercise of the author's right by its beneficiaries.'

259. Some provisions are common to all beneficiaries of neighbouring rights; others are specific to each of the three categories.

§1. Common Provisions

260. Five provisions apply to all neighbouring rights:

(1) Article L. 211-2 is intended to complete the principle set in Article L. 211-1: in case of conflict between beneficiaries of author's right and of neighbouring rights or if the beneficiary of the neighbouring right is unknown (especially in case of vacant succession) or in other case, the judicial authorities may adopt any appropriate measure on the request of the Ministry of Culture or of any person having a justified interest.

(2) Article L. 211-3 lists the exceptions to the exercise of neighbouring rights. They coincide with most of the exceptions provided under Article L. 122-5 for copyright: (1) private and free performance in family circle; (2) private copies; (3) subject to adequate elements of identification of the source, analysis, and short citations, press reviews, dissemination of official speeches; public communication or reproduction of extracts for purpose of illustration for teaching or scientific research; (4) parody, pastiche, and caricature; (5) technical copies; (6) public communication or reproduction of a phonogram, a videogram, or an audiovisual programme for the benefit of people with a disability; (7) safeguard copies of a phonogram, a videogram, or an audiovisual programme; *see supra* paragraphs 225 et seq.). All those exceptions shall satisfy the so-called three-steps test which requires that any such exception must not go beyond 'normal exploitation of the performance, phonogram, videogram or audiovisual programme nor unreasonably prejudice the legitimate interests of the performing artist, producer and audiovisual communication enterprise'.

(3) Article L. 211-4 (last modified by the Act No. 2015-195 of 20 February 2015) limits the duration of neighbouring rights:

(a) the duration of the economic rights of performing artists is fifty years from 1 January of the calendar year following that of the performance; however, if a fixation in a videogram or a phonogram of the performance is made available to the public, through material supports or its communication to the public, within the above period of time, the economic rights of the performing artist expire only fifty years (in case of a fixation in a videogram) or seventy years (in case of a fixation in a phonogram) after 1 January of the calendar year following the first of those facts;
(b) the duration of the economic rights of phonograms producers is fifty years from 1 January of the calendar year following that of the first fixation of a sequence of sounds; however, if a phonogram is made available to the public, through material supports or its communication to the public, within the above period of time, the economic rights of the phonogram producer expire only seventy years after 1 January of the calendar year following the date when the phonogram was made available to the public or, failing this, following its first communication to the public;
(c) the duration of the economic rights of videograms producers is fifty years from 1 January of the calendar year following that of the first fixation of a sequence of images with or without sound; however, if a videogram is made available to the public, through material supports or its communication to the public, within the above period of time, the economic rights of the videogram producer expire only fifty years after 1 January of the calendar year following the first of those facts;
(d) the duration of the economic rights of audiovisual communication enterprises is fifty years from 1 January of the calendar year following that of the first communication of the programmes to the public.

(2) Article L. 211-6 applies the exhaustion of right to neighbouring rights. Once a physical copy of a fixation protected by a neighbouring right was sold with the rightholder's consent on the territory of a Member State of the European Economic Area, the sale of such copy may no longer be prohibited in the Member States of the European Economic Area.
(3) Article L. 211-7 applies the new chapter relating to certain uses of orphan works (Article L. 135-1–L. 135-7, *see supra* paragraph 127) to neighbouring rights.

261. The sanctions of the neighbouring rights are very similar to those of author's rights (*see infra*), although the legislation does not use the word 'infringement', in order to underline the distinction between author's rights and neighbouring rights. Criminal sanctions are foreseen under Article L. 335-1 and L. 335-4–L. 335-9: they are the same as for violation of copyright (*see infra*). However, the law takes into account the structural specificity of some neighbouring rights. Consequently, Article L. 335-4 distinguishes between fixation, reproduction, communication to the public, putting at public disposal, and telediffusion, whereas Article L. 335-2 and L. 335-3 sanctioning violation of author's rights mention only reproduction, performance, and diffusion.

262. The specific procedure of counterfeit-seizure ('saisie-contrefaçon') as provided for in Article L. 332-1 (*see infra*) does apply to violation of neighbouring rights (Article L. 332-1, §6). Further, Article L. 335-1 provides that as soon as the offences have been established, the competent police officers may effect seizure of the unlawfully reproduced phonograms and videograms, of the copies and articles manufactured or imported unlawfully, of any means of circumvention of technological measures (*see infra*) and of the equipment specially installed for the purpose of such acts.

§2. Rights of Performing Artists

263. Article L. 212-1 defines the performing artist as 'the person who acts, sings, recites, declaims, plays or executes in any other way a literary or artistic work, a variety, circus or puppet show'.

264. The protection of a performing artist implies the performance of a work. Consequently, sportsmen are not considered as performing artists. Only the persons who participate directly in the performance may benefit from such protection: technicians are not considered as performing artists either. Article L. 212-1 expressly excludes 'ancillary artists' ('artistes de complément') considered as such under professional custom.[206] The qualification should not be based only on the clauses of the contract of employment, but on the originality of the performance,[207] and also on its importance and duration.[208]

I. Exploitation Rights

265. The performing artists enjoy an exclusive right to prohibit or to authorize the fixation, reproduction and communication to the public of their performances, as well as any separate use of the sounds or images of the performance, when the latter has been fixed for both (Article L. 212-3). Any such act of exploitation must be authorized in writing by the performing artist.

266. As for the artist's remuneration, Article L. 212-3, §2 sends back to Article L. 762-1 and L. 762-2 of the Labour Code. The first of these two texts presumes that the contract entered into with a performing artist is a contract of employment. This presumption applies also to foreign artists.[209]

267. Article L. 212-3-5 provides for a special exception to the performing artist's exclusive rights. The artists may not prohibit the reproduction or public communication

206. For example, for theatre or cinema, the role of an ancillary artist must not exceed thirteen lines of text.
207. Paris, 18 Feb. 1993: D. 1993, jur., p. 397, note Wekstein-Steg; RIDA, October 1993, p. 214; Cass. Civ. 1, 6 Jul. 1999, D. 2000, jur., p. 209, concl. Sainte-Rose.
208. Paris, 11 May 1994: D. 1995, jur., p. 185, note Ravanas.
209. Cass. soc., 1 Apr. 1993: RIDA, October 1993, p. 197, obs. Kéréver.

of their performance, if it is accessory to an event, which is the main subject of a sequence of a work, or of an audiovisual document. This rule aims at protecting the right of public information, but it does not give indications as to the nature of the 'event' in consideration.

268. Article L. 214-1, §1 provides for another exception to the performing artists' exclusive rights. Under this rule, when a phonogram has been published 'for commercial purposes', the artist may not forbid the exploitation of the phonogram in the following circumstances: (1) its direct communication in a public place where it is not used in an entertainment; (2) its broadcasting, the simultaneous and integral cable distribution of such broadcast as well as its reproduction for those sole purposes, realized by or for audiovisual communication enterprises to add sound tracks to their own programmes broadcasted on their own station as well as on the stations of audiovisual communication enterprises which pay the 'equitable remuneration'; (3) its communication to the public by a radio service within the meaning of Article 2 of Law No. 86-1067 of 30 September 1986 on the freedom of communication, except radio services whose main programme is dedicated mainly to one performer, one author, one composer, or even comes from the same phonogram.

269. In these three cases, the user of the phonogram does not have to request the artist's authorization since he benefits of a 'legal license'. This solution complies with the Rome Convention on neighbouring rights (Article 12) and with the EEC Directive No. 92/100 of 19 November 1992, relating to the rental right and lending right and to certain neighbouring rights in the field of intellectual property.[210] In exchange for such licence, the performing artists are entitled to a so-called equitable remuneration. Its amount is assessed on the revenue from exploitation or, failing that, calculated as a lump sum in the cases laid down in Article L. 131-4 (*see supra* paragraph 156). The schedule of remuneration and the conditions of payment of the remuneration are normally laid down by specific agreements for each branch of activity between the organizations representing the performers and producers and the persons using phonograms (Article L. 214-3). In absence of agreement, the schedule of remuneration and the conditions for paying the remuneration are decided by a special commission presided by a State's representative and composed of an equal number of representatives of performers', producers', and users' association (Article L. 214-4).

270. The proceeds from the 'equitable remuneration' are collected and dispatched between the beneficiaries by collecting societies (Article L. 214-5). To this aim, the performing artists and the producers have created the SPRE ('Société civile pour la Perception de la Rémunération Equitable de la communication au public de phonogrammes du commerce'). According to Article L. 214-1, §6, the remuneration is to be shared by halves between the artists and the producers. The nationality of the performing artist does not matter but, under reservation of the international conventions, only the artists whose performance has been fixed on a phonogram for the first time in a Member

210. EEC Directive No. 92/100 of 19 Nov. 1992 on rental right and lending right and on certain rights related to copyright in the field of intellectual property, OJEC, No. L. 346, 27 Nov. 1992, pp. 61–66, repealed and replaced by the EC Directive 2006/115 of the European Parliament and of the Council of 12 Dec. 2006 on rental right and lending right and on certain rights related to copyright in the field of intellectual property (codified version), OJEC, No. L. 376, 27 Dec. 2006, pp. 28–35.

State of the EU can receive a share of the equitable remuneration (Articles L. 214-2 and L. 311-2).

271. The Act No. 2016-925 of 7 July 2016 has created the 'music mediator' ('*médiateur de la musique*') charged with a mission of conciliation in any dispute relating to the interpretation or implementation of: (1) an agreement between the performers whose performance is fixed in a phonogram, phonogram producers, and editors of public communication services online providing musical works; (2) a contract between a performing artist and a producer of phonograms; (3) a contract between a producer of phonograms and an editor of public communication services online providing musical works; (4) a contract between a producer of phonograms and a show producer. It doesn't prevent the parties to such disputes from directly going to court. When the music mediator finds an agreement between the parties, he writes a conciliation report detailing the steps to implement it. Failing agreement between the parties, the mediator may issue a recommendation proposing measures to put an end to the dispute. He may make public the conciliation or recommendation, subject to the information covered by professional secrecy. He also has to submit an annual report on its activities to the Minister responsible for culture and may make proposals.

II. Moral Rights

272. Article L. 212-2, inspired from Article L. 121-1 states that 'the performing artist has the right to respect of his name, his quality and his performance'. It adds that this right is perpetual and may not be transferred *inter vivos*; it is transmissible to the artist's heirs as for the protection of the interpretation and the memory of the deceased.

273. In this respect, French law goes beyond the Rome Convention on neighbouring rights, which is silent as for the moral rights of performers. This right is, however, more limited than the author's moral right, since it does not include the right to disclose the work and the right to reconsider or to withdraw.

274. Finally, since neighbouring rights may not damage the author's rights, the performing artist may not claim his own moral right to justify alterations of the interpreted work – such as modifications or suppressions – a mere warning after the credit list of the film where interpreted music is incorporated is a satisfactory measure.[211]

III. Transfer of Rights

275. Performing artists usually transfer their rights to producers or audiovisual communication firms. French legislation aims at protecting their interests in such contracts.

211. TGI Paris, 10 Jan. 1990: D. 1991, jur., p. 206, note Edelman, D. 1991, som., p. 99, obs. Colombet; in the Rostropovitch case.

A. General Rules

276. Article L. 212-3, §1 requires the artist's 'written authorization' for the fixation of his performances, their reproduction, communication to the public, and the separate use of the sounds and images if the performance was fixed for both ways. This rule means that the transfer of rights may not be implicit but must be made in a written form. However, no specific mentions are required by law. In case of 'joint performance', each 'co-performer' must give his authorization.

277. Usually performing artists entrust collecting societies with the task of managing their rights. Two such firms exist in France: ADAMI ('*Société Civile pour l'Administration des Droits des Artistes et Musiciens Interprètes*') and SPEDIDAM ('*Société de Perception et de Distribution des Droits des Artistes-Interprètes de la Musique et de la Danse*'). The first one manages the rights of artists whose name appears on the labels of sound recordings and in the credits of audiovisual works, whereas the second takes care of artists whose name does not appear.

B. Rules Specific to the Contract for Production of an Audiovisual Work

278. According to Article L. 212-4, §1, the conclusion of a contract between a performing artist and a producer for the making of an audiovisual work entails authorization to fix, reproduce, and communicate to the public the artist's performance. This presumption of transfer does not apply to contracts relating to a live performance,[212] or to the multimedia work derived from an audiovisual work,[213] or to the attendance sheet, which does not contain any mention or clause except the date of diffusion.[214] This presumption is in theory rebuttable, but performing artists have seldom the power to make their interests prevail.

279. Article L. 212-4, §2 states that: 'The contract provides for a separate remuneration for each mode of exploitation of the work.' This rule aims at ensuring to the artist an effective revenue for the various types of exploitation of his performance. If the remuneration is not mentioned for one or several types of exploitation, it will be determined by reference to schedules established under specific agreements concluded in each sector of activity between employees' (performers') and employers' (producers') associations (Article L. 212-5). If no such agreement exists, or at the date of expiry of the prior agreement, the modes and bases of remuneration are determined, for each sector of activity by a commission consisting of two judges, one 'qualified personality', and an equal number of representatives of employees' (performers') and employers' (producers') associations (Article L. 212-9).

212. Paris, 16 Jun. 1993: D. 1994, jur., p. 218, note Edelman.
213. TGI Paris, 26 Mar. 2003, Légipresse 2003, No. 205, I, p. 131.
214. Paris, 18 Sep. 2002, D. 2002, AJ., p. 3208.

§3. Rights of Producers of Phonograms and Videograms

I. Definitions

A. Definition of Producers of Phonograms

280. Article L. 213-1, §1 defines the producer of phonogram as 'the legal or natural person who takes the initiative and responsibility for the first fixation of a sequence of sounds'. A phonogram is then a fixed sequence of sounds, but the law does not require that the sequence of sounds should be a work of art: for instance, the fixation of birds' songs might be protected under Article L. 213-1. The word 'fixation' is not defined so as to embrace all new techniques.

B. Definition of Producers of Videograms

281. Article L. 215-1, §1 defines the producer of videograms as 'the legal or natural person who takes the initiative and responsibility for the first fixation of a sequence of images, whether accompanied by sounds or not'. This definition seems to encroach upon the definition of an audiovisual work of Article L. 112-2 (*see supra* paragraph 61), except that Article L. 112-2 mentions 'animated' sequences of images. It is, therefore, necessary to define the relations between both notions. It should be reminded that a videogram is only a fixed sequence of images, accompanied by sounds or not, but is not a work in itself. On the other hand, Article L. 112-2 does not state that any animated sequence of images is a work, but only that works consisting of such sequences are said 'audiovisual works'.

II. Content of Rights

A. Principles

282. In spite of the differences in definition, producers of phonograms and videograms receive the same legal treatment.

283. Under Articles L. 213-1, §2 and L. 215-1, §2, producers of phonograms and videograms have the exclusive reproduction right. They can authorize or prohibit direct or indirect, temporary or permanent reproduction by any means and in any form, in whole or in part. They also enjoy the right to make the phonogram or videogram available to the public, by means of sale, exchange, or rental. These articles create a specific right of distribution, which is not exhausted after the first sale made with the consent of the rightholder. They recognize to the producers a right to control some forms of marketing after the first sale of the phonogram or videogram. The Supreme Court held that the protection of producers such as organized by French law, which grants rights other than these listed in the Rome Convention of 26 October 1961 is not contrary to this Convention which only provides for a minimum and authorizes the Member States to create a wider protection.[215]

284. Finally, Articles L. 213-1 and L. 215-1 grant to the producer the right to authorize any communication to the public of the phonogram or videogram. For example, they can prohibit the use of the phonogram or videogram for public performance. New Article L. 213-2 (Act No. 2016-925 of 7 July 2016) rules specifically the contract concluded by the producer of a phonogram and an editor of public communication services online providing musical works. This contract must set the conditions for the exploitation of the phonograms in an objective and fair manner. These conditions shall not include discriminatory clauses not justified by actual counterparts.

285. Producers of phonograms or videograms enjoy no moral rights.

B. The Legal Licence Relating to Phonograms Published for Commerce

286. Article L. 214-1 provides for an exception to the phonogram producers' exclusive rights. Under this rule, when a phonogram has been published 'for commercial purposes', the producers may not forbid the exploitation of the phonogram in the following circumstances: (1) its direct communication in a public place where it is not used in an entertainment; (2) its broadcasting, the simultaneous and integral cable distribution of such broadcast as well as its reproduction for those sole purposes realized by or for audiovisual communication enterprises to add sound tracks to their own programmes broadcasted on their own station as well as on the stations of audiovisual communication enterprises which pay the 'equitable remuneration'; (3) its communication to the public by a radio service within the meaning of Article 2 of Law No. 86-1067 of 30 September 1986 on the freedom of communication, except radio services whose main programme is dedicated mainly to one performer, one author, one composer, or even comes from the same phonogram.

287. In these three cases, the user of the phonogram does not have to request the producer's authorization since he benefits of a 'legal license'. This solution complies with the Rome Convention on neighbouring rights (Article 12) and with the EEC Directive No. 92/100 of 19 November 1992, relating to the rental right and lending right and to certain neighbouring rights in the field of intellectual property.[216] In exchange for such licence, the phonogram producers' are entitled to a so-called equitable remuneration. Its amount is assessed on the revenues from exploitation (Article L. 214-1, §5), or failing that, calculated as a lump sum in the cases laid down in Article L. 131-4 (*see supra* paragraph 156). The schedule of remuneration and the conditions of payment of the remuneration are normally laid down by specific agreements for each branch of activity between the organizations representing the performers and producers and the persons using phonograms (Article L. 214-3). In absence of agreement,

215. Cass. crim., 2 Feb. 1994: RIDA, April 1994, p. 321.

216. EEC Directive No. 92/100 of 19 Nov. 1992 on rental right and lending right and on certain rights related to copyright in the field of intellectual property, OJEC, No. L. 346, 27 Nov. 1992, pp. 61–66, repealed and replaced by the EC Directive 2006/115 of the European Parliament and of the Council of 12 Dec. 2006 on rental right and lending right and on certain rights related to copyright in the field of intellectual property (codified version), OJEC, No. L. 376, 27 Dec. 2006, pp. 28–35.

the schedule of remuneration and the conditions for paying the remuneration are decided by a special commission presided by a State's representative and composed of an equal number of representatives of performers', producers', and users' association (Article L. 214-4).

288. The proceeds from the 'equitable remuneration' are collected and dispatched between the beneficiaries by collecting societies (Article L. 214-5). To this aim, the performing artists and the producers have created the SPRE ('*Société civile pour la Perception de la Rémunération Equitable de la communication au public de phonogrammes du commerce*'). According to Article L. 214-1, §6, the remuneration is to be shared by halves between the artists and the producers. The nationality of the producer does not matter but, under reservation of the international conventions, only the producers whose phonogram has been fixed for the first time in a Member State of the EU can receive a share of the equitable remuneration (Articles L. 214-2 and L. 311-2).

289. The Act No. 2016-925 of 7 July 2016 has created the 'music mediator' ('*médiateur de la musique*'), charged with a mission of conciliation in any dispute relating to the interpretation or implementation of: (1) an agreement between the performers whose performance is fixed in a phonogram, phonogram producers, and editors of public communication services online providing musical works; (2) a contract between a performing artist and a producer of phonograms; (3) a contract between a producer of phonograms and an editor of public communication services online providing musical works; (4) a contract between a producer of phonograms and a show producer. It doesn't prevent the parties to such disputes from directly going to court. . When the music mediator finds an agreement between the parties, he writes a conciliation report detailing the steps to implement it. Failing agreement between the parties, the mediator may issue a recommendation proposing measures to put an end to the dispute. He may make public the conciliation or recommendation, subject to the information covered by professional secrecy. He also has to submit an annual report on its activities to the Minister responsible for culture and may make proposals.

III. Transfer of Rights

290. Transfers of rights by the producers are in principle subject to the rules of general contract law. No specific form or mentions are required. As for videograms, Article L. 215-1, §3 provides for a specific rule: 'The rights afforded to the producer of a videogram under the preceding paragraph, the author's rights and the performers' rights of which he disposes in respect of the work fixed on the videogram may not be assigned separately.'

291. This rule applies in the situation where all the author's rights and the neighbouring rights belong to the same person (producer or his successor in rights). In such a case, these rights may only be transferred globally, as for all the persons (author, performing artists, producer). The rule aims at avoiding the risk of speculation by the producer who would assign separately the various rights, which might trouble the exploitation of the work. It is not, however, forbidden to limit the transfer to a part of the work, or to one or several ways of exploitation.

§4. Rights of Audiovisual Communication Firms

292. The audiovisual communication enterprise is defined by Article L. 216-1, §2 as a firm which provides a service of audiovisual communication within the meaning of the Act No. 86-1067 of 30 September 1986 relating to the freedom of communication, whatever the legal rules applicable to such service. This enterprise holds a neighbouring right on its programmes (Article L. 216-1, §1). The notion of 'programme' is wider than the one of 'work', but the qualification may be difficult in some marginal cases, such as multimedia products.

293. The neighbouring right recognized to an audiovisual communication enterprise allows it to benefit of an exclusive right even on programmes which the firm did not fix itself. Such an enterprise may, moreover, cumulate this right with the one it may enjoy as producer of phonograms or videograms, if it fulfils the conditions (i.e., has taken the initiative and responsibility for the first fixation of a sequence of sounds or images: *see supra* paragraphs 280 et seq.). Consequently, third parties may not reproduce; make the programmes available to the public by means of sale, exchange, or rental without the enterprise's authorization.

294. The enterprise also enjoys the exclusive right to telediffuse its programmes (Article L. 216-1) and to authorize their communication to the public, but only 'in a place accessible to the public for payment of an entry fee'.

295. The Act No. 2006-961 of 1 August 2001, to break a contrary decision of the 'Cour de cassation',[217] has added a new Article L. 216-2 which provides that authorization to telediffuse a performance of a performing artist, a phonogram, a videogram, or the programmes of an audiovisual communication enterprise by electromagnetic waves shall include its non-commercial distribution towards the networks of buildings or groups of buildings for habitation use installed by the owners or co-owners, when it is intended only to permit the connection of each flat to collective receiving installations.

296. As for the transfer of their rights, audiovisual communication enterprises are subjected to the same rules than the phonogram or videogram producers. Transfers of rights are in principle subject to the rules of general contract law, so that no specific form or mentions are required. And moreover if the audiovisual communication enterprise is producer of a videogram, disposes of the author's right and of the performer's right, Article L. 215-1, §3 is applicable.

217. Cass. civ. 1, 1 Mar. 2005: Bull. civ. I, No. 105 and 106; *JCP* G 2005 II 10053, note Caron; CCE 2005, comm. No. 80, note Caron.

Chapter 10. Infringement, Procedure, and Remedies

§1. Infringement

297. Infringement consists, *stricto sensu*, in the violation of the author's right of reproduction or performance or of the *'droit de suite'*. However, the sale, import, or export of infringing works is also treated as infringement. Criminal sanctions also apply to the violation of neighbouring rights.

I. Violation of the Reproduction Right

298. According to Article L. 335-3 and L. 335-2, any reproduction by any means of a work of the mind, any edition of writings, musical compositions, drawings, paintings, or any other printed or engraved production made in violation of rules protecting the authors' right is an infringement: any infringement is an offence (and more precisely a 'délit').

299. Therefore, the material act of infringement consists of a reproduction unauthorized by the rightholder. Such a reproduction may concern a number of copies, but a single copy is enough to constitute an infringement.[218] The infringing reproduction may be made by any technical means (printing, recording, photography, etc.); it may be total or partial.[219] The reproduction is also illicit if it has a destination different from the one authorized by the author (e.g., broadcasting of records whereas the author authorized only their public sale; *see supra* paragraphs 221 et seq.).

300. An attempt to reproduce is not an infringement.[220]

301. According to a steady line of cases, copyright infringement is an 'intentional misdemeanour': criminal sanctions apply only if the violation was intentional.[221] However, French courts presume the defendant's bad faith.[222] The presumption is rebuttable and the plaintiff may evidence his good faith.[223] Such a proof is difficult, especially when the plaintiff is a professional, who is supposed to seek information as to the legal status of the works he reproduces.[224] If such good faith is evidenced, criminal sanctions do not apply, but the defendant may nevertheless be liable in torts.[225]

218. Paris, 21 Jan. 1963: JCP 1963 II 13235, note Delpech.
219. Cass. civ. 1, 3 Jun. 1997: Bull. civ. I, No. 184; D. 1998, jur., p. 166, note Daverat; JCP ed. E, 1998, Chron., p. 1250, note Bougerol, the reproduction in a newspaper of a photograph of a scene of a film is a violation of the producer's rights.
220. Paris, 5 Aug. 1884: DP 1893, 2, 177.
221. Cass. crim., 1 Feb. 1912: Gaz. Pal. 1912, 1, jur., p. 438.
222. Cass. crim., 1 Feb. 1912, *supra* – Cass. crim., 1 May 1940: DA 1941, 116. – Cass. crim., 25 Mar. 1957: Bull. crim., p. 152.
223. Cass. crim., 10 Dec. 1958: Bull. crim., No. 735.
224. Paris, 1 May 1975: RTD com. 1977, 503, obs. Desbois.
225. Cass., 7 Dec. 1900: D. 1901, jur., p. 339. -Versailles, 21 Oct. 1992: RIDA, 1994, No. 159, p. 350.

II. Violation of the Performing Right

302. Article L. 335-3 also sanctions any performance or diffusion violating author's rights. In order to determine whether the performance is illegal, the judge must refer to Article L. 122-2, which defines the various means of communication to the public (*see supra* paragraphs 210 et seq.). Fraudulent intention is also required here, and is presumed, as in the case of violation of the reproduction right.[226]

303. The law facilitates the evidence of violation: according to Article L. 331-2, the proof of material violation of the provisions of the Books 1, 2, and 3 may be brought, not only by reports drawn up by police officers, but also by statements made by sworn agents appointed, as appropriate, by the Centre National du cinema et de l'image animée, by the regularly constituted bodies for professional defence referred to in Article L. 331-1 and by the collecting societies mentioned under Title 2 of Book 3 (*see supra* paragraphs 159 et seq.). Such agents must be agreed by the Ministry of Culture.

304. These provisions do not exclude the proof by the means provided for by the rules of criminal procedure.[227]

III. Violation of the 'Droit de Suite'

305. The violation of the *'droit de suite'* occurs when, on the occasion of a resale act, the artist does not receive his resale royalty. Article L. 334-1 states that 'in the event of infringement of Article L. 122-8, the buyer and the auctioneer may be pronounced jointly liable for damages in favour of the beneficiaries of the *droit de suite'*. A penal fine is foreseen against the art market professionals who do not pay the royalty to its beneficiary or do not give the necessary informations to the beneficiary or a collecting society (Article R. 122-11).

IV. Violation of Moral Right

306. The legislation does not provide for a specific solution to the question whether a violation of moral right may entail criminal sanctions. In spite of the principle of strict interpretation of penal law, French courts apply the same criminal sanctions as for the violation of the exploitation rights.[228]

226. Paris, 3 Nov. 1956: Gaz. Pal. 1956, jur., p. 324.
227. Cass. crim., 5 Sep. 1989: RIDA, April 1990, p. 201.
228. Paris, 25 Jan. 1968: RIDA, July1968, p. 174; RTD com. 1968, 344, obs. Desbois. Paris, 23 Mar. 1992: RIDA, January 1993, p. 181, obs. Kéréver, where the authorship of a work was falsely attributed to the sculptor Rodin. Cass. crim., 13 Dec. 1995: RIDA, July 1996, p. 307; RTD com. 1996, p. 442, obs. Françon. Cass. crim., 24 Sep. 1997: Gaz. Pal. 1998, 2, jur., p. 259, note Leclerc.

V. Offer to the Public, Export and Import

307. Under Article L. 335-2, §3, are sanctioned the offer to the public, export and import of infringing works. This provision aims at sanctioning all the persons who participate in the public diffusion of an infringing work, even if they did not take the initiative of its reproduction.[229] This offence is independent from the violation of reproduction and performing rights. It consists of the act to offer to the public an infringing work, either by sale, exhibition, or rental.

308. Similarly, imports and exports of infringing works are sanctioned. This means that sanctions of French law apply to the infringement in France of works which will be used abroad, and to exploitation in France of works infringed abroad, whatever their place of publication. The transit is treated as importation.[230]

309. As for the requirement of fraudulent intention, the courts make a distinction between various professionals.

310. The mere bookshop keeper is not presumed to have acted in bad faith,[231] nor is an unprofessional person.[232] However, an antique shopkeeper has been sanctioned whereas he should have checked the legality of the reproductions he sold.[233] Printers[234] and shops selling infringing phonograms and videograms are presumed to act fraudulently.[235] As for the importer, he is supposed to show that he sought all the information which would allow him to avoid the risk of infringement.[236]

VI. Violation of the Neighbouring Rights

311. Article L. 335-4 defines the violations of the neighbouring rights. It consists of:

- any fixation, reproduction, communication, or making available to the public, on payment or free of charge, or any telediffusion of a performance, a phonogram, a videogram, or a programme made without authorization, where such is required, of the performer, the phonogram or videogram producer or the audiovisual communication enterprise.
- any importation or exportation of phonograms or videograms made without the authorization of the producer or the performer, where such is required.
- failure to pay the remuneration due to the performer or the phonogram or videogram producer in respect of private copying (*see supra* paragraph 260) or public communication or of the telediffusion of phonograms.

---

229. Cass. crim., 27 May 1986: RIDA, July 1987, p. 181; criminal sanctions apply to an offer for sale of a copyrighted model, even if the defendant did not manufacture it.
230. Cass. crim., 7 Oct. 1985: D. 1986, I.R., p. 188, obs. Colombet.
231. TGI Paris, 21 Feb. 1975: RIDA, July 1976, p. 144.
232. Paris, 17 Feb. 1988: D. 1989, som., p. 50, obs. Colombet; JCP 1989 I 3376, No. 1, obs. Edelman.
233. Paris, 28 May 1979: RIDA, October 1979, p. 145.
234. Cass. civ., 1 Jul. 1970: D. 1970, jur., p. 734, note Edelman.
235. TGI Paris, 2 May 1983: RIDA, October 1983, p. 247.
236. Cass. com., 16 Jun. 1992: RIDA, January 1993, p. 176, obs. Kéréver.

312. It is also possible to infringe the moral right of the performing artist. But, in the absence of a specific text, that violation cannot be penally sanctioned; only civil remedies are possible.

313. The violations of neighbouring rights are, like copyright infringement (*see supra* paragraph 301), 'intentional misdemeanour' and French courts also presume the defendant's bad faith[237] (rebuttable presumption).

§2. Procedure

314. The persons entitled to sue the infringers are: the author, his assignee, and the collecting societies.[238] Firms such as the SACEM (*see supra* paragraph 160) may sue for infringement and seize works which belong to their repertory and are exploited without their authorization.[239] Collective firms entrusted with the management of neighbouring rights may also sue for the violation of such rights.[240] However, the Cour de cassation held that the authors who transferred their rights to the SACEM keep nevertheless their right to sue the infringers individually.[241] The juristic person who discloses and exploits commercially a work is presumed to own a copyright on this work and may sue the infringers.[242]

315. As for foreigners, they may bring actions in France on condition they have a right for the French territory.[243]

316. The choice of forum is determined according to Article L. 331-1, §1 which has been modified by the Act No. 2011-525 of 17 May 2011: 'Civil actions and claims relating to literary and artistic property, even when they also address a related issue of unfair competition, are exclusively brought before the "tribunaux de grande instance" determined by regulation'. The commercial courts have no more jurisdiction for such disputes; and only ten selected 'tribunaux de grande instance' have an exclusive jurisdiction. Arbitration is allowed in the conditions of Articles 2059 and 2060 of the Civil Code (the matter should not relate to a question of public order) (Article L. 331-1 §4).

237. Cass. crim., 13 Dec. 1995: RIDA, July 1996, p. 279; D. 1997, jur., p. 196, note Edelman.
238. Cass. civ. 2, 6 Dec. 1966: JCP 1967 II 14937, concl. Lindon; D. 1967, jur., p. 381, note Desbois; two decisions; the collecting societies may act only for the defence of the interests which they are mandated to defend according to their charter. Paris, 25 Jun. 1997: JCP ed. E, 1997, pan. No. 1348; The Centre Français d'Exploitation du Droit de Copie may bring action against a self-service photocopy shop.
239. Cass civ. 1, 10 Feb. 1987: Bull. civ. I, p. 49.
240. Cass. com., 16 Jun. 1992: RIDA, January 1993, p. 176, obs. Kéréver; Reims, 29 May 1996: JCP ed. E, 1997, pan. No. 341; the SPRE has an interest to sue and its action is not an abuse of a dominant position on the French market.
241. Cass. civ. 1, 24 Feb. 1998: RIDA, July 1998, p. 213, obs. Kéréver; RTD com. 1998, 592, obs. Françon.
242. Cass. civ. 1, 3 Jul. 1996: RIDA, January 1997, p. 315, obs. Kéréver; RTD com. 1997, 267, obs. Françon.
243. Cass. civ. 1, 29 Apr. 1970: Rev. crit. DIP 1971, 270, note Batiffol, an Italian citizen assignee of copyright, may not sue for infringement in France where he has no rights.

317. Regularly constituted bodies for professional defence shall be entitled to institute legal proceedings to defend the interests entrusted to them under their statutes (Article L. 331-1, §2). The beneficiary of an exclusive exploitation right may, unless otherwise provided for in the licence contract, also institute infringement proceedings (Article L. 331-1, §3). The 'Centre national du cinema et de l'image animée' may institute penal proceedings against acts of infringement of audiovisual works (Article L. 331-3).

318. If the claimant can give reasons that circumstances are likely to compromise the payment of damages, the court shall order the sequestration of the alleged infringer's movable or immovable assets, including the freezing of the bank accounts and other assets, under the general rules of law. To determine the goods likely to be seized, the court may order the submission of banking, financial, accounting or commercial documents or the access to relevant data (Article L. 331-1-1).

319. If so required, the court hearing civil proceedings provided for by Books I, II, and III (copyright, neighbouring rights, sui generis right of the producer of databases) shall order, under penalty of a daily fine if necessary, in order to determine the origin and the distribution networks of the infringing goods or services which allegedly prejudice the claimant's rights, the communication of any document or information held by the defendant or by any person who was found in possession of such allegedly infringing goods or who provides services which allegedly prejudice the claimant's rights or was reported to take part to the production, manufacturing, or distribution of such products or the supply of such services ('Right of information'). The communication of documents or information shall be ordered if there is no legitimate hindrance. The documents or information sought relate to: (a) The name and address of the producers, manufacturers, distributors, suppliers, and other previous holders of the products or services, as well as the intended wholesalers and retailers. (b) The quantities produced, commercialized, delivered, received, or ordered, as well as the price obtained for the products or services in question (Article L. 331-1-2).

320. Evidences of infringement may be collected through a specific procedure of seizure: counterfeit-seizure ('saisie-contrefaçon': Article L. 332-1–L. 332-4). That procedure is reserved to the author of a protected work, his assignees, or successors (Article L. 332-1, §1). According to Article L. 321-2 the collecting societies duly established are entitled to take legal action to defend the rights for which they are responsible under their statutes. Consequently, they can also ask for counterfeit-seizure.[244]

321. The plaintiff must first request the authorization to seize from the President of the 'Tribunal de grande instance'. It is necessary to invoke a creation, to give some clues to it and to claim a violation of the exploitation rights[245] or of the moral right.[246] The judge may not refuse the authorization, but only define its scope and order the payment of a warranty. The judge may condition the implementation of the measures it ordered to the furnishing by the claimant of security to ensure, if necessary, the defendant's compensation if the infringement action is subsequently held unfounded or the seizure is cancelled (Article L. 332-1, §5). The seizure is executed by a bailiff

244. Cass. civ. 1, 10 Feb. 1987: Bull. civ. I, No. 49.
245. Paris, 23 Mar. 1978: RIDA, July 1979, p. 127.
246. Paris, 17 May 1993: Rev. dr. propr. Ind. 1993, No. 49, 78.

who may be assisted by an expert and a police officer if necessary. He may proceed in any place with either the detailed description, with or without taking samples, or the effective seizure of the allegedly infringing works as well as any related document, according to what was authorized by the president. The court shall authorize the effective seizure of any document related to the allegedly infringing works, even in the absence of the latter. The court shall also order, for the same evidential purposes, the detailed description or the effective seizure of equipment and tools used to manufacture or distribute the allegedly infringing works (Article L. 332-1, §2). In literary and artistic property (with the exception of softwares and databases, *see infra*), the counterfeit-seizure is not only a probative measure, it is also a protective measure. The President may order: 1° seizure of the copies constituting an unlawful reproduction of a work or of any means of circumvention of technological measures; 2° seizure, whatever the day or time, of the copies constituting an unlawful reproduction of a work, whether already manufactured or in the process of manufacture, of any means of circumvention of technological measures, whether already manufactured or in the process of manufacture, of the receipts obtained and of copies unlawfully used; 3° seizure of receipts (within the limits defined by Articles L. 333-1 et seq.) from any reproduction, performance or dissemination, by any means, of a work of the mind, carried out in violation of the author's rights or from any circumvention of technological measures;[247] 4° effective seizure of unlawful works or goods suspected of infringing an author's right, or their delivery up so as to prevent their entry into or movement within the channels of commerce (Article L. 332-1, §3). The bailiff drafts a report which must be delivered to the defendant. An irregular seizure may be declared invalid and the plaintiff sentenced to pay damages to the defendant. Still because of its protective nature, the counterfeit-seizure may also be completed by some orders which exclusively aim at blocking the infringing activity, the President may order: (a) delay or suspension of public performances which are in progress or which have already been announced; (b) suspension of all manufacture in progress serving the unlawful reproduction of the work or the circumvention of technological measures.

322. The distrainee or the garnishee may ask the President of the 'Tribunal de grande instance' to lift the seizure or to limit its effects or to authorize the resumption of manufacture or of the public performances of the work, under the authority of an administrator appointed as receiver, to hold the proceeds from such manufacture or performance on behalf of the person to whom the work belongs. Such a claim must be submitted to the President within twenty working days or thirty-one civil days if this time limit is longer, as from the day on which the detailed description or the effective seizure is realized (Article R. 332-2). In such a case, if the President allows the request of the distrainee or garnishee, he may order the petitioner to deposit a sum as a guarantee for any damages to which the author might be entitled (Article L. 332-2, §2). The distrainee or garnishee can also ask the President to lift the seizure, without any time limit, if the distrainer does not submit the matter to the competent court within twenty working days or thirty-one civil days if this time limit is longer, as from the day on which the detailed description or the effective seizure is realized (Article L. 332-3 and R. 332-3).

247. Cass. civ. 1, 10 Feb. 1987: Bull. civ. I, No. 49.

323. When the copyrighted work is a software or a database[248] (Article L. 332-4), the procedure of counterfeit-seizure has exclusively a probative nature. The President of the 'Tribunal de grande instance' may condition the implementation of the measures it ordered to the furnishing by the claimant of security to ensure, if necessary, the defendant's compensation if the infringement action is subsequently held unfounded or the seizure is cancelled (Article L. 332-4, §5). The seizure is executed by a bailiff who may be assisted by an expert and a police officer if necessary. He may proceed in any place with either the detailed description, with or without taking samples, or the effective seizure of the allegedly infringing software or database as well as any related document, according to what was authorized by the president. The detailed description may take the form of a copy of the allegedly infringing software or database (Article L. 332-4, §2). The court shall also order, for the same evidential purposes, the detailed description or the effective seizure of equipment and tools used to manufacture or distribute the allegedly infringing software or database as well as any related document (Article L. 332-4, §3). The President may order the effective seizure of any document related to the software, database, equipment, or tools, even in the absence of the latter (Article L. 332-4, §4). The counterfeit-seizure must be followed by the introduction of the action for infringement – either a civil or criminal action – within twenty working days or thirty-one civil days if this time limit is longer, as from the day on which the detailed description or the effective seizure is realized (Article R. 332-4). If not, the entire seizure, including the description, shall be void upon the defendant's request, without its having to motivate its request and without prejudice to the damages which may be claimed (Article L. 332-4, §5). A void seizure may not be used as evidence during the proceedings.

324. According to Article L. 336-1, §3, the specific procedure of counterfeit-seizure of Article L. 332-4 may also be used against infringement committed through peer-to-peer softwares even if the infringed work is not necessarily a software or a database (it is more often a musical or audiovisual work).

325. The French customs administration may withhold in the course of its inspections allegedly infringing goods. This French system of customs measures apply, in principle, to goods crossing the French border and coming from another Member State of the EU, with the exception of goods legally manufactured or put on the market on the territory of a Member State of the EU and destined, after their transit on the French territory, to be exported outside of the EU or to be put on the market of another Member State of the EU, in order to be there legally commercialized (Article L. 335-10 *in fine*).

326. Under Article L. 335-10, the customs administration may withhold in the course of its inspections the allegedly infringing goods upon the rightholder's request (holder of a copyright or of a neighbouring right). The Public Prosecutor, the plaintiff, and the party declaring or in possession of the goods shall be informed without delay by the customs service of the withholding measure that it has taken.

327. The withholding measure shall be lifted as of right where the plaintiff fails, within ten working days (three working days in case of perishable goods) following notification of the withholding of the goods, to prove to the customs service: either that precautionary measures have been taken; or that he has instituted proceedings

248. Cass. civ. 1, 20 Jan. 2004: RJDA May 2004, p. 474, note Bouche.

before the civil court or the court of misdemeanours and has provided the necessary guarantees to cover his liability in the event of the infringement claim being eventually considered unfounded; or that he has filed a complaint with the Public Prosecutor. The customs administration may extend the period of ten working days by a maximum of ten new working days at the request duly motivated of the plaintiff.

328. For the purpose of the institution of the legal proceedings referred to in the foregoing paragraph, the plaintiff may require the customs administration to communicate the names and addresses of the sender, the importer and the consignee of the goods withheld, or of the holder thereof, images of the goods, and also information on their quantity, origin, provenance, and destination, notwithstanding the provisions of Article 59*bis* of the Customs Code concerning the professional secrecy to which officials of the customs administration are bound.

329. The customs administration may also withhold in the course of its inspections the allegedly infringing goods (with the exception of perishable goods) ex officio, without any rightholder's request (Article L. 335-11). The withholding is immediately notified to the holder of the copyright or of the neighbouring right (with images of the goods and information on their nature and quantity) and the Public Prosecutor is informed thereof. The withholding measure shall be lifted as of right if the rightholder, within four working days following notification of the withholding of the goods, does not start by a written request the normal customs measures proceeding as described above. The period of time of ten working days, during which the rightholder shall prove to the customs service his precautionary measures, civil or penal proceedings or complaint with the Public Prosecutor, starts from the acceptance of this request by the customs administration.

330. During the withholding period, the rightholder may inspect the goods withheld, upon his request or upon the customs administration's request. He may also realize a counterfeit-seizure against the withheld goods (*see supra* paragraph 323). On the occasion of the control of the goods withheld, the customs administration may take samples which may be transferred, upon request, to the holder of the trademark or the exclusive licensee for the sole purpose of analysis and to facilitate his civil or criminal action. The withheld goods may also be destroyed under the control of the customs administration (under some conditions listed in Article L. 335-14 and L. 335-15).

331. Special procedures have been created in order to fight against infringement committed through peer-to-peer softwares and Internet. The Acts No. 2009-669 of 12 June 2009 and No. 2009-1311 of 28 October 2009 have created the 'Haute Autorité pour la diffusion des oeuvres et la protection des droits sur Internet' ('High Authority for the Dissemination of Works and Protection of Rights on the Internet HADOPI'), an independent public authority having three missions: (1) a mission of encouraging the development of the legal offer and observation of the lawful and illicit use of works and objects to which a copyright or a neighbouring right is attached on the electronic communications networks used for the provision of on-line public communication services; (2) a mission to protect these works and objects with regard to attacks on these rights committed on electronic communications networks used for the provision of online communication services to the public; (3). a regulatory and monitoring mission in the field of technical measures for the protection and identification of works and objects protected by copyright or by a neighbouring right.

332. Against infringements committed through peer-to-peer, the Hadopi monitors the subscribers of the Internet access ('Hadopi procedure': sworn agents monitor networks and retrieve IP addresses of lines used for illegal downloads; these informations are transmitted to the Hadopi which obtains from the access providers the identity of the concerned subscribers; the Hadopi issues a warning to the subscribers in order to warn them of these acts and to ask them to secure their line so that illegal downloads do not happen again; in case of recidivism, and after further warnings, the Hadopi may transmit the file to the Public Prosecutor who may, by means of a criminal order, impose a penalty, up to EUR 1,500, on the subscriber), and rightholders may also engage actions against the Internet user who uploads or downloads (infringement actions as uploading may be an illicit communication to the public and downloading may be an illicit reproduction), against the Internet access provider (in order to find technical solutions to prevent the infringement) or against peer-to-peer softwares.

333. According to Article L. 335-2-1, is punished by three years imprisonment and a fine of EUR 300,000, the fact: (1) to publish, make available to the public, or to communicate to the public, knowingly and in any form whatsoever, software clearly intended for the making available to the unauthorized public of protected works or objects; (2) to induce knowingly, including through an advertisement, the use of such a software. According to Article L. 336-1, when a software is mainly used for illicitly making available to the public works or objects protected by a right of literary and artistic property, the President of 'Tribunal de grande instance', in emergency interim proceedings, may order all necessary measures to the protection of this right and in accordance with the state of the art. The measures ordered shall not have the effect of distorting the essential characteristics or the original purpose of the software. And, pursuant to Article L. 336-2, when an infringement of a copyright or neighbouring right is committed through the content of a public online communication service, the 'Tribunal de grande instance' may order all appropriate measures to prevent or stop such infringement, against any person. The request may be formed by the rightholders, their heirs, the 'Centre national du cinéma et de l'image animée', collecting societies, or bodies for professional defence referred to in Article L. 331-1.

§3. Remedies

334. Infringement of copyright may entail criminal and civil sanctions.

I. Criminal Sanctions

A. Principal Remedies

335. Under Article L. 335-2 copyright infringement is sanctioned by a term of three years imprisonment and a fine of EUR 300,000. A same sanction applies to peer-to-peer softwares' editors (who edit, make available, or communicate to the public, knowingly and in any form, a software obviously destined to make available to the public protected works or objects, and knowingly incite to the use of such a software; Article L. 335-2-1). The infringement is punished by a term of seven years' imprisonment and a fine of EUR 750,000 where it is committed by an organized gang. The same sanctions apply as for the violation of the exclusive neighbouring rights (Article L. 335-4) except for the failure to pay the remuneration due to the author, the performer, or the phonogram or videogram producer in respect of private copying or public communication or of the telediffusion of phonograms, which is only sanctioned by a fine of EUR 300,000 and no imprisonment. When the infringer is or was linked by contract with the plaintiff (e.g., former licensee or employer of the author), the sanctions are doubled (Article L. 335-9).

336. Juristic persons may be penally liable and sanctioned in the conditions of Article 121-2 of the Penal Code. Article L. 335-8 of the I.P. Code, which sends back to Articles 131-38 of the Penal Code, allows the judge to order against a juristic person a fine increased fivefold EUR 1,500,000. Juristic persons shall also be liable to the penalties referred to in Article 131-39 of the Penal Code (*see supra,* paragraph 106) Moreover, the director, a natural person, may also bear the usual sanctions (Article 121-2, Penal Code).

B. Supplementary Sanctions

337. Natural or juristic persons penally liable may be further obliged, at their own costs, to remove from the channels of commerce the goods found to be infringing and all things which were used or intended to commit the infringement (Article L. 335-6, §1 and L. 335-8, §3). The courts may also order the destruction, at the expense of the infringer, or the delivery up to the injured party of the goods removed from the channels of commerce or seized, without prejudice to the damages which may be claimed (Article L. 335-6, §3 and L. 335-8, §4). The court may order, against natural persons, the seizure of the proceeds coming from the infringement (Article L. 335-6, §2). This is understood as 'the profit' and not as the total product issued from the unlawful exploitation of the work.[249] It may also order the seizure of all the infringing items as well as of the equipment specially used for the infringement.[250]

338. The plaintiff may also request the posting of the judgment on the defendant's door (combination of Article L. 335-6, §4 I.P. Code and Articles 131-35 Penal Code), and the publication of the judgment (in whole or by excerpts) in newspapers at the defendant's expense without, however, the costs of such publication exceeding the maximum amount of the fine incurred.

339. Moreover, Article L. 335-5 authorizes the court to order the total or partial, permanent or temporary (for a period not exceeding five years) closure of the establishment that has served for the commission of the offence. Temporary closure may not be a cause of either termination or suspension of employment contracts, or of any monetary consequence prejudicial to the employees concerned. And in case of

249. Cass. Ch. mixte, 5 Nov. 1976: D. 1977, jur., p. 221, note X.L.; RTD com. 1976, 728, obs. Desbois.
250. *See* , for example, Cass. crim., 13 Dec. 1995: D. 1996, I.R., p. 42.

a permanent closure, the rights of the employees are protected according to Article L. 122-14-4 and L. 122-14-5 of the Labour Code.

C. Criminal Protection of Technological Measures and Rights-Management Information

340. The Act No. 2006-961 of 1 August 2006, implementing into French law the EC Directive No. 2001/29,[251] has created, among the provisions which are common to copyright and neighbouring rights, a new section (Articles L. 331-5 et seq.) especially devoted to the definition and regulation of the technological measures and rights-managements information. Specific criminal sanctions have been created to protect such technological measures and rights-managements information.

341. 'Technological measures' (Article L. 331-5) means any technology, device or component that, in the normal course of its operation, is designed to prevent or restrict acts, in respect of works (other than software) or other subject-matter (a performance, a phonogram, a videogram, or an audiovisual communication programme), which are not authorized by the rightholder of any copyright or any right related to copyright as provided for by law. They shall be deemed effective where the use of a protected work or other subject matter is controlled by the rightholders through application of an access control or protection process, such as encryption, scrambling, or other transformation of the work or other subject matter or a copy control mechanism which achieves the protection objective. Such technological measures must preserve the effective interoperability and respect the various exceptions or limitations provided for. And criminal sanctions are provided for by Article L. 335-3-1 (copyright) and L. 335-4-1 (neighbouring rights) against the circumvention and the supplying or offer of means especially intended or adapted for the circumvention of any effective technological measures, which the person concerned carries out in the knowledge that he or she is pursuing that objective.

342. 'Rights-management information' (Article L. 331-11) means any information provided by rightholders which identifies the work (other than software) or other subject matter (a performance, a phonogram, a videogram, or an audiovisual communication programme), the author or any other rightholder, or information about the terms and conditions of use of the work or other subject matter, and any numbers or codes that represent such information. Criminal sanctions are provided for by Article L. 335-3-2 (copyright) and L. 335-4-2 (neighbouring rights) against any person knowingly performing without authority any of the following acts: (a) the removal or alteration of any rights-management information; (b) the supplying or offer of means especially intended or adapted for the removal or alteration of rights-management information; (c) the distribution, importation for distribution, broadcasting, communication, or making available to the public of works or other subject matter from which rights-management information has been removed or altered without authority.

---

251. EC Directive 2001/29 of the European Parliament and of the Council of 22 May 2001 on the harmonization of certain aspects of copyright and related rights in the information society, OJEC, No. L. 167, 22 Jun. 2001, pp. 10–19.

II. Civil Remedies

343. The rightholder may first claim for the cessation of the infringing acts. But he may also claim for damages. Since the Act No. 2007-1544 of 29 October 2007 and its revision by the Act No. 2014-315 of 11 March 2014, Article L. 331-1-3 states that 'To set the damages, the court takes into account separately: 1° the negative economic consequences of the rights infringement, including the loss of profit and loss suffered by the injured party; 2° the moral prejudice caused to the latter; 3° the profits made by the infringer, including economies of intellectual investments, material and promotional economies due to the infringement'. The legislator's intention was to break with the old general rules of the Civil Code about torts and especially with the traditional rule that damages are covering all the loss suffered but only such loss. Because of this old rule, the profits made by the infringer were of no relevance, so that the infringer, even paying damages, could still have interest to infringe. Thanks to the new rule of Article L. 331-1-3, it is now possible to award to the injured party a sum covering all his loss (economic or moral prejudice) but also a part of or all the profits made by the infringer because of the infringement. After a short time of hesitation, French courts now frequently use this possibility in order to repair and discourage intellectual property rights infringement.

344. The judges may also, if required by the injured party, use another method of evaluation of the indemnity to be paid by the infringer: it consists of a lump sum superior to the royalties amount which the infringer would have to pay to receive the rightholder's authorization. Article L. 331-1-3, §2 states 'The court, however, shall, as an alternative and upon request of the injured party, award as damages a lump sum. This sum is higher than the amount of royalties or fees which would have been due if the infringer had requested authorization to use the right which it has prejudiced. This sum is not exclusive of compensation for the moral prejudice caused to the injured party.'

345. Article L. 331-1-4, §1 adds that 'In the case of civil liability for infringement, violation of a neighbouring right or of the database producer's rights, the court may order, at the injured party's request, the recall from the channels of commerce, the definitive removal from such channels, the destruction and the confiscation, in favour of the injured party, of the products recognised as infringing, of the media used to collect the unlawfully extracted content of a database and of the materials and implements principally used in their creation or their manufacturing.' The court may also order 'any appropriate publicity measure of the judgment, in particular its display or its publication, in whole or in part, in such newspapers or over such inline services of communication to the public it may designate, pursuant to the conditions it specifies' (Article L. 331-1-4, §2). The measures mentioned in the first two paragraphs are ordered at the cost of the infringer (Article L. 331-1-4, §3). The court may also order the seizure of receipts from the infringement, from the violation of a neighbouring right or of the database producer's rights. These receipts are to be remitted to the plaintiff or his successors in rights (Article L. 331-1-4, §4).

346. The Cour de cassation has also decided that the infringing products cannot be the object of conventions ('choses hors du commerce', *see* New Article 1162 Civil Code).[252]

252. Cass. com., 24 Sep. 2003, Bull. civ. IV, No. 147.

Chapter 11. Relation to Other Intellectual Property Rights

347. A likelihood of overlapping may occur between copyright on the one hand, designs and models, trademarks, or patents on the other hand.

§1. Copyright and Registered Designs and Models

348. The protection by copyright may be cumulated with the protection by registration. Article L. 513-2 embodies the famous French principle of 'Unity of Art' ('unité de l'art'), according to which an original work of art may always be protected by copyright, whatever its destination or merit (*see infra*). Thus, the author of an original design or model who chooses to register it with the 'Institut National de la Propriété Industrielle' does not renounce the copyright protection, which he may always claim alternatively or in cumulation with the protection flowing from the registration. He may have such an interest in claiming copyright protection when the registration is void or expired after its normal duration of five years renewable until a maximum of twenty-five years.[253]

§2. Copyright and Trademarks

349. If a sign covered by copyright is later registered as trademark by a third person, without the copyright's holder authorization, the trademark is void (Article L. 711-4 e; *see infra*).[254]

§3. Copyright and Patents

350. The text of a patent is a copyrightable work; on the contrary, a technical characteristic may not be protected by copyright, but only by a patent, if it fulfils the conditions of patentability.

253. Cass. 2 May 1961: D. 1962, jur., p. 163, note P. Greffe.
254. *See* , for instance: Paris, 20 Sep. 1994: RIDA, April 1995, 362.

Part II. Patents

351. A patent is a title granted by the State to the possessor of an industrial useful creation. It confers to its holder an exclusive right to use the protected invention for a limited time on the territory of the State which granted it.

352. Patenting inventions is by no means compulsory, but an unpatented invention is not protected by an exclusive right sanctioned by an action for infringement. Such an unpatented invention is a mere know-how, having an economic value as long as it is a secret and not immediately accessible to the public (*see infra*).

Chapter 1. Sources: Legislation

353. Patents covering the French territory may be granted either by the French Office of Industrial Property (Institut National de la Propriété Industrielle), which is part of the Ministry of Industry, or by the European Patent Office in Munich, Germany, when the application was made for the grant of an European patent for France according to the Munich Convention of 5 October 1973, revised on 29 November 2000 (European Patent Convention 2000, entered into force on 13 December 2007).

354. The Act of 5 July 1844 was the first French statute relating to patents; it stayed in force until the Act of 2 January 1968 (entered into force on 1 January 1969). This statute was modified by the Act of 13 July 1978 (in force since 1 July 1979) and by the Act of 26 November 1990. All these legal provisions were abrogated by the Act of 1 July 1992, instituting the Intellectual Property Code. The Code collects all the former provisions under a systematic numbering.

355. The Munich Convention on the grant of European patents was introduced in France by the Act No. 77-683 of 30 June 1977 (Article L. 614-1–L. 614-16 of the I.P. Code). European patents for France are subject to the provisions of the EPC 2000 (with the very rare exceptions of some rules of the Munich Convention 1973 which still apply) as for their validity, and to the I.P. Code as for their working and remedies for infringement.

356. The Washington Treaty of 19 June 1970 relating to the patent co-operation (PCT) allows by the filing of a sole patent application with the International Bureau of the WIPO, to obtain patents in several Member States. This Treaty was introduced in France by the Act No. 77-682 of 30 June 1977 (Article L. 614-17–L. 614-24 of the I.P. Code). The designation of France through the international procedure of the Patent Cooperation treaty is deemed to be an application for a European patent for France (I.P.Code, Article L. 614-24).

357. In 2015, 16,272 French patent applications were filed with the INPI; on 31 December 2014, 510,490 patents were in force in France.

Chapter 2. Patentable Subject Matter

358. Some useful creations, although interesting the industry, may not be protected by a patent. Such is the case for creations which are not legally qualified as inventions, for inventions contrary to public order or good morals, and for inventions excluded from patentability by law.

§1. Creations Not Deemed as Inventions

359. In order to be patentable, a creation must be an invention in the legal meaning. The Code does not provide for a definition of an invention, but only lists creations which are not considered as inventions (Article L. 611-10). This list covers five series of creations but is not exhaustive. These creations are excluded from patentability only if they are claimed 'as such'.

I. Discoveries, Scientific Theories, and Mathematical Methods

360. A discovery consists of establishing a phenomenon which existed in the nature, but was unknown. It is unpatentable as such, but the industrial applications of a discovery may be patented.[255]

II. Aesthetic Creations

361. Creations which are exclusively aesthetic, without any useful aspect (e.g., paintings, sculptures, etc.), are not patentable (they may eventually be protected under copyright if they are original: *see supra* paragraphs 119 et seq.). If aesthetic elements are associated with technical aspects, a patent may be granted (as for the possibility of protection by the law of designs and models, *see infra* paragraphs 879 et seq.).

III. Plans, Principles, and Methods as Well as Presentation of Information

362. This exclusion aims at purely abstract creations, without any material realization. Under French case law, business methods are not patentable.[256]

255. Cass. com., 31 Mar. 1954: Ann. propr. Ind. 1954, 266.
256. Paris, 21 Mar. 2001: PIBD 2001, III, 397, sales method.- Rennes, 7 Oct. 2003: JCP ed. E, 2004, No. 562, p. 619, method of treatment of data. – Paris, 15 Mar. 2006: PIBD 2006, III, 348.

IV. Computer Software

363. Because computer softwares are protected by copyright, such creations may not be patented as such, i.e., a patent application may not claim exclusively a computer program. But an invention may be patentable if some of its elements are activated by a computer involving a program.[257] This exclusion receives a very narrow interpretation by the European Patent Office (and also the French INPI) which considers that a computer software is not excluded from patentability if it is capable of bringing about, when running on a computer or loaded into a computer, a 'further technical effect' going beyond the 'normal' physical interactions between the computer program and the computer hardware on which it is run.[258]

V. Presentation of Information

364. Information as such or its method of presentation is not patentable.[259]

§2. Inventions Contrary to Public Order or Good Morals

365. When the commercial exploitation of an invention would be contrary to dignity of the human person, public order or good morals may not be patented. From this point of view, a patent may not be refused only because the working of the invention is legally prohibited (Article L. 611-17). For instance, a patent on a hooking device for towing vehicles which does not comply which the technical norms is valid.[260]

366. The INPI may refuse an application obviously unpatentable under this rule (Article L. 612-12, 4°), or may suppress the elements which seem to be contrary to public order or good morals. Case law on the question is almost non-existent: an old decision may be cited, avoiding a patent on an opium pipe.[261]

§3. Medicine

367. Ethical considerations, public health, and public interest are also at the origin of another exclusion from patentability. Article L. 611-16 states that 'Methods for treatment of the human or animal body by surgery or therapy and of diagnosis practiced on the human or animal body are not patentable. This provision shall not apply to products, in particular substances or compositions, for use in any of these methods.' Case law is not abundant in this matter. It was held, for instance, that an

257. Paris, 15 Jun. 1981: PIBD 1981, III, 175.
258. OEB Technical Board of Appeal, 1 Jul. 1998, JO OEB 1999, p. 609.
259. Cass. com., 13 Feb. 1973: JCP 1974 II 17626, note Pérot-Morel; presentation of information on the labour market. – TGI Paris, 7 Jun. 2013: PIBD 2013, III, 1421.
260. Paris, 11 Mar. 1982: Dossiers Brevets, 1983, 1, 1.
261. T. com. Seine, 25 Nov. 1913: Ann. propr. Ind. 1915–1919, 2, p. 16.

invention designated to fight animal parasites is not a method of therapeutic treatment, but an industrially applicable process and is, therefore, patentable.[262]

§4. Biotechnologies

368. Article L. 611-16–L. 611-19 has been modified by the Act No. 2004-1338 of 8 December 2004 implementing into French law the EC Directive No. 98/44 of 16 July 1998.[263] Some exclusions from patentability in the field of biotechnology are listed in these articles:

- The human body, at the various stages of its formation and development, and the simple discovery of one of its elements, including the sequence or partial sequence of a gene, cannot constitute patentable inventions (Article L. 611-18, §1).
- Shall also be considered unpatentable in particular: (a) processes for cloning of human beings; (b) processes for modifying the germ line genetic identity of human beings; (c) uses of human embryos for industrial or commercial purposes; (d) total or partial sequences of a gene as such[264] (Article L. 611-18, §3).

However, 'an invention constituting a technical application of a function of an element of the human body may be protected by a patent. This protection shall cover the element of the human body only to the extent necessary to the realization and the exploitation of this particular use. Such use must be disclosed in the patent application in a concrete and precise manner' (Article L. 611-18, §2):

- Shall also be considered unpatentable the methods for treatment of the human or animal body by surgery or therapy and the diagnostic methods practiced on the human or animal body. This provision shall not apply to products, in particular substances or compositions, for use in any of these methods (Article L. 611-16).

369. As for animal and plants, Article L. 611-19 I states that shall be unpatentable:

- 1° animal varieties; animal varieties may not be protected either by a patent, or by any other title.[265] An exception is admitted to the principle of non-patentability,

262. Paris, 24 Sep. 1984: PIBD 1984, III, 252; Ann. propr. Ind. 1985, 103, obs. Mathély: RTD com. 1985, 105, obs. Chavanne and Azéma.- Paris, 31 Jan. 2001: Ann. propr. Ind., 2001, n. 1, p. 43, is patentable a method of cleaning teeth for an aesthetic aim. – Paris, 28 Jun. 2006: PIBD 2006, III, 641, is patentable an hygienic method.
263. EC Directive No. 98/44 of the European Parliament and of the Council of 6 Jul. 1998 on the legal protection of biotechnological inventions, OJEC, No. L. 213, 30 Jul. 1998, pp. 13–21.
264. This last exclusion to patentability does not conform to the EC Directive 98/44 which excludes from patentability only the total or partial sequences of a gene in the human body, i.e., in its 'natural environment' (Recital 20).
265. Nevertheless, the INPI granted a patent on a transgenic animal: Transgene Patent, No. 87-086-23, 21 Sep. 1991.

as for microorganisms: living organisms, whether animal or vegetal, may be patented if they are microscopic, or are obtained by a microbiological process;
- 2° plant varieties as defined in Article 5 of Regulation (EC) No. 2100/94 on Community plant variety rights; plant varieties may not be protected by a patent, but by a plant variety right ('certificat d'obtention végétale': *see infra*). An exception is admitted to the principle of non-patentability, as for microorganisms: living organisms, whether animal or vegetal, may be patented if they are microscopic, or are obtained by a microbiological process;
- However, inventions which concern plants or animals shall be patentable if the technical feasibility of the invention is not confined to a particular plant or animal variety (Article L. 611-19 II).
- 3° essentially biological processes for the production of plants and animals (i.e., natural processes where the human intervention is non-existent or limited). A process that consists entirely of natural phenomena such as crossing or selection shall be regarded as biological process. This exclusion does not prejudice to the patentability of inventions which concern a technical process, in particular a microbiological one; any process involving or resulting in or performed upon a microbiological material shall be regarded as microbiological process (Article L. 611-19 III). Normally, this exclusion should also not prejudice to the patentability of a product obtained by means of such an essentially biological process (*see* EPO Enlarged Board of Appeal, 25 March 2015, decision G2/13). However, in reaction against this decision G2/13, the Act No. 2016-1087 of 8 August 2016 adds that 'products exclusively obtained by essentially biological processes, including the elements that make these products and genetic information they contain' are unpatentable (L. 611-19 I *3°bis*);
- 4° processes for modifying the genetic identity of animals which are likely to cause them suffering without substantial medical benefit to man or animal, and also animals resulting from such processes.

§5. The Second Therapeutic Application

370. For a long time, the invention consisting of a new therapeutic application of an already known medicine was not patentable under French law.[266] Since the Act No. 2008-776 of 4 August 2008,[267] the 'second therapeutic application' is patentable. Shall be patentable:

- any substance or composition, comprised in the state of the art, for use in a method for treatment of the human or animal body by surgery or therapy and of diagnosis practiced on the human or animal body, provided that its use for any such method is not comprised in the state of the art (Article L. 611-11, §4);
- any substance or composition comprised in the state of the art for use in any of a method for treatment of the human or animal body by surgery or therapy and of diagnosis practiced on the human or animal body, provided that its use in any

266. J. Azéma, 'La brevetabilité de la seconde application thérapeutique', JCP 1989 I 3382.
267. Act No. 2008-776 of 4 Aug. 2007, JORF No. 0181, 5 Aug. 2008, p. 12471.

one of these methods is not comprised in the state of the art (Article L. 611-11, §5).

§6. Inventions Made or Used in Outer Space

371. The Act No. 2008-518 of 3 June 2008 has expressly affirmed the patentability of inventions made or used in outer space, introducing a new §4 in Article L. 611-1:

> Unless otherwise provided for in an international agreement to which France is a party, the provisions of this Article shall apply to the inventions made or used in outer space including on celestial bodies or in or on space objects placed under national jurisdiction pursuant to Article VIII of the Treaty of 27 January 1967 on the principles governing the activities of States in the exploration and use of outer space, including the moon and other celestial bodies.

Chapter 3. Conditions of Patentability

372. In order to be patentable an invention must fulfil three conditions: novelty, inventive step, and industrial application.

§1. Novelty

373. According to Article L. 611-11, 'An invention shall be considered to be new if it does not form part of the state of the art.' Consequently, novelty within the meaning of patent law requires a comparison between the invention and the state of the art, in order to determine whether the former is exterior to the latter.

I. The Invention Must Be Compared to the State of the Art

374. The state of the art consists of all the information accessible to the public prior to the date of the patent application.

375. The state of the art includes only information accessible to the public.

376. The 'public' consists of all the persons not bound by a duty to keep the information received confidential. As long as the knowledge of the invention remains limited only to persons supposed to keep the information secret, such technical information is not accessible to the public and the invention stays new. For instance, if a research laboratory is open only to research staff and other personnel, the information is not accessible to the public. But the disclosure of the invention, be it to only one person not bound by an obligation of secrecy, destroys the novelty.[268]

377. The invention is accessible to the public if it has been disclosed in a way complete enough to enable a man skilled in the art to reproduce it. A non-precise disclosure does not destroy novelty (e.g., remote photos of a machine). The invention is 'accessible' if the public was able to know it; it is not necessary to evidence actual knowledge.[269]

378. An exception to the necessity of accessibility to the public is provided for by Article L. 611-11, §3, dealing with the so-called problem of double patenting. This problem arises when two successive patent applications are made for the same invention, whereas the first one is not yet published at the date of the second one. In such a situation it is necessary to avoid the grant of two competing patents. The solution to the conflict consists of fictitiously considering the content of the first application as accessible to the public; consequently, the invention is no longer new and the second

268. Lyon, 10 Jan. 1973: Ann. propr. Ind. 1974, 106: the delivery of a prototype to a client without providing for a duty of secrecy is a public disclosure of the invention which loses its novelty.- Paris, 29 Oct. 1999: PIBD 2000, III, 219, industrial site open to the outside.

269. Paris, 26 Jan. 1974: PIBD 1974, III, 228; RTD com. 1974, 266, obs. Chavanne and Azéma; in this case, a bandage was experienced in a hospital; it was made accessible to the public prior to the patent application, because patients could leave with such a bandage on a wound.

patent may not be granted. However, this rule applies only to the evaluation of novelty and not for non-obviousness of the invention (Article L. 611-14).

379. Conflicts between two European patent applications designating France (EPC 2000, Articles 54, §3 and 56), or between a French and a European patent application (EPC 2000, Article 139) are solved in the same way.

380. The state of the art contains all the information accessible to the public.

381. French law requires an 'absolute novelty': in order to be patentable, the invention must not have been accessible to the public at any time, place, and by any means prior to the patent application. Consequently, any prior information accessible to the public destroys the novelty of the invention, whatever the place, date, author, or means of disclosure. Especially it should be noted that French law does not protect the inventor against his own disclosures.[270]

382. Disclosure destroying novelty may have been made by any means: written documents, oral explanation, schemes, photos, experiments,[271] public use of the invention, and any other public communication of the invention.[272]

383. The disclosure may be evidenced by all means of proof: witnesses, presumptions, etc. The burden of proof stays with the person who wishes to have the patent declared invalid (e.g., a competitor), or the patent application refused (the French Patent Office, INPI).

384. Exceptionally, some information, although accessible to the public, does not belong to the state of the art and, therefore, does not destroy novelty of a further patent application: such is the case for an abusive disclosure, disclosure during a public exhibition, or disclosure covered by a right of priority.

A. Abusive Disclosure

385. Article L. 611-13 a) states that disclosure of the invention shall not be taken into consideration if it occurred within the six months preceding filing of the patent application or if it is the result of publication, after the date of that filing, of a prior patent application and if, in either case, it was due directly or indirectly to 'an obvious abuse against the inventor or his predecessor in rights'. Industrial spying is the most evident example of such an abuse.

B. Disclosure at a Public Exhibition (Article L. 611-13, b)

386. An invention which has been accessible to the public during an international exhibition within the meaning of the Paris Convention of 1928 may still be patented. Article L. 611-13 b) states that disclosure of the invention shall not be taken into

270. Cass. com., 27 Oct. 1964: Ann. propr. Ind. 1967, 3.
271. TGI Paris, 29 May 1981: Dossiers Brevets 1981, 4, 1; JCP ed. CI, 1982 II 11084, obs. Burst and Mousseron.
272. Cass. com., 19 May 1987: D. 1987, I.R., p. 136; JCP ed. E 1988 II 15143, obs. Burst and Mousseron; RTD com. 1987, 501, obs. Chavanne and Azéma, novelty was destroyed by the communication to a client of an estimate containing the elements of the invention. – Cass. com., 15 May 2007: PIBD 2007, III, 857, novelty was destroyed by the marketing of a product whose analysis makes it possible to discover its composition.

consideration if it occurred within the six months preceding filing of the patent application or if it is the result of publication, after the date of that filing, of a prior patent application and if, in either case, it was due directly or indirectly to the fact that the applicant or his legal predecessor had displayed the invention at an official, or officially recognized, international exhibition falling within the terms of the revised Convention on International Exhibitions signed at Paris on 22 November 1928. The applicant may enjoy this exhibitor's right if he furnishes within four months as from the filing date of the patent application an attestation issued during the exhibition by the authority responsible for ensuring protection of industrial property at that exhibition and confirming that the invention has in fact been displayed at that exhibition. The attestation shall state the opening date of the exhibition and, where appropriate, that of first disclosure of the invention if the two dates should not be the same. It shall be accompanied by documents that enable the invention to be identified and bearing authentication by the above-mentioned authority (Article R. 612-22).

C. Disclosure Covered by a Priority Right

387. The Paris Convention on the Protection of Industrial Property of 1883 (Article 4B), created the so-called priority right, which aims at facilitating the international patenting.

388. According to this provision, the author of a first patent application made in or for one Member State may file further applications for the same invention in other Member States within twelve months. According to the TRIPs Agreement, the priority right now applies between the World Trade Organization Member States (TRIPs Agreement, Article 2). A disclosure made after the first application ('priority date') does not destroy the novelty of the invention as for the subsequent applications.

389. If the first patent applicable has not been made in or for a Member State of the Paris Convention or of the TRIPs Agreement, the benefit of the priority right is still possible under a reciprocity condition. Article L. 611-12 states that:

> Where the first filing has been made in a State which is not a party to the Paris Union or to the World Trade Organization, it shall not be possible to grant a priority right in regard of such filing having effects equivalent to those afforded by the Paris Convention under the same conditions unless such State affords an equivalent priority right on the basis of the first filing of a French patent application, an international application or a European patent application in which France is designated.

390. The benefit of the priority right is not automatic; it must be claimed at the time of the subsequent applications; proper justification must be produced by the applicant (Article L. 612-7 and R. 612-24).

391. The Act of 26 November 1990 (Article L. 612-3, I.P. Code) introduced into French law the 'internal priority'. According to this provision, an applicant may file a second French patent application for the same invention within twelve months and claim the benefit of the date of the first application. This system allows him to perfect an early first application.

II. The Invention Must Be External to the State of the Art

392. According the Article L. 611-11, §1, an invention is new if 'it does not form part of the state of the art'. Therefore, novelty implies that the invention is different from the technical information accessible to the public at the date of the patent application. These differences are evaluated in an objective way, without reference to originality of the invention or its non-obviousness.

393. The invention is 'included in the state of the art' if it is entirely known as such, with the same technical components, arranged in the same way, and exercising the same technical function in order to produce the same result.[273] Such an information entirely included in the state of the art is called 'All pieces anteriority' ('anteriorité de toutes pièces'). Novelty may be destroyed only upon evidence of such an 'All pieces anteriority,' it is not possible to combine several partial anteriorities.[274]

§2. Inventive Step (Non-obviousness)

394. This condition was introduced into French law by the statute of 2 January 1968 (Articles 6 and 9). Inventive step has to be evaluated separately from novelty.[275] An invention implies an inventive step if, 'for a man skilled in the art, it does not result in an obvious way from the state of the art' (Article L. 611-14).

I. The Invention Must Be Compared to the State of the Art

395. The state of the art used for the evaluation of the inventive step does not include the content of prior patent applications not yet published at the date of the discussed application. Thus information contained in such an unpublished application may not be used to discuss the inventive step implied by a further application.[276] On the contrary, such an information may be used for the evaluation of novelty (*see supra*: 'Double patenting', paragraph 378).

396. In this state of the art, the judge does not look for an 'all pieces anteriority', but may combine several partial information in order to evaluate the non-obviousness of the invention for a man skilled in the art.[277]

273. Cass. com., 12 Mar. 1996: PIBD 1996, III, 273. – Cass. com., 19 Feb. 1991: PIBD 1991, III, 295. – Cass. com., 15 May 2007: PIBD 2007, III, 857. – Paris, 19 Mar. 2014: PIBD 2014, III, 491.
274. Cass. com., 19 Feb. 1991, *supra*.
275. Cass. com., 6 Mar. 1979: Bull. civ. IV, No. 88.
276. Cass. com., 3 Jan. 1985: Ann. propr. Ind. 1985, 67, obs. Mathély.
277. Paris, 9 Nov. 1994: PIBD 1995, III, 57. – Paris, 4 Jul. 2003: PIBD 2003, III, 495.

II. The Invention Must Not Be Obvious as Compared to the State of the Art

397. The judge must refer to the knowledge of a man skilled in the art (Article L. 611-14). The courts define him as 'the man who possesses the normal knowledge in the technical area of the invention and is able, using this knowledge, to conceive the solution of the problem which the invention attempts to solve'.[278] Consequently, the invention which remains within the ordinary knowledge of such a man skilled in the art is obvious for him and not patentable.

398. The main difficulty is to determine the criteria of non-obviousness, which are not provided by the statute. The French courts sometimes apply the so-called problem-and-solution approach (applied in the European Patent Office). In the problem-and-solution approach, there are three main stages:(i) determining the 'closest prior art'; (ii) establishing the 'objective technical problem' to be solved; and (iii) considering whether or not the claimed invention, starting from the closest prior art and the objective technical problem, would have been obvious to the skilled person. More frequently, French courts use objective criteria of non-obviousness:

- the technical problem was not raised in the prior state of the art;[279]
- long delay between the knowledge of the technical means and their combination in order to solve the problem;[280]
- the important number of anteriorities and their dissemination in the state of the art;[281]
- breaking away from traditional methods and techniques;[282]
- important prejudice against the solution;[283]
- important and unexpected technical progress.[284]

399. This list is not exhaustive, as these are the most frequent signs of non-obviousness used by the courts. In no way are such signs to be considered as independent conditions of patentability.

400. Other criteria are generally accepted in order to conclude that the invention was obvious for a man skilled in the art and, therefore, did not imply any inventive step:

- the invention is the result of mere execution operations;[285]

---

278. Cass. com., 17 Oct. 1995: Bull. civ. IV, No. 232; Ann. propr. Ind. 1996, 1, obs. Mathély. RTD com. 1996, 675, obs. Azéma.
279. Paris, 22 Mar. 1990: PIBD 1990, III, 411.- 27 May 1998: PIBD 1999, III, 105.
280. Paris, 29 Mar. 1984: Ann. propr. Ind. 1984, 14, note Mathély; D. 1986, som., p. 136, obs. Mousseron and Schmidt.
281. Cass. com., 18 Oct. 1994: PIBD 1995, III, 5.
282. Paris, 14 Feb. 1989: PIBD 1989, III, 282.
283. Paris, 25 Apr. 1990: PIBD 1991, III, 333.- Cass. com., 12 Dec. 1995: Bull. civ. IV, No. 292.- Cass. com., 19 Dec. 2000: Ann. propr. Ind., 2001, No. 2, p. 146.
284. Paris, 5 Jul. 1990: PIBD 1990, III, 637.
285. Cass. com., 21 Mar. 1989: PIBD 1989, III, 401. Cass. com., 5 May 1998: PIBD 1998, III, 397. – Paris, 1 Mar. 2006: PIBD 2006, III, 313.

- the invention applies technical elements known in their structure and function;[286]
- the invention uses known structural means which are technically equivalent to those in the state of the art.[287]

401. In conclusion, it should be recalled that the inventive step is evaluated at the trial judge's discretion.[288] The French Supreme Court only requires that the lower courts motivate their decision and quash those grounded on general statements.[289]

§3. Industrial Application

402. Following the Munich Convention of 1973 on the grant of European patents, French law requires that the patentable invention be able of industrial application. This condition is fulfilled when 'the object of the invention may be manufactured or used in any kind of industry, including agriculture' (Article L. 611-15). This condition is independent from the quality of the industrial result produced by the invention.[290] The Supreme Court held that a plasmid expressing a hormone of human growth without a foreign protein does fulfil the condition, since it may be manufactured or used in the industry.[291] As for inventions relating to genetic sequences, Article 5 of the EC Directive No. 98/44[292] provides: 'The industrial application of a sequence or a partial sequence of a gene must be disclosed in the patent application.' The ability of industrial application is not enough, the industrial application must be clearly exposed as from the filing date. Recital 23 of the directive, concerning the patentability of DNA sequence, explains that if there is no indication of a function, it does not contain any technical information and is, therefore, not a patentable invention. Recital 24 explains that where a sequence or partial sequence of a gene is used to produce a protein or part of a protein, to specify which protein or part of a protein is produced or what function it performs. The EPO Technical Board of Appeal has decided that the only 'prediction' of the ability of a protein to act as a receptor did not satisfy the requirement of industrial application.[293]

286. Cass. com., 13 Dec. 1994: PIBD 1995, III, 141.
287. Cass. com., 3 Mar. 1978: Ann. propr. Ind. 1978, 157. – Paris, 20 May 2005: PIBD 2005, III, 490.
288. Cass. com., 9 Mar. 1993: PIBD 1993, III, 412. – Cass. com., 12 Dec. 1995, Bull. civ. IV, No. 292.
289. Cass. com., 21 Mar. 1989: Bull. civ. IV, No. 91.
290. TGI Paris, 8 Apr. 1994: PIBD 1994, III, .399. -11 Mar. 1998: PIBD 1998, III, 398. – Paris, 28 Oct. 2005 : PIBD 2006, III, 1. – Paris, 6 Jan. 2006 : PIBD 2006, III, 160.
291. Cass. com., 19 Dec. 2000: JCP ed. E 2001, p. 303; PIBD 2001, III, 271; RTD com. 2001, p. 692, obs. Azéma and Galloux.
292. EC Directive No. 98/44 of the European Parliament and of the Council of 6 Jul. 1998 on the legal protection of biotechnological inventions, OJEC, No. L. 213, 30 Jul. 1998, pp. 13–21.
293. OEB Technical Board of Appeal, 20 Jun. 2001, JO OEB 2002, p. 293.

Chapter 4. Formalities

403. In order to receive a patent protection, the interested person must file an application with the competent administrative body. Then starts the procedure of grant, which may lead either to the grant or to the refusal of a patent.

§1. Filing of a French Patent Application

404. Formally, the patent application consists of a file the content of which is regulated by Article L. 612-1–L. 612-7 supplemented in detail by Article R. 612-1–R. 612-25.

I. The Applicant

405. The application may be filed by the applicant in person or by a representative having his place of residence, his place of business, or an establishment in a Member State of the EU or in a State party to the Agreement on the European Economic Area. Natural or legal persons not having their place of residence or their place of business in a Member State of the EU or in a State party to the Agreement on EEA shall be required to appoint a representative who satisfy this condition within two months as from the date of receipt of the notification addressed to them for that purpose. In the event of more than one applicant, a common representative shall be appointed. If the latter is not one of the applicants, he must meet the conditions provided in the first paragraph (Article R. 612-2).

406. Since the Act of 26 November 1990, the agency is the monopoly of professionals qualified as 'conseils en propriété industrielle' ('industrial property counsels', Article L. 422-2 and Article R. 612-2, §1). However, the persons listed under Article L. 422-4 and L. 422-5 may also act as agents with the French INPI: an attorney ('avocat'), a company or public organization with which the applicant is contractually bound, a specialized professional organization, or a professional established within the territory of a Member State of the EU or of a State party to the Agreement on EEA acting on an occasional basis and authorized to represent persons before the central industrial property office in this State.

II. The Place of the Application

407. The patent application may be filed either with the INPI (National Institute of Industrial Property) in Courbevoie. The filing may also result from a mailing to the INPI by registered letter with advice of delivery or by a message using any type of remote transmission (fax) according to the conditions defined by Director General of the Institute to guarantee, in particular, the safety of mailing. In such cases, the date of submission of the documents shall be the date of receipt at the INPI. The Director

General of the INPI may require a filing by an electronic means where this simplifies the examination and publication of the patent application. An online application is also possible and now very usual (Article R. 612-1). The filing of European and international applications by persons having a domicile or head office in France must also be done through the INPI (Article R. 614-1 and R. 614-21).

III. The Content of the Application

A. General Rules

408. The application is to be drafted in French language, with the exception of the descriptions and of the claims which may be drafted in a foreign language if the applicant is (Article R. 612-21): citizen of a State granting equivalent treatment to French citizens or assignee of a patent application filed abroad or of a priority right on such an foreign application, on condition that the foreign country in question grants equivalent treatment to French citizens. However, in all the above cases, a French translation must be provided within three months as from the filing date of the patent application.

409. A filing date and number are granted when the applicant has filed the documents containing (Article L. 612-2 and R. 612-8):

- an indication that a patent is sought;
- information sufficient to enable the applicant to be identified or contacted;
- a description of the invention or a reference to an earlier application made in accordance with the conditions laid down by regulation.

Since the Ordinance No. 2008-1301 of 11 December 2008 a filing date may be granted even in the absence of claims, which may be furnished later, in a period of time set by INPI.

B. The Request

410. The request for grant of a French patent must contain the following information (Article R. 612-10):

- identification of the applicant, of the inventor(s) and, if any, of the representative;
- identification of the invention by a title;
- identification of the type of protection requested.

411. The applicant has the choice between a patent (exclusive right for twenty years), a certificate of utility (exclusive right for six years), supplementary protection certificate linked to a pharmaceutical patent (Article L. 611-2, §3: *see infra*, paragraph 568), or to a patent for a phytopharmaceutical product.[294] The additional certificate

294. EC Regulation No. 1610/96 of 23 Jul. 1996: OJEC, No. L. 198, 8 Aug. 1996.

('certificat d'addition') title linked to a patent or a certificate of utility was suppressed by the Act of 26 November 1990.

412. The request may also contain the following optional information:

- request for a delayed procedure of search;
- request for extension of the period for payment of search fees;
- request for reduction in filing fees;
- priority documents if a priority right is claimed;
- priority of a disclosure of the invention in an international exhibition.

C. *The Description*

413. The description of the invention is important, since it discloses the new technology to the public, thus allowing further research.

1. The Physical Requirements

414. Unless the nature of the invention means that a different manner or a different order would afford a better understanding and a more economic presentation (Article R. 612-13), the description must mention: (1) a statement of the technical field to which the invention relates; (2) a statement of the background art known to the applicant and which can be regarded as useful for understanding the invention and drawing up the search report; the documents reflecting the prior art shall be cited wherever possible; (3) disclosure of the invention, as claimed, in such terms that the technical problem and the solution proposed can be understood; where appropriate, any advantageous effects of the invention with reference to the prior art shall be stated; (4) a brief description of the drawings, if any; (5) a detailed description of at least one way of carrying out the invention; the description should normally be accompanied by examples and references to the drawings, if any; (6) a statement of the way in which the invention is capable of exploitation in industry if such exploitation is not obvious from the description or the nature of the invention (Article R. 612-12). The applicant may optionally annex at the end of the description: (1) short extracts from computer programs presented in the form of lists written in current programming languages, where necessary for the understanding of the invention; (2) lists of nucleotide and/or amino acid sequences; (3) chemical or mathematical formulae (Article R. 612-13). If the patent application relates to a microorganism or more generally to a biological material which is not available to the public and which cannot be described in such a manner as to enable the invention to be performed by a person skilled in the art, the description shall be considered inadequate unless the biological material has been deposited with the recognized depository institution (such as, e.g., Institut Pasteur), this deposit must be identified in the description of the invention and the description must provide the information as to the characteristics of the biological material (Article L. 612-5, §2 and R. 612-14, R. 612-15). France ratified the Budapest treaty of 28 April 1977 on the international recognition of deposit of microorganisms in view of patent procedure.[295]

295. Published by Decree No. 80-954 of 25 Nov. 1980: JORF, 2 Dec.; in force since 19 Aug. 1980.

2. Characters of the Description

415. Article L. 612-5 states 'The patent application must disclose the invention in a manner sufficiently clear and complete for it to be performed by a person skilled in the art' and Article R. 612-12, 3° requires that the disclosure of the invention permits to understand 'the technical problem and the solution proposed'. This rule is sanctioned by the refusal of the patent application by the INPI (Article L. 612-12, §6). The patent granted on the basis of an insufficient description may be declared void.[296] When the invention is a biological material which is not available to the public and which cannot be described in such a manner as to enable the invention to be performed by a person skilled in the art, the description is deemed sufficient only after the deposit of this biological material in a permanent culture, according to Article L. 612-5, §2.

416. The description is unchangeable. The description initially provided on the filing date, may be amended only in strictly limited cases:

- during the search procedure following a change of claims, the description may be restricted upon request by the applicant and with the authorization of INPI (Article R. 612-59–R. 612-61);
- until the date of payment of the patent grant fee, the applicant may, under motivated request, correct obvious material errors. A special fee is due (Article R. 612-36);
- after the examination by the INPI, the description may be amended to the extent required to remedy the irregularities that have been determined (Article R. 612-37).

D. The Claims

417. The claims are sentences whereby the patent applicant defines the matter for which protection is sought (Article L. 612-6).

1. Formal Requirements (Article L. 612-6)

418. The application may include several claims (under condition of unity: *see infra*). According to Article R. 612-17, a claim should be drafted in two parts:

- a preamble mentioning the state of the art which the invention purports to change ('A preamble giving the designation of the subject matter of the invention and those technical features which are necessary for the definition of the claimed elements but which, in culmination, are part of the prior art');
- the exposure of the technical characteristics for which the exclusive right is claimed (the 'characterizing portion, preceded by an expression of the type "characterized by" stating the technical features for which, in combination with the features stated in item 1, protection is sought').

296. For example, Cass. com., 13 May 1997: PIBD 1997, III, 424; RTD com. 1997, 642, obs. Azéma. – 20 Mar. 2002: PIBD 2002, III, 337.

419. The drafting may, however, be done in a different presentation 'if the nature of the invention so justifies' (Article R. 612-17). The statute does not provide for any definite style of drafting: the claims may be drafted in a general and abstract way ('functional style') or in a specific way ('structural style'). Whatever the language used the claims must be 'clear and concise' (Article L. 612-6).

2. Substantive Requirements

420. The applicant may not claim technical elements which are not included in the description (claims shall be 'clear and concise and be supported by the description', Article L. 612-6). This rule is sanctioned either by the refusal of the application (Article L. 612-12, §8) or by the judicial invalidation of such claims (Article L. 613-25, c).[297]

421. The applicant may claim only one invention in each patent application. This principle of unity of invention is, however, broad enough to allow the grouping of several inventions in one application, provided that they form a single general inventive concept (Article L. 612-4). Such a concept allows to apply for: either several independent claims of the same category (product, process, or use) (Article R. 612-19, §1) (but the application can contain several independent claims of the same category only if the subject matter of the application relates to several linked products, or to different uses of a product or a device, or to alternative solutions to a particular problem which cannot be covered by only one claim, Article R. 612-17-1) or several claims of different categories (Article R. 612-19, §2 and §3).

422. The rule of unity of invention is sanctioned by the refusal of the complex application, unless the applicant divides it at the request of the INPI within the time limit granted to him (Article L. 612-4, §2 and L. 612-12, §2). The divisional applications benefit from the filing date or from the priority date of the initial application.

423. The claims must define the invention in a way precise enough to allow the drafting of the search report. This rule is sanctioned by the refusal of the application (Article L. 612-12, §6). If the invention relates to a technical application of a function of an element of the human body, this technical application must be disclosed in the patent application in a concrete and precise manner (Article L. 611-18, §2).

3. Adaptation of the Claims

424. Before the grant of the patent, claims may be adapted according to the conditions set by Article L. 612-13:

- until the date of the beginning of the preliminary search procedure;
- as for certificates of utility, the claims may be adapted until the grant of the title;
- during the search procedure (*see infra*).

Moreover, if a patent claim is partially declared invalid, the court may order the patent holder to provide for a new draft of the claims amended according to the judgment (Article L. 613-27, §3).

297. Paris, 7 Jul. 1995: PIBD 1995, III, 517; RTD com. 1996, 676, obs. Azéma.

425. As long as the patent application is not published, the claims such as notified to the infringer are effective as against third persons (Article L. 615-4, §1). After the publication of the application, only restrictive adaptations are demurrable against third parties (Article L. 615-4, §1 1°) and where the patent concerns the use of a microorganism, it cannot be invoked until the day on which the microorganism has been made available to the public (Article L. 615-4, §1 2°). After the publication of the grant of the patent, even the extensive adaptations are effective against third parties.[298]

E. The Drawings

426. Drawings are optional. According to Article L. 613-2, §1, the drawings shall be used to interpret the claims.

427. They are to be filed only if the description or the claims refer to such drawings. The filing date is in such a case the date of filing of the drawings (Article R. 612-9). If they are not provided, references to the drawings are cancelled in the patent application.

F. The Abstract

428. The abstract is a summary of the invention and plays an informative role (Article R. 612-20) to facilitate the classification and consultation of patents. It may not be taken into account for any other purpose, in particular not for the purpose of interpreting the scope of the protection sought or for the purpose of determining the patentability of the invention. The final content of the abstract shall be drafted, where necessary, by the INPI.

G. Justification of Payment of Fees

429. The various fees are the following (Article R. 411-17):

- Application fee: it covers the first annual fee (Article R. 613-46); unless the payment is made within one month from the filing date (Article R. 612-5), the patent application is refused (Article R. 612-45, 2°).
- Search fee: unless the payment is made within one month from the filing date (Article R. 612-5), the patent application is refused (Article R. 612-45, 2°).
- New claim fee: if a new claim entails a supplementary search report, a special fee is due.
- Supplementary claims fee: if there are more than 10 claims, an additional fee is due for each additional claim.

430. The amount of fees may be reduced in the cases listed in Articles L. 612-20 and R. 613-63. The reduction is as of right for natural persons.

298. Paris, 21 Jun. 1990: Ann. propr. Ind. 1992, 306.

§2. Processing of a French Patent Application

431. A French patent is either refused or granted after an administrative procedure which consists of four stages: examination, search, publication, and grant.

I. Examination

A. Examination by the Ministry of Defence

432. Within fifteen days from the filing date, the INPI discloses the patent applications to the French Ministry of Defence (Article L. 612-8 and R. 612-26) which examines their utility for defence purposes. During the time of this examination, the patent application is kept secret, the search procedure does not start, the invention may not be publicly used under penal sanctions (a fine of EUR 4,500, and where the violation has prejudiced national defence, an imprisonment of five years Article L. 615-13), and no official copy of the application is delivered by the INPI (Article L. 612-9).

433. The authorization to disclose and use the invention is implied after five months as from the filing date; it may be given earlier, at the applicant's request. The Ministry of Defence may extend the prohibition in time (an indemnity is then due to the applicant: Article L. 612-10, §2). At any time, the French State may obtain a compulsory licence, or expropriate the patent (*see infra*, paragraphs 545 et seq).

B. Examination by the INPI

434. All the applications are subject to a minimal technical examination by the INPI. The statute does not provide for the content of the examination, but only lists the cases when the application may be refused (Article L. 612-12). First, the INPI grants a time for correction of defects in the application. Then the decision of refusal is taken by the Director General of the INPI. It cancels the application retroactively.

435. The causes of refusal are the following:

- formal defect (Article L. 612-12, 1° and R. 612-46);
- violation of the rule of unity of invention (Article L. 612-12, 2° and 3°; R. 612-33 and R. 612-48);
- a structural defect which makes the drafting of the search report impossible (Article L. 612-12, 6°);
- lack of support of the claims by the description (Article L. 612-12, 8°);
- an obvious lack of patentability of the invention (Article L. 612-12, 4°, 5°, 7°); however, lack of novelty is sanctioned only if it appears obvious from the search report; the INPI does not check inventive step;
- finally, the application may be refused when the applicant did not make any remarks or filed amended claims during the search procedure, although he was invited to do so by the INPI (Article L. 612-12, 9°).

436. The appeals which may be made by the applicant against the decisions taken by the INPI are filed either with the INPI, or with French courts.

437. Two kinds of appeals may be filed with the INPI: appeal for continuation of the proceeding and appeal for restoration.

438. Appeal for continuation of the procedure can be brought when the application was or may be refused because of the non-respect of a deadline granted by the INPI to the applicant (Article R. 612-52). A special fee is due (Article R. 411-17).

439. Appeal for restoration (restitutio in integrum) may be filed when the application was refused, or a request rejected, or another right lost because of non-respect of a legal deadline. Restoration is excluded in some cases (priority right renewal fees or request for search procedure). The appeal for restoration requires the proof of an excuse which justifies the non-respect of the deadline (Article L. 612-16).

440. Decisions taken by the Director General of the INPI may be appealed against in the 'Cour d'appel' of Paris (new Article D. 411-19-1). A further appeal to the Supreme Court (Cour de cassation) is open on legal grounds.

II. Documentary Search

441. The procedure of grant of French patents includes a documentary search, designed to reveal prior art likely to affect novelty or inventive step of the proposed invention. This procedure does not apply to certificates of utility.

442. Immediately after the filing date, the search procedure begins (the possibility for the applicant to request a delay of eighteen months for the search procedure has been abolished by the 'Ordonnance' No. 2008-1301 of 11 December 2008 which deleted the §1 of Article L. 612-15). The only way to elude the search procedure is to transform the patent application in a certificate of utility application (Article L. 612-15).

443. The search is done for the INPI by the Search Division of the European Patent Office in The Hague. First, a preliminary search report is drafted by the INPI, listing the relevant prior art. It shall cite the documents that may be taken into consideration to assess the patentability of the invention that constitutes the subject matter of the patent application. It is accompanied of an opinion on the patentability of the invention according to the cited documents. This opinion shall be accessible to any third party. The preliminary search report and the opinion are made on the basis of the claims as filed, taking into account the description and, where appropriate, the drawings. Each citation shall be made in relation to the claims that it relates to. If necessary, the pertinent sections of the cited document shall be identified by giving, in particular, the page, column, and lines or the figures. The preliminary search report shall distinguish between the cited documents that were published before the priority date, between the priority date and the filing date, on the filing date, and subsequent thereto. Any document referring to an oral disclosure, to a use, or to any other disclosure that has taken place before the filing date of the patent application shall be cited in the preliminary search report stating the publication date of the document and that of the non-written disclosure (Article R. 612-57). It is notified to the applicant. If no prior art is discovered, the patent may be granted immediately. If such prior documents appear, it is up to the applicant to answer within three months (Article R. 612-59), either by formulating remarks, or by adapting the patent claims. In absence of answer, the INPI may refuse the application (Article L. 612-12, 9°). However, if the draft search report shows an obvious lack of novelty, the INPI may order that the applicant modifies the claims under the sanction of refusal of the application (Article L. 612-12, 7°).

444. The draft report is published together with the patent application. Third parties may then address remarks to the INPI within three months. Then the final search report is drafted, taking into account the last set of claims and the remarks formulated by the applicant and the third parties. It is annexed to the patent when granted. This report does not produce any legal consequence. The INPI grants the patent even when a great number of prior documents are listed except in the case above. It does not provide for an opinion on the pertinence of the listed documents. Nor is a court bound by the results of the search: the report has mainly an informative function as to the probable validity of the patent.

III. Publication of the Application

445. Patents play an important technical information role in allowing the public to know the content of new technologies. The INPI is in charge of 'diffusing the inventions' (Article L. 612-21–L. 612-23 and R. 612-74–R. 612-75), by organizing the publication of patent applications. Unless the applicant requests an anticipated publication, the application is published eighteen months after the filing date or the date of priority. The whole file is then accessible to the public, including the 'subsequent acts of procedure' (Article L. 612-21, 3°).

446. During three months from publication, third parties may address remarks to the INPI; the applicant may (but does not have to) then adapt the patent claims.

447. From the date of publication, the applicant may bring actions for infringement, without notifying to the defendant a copy of the patent application (Article L. 615-4).

IV. Grant of the Patent

448. If the application complies with all the legal conditions, the title of protection of the invention is granted by the INPI. The applicant must pay grant and printing fees (Article R. 411-17). In the event of lapse of the rights deriving from a patent application due to failure to pay the first annual fee, the patent granting procedure shall be terminated (Article R. 612-72). The decision of grant is notified to the applicant who receives a certified copy of the title. It is published in the 'Bulletin officiel de la propriété industrielle' (BOPI). The grant gives to the patent its final content; the right is presumed valid until a court decides to invalid it upon action by an interested person.

449. The exclusive right takes effect as from the date of filing of the application, and not from the date of grant (Article L. 613-1).

450. Third parties may appeal the INPI's decision to grant a patent, if such a grant causes them a damage.[299]

451. After the grant, any interested person may request from the INPI (upon payment), an opinion ('avis documentaire') on the pertinence of the prior art citations in the search report (Articles L. 612-23 and R. 613-60–R. 613-62).

299. Paris, 11 Oct. 1982: PIBD 1982, III, 247.-Bordeaux, 15 Feb. 1999: PIBD 1999, III, 403.

Chapter 5. Scope of Exclusive Rights

452. The IP Code states, in its Article L. 611-1: 'Any invention may be the object of a title of industrial property (…) which confers to its holder or to his successors in right, an exclusive right to exploit the invention.' The exclusive character of the patent right implies that the holder may prohibit to any third person the use of the protected invention. He may also authorize such a use, through a contractual agreement with the interested party (*see infra*, paragraphs 514 et seq.). The inventor enjoys a very simple moral right which only consists of a right to paternity: the inventor has the right to be mentioned as such in the patent (Article L. 611-9; he may also refuse to be mentioned in such a quality). Therefore, patent confers essentially economic rights.

453. The protection granted by a French patent covers only the territory of France: the principle of territoriality of the industrial property rights applies.

454. The exclusive right covers the invention such as defined by the patent claims, eventually interpreted in view of the description and the drawings (Article L. 613-2). However, the scope of this exclusive right may be modified through the renunciation to or the limitation of a patent claim. 'Any violation of the patentee's rights such as defined in Article L. 613-3–L. 613-6 is an infringement' (Article L. 615-1, §1). The list of rights contained in these articles is exhaustive. The patentee's rights are more or less effective: in some cases he may prohibit the working of the protected invention without having to evidence the infringer's bad faith; in other cases, he must show such a bad faith.

§1. Renunciation to or Limitation of a Patent Claim

455. The scope of a granted patent shall be first reduced by a court's decision pronouncing its partial nullity, i.e., the nullity restricted to one or some of the patent claims (*see infra*). Such a reduction shall also be obtained through the voluntary renunciation of the patentee to one or some of the patent claims (Article L. 613-24). The owner of a patent may at any time relinquish either the entire patent or one or more claims under the patent. In practice, the renunciation to the entire patent is not very useful as the same result may be obtained much easier through non-payment of the annual fees (*see infra*). The partial renunciation is useful as it may abort a nascent litigation about the patent validity. The renunciation shall be effected by the patent owner or joint owners in writing with the National Institute of Industrial Property (INPI) but also with the consent of the beneficiaries of real property rights, pledge or licence, entered in the National Registry of Patents. If an action for vindication of the patent ownership is pending, the consent of its author to the requested renunciation is necessary. The renunciation must originate from the owner of the patent, registered in the National Registry of Patents on the day of the request, or his agent who, unless he has the capacity of 'conseil en propriété industrielle' ('industrial property counsel') or of 'avocat' (attorney), must justify a special power (Article R. 613-45). The partial renunciation shall have retroactive effect, as from the date on which the patent application has been filed.

456. The patentee may also modify the writing of one or some of the patent claims (of a French patent or of the French designation of a European patent). Legal security of third parties implies that such a modification shall only be a patent claim limitation. For a long time, such a limitation could only result from a court decision partially annulling a claim and referring the owner of the patent to the INPI for redrafting in accordance with the operative part of the judgment. The Act No. 2008-776 of 4 August 2008, incorporating into French law a mechanism newly introduced in the EPC, added a possibility of voluntary limitation in Article L. 613-24 of the Intellectual Property Code. The request for limitation, submitted to the INPI must be made by a written declaration. It must originate from the owner of the patent, registered in the National Registry of Patents on the day of the request, or his agent who, unless he has the capacity of 'conseil en propriété industrielle' ('industrial property counsel') or of 'avocat' (attorney), must justify a special power (Article R. 613-45). If the patent belongs to several persons (joint ownership), the request must be made by all of them. It must be accompanied by the justification for the payment of the prescribed fee, cover only one patent, be accompanied, where appropriate, by the consent of the beneficiaries of real property rights, pledge or licence, entered in the National Registry of Patents. It shall be accompanied by the full text of the amended claims, and where applicable, the description and drawings as amended.

457. Such a limitation request shall also be made in the course of a pending action for patent revocation; the limited patent will then become the object of this action. However, a party who, in a single proceeding, imposes several limitations on his patent, in a dilatory or abusive manner, may be sentenced to a civil fine not exceeding EUR 3,000 (Article L. 613-25).

458. If it appears that the amended claims do not constitute a limitation by comparison with the earlier claims of the patent or if these modified claims are not based on the description or do not clearly define the subject matter of protection (L. 612-6), a notification shall be sent to the applicant with a time limit to regularize his request or to submit observations. In the absence of regularization or convincing observations, the application is rejected by decision of the Director of INPI. If the limitation request is accepted, it is entered in the National Registry of Patents and a notice of registration is sent to the author of the limitation.

§2. Acts Prohibited Without Condition of the Infringer's Bad Faith

459. This rule relates to the unauthorized working of the patent either by a manufacturer or by an importer.

460. If the patent covers a product, it is forbidden to manufacture such a product without the patentee's authorization (Article L. 613-3, a). The material reproduction of the product is necessary,[300] but also sufficient for the infringement to exist. Neither the process used to reproduce the product, nor the destination of the product are

300. Cass. req., 9 Jul. 1908: S. 1908, 184: preparatory acts do not infringe the patent.

material.[301] Infringement may consist of the reproduction of one or several elements of the product, on condition that they are protected as such.[302] When the patent covers a combination of elements, infringement may consist of an equivalent combination, using different elements, but which fulfil the same technical function.[303] Are also forbidden: the offer, the marketing, the use, the importation, the exportation, the transshipment or the possession of the patented product in view of one of these aims. However, importation from a Member State of the European Economic Space may be lawful if the patentee's right is exhausted (*see infra*).

461. If the patent covers a process, it is prohibited to use this process without the patent holder's consent (Article L. 613-3, b). And because such a process patent covers the products directly obtained by the process (Article L. 613-2, §2), the offer, marketing, use, importation, exportation, transshipment, or possession of such a product (directly obtained by the process) in view of one of these aims, is also prohibited. (Article L. 613-3, c). Whatever the object of the patent, infringement exists only if the essential elements of the invention were reproduced. Consequently, an improvement is an infringement, because it reproduces such elements of the patented invention.

§3. Acts Prohibited under Condition of the Infringer's Bad Faith

462. Some exploitations of the patent are infringement only if they are done by a person who acted in bad faith, knowing the existence of an exclusive right and the infringing character of the acts he performed.

463. As for product patents, Article L. 615-1, §3, the offer, the sale, the use, the possession in view of use, or sale of an infringing product are sanctioned only if they are committed by a person other than the manufacturer of the infringing product. As for process patents, Article L. 613-3, b) adds the offer of exploitation of the process on the French territory.

464. Whatever the patent's object, it is illegal to supply or offer to supply, on French territory,[304] to a person other than a person entitled to exploit the patented invention, the means of implementing, on that territory, the invention with respect to an essential[305] element thereof where the third party knows, or it is obvious from the circumstances, that such means are suitable for putting and are intended to put the

301. Paris, 14 Feb. 1967: Ann. propr. Ind. 1967, 15; the product is infringing even when it was not subsequently sold.
302. Cass. com., 19 Feb. 1991: JCP ed. E. 1992 II 312, note Martin.-15 Jan. 1997: D. 1997, som., obs. Mousseron.
303. Cass. com., 26 Jan. 1993: JCP 1993 IV,87.-16 Jan. 1996: PIBD 1996, III, 175 .-Paris, 9 Jun. 2000: PIBD 2000, III, 465.
304. Paris, 19 Jan. 2000 : PIBD 2000, III, 303, no acts committed on the French territory.
305. Examples of essential elements, Paris, 14 Apr. 2015: PIBD 2015, III, 405. – TGI Paris, 30 Sep. 2009: PIBD 2010, III, 14. – Paris, 22 May 2013: PIBD 2013, III, 1313. – Cass. com., 12 Feb. 2008: Propr. industr. 2008, comm. 38, obs. M. Boizard. Examples of non-essential elements, Lyon, 19 Sep. 2002: PIBD 2003, III, 281. – Paris, 25 Nov. 2014: PIBD 2015, III, 101. – Paris, 19 Mar. 2014: PIBD 2014, III, 491.

invention into effect[306] (Article L. 613-4, §1). The providing of such means is lawful if the receiver is authorized to exploit the patent (e.g., a licensee). It is also lawful where the means of implementation are staple commercial products, except where the third party induces the person supplied to commit acts prohibited by Article L. 613-3 (these are acts accomplished by the manufacturer: *see supra* paragraph 459). It was decided, for instance, that the delivery to a farmer of two products which could be mixed together in order to obtain the patented product amounted to an infringement by 'providing of means'.[307]

465. Bad faith may be evidenced by all means of proof by the patent holder. It may be evidenced, for instance, by warnings,[308] or a counterfeit-seizure against the defendant.[309] It may also be presumed from the defendant's profession.[310]

306. It is not necessary to be aware of the existence of the infringed patent, Paris, 22 May 2013: PIBD 2013, III, 1313.
307. Paris, 14 Feb. 1989: JCP ed. E, 1990 II 15698, obs. Burst and Mousseron.
308. Paris, 21 Jan. 1993: PIBD 1993, III, 314.
309. TGI Paris, 12 Feb. 1987: PIBD 1987, III, 157.
310. Cass. com., 13 Feb. 1985: PIBD 1985, III, 181.

Chapter 6. Ownership and Transfer

§1. Ownership

I. General Rules

466. The applicant being the inventor designated in the patent application is presumed to be the owner of the patent. Ownership may be claimed by a third person who shows that the invention was stolen from the true inventor, or that the patent application was filed in violation of a legal or a contractual obligation (Article L. 611-8).[311]

467. In case of concomitant inventions, made simultaneously by independent inventors, the right to the patent belongs to the one who first filed the patent application (Article L. 611-6). The first and true inventor may neither act for invalidity of such a patent,[312] nor act for recovery of ownership.

468. The action for vindication of the patent ownership is to be brought within five years from the publication of grant of the patent. However, in case of bad faith at the time of grant or of the acquisition of title, this time limit is computed from the expiration of the patent (Article L. 611-8, §3).

469. If the action succeeds, the ownership of the patent is transferred to the plaintiff with retroactive effect, such a decision being published in the 'Registre National des brevets' (National Registry of Patents). All the contracts passed by the usurper are cancelled as from the date of the publication of the judgment.[313] Foreign patents parallel to the French ones may also be claimed, as well as all the earnings.[314]

II. Joint Ownership

470. The patent right may belong to several persons (natural or legal), being joint owners. Such a situation may be the result of a joint filing of the patent application, of a partial transfer of the patent, or a legal joint ownership (e.g., following a succession). It may also be the consequence of a judicial decision transferring partially the ownership of a patent in the cases listed under Article L. 611-8 (*see supra* paragraph 466).

471. The IP Code provides for specific rules (Article L. 613-29–L. 613-31), derogatory to the ordinary rules from the Civil Code (Articles 815 et seq., 883 et seq., 1873-1 et seq.) relating to joint ownership (Article L. 613-30). However, the joint

311. Paris, 24 May 1994: PIBD 1994, III, 496. – Cass. com., 21 Feb. 1995: Bull. civ. IV, No. 50. -24 Feb. 1998: PIBD 1998, III, 263. -3 Jun. 1998: PIBD 1998, III, 531.
312. Paris, 23 Apr. 1992: PIBD 1992, III, 605.
313. Cass. com., 7 Feb. 1995: Dossiers Brevets 1995, 1, 4; RTD com. 1996, 266, obs. Azéma.
314. Cass. com., 18 Jan. 1994: Bull. civ. IV, No. 23.- Cass. Com., 28 Apr. 2004: JCP ed. E 2004, No. 908, p, 988.

owners may derogate from all the specific rules of Article L. 613-29–L. 613-31 at any time by means of a joint ownership agreement (Article L. 613-32).

472. All the joint owners must consent to the decisions relating to the existence or content of the patent, such as: adaptation of patent claims, withdrawal of the application, assignment of the totality of the rights, and grant of an exclusive licence (Article L. 613-29, d).

473. Each joint owner may bring actions against infringers. He must only notify such actions to the other joint owners (Article L. 613-29, b).

474. Each joint owner may exploit the invention for himself, but must indemnify the others who do not exploit it personally, or who do not granted licences (Article L. 613-29, a).

475. Each joint owner may grant a non-exclusive licence, but must indemnify the others as said above (Article L. 613-29, c). However, the draft of licence has to be notified to the others, who may oppose the grant of such licence, but must then acquire the part of the one who initiated the project.

476. Each co-owner may at any time transfer his fraction in the patent (Article L. 613-29, e). He must notify this project of transfer to the others, who may exercise their pre-emption right within three months. If an agreement cannot be reached, the price is set by the tribunal. However, within one month from the notification of the judgment, the parties may renounce the transfer.

477. Each co-owner may give up his rights in the patent, after notification to the others (Article L. 613-31).

III. Ownership in Employees' Inventions

478. Ownership in such inventions is regulated by Articles L. 611-7 and L. 615-21. This regime is a minimum, the parties may agree on solutions more favourable to the employee. Ownership is determined according to a legal system of classification of employees' inventions.[315] A specific dispute resolution procedure is also provided.

A. Classification of Employees' Inventions

1. Criterias of Classification

479. The statute provides for two categories of employee's inventions: the 'mission inventions' and all the other inventions. Into the first category fall all inventions made by an employee in the execution of an employment contract comprising an inventive mission corresponding to its effective functions or of studies and research which have been explicitly entrusted to him by the employer.[316]

315. A very similar system applies to inventions made by civil servants of the French State and public entities (IP Code, Arts R. 611-11 et seq.); their remuneration is set forth by IP Code., Art. R. 611-14-1. *See* : Paris, 17 Dec. 1997: PIBD 1998, III, 160.

316. Cass. com., 15 Nov. 1994: PIBD 1995, III, 55: a 'service note' entrusted the employee with studies and research.

480. Such inventions belong to the employer, who decides whether he wishes to apply for a patent. However, the employer must inform the employee when he files an application and when the patent on the invention is granted. The employee inventor may claim a specific remuneration the conditions of which are to be determined by the contract for employment or collective labour agreements.[317] He always keeps right to paternity of the invention and may require to be mentioned as inventor.

481. All other inventions belong, in principle, to the inventor. However, when the invention was made by an employee 'during the execution of its functions or in the field of activity of the company or by reason of knowledge or use of technologies or specific means of the company or of data acquired by the company', the invention is 'attributable' to the employer: the employer may attribute to himself the right to apply for a patent, or a right to exploit the invention.

482. The employee inventor is entitled to an 'equitable price' to be agreed by the parties or by the 'Commission Nationale des Inventions de Salariés' (CNIS, National Commission for Employees' Inventions) (*see infra*). It should be computed taking into account each party's input and the commercial and industrial utility of the invention (Article L. 611-7, § 2).

2. Procedure of Classification

483. Any employee must immediately inform his employer that he made an invention, whatever its nature and content. In this notification, he must propose a classification of the invention in one of the legal categories. When the employer does not answer within two months, he is deemed to accept the proposed classification (Article R. 611-6). In case of disagreement, each party may refer the matter to the CNIS.

484. If the invention is classified as 'attributable' to the employer, he must exercise his rights within four months from the reception of the notification (Article R. 611-7).

B. Dispute Resolution

485. Any dispute relating to an employee's invention may be brought, upon a party's request, in the 'National Commission of Employees' Inventions' ('Commission Nationale des Inventions de Salariés'), consisting of representatives of employers and employees and chaired by a judge (Article L. 615-21). Its functioning is regulated by Article R. 615-6–R. 615-31.

486. The procedure is contradictory. Within six months, the Commission proposes a reconciliation draft, which replaces the parties' agreement if no party has brought the dispute to a tribunal within six months. This agreement may be made enforceable by the president of the tribunal, upon request.

487. If a patent was granted in violation of the classification of the invention, the rights may be vindicated in courts by the entitled person (either the employer or

317. Paris, 19 Nov. 1997: PIBD 1998, III, 157.- Cass. com., 21 Nov. 2000: JCP ed. E 2001, p. 275, note Galloux; D. som., p. 1188, obs. Raynard; RTD com., 2001, p. 87, obs. Azéma and Galloux; PIBD 2001, III, 101, the remuneration is not necessarily based on the salary.

the employee, depending on the classification of the invention: *see supra*, paragraphs 478 et seq.).

IV. Ownership in Officials' or Public Servants' Inventions

488. As for inventions made by officials or public servants, the solutions are very similar to Article L. 611-7 with some specific rules set in Article R. 611-11–R. 611-14-1, unless more favourable contractual provisions govern the industrial property rights in inventions they make.

489. Inventions made by an official or public servant in the execution either of tasks comprising an inventive mission corresponding to his attributions, or of studies or research explicitly entrusted to him shall belong to the public person on behalf of whom he carries out those tasks, studies, or research. However, if the public person decides not to develop the invention, the official or public servant who has made the invention may enjoy the economic rights deriving from the invention in accordance with the conditions laid down in an agreement concluded with the public person (Article R. 611-12, §1).

490. All other inventions shall belong to the official or public servant. However, the public employer shall have the right to have attributed to him all or a part of the rights deriving from the patent protecting the invention where the invention has been made by an official or a public servant: Either in the course of carrying out his duties; Or in the field of activity of the public body concerned; Or through knowledge or use of techniques, specific means of such body or of data obtained by that body (Article R. 611-12, §2).

491. Where the same public servant carries out his activities on behalf of more than one public person, those public persons shall act concertedly in accordance with the conditions to be determined by order or by an agreement brought to the knowledge of the servants concerned for the exercise of their rights and the execution of their obligations (Article R. 611-13).

492. An official or public servant who makes an invention shall immediately declare the invention to the authority empowered by the public person to which it belongs. The provisions of Article R. 611-1–R. 611-10 relating to the obligations of employee and employer shall apply to officials and public servants and to the public persons concerned (Article R. 611-14).

§2. Transfers

493. Ownership of a patent implies not only the right to exploit personally the protected invention and to forbid its exploitation to others, but also the right to authorize such exploitation by third parties upon a contractual agreement. Such agreements are subject to the ordinary rules of contract law; they may consist of any kind of contract: assignment, exchange, rental (licence), donation, contribution to a corporation, pledge, etc. The IP Code does not regulate in detail such contracts, but only expressly states that rights implied by a patent or a patent application may be assigned or licensed

(Article L. 613-8). These two contracts which are the most frequent in practice, are studied hereafter.

I. Assignment of a French Patent

494. This is a contract whereby the patentee transfers his rights in exchange for the payment of a price. It is subject to the rules of sales contracts (Articles 1582–1701-1 Civil Code), and to some scarce rules of the IP Code.

A. Conditions of the Assignment

1. Formal Conditions

495. Assignment must be done in writing as a condition of its validity (IP Code, Article L. 613-8, §5). In order to be demurrable against third parties, the contract must be registered in the National Register of Patents (Article L. 613-9 and Article R. 613-53–R. 613-59). This formality is to be done for any assignment of a French patent even if the contract is international, or is subject to a foreign law and was concluded abroad.[318]

496. If one of the parties is domiciled abroad, the contract must be notified to the Foreign Trade Ministry within one month from its conclusion (Article R. 624-1–7). This formality applies to all technology transfers (i.e., also to transfers of unpatented know-how).

2. Substantive Conditions

497. The seller must be the owner of the transferred patent rights and capable to assign them. A joint owner may assign only his fraction of the right: the other co-owners have a right of pre-emption (*see supra,* paragraphs 470 et seq.).

498. The assignment may have as its object either a patent or a patent application. It may be total or partial, when, for instance, only the rights in some manners of working of the invention are transferred (e. g. sales but not manufacturing). If the technology is unpatented, the contract is not a sale, but a communication of know-how, subject to the rules of contracts for services (*see infra*). The assignment of a void or expired patent is void for lack of object. The invalidated contract is retroactively cancelled and the transferor has to restitute the received price, unless the parties provided for a clause 'on buyer's own risks'[319]

499. Unless a contrary provision is agreed upon, the following rights are not included in an assignment:

- patents on improvements;
- priority right;
- foreign parallel patents;

318. Trib. civ. Seine, 18 Jun. 1955: Ann. propr. Ind. 1956, 6.

319. Cass. com., 3 May 1978: D. 1979, jur., p. 247, note Burst.

- know-how relating to the patented invention;
- in any case, the inventor's moral right is not transferrable.[320]

B. Effects of the Assignment

1. Transfer of Rights

500. The patent right is transferred from the seller to the buyer as from the moment of signature of the contract. The transfer is demurrable against third parties as from the date of its registration in the National Patent Register. Consequently, the transferee may not, for instance, claim from an infringer compensation of the loss suffered prior to the registration of the contract of assignment.[321]

2. Parties' Obligations

501. The obligations characteristic of a contract of sale apply to the assignment of patents. The parties are free to add other obligations or to modify them, in respect of the public order and competition law.

a. The Transferor's Obligations

502. (a) Delivery The duty to deliver the object of the sale consists here of the handling over the title representing the patent.

503. (b) Warranty According to the Civil Code (Article 1625), the seller guarantees the buyer against eviction and against hidden defects.

504. Eviction consists of a trouble in the possession of the patent right acquired by the assignee.

505. The transferor should not personally cause such a trouble: he may not, for instance, exploit the invention after the assignment of the patent without the assignee's authorization.[322] He may not either challenge the assignee's right, for instance, by claiming avoidance of the sold patent. This seller's personal warranty is mandatory and may not be set aside by contract (Article 1628, Civil Code).

506. The seller must also warranty the buyer against eviction by third persons. This warranty covers the troubles having their legal ground prior to the assignment. For instance, if a third party brings an action against the assignee for vindication of the patent, the assignee may call upon the seller who will have to help him to win the dispute. If he fails to do so, the seller will have to indemnify the buyer for all the loss he suffered as the consequence of the third party's action.

507. On the contrary, the so-called factual troubles caused by third parties are not covered by the seller's warranty: being the new owner of the patent, the assignee must act by himself against infringers and may not call the seller for warranty.

508. This warranty against eviction by third parties is not mandatory and may be excluded or amended by contract in the ordinary conditions of French contract law.

---

320. Cass. com., 23 Nov. 1964: Bull. civ. IV, No. 513.
321. Paris, 1 Dec. 1992: PIBD 1993, III, 220.
322. Paris, 2 Oct. 1978: D. 1980, jur., p. 139, note Mousseron.

509. Hidden defects are defects which could not be detected by the buyer at the time of the sale, and which make the thing unfit for its use. Such a defect affecting a patent may be either a legal defect (nullity of the patent), or a material one (the invention is impossible to work). From this point of view, only defects in the conception of the invention are warranted, and not those due to the manufacturing of the patented product or the use of the process.[323] The seller of a patent does not warranty its commercial success.[324] It was held that the warranty covers the prohibition by the Ministry of Health of marketing of some applications of a patented medicine.[325]

510. Failure to warranty such defects is sanctioned by the rescission of the assignment or the reduction in price, eventually completed by damages. The action for warranty must be brought within two years following the discovery of the defects (Article 1648 of the Civil Code).

511. Warranty of hidden vices may be excluded or amended by agreement, at least between professional parties, which is usually the case as for patent assignments.

b. The Transferee's Obligations

512. The transferee's main obligation is to pay the sale price. In order to be valid a contract of sale must provide for a price which is either determined or at least determinable by reference to objective elements allowing its computation (Article 1583, Civil Code).

513. Other obligations may also be provided in compliance with public order (within the meaning of French law) and with French and eventually EU competition rules (EU Regulation No. 316/2014, 21 March 2014: OJEC, No. L 93, 28 March 2014, p. 17). However, a contract of assignment, which does not imply continuous relations between the parties, is less at risk of violating competition law than a licence contract.

II. French Patent Licence

514. A licence is a contract whereby the patentee authorizes a licensee to exploit his patent in exchange for payment of a price (royalty). It belongs to the category of contracts of rental and is, therefore, subject to the rules specific to rentals (Articles 1708 et seq., Civil Code).[326] The IP Code provides for some scarce rules in its Article L. 613-8. The combination of these rules allows to define the conditions and effects of the patent licences in French law.

323. Cass. civ. 3, 24 Jun. 1975: D. 1976, jur., p. 193, note J. Schmidt.
324. Cass. com., 12 Dec. 1984: JCP ed. E, 1985 II 14139.
325. Paris, 29 Oct. 1987: Ann. propr. Ind. 1988, 300.
326. Paris, 21 Oct. 1999: PIBD 2000, III, 181.

A. Conditions of the Patent Licence

1. Formal Conditions

515. These conditions are identical to those required from the assignment (*see supra* paragraph 495): the contract must be written, entered in the National Register of Patents, and notified to the administration if one of the parties is a foreign resident.

2. Substantive Conditions

a. Conditions Relating to the Parties

516. The licensor must hold a right in the patent. Most often, the licensor is the owner of the patent (for joint ownership: *see supra*, paragraphs 470 et seq.). However, the licence may also be granted by a tenant for life (usufructuary of the patent), or a licensee, granting a sub-licence with the licensor's consent.

517. Each party must be capable to make acts of administration on his assets.

518. The so-called system of 'legal license' (licence de droit), whereby a patentee made a public offer of licence through the intermediary of the INPI has been abolished by the Act no. 2005-842 of 26 July 2005 (repealed Article L. 613-10, R. 613-1–R. 613-9).

519. It should be noted that when a licence is granted to a corporation belonging to a conglomerate, such licence does not benefit to the other corporations of the same group. According to French law, each such corporation is a separate legal person, whereas the conglomerate has no legal personality.

b. Conditions Relating to the Object

520. The licence may have as its object either an already granted patent, or a patent application. In the latter case, the contract's effects are suspended until the final decision of grant by the INPI. If the licensed patent is declared invalid by a judgment, the licence itself becomes void for lack of object.[327] It was held that the impossibility of exploitation of the invention is not only a defect of the patent, but also alters the essential characteristic of the licence: the licensee may in such a case seek nullity of the contract.[328]

521. However, if the parties considered the validity as aleatory, they do not have to restitute what was delivered or paid when the contract is invalidated.[329]

522. When the licensee keeps working the invention after the revocation of the patent (and of the licence) he does not infringe, but may be held liable for unfair competition upon evidence of a wrongdoing (*see infra*, paragraph 608).

523. The licence may be either total (the entire patent is licensed) or partial (only some applications are licensed). It may be limited to a portion of the French

327. Cass. com., 8 Jul. 1970: Bull. civ. IV, p. 204.
328. Cass. civ. 3, 24 Jun. 1975: D. 1976, jur., p. 196, note J. Schmidt.
329. Cass. com., 3 May 1978: D. 1979, jur., p. 247, note Burst.

territory. As for the ancillary object of the licence, the solutions are the same as for the assignment (*see supra*, paragraph 493).

B. *Effects of the Patent Licence*

524. Unlike the assignment, the licence does not transfer the ownership in the patent, but only creates obligations binding the parties during a limited time (the maximum duration is that of the patent).

1. The Licensor's Obligations

a. Delivery

525. The licensor must deliver to the licensee the text of the patent application, in order to allow him to have knowledge of the technical information contained in these documents. This information should by itself allow the exploitation of the patent, since the description of the invention must be clear and complete enough to allow a man skilled in the art to reproduce the invention (*see supra*, paragraph 415).

526. The licensor must let the licensee exploit the patented invention. Unless a more limited scope is provided for, the licence is in principle total: it covers all the elements of the patent, for the whole French territory and for the remaining total duration of the exclusive right. If the licence is limited in one or more of these aspects (object, territory, or duration), the licensee infringes the patent if he works the invention outside of the contractual limits (Article L. 613-8, §3).

527. If the licence covers several parallel patents in France and abroad, each of them is subject to the law of the State which granted the right, as far as validity or ownership are concerned. The parties may subject their contractual obligations to the legal system of their choice. In absence of an express choice of law, French courts will determine it according to the Rome Convention of 19 June 1980 on the law applicable to contractual obligations, ratified by France, or according to the Rome I Regulation No. 593/2008 of 17 June 2008 on the applicable law to contractual obligations, which applies to contracts concluded as from 17 December 2009 (Article 28).[330]

b. Warranty

528. (a) Warranty of peaceful enjoyment (Article 1719, §3, Civil Code) The licensor should not trouble the peaceful enjoyment of the patent by the licensee: he must, for instance, pay the renewal fees in order to maintain his title in force. He remains the owner of the patent and may exploit it himself, unless a contrary clause is provided for.

529. The licensor must also warranty the licensee against factual or legal trouble coming from third parties. He must, therefore, take the necessary measures against infringers if the licensee so requests (the licensee may bring actions for infringement

330. JOCE, 9 Oct. 1980, No. L. 266, p. 1. It is applicable in France since 1 Apr. 1990, as for contracts entered into after that date; JOCE, 4 Jul. 2008, No. L. 177, p. 6.

only in limited situations: *see infra*, paragraph 582). If the licensee is sued for infringement by a third party, he may call up the licensor for warranty.

530. (b) Warranty against hidden defects Hidden defects are defined as in the contract for assignment (*see supra,* paragraph 503). The content of the warranty in licence contracts is the one provided for by the Civil Code for rental contracts (Article 1721, Civil Code). The hidden vice may consist of a 'legal defect' of the patent: the nullity of the patent entails rescission of the licence and the licensor must compensate the licensee for the loss he sustained.[331] Most often the disputes between the licensee and the licensor deal with difficulties in the exploitation of the patent.

531. In such cases the warranty is limited to conceptual defects of the invention, which either make its operation impossible,[332] or cause the manufacturing of defective products.[333] However, the licensee may not complain about difficulties of exploitation of the invention when he made preliminary tests which were satisfactory.[334] Mere technical adjustments are not hidden vices and must be sustained by the licensee, unless they go beyond the normal know-how of a man skilled in the art.[335] Absent a contrary provision of the contract, the licensor does not warranty the industrial and commercial value of the invention.[336]

532. The warranty of hidden defects may be amended by contract. It may be excluded or limited, unless the licensor knew the defect: according to the rules of civil law, bad faith excludes the benefit of such clauses.

533. A clause may validly limit the warranty to the mere existence of the patent and exclude the patent's validity and put its exploitation at the licensee's risk.[337]

c. Other Obligations

534. The licensor may undertake other obligations towards the licensee, according to the parties' needs. Any such obligation must comply with public order and competition law. If it is at risk of distorting competition within the EU, such clauses must no longer be notified to the European Commission, since the EC Council Regulation No. 1/2003 of 16 December 2002[338] which suppressed such an obligation. As from 1 May 2004, all the contracts are presumed valid, unless a third party (or public authority) shows the contrary. No new exemptions will be granted under the EC Regulation No. 240/96 of the Commission of 31 January 1996 relating to the application of Article 85, §3 of the Rome Treaty to certain categories of technology transfer agreements.[339] The EC Regulation No. 240/96 has been repealed and replaced by the EC Regulation No.

331. Lyon, 12 Jan. 1989: Ann. propr. Ind. 1989, 45.
332. Cass. com., 11 Jul. 1988: D. 1988, I.R., p. 238.
333. Besançon, 30 Sep. 1994: JCP ed. E, 1995 pan. 336: the patentee is liable together with the seller of the defective products towards persons who suffered a damage.
334. Paris, 16 Mar. 1963: Ann. propr. Ind. 1963, 385.
335. Paris, 2 Jun. 1988: D. 1988, I.R., p. 202.
336. Paris, 27 May 1993: PIBD 1993, III, 580; D. 1996, som., p. 20, obs. Mousseron and Schmidt.
337. TGI Paris, 14 Dec. 1994: PIBD 1995, III, 183.- Cass. com., 11 Mar. 1986: Bull. civ. IV, No. 43; Ann. propr. Ind. 1986, 266.
338. Council Regulation (EC) No. 1/2003 of 16 Dec. 2002 on the implementation of the rules on competition laid down in Arts 81 and 82 of the Treaty, OJEC, No. L. 1, 4 Jan. 2003, pp. 1–25.
339. JOCE, No. L. 31, 9 Feb. 1996.

772/2004 of 27 April 2004 which, in turn, has been repealed and replaced by the EU Regulation No. 316/2014 of 21 March 2014.[340]

535. The most frequent additional clauses provide for the exclusivity of the licence: the licensor undertakes the obligation not to grant other licences on the same patent to third parties.

536. The licensor frequently also accepts to communicate to the licensee the improvements which may be brought in the future to the patented invention and undertakes the duty to grant to him licences on such improvement patents.

2. The Licensee's Obligations

a. Obligation to Pay the Price

537. The licence is granted in consideration of a price; otherwise it would be a loan of the patent. The price may consist either of a lump sum, or of royalties assessed on the results of exploitation, most often of a combination of both. The licensee frequently pays a minimum annual royalty independent from the exploitation of the invention: such clauses are held valid.[341]

538. The payment of royalties is due until the date of termination of the licence, if this date is earlier than the one of expiration of the patent. But payment may not be due after the licensed patent is expired.[342] Such a provision is also held to violate French competition law.[343] Payment after expiration of the patent may, however, be justified in so-called mixed contracts, which associate a patent licence and a communication of know-how (*see infra*, paragraph 1053).

b. Obligation to Exploit the Patent

539. French courts decide that the licensee must exploit the patent, even in absence of such provision in the contract.[344] The exploitation must be effective and serious considered the technical means at the licensee's disposal.[345] Only absolute impossibility which amounts to a force majeure may excuse lack of exploitation.[346]

---

340. Commission Regulation (EU) No. 316/2014 of 21 Mar. 2014 on the application of Art. 101(3) of the Treaty on the Functioning of the European Union to categories of technology transfer agreements, OJEC, No. L. 93, 28 Mar. 2014, pp. 17–23.
341. Cass. com., 1 Feb. 1994: Ann. propr. Ind. 1995, 84, note Mathély; RTD com. 1995, 772, obs. Azéma.
342. Paris, 22 May 1990: D. 1993, som., p. 378, obs. Mousseron and Schmidt.
343. Commission Nationale de la Concurrence, opinion of 26 May 1983; BOSP, 8 Nov. 1983: Dossiers Brevets 1983, 4, 6.
344. Cass. com., 16 May 1961: Bull. civ. IV, No. 212.
345. Paris, 8 Apr. 1964: JCP 1964 II 13876, note R. Plaisant.
346. Cass. com., 1 Oct. 1996: D. 1997, som., p. 336, obs. J. Schmidt.

c. Other Obligations

540. Other obligations may be provided for by the contract, such as a duty not to manufacture or sell competing products, an obligation not to question the validity of the licensed patent,[347] an obligation to buy the row materials or other products from the licensor if they are necessary to maintain the quality of the patented goods, etc. Validity of such supplementary clauses must be checked towards French and eventually EU competition law.

347. Such clauses are valid: Cass. com., 11 Mar. 1986: Bull. civ. IV, No. 43.

Chapter 7. Limitations and Exceptions: Compulsory Licences

§1. Limitations and Exceptions to the Scope of Patent Protection

541. The statute provides for some cases where the patentee may not prohibit the exploitation of the patent by third parties. Such exceptions are justified either in consideration of the aim of the exploitation, or of the quality of the operator.

542. Considering the aim of the exploitation, Article L. 613-5 states that 'the rights afforded by a patent shall not extend to':

- acts done privately and for non-commercial purposes;
- acts done for experimental purposes relating to the subject matter of the patented invention;
- extemporaneous preparation in a pharmacy of a medicine for an individual in accordance with a medical prescription or acts concerning the medicine so prepared;
- the studies and assays required to obtain a market authorization for a medicine, as well as the acts necessary to their completion and for obtaining the market authorization;
- the acts necessary for the advertising's visa referred to in Article L. 5122-9 of the French Code of Public Health;
- objects designed to be launched in the outer space introduced on the French territory.

The Act No. 2004-1338 of 8 December 2004 has introduced new exceptions:

- patents on a product containing or consisting of genetic information, patents on a biological material possessing specific characteristics as a result of the invention and patents on a process that enables a biological material to be produced possessing specific characteristics as a result of the invention, do not prohibit the use by the farmer of the product of its harvest for the propagation or multiplication by it on its own holding (Article L. 613-5-1), do not prohibit the use by the farmer of the protected live-stock for an agricultural purpose but not for sale within the framework of a commercial reproduction activity (Article L. 613-5-2), and do not prohibit the deeds performed in order to create or discover and develop other plant varieties (Article L. 613-5-3).

543. This list is exhaustive: an unauthorized user of the patented invention might not claim other excuses, such as the fact that he did not seek to make a profit,[348] etc.

544. A third party sued for infringement may also raise an excuse grounded on the so-called prior personal possession right ('*droit de possession personnelle antérieure*'). According to Article L. 613-7, this defence benefits to any person who possessed the

348. Cass. com., 14 Apr. 1964: Ann. propr. Ind. 1964, 105.

invention in good faith prior to the patent application filing date or to the priority date. The beneficiary may continue with the exploitation, even industrial or commercial, of the invention even after a patent was granted to a third person. The 'personal possession' must exist on the French territory.[349] The benefit of this right is exclusively personal. Under Article L. 613-7, §2, the right may be transferred only together with the business, the enterprise or the part of the enterprise to which it belongs.

§2. Compulsory Licences

545. The patent holder may be deprived from his right without his consent, either as a consequence of an expropriation, or of a compulsory licence decided by the public authority.

I. Expropriation

546. The French State may expropriate totally or partially a patent owner from his rights, in the interest of the National Defence (Article L. 613-20). The Ministry has a discretionary power as to the opportunity of such a measure. A compensation is to be paid to the patentee. Failing amicable agreement, compensation for expropriation shall be fixed by the 'Tribunal de Grande Instance'.

II. Compulsory Licences

547. In order to favour some aspects of public interest, compulsory licences may be granted without the patentee's consent. The decision is taken either by the judicial or by the administrative authority. These compulsory licences are nonexclusive (Article L. 613-13).

A. Compulsory Licences of Judicial Origin

548. Such licences are granted at the request of an interested person by the First Instance Court (Tribunal de grande instance) in two situations: lack of exploitation of the patent or dependency towards a prior dominant patent.

1. Compulsory Licence for Lack of Exploitation (Article L. 613-11–L. 613-14)

549. The licence is granted upon the following conditions (cumulative):

- lack of exploitation or of at least serious preparation to exploitation of the patent three years after the grant, or four years after the filing of the application; the same shall apply where exploitation has ceased for more than three years;

349. Paris, 18 Feb. 1986: PIBD 1986, III, 264.

- on the territory of a Member State of the EU or of the European Economic Area;
- lack of marketing of the product in a quantity sufficient to satisfy the needs of the French market;
- evidence that the plaintiff could not obtain a licence from the patent holder and that he is able to exploit the patent in an effective and serious manner.

550. The claim is brought in the Tribunal de grande instance of Paris. The defendant may escape the compulsory licence by showing a legitimate excuse for non-working his patent. The importation of products from a Member State of the World Trade Organization amounts to the working of the patent (IP Code, Article L. 613-11, § 3, resulting from the introduction of the TRIPs Agreement).

551. The judicial licence is not exclusive (however, the licensee may bring action for infringement under Article L. 615-2, §4). Its content is decided by the tribunal (Article L. 613-12). Such a licence may be transferred only together with the business, the company, or the part of the company to which it belongs (Article L. 613-13). In case of non-performance of his obligations by the licensee, the tribunal may decide to terminate the compulsory licence (Article L. 613-14).

552. This system has received very rare applications: usually, the interesting patents are worked either by the owner himself, or by a licensee under a contractual licence.

2. Compulsory Licence for Dependency (Article L. 613-15)

553. This licence may be granted to a person who owns a patent on an improvement relating to a prior patent belonging to a third party. The improvement patent may not be exploited without the prior patent owner's consent ('to improve is to infringe'). Thus, if the holder of the prior patent refuses to authorize the working of the improvement patent, the latter's exploitation is blocked. In order to solve such a conflict, a court may grant a compulsory licence on the prior patent to the holder of the improvement patent.

554. However, the licence for dependency may be granted only if public interest requires it, because the improvement involves a substantial technical advance and is of considerable economic interest.

555. The application for a compulsory licence shall be made to the Tribunal de Grande Instance of Paris; it must be accompanied by evidence establishing that the applicant has been unable to obtain a licence from the owner of the patent and that it is in a position to exploit the invention in an effective and serious manner.

556. The compulsory licence shall be granted on fixed terms, particularly in respect of its duration, its field of application, and the amount of the royalties to be paid in consideration thereof. Those terms may be amended by court decision following a request by the owner or the licensee. However, the dependency licence is granted only within the limits necessary to the exploitation of the invention. The licence granted to the holder of the subsequent patent may be transferred only together with the said patent. The holder of the prior patent may also obtain a reciprocal compulsory licence on the improvement patent. In case of non-performance of his obligations by the licensee, the tribunal may decide to terminate the compulsory licence (Article L. 613-14).

557. Under the Act No. 2004-1338 of 8 December 2004 a new compulsory licence was introduced in Article L. 613-15-1 for the holder of a plant variety right: 'Where a breeder cannot acquire or exploit a plant variety right without infringing a prior patent, it may request the license of this patent inasmuch as the license is necessary for the exploitation of the plant variety to be protected and in so far as the variety constitutes with regard to the invention asserted in this patent an important technical advance and is of considerable economic interest.'

558. The application for a compulsory licence shall be made to the Tribunal de Grande Instance of Paris; it must be accompanied by evidence establishing that the applicant has been unable to obtain a licence from the owner of the patent and that it is in a position to exploit the invention in an effective and serious manner.

559. The compulsory licence shall be granted on fixed terms, particularly in respect of its duration, its field of application and the amount of the royalties to be paid in consideration thereof. Those terms may be amended by court decision following a request by the owner or the licensee. Where such a licence is granted, on application brought before the court, the holder of the patent will be entitled, under equitable conditions, to a cross-licence to use the protected variety. In case of non-performance of his obligations by the licensee, the tribunal may decide to terminate the compulsory licence (Article L. 613-14).

B. *Compulsory Licences of Administrative Origin*

1. Automatic Licence in the Interest of Public Health (Article L. 613-16 and L. 613-17-1)

560. For any patent on a medical product, a medical device, a medical device for in vitro diagnosis, a subsidiary therapeutic product or on their process for obtaining the same, a product necessary for obtaining the same or a process for manufacturing such a product or on an ex vivo diagnostic method, the Minister responsible for industrial property, at the request of the Minister responsible for health, may, by way of an order, place that patent under the regime of automatic licence ('licence d'office'). The patents of these products, processes, or diagnostic methods may be subjected to public interest licence scheme in the interest of public health only where these products, products resulting from these processes or these methods are made available to the public in insufficient quantity or quality or at abnormally high prices, or where the patent is exploited under conditions contrary to the interest of public health or is judged as an anti-competitive practice by a final administrative or court decision. Following such a decision of the Minister, any qualified person may request from the Minister responsible for industrial property the grant of a licence the content of which is determined by this Minister particularly in respect of its duration and field of application, but not in respect of the amount of the royalties to be paid in consideration thereof. The licence shall take effect from the date of notification of the order to the parties. In the absence of an amicable agreement approved by the Minister responsible for industrial property and the Minister responsible for health, the amount of the royalties shall be fixed by the Tribunal de Grande Instance. But where the purpose of the licence is to remedy an anti-competitive practice or in urgent cases, the Minister responsible for patent rights shall not be required to seek an amicable agreement.

561. The application for a compulsory licence, made pursuant to Regulation (EC) No. 816/2006 of the European Parliament and of the Council of 17 May 2006, on the compulsory licensing of patents relating to the manufacture of pharmaceutical products for export to countries with public health problems[350] shall be submitted to the governmental authority. The licence is granted in accordance with the conditions established by Article 10 of such Regulation. The order granting the licence fixes the royalties to be paid. The licence shall take effect on the latest date the order is notified to the applicant and to the right-holder (Article L. 613-17-1).

2. Automatic Licence in the Interest of Economic Development (Article L. 613-18)

562. The Minister responsible for industrial property may give formal notice to the owners of patents other than those referred to in Article L. 613-16 to undertake the exploitation of such patents so as to satisfy the requirements of the national economy. If no action is taken within a period of one year to comply with such notice and if the failure to exploit the invention or the lack of quality or quantity of the exploitation seriously prejudices economic development and the public interest, the patents in respect of which formal notice has been given may be subjected to public interest licences by decree in Conseil d'État. The Minister responsible for industrial property may extend the one-year period referred to above if the holder of the patent can produce legitimate reasons consistent with the demands of the national economy. As from the date of publication of the decree subjecting the patent to public interest licences, any qualified person may apply to the Minister responsible for industrial property for the grant of a licence to exploit the patent. The licence can only be non-exclusive: it shall be granted by an order of the above-mentioned Minister on fixed conditions with regard to its duration and field of application, but not in respect of the amount of royalties to be paid in consideration thereof. The licence shall take effect from the date of notification of the order to the parties. Failing amicable agreement, the amount of the royalties shall be fixed by the Tribunal de Grande Instance.

3. Automatic Licence in the Interest of National Defence (Article L. 613-19)

563. The State may at any time, in order to meet its defence requirements, obtain a licence ex officio to exploit an invention that is the subject of a patent application or a patent, whether the exploitation is to be done by the State itself or on its behalf. The public interest licence shall be granted at the request of the Minister responsible for defence by order of the Minister responsible for industrial property. The order shall lay down the conditions of the licence, excluding those relating to the amount of

350. Regulation (EC) No. 816/2006 of the European Parliament and of the Council of 17 May 2006 on compulsory licensing of patents relating to the manufacture of pharmaceutical products for export to countries with public health problems, OJEC, No. L. 157, 9 Jun. 2006, pp. 1–7.

royalties to be paid in consideration thereof. The licence shall take effect on the date of the application for the public interest licence. Failing amicable agreement, the amount of the royalties shall be fixed by the Tribunal de Grande Instance. Proceedings at all levels of jurisdiction shall take place in court chambers.

4. Automatic or Compulsory Licence in the Interest of Competition

564. Under the TRIPs Agreement a new compulsory licence or automatic licence was introduced in Article L. 613-19-1, on the semi-conductor chips titles. Such is the case for a use for public non-commercial aims or to remedy an anti-competitive practice qualified as such by a court.

Chapter 8. Duration of Protection

565. The patent right is temporary: it is effective between the date of coming into force and the date of termination.

§1. Date of Coming into Force of Patent Rights

566. The exclusive right of the patent takes effect as from the filing date. As from this date, the applicant may bring actions against infringers. However, until the grant of the patent, the right is weakened, since the applicant may not obtain a judgment against third parties: the tribunal must suspend its proceedings until the INPI's decision.

567. Unauthorized acts by third parties done prior to the grant are illicit only if they follow the publication of the application, or a notification to the infringer of a certified copy of the application (such copies are not delivered by the INPI until the end of the inspection by the Ministry of Defence: *see supra*, paragraph 432). In any case, the tribunal must suspend the proceedings until the grant of the patent (Article L. 615-4, §3).

§2. Date of Termination of Patent Rights

I. Total Termination of Rights

568. Normal termination occurs at the expiration of the legal duration of each category of titles:

- patents expire twenty years after the filing date;
- certificates of utility expire six years after the filing date;
- supplementary protection certificates for medicinal products or for phytopharmaceutical products[351] take effect on the termination date of the patent which they supplement for a duration equal to the time elapsed between the date of filing of the patent application and the date of the first authorization to market the product within the EU (or European Economic Area), reduced by a period of five years. Notwithstanding, the duration of the certificate may not exceed five years from the date on which it takes effect.

569. Anticipated termination may occur in case of non-payment of the renewal fees by the patent owner (Article L. 612-19). Renewal fees are due for any industrial property title. The first one is to be paid on the filing date; the following ones are due on the last day of the anniversary month of the filing date (Article R. 613-46). Their amount is graduated (from EUR 36 for the first year to EUR 760 for the twentieth).

351. EC Regulation No. 1610/96 of 23 Jul. 1996: OJEC, No. L. 198, 8 Aug. 1996; EC Regulation No. 469/2009 of 6 May 2009: OJEC, No. L. 152, 1, 16 Jun. 2009.

Natural persons, small- or medium-sized businesses, non-profit institution of the teaching or research sector may benefit from reduced fees (Article L. 612-20). The right for reduction shall be acquired on simple declaration. All misrepresentation shall be recorded, at any time and at the end of an adversary proceeding, by a decision of the director of the National Institute of Industrial Property under the conditions provided for in Article L. 411-4. This decision shall be accompanied by an administrative fine whose amount may not exceed ten times the amount of the fees due and the proceeds shall be handed over to the National Institute of Industrial Property.

570. The sanction of non-payment consists of the forfeiture of the patent (L. 613-22), the patentee being presumed in such a case to abandon his right. However, several rules aim at preventing such a sanction.

571. Where the payment of an annual fee is not made by the normal due date, a reminder shall be addressed to the owner of the patent application or the patent advising him that he is liable to lose his rights if the payment, accompanied by payment of the fee for late payment, is not made before the expiry of a six-month period (Articles L. 612-19 and R. 613-47, R. 613-48). The lack of a reminder shall not imply the liability of the INPI and shall not constitute grounds for restoring the rights of the patent owner. In case of non-payment, forfeiture is established by the Director General of the INPI, or at the request of the patentee, or of a third party (Article L. 613-22 and R. 613-49). The forfeiture is notified to the patentee (R. 613-49) and published in the National Register of Patents (R. 613-50). The right is terminated as from the falling date of the unpaid fee (Article L. 613-22).

572. The forfeited patent owner may still appeal for restoration in his rights. The appeal is to be addressed to the Director of the INPI and be motivated by a 'legitimate excuse' of the non-payment (e.g., the representative's error or a computer failure, etc.), within two months of the hindrance ceasing to exist. The appeal shall only be admissible within a period of one year from expiry of the time limit not complied with (Article L. 612-16). Restoration shall be granted by the Director of the INPI on condition that the annual fee or fees be paid. A decision refusing the restoration may be appealed against in the 'Cour d'Appel' of Paris (Article R. 411-19 and R. 411-20).

573. Restoration cancels the forfeiture of the patent as from the date of the unpaid renewal fee.

574. When a French patent covers an invention for which a European patent was granted to the same person, the French patent ceases to produce effect either at the expiration of the opposition time limitation, or at the end of such a procedure (Article L. 614-13).[352]

II. Partial Termination of Rights (Exhaustion)

575. The statute of 13 July 1978 introduced into French law the rule of exhaustion of patent rights (Article L. 613-6). The patent owner may not enforce his exclusive right as for products which he marketed or agreed to be marketed either in France or

352. Cass. com., 17 Oct. 1995: PIBD 1996, III, 32; RTD com. 1996, 267, obs. Azéma. – Paris, 2 Jul. 2010: PIBD 2010, III, 730.

in a Member State of the European Economic Area. Such products circulate freely in this Space.

576. Consequently, he may only control the circulation of products marketed without his consent: infringing products,[353] or products marketed (even with his consent) outside the EEA as long as he did not agree to their introduction into the European space.[354]

353. Paris, 21 Jan. 1993: PIBD 1993, III, 314.
354. Paris, 17 Jan. 1996: PIBD 1996, III, 178.

Chapter 9. Infringement and Remedies

577. Whereas the sanctions of infringement were strengthened, third parties' interests are protected by an action for 'declaration of non-infringement'.

§1. Action for Declaration of Non-infringement

578. This preventive action was introduced by the Act of 27 June 1984 (Article L. 615-9). It is open to any person who works or prepares for working an invention on the territory of a Member State of the EU.

579. During the first stage, the interested party must invite the patent owner to take position as to the infringing character of the exploitation. If no answer is given within three months, or if he questions the answer, the petitioner may bring an action in the First Instance Court (Tribunal de grande instance) of Paris, competent for patent matters, requesting a decision stating that his exploitation is not infringing the defendant's patent, without prejudice to any proceedings for the nullity of the patent or subsequent infringement proceedings if the working is not carried out in accordance with the conditions specified.

580. If the action is dismissed, the petitioner is not for all that an infringer. If the action is well-grounded, the petitioner may not be sued for infringement as for this specific exploitation.

§2. Action for Infringement

581. This action, which allows the patentee to enforce his exclusive right, is subject to specific procedural rules as for its starting, development, and outcome.

I. The Starting of the Action

582. The person entitled to bring an action for infringement is in principle the patentee (for joint owners: *see supra*, paragraph 470). A licensee may act only when the following conditions are fulfilled:

- the licence is exclusive;
- the licence agreement does not provide for a clause whereby the licensee may not bring such action;
- the licensee has unsuccessfully summoned the patentee to act against the infringer;
- the licence was entered into the National Registry of Patents.

The holder of a compulsory licence may bring an infringement action if, after a formal notice, the owner of the patent does not institute such proceedings (Article L. 615-2, §4).

583. Since the Decree No. 2008-624 of 27 June 2008, jurisdiction for civil actions belongs exclusively to the First Instance Court ('Tribunal de grande instance') of Paris (Article D. 631-2). Jurisdiction for criminal actions belongs to the criminal Court of First Instance ('Tribunal correctionnel') designated under the ordinary rules of procedure. Actions for unfair competition connected to the action for infringement are brought in the same court (Article L. 615-17). Where an invention which is the subject of a patent application or of a patent is worked, in order to meet the requirements of national defence, by the State or its suppliers, subcontractors, and subsidiary suppliers, without a licence having been afforded to them, the civil proceedings shall be brought before the 'Tribunal de Grande Instance' sitting in chambers (Article L. 615-10, §1).

584. Article L. 615-17 §2 states that the above rules of jurisdiction do not exclude arbitration. However, patent matters may be arbitrated following the conditions of Articles 2059 and 2060 of the Civil Code, which prohibit arbitration in matters interesting public order. It is thought that infringement affects only private interests and is, therefore, arbitrable.

585. The judicial action for infringement is admissible if the plaintiff brings justification that his right is demurrable to third parties (Article L. 615-4). In the case of infringement proceedings instituted on the basis of an application for a utility certificate, the plaintiff shall be required to produce a search report drawn up under the same conditions as the report provided for in Article L612-14 (Article L. 615-6). When the action is based on a European patent for France, the holder may exercise his rights as from the date of the publication of the European patent application, on condition a translation of the claims in French language was published by the INPI (Article L. 614-9).

586. The action may be brought within five years from each illicit act of exploitation of the patent (Article L. 615-8).

II. The Development of the Action

587. The tribunal follows its ordinary rules of procedure. It must, however, suspend the proceedings until the grant of the patent (Article L. 615-4, §2).

A. The Plaintiff's Arguments

588. The plaintiff has to evidence that the technique worked by the defendant is similar to the one protected by his patent.

1. Determination of the Protected Technique

589. The scope of the invention protected by the exclusive right is determined by the patent claims, interpreted in the light of the description and the drawings (Article L. 613-2). If the claims were extended after the date of publication of the application or of the notification of a copy to the infringer, such extensions are not demurrable to third parties (Article L. 615-4).

2. Determination of the Infringing Technique

590. This determination may be made by all means of evidence: witnesses, presumptions, etc. However, the law organizes a specific procedure of counterfeit-seizure ('saisie-contrefaçon') designed to facilitate the proof of infringement (Articles L. 615-5 and R. 615-2 et seq.). Even if the counterfeit-seizure is very common in practice, it is not a compulsory procedure. That is the reason why the Act no. 2014-315 of 11 March 2014 added Article L. 615-5-1-1 to precise that a court may order, on its own initiative or at the request of any person having quality, all legally admissible investigative measures, even if a counterfeit-seizure has not previously been ordered. However, given the energetic character of this procedure, several safeguards are provided for.

591. The plaintiff must first request the authorization to seize from the President of the 'Tribunal de grande instance' of Paris. The judge may not refuse the authorization, but only define its scope and order the payment of a warranty. The judge may condition the implementation of the measures it ordered to the furnishing by the claimant of security to ensure, if necessary, the defendant's compensation if the infringement action is subsequently held unfounded or the seizure is cancelled (L. 615-5, §4). However, when an invention which is the subject of a patent application or of a patent is worked, in order to meet the requirements of national defence, by the State or its suppliers, subcontractors and subsidiary suppliers, without a licence having been afforded to them, and where the President of the Court orders an expert opinion or a description with or without effective seizure, as provided for in Article L. 615-5, the appointed law officer shall refrain from proceeding with seizure, description and any investigation into the archives and documents of the business if the contract for research or manufacture comprises a defence security classification (Article L. 615-10, §2). The same shall apply to research or manufacture carried out in military establishments (Article L. 615-10, §3). The President of the first instance court may, if so requested by the entitled person, require an expert opinion which may only be carried out by persons authorized by the Minister responsible for defence and in the presence of his representatives (Article L. 615-10, §4).

592. The seizure is executed by a bailiff who may be assisted by an expert and a police officer if necessary. He may proceed in any place with either the detailed description, with or without taking samples, or the effective seizure of the allegedly infringing articles or processes as well as any related document, according to what was authorized by the president. The order may authorize the effective seizure of any document relating to the allegedly infringing goods or processes, even in the absence of the latter. The court shall also order, for the same evidential purposes, the detailed description or effective seizure of equipment and tools used to manufacture or distribute the goods or to implement the allegedly infringing processes. The bailiff drafts a report which must be delivered to the defendant. An irregular seizure may be declared invalid and the plaintiff sentenced to pay damages to the defendant.[355]

355. Cass. com., 19 May 1987: PIBD 1987, III, 485.- However, the automatic nullity affects only the real seizure of products and not the description made by the process-server: Paris, 13 Oct. 2000: PIBD 2001, III, 166; RTD com. 2001, 692, obs. Azéma and Galloux.- 14 Jun. 2002: PIBD 2002, III, 464.

593. The seizure must be followed by the introduction of the action for infringement – either a civil or criminal action – within twenty working days or thirty-one civil days if this time limit is longer, as from the date of the report of seizure. If not, the entire seizure, including the description, shall be void upon the defendant's request, without its having to motivate its request and without prejudice to the damages which may be claimed. A void seizure may not be used as evidence during the proceedings.

594. And since the Act No. 2007-1544 of 29 October 2007, if so required, the court hearing civil proceedings relating to patent, shall order, under penalty of a daily fine if necessary, in order to determine the origin and the distribution networks of the infringing goods or processes which prejudice the claimant's rights, the communication of any document or information held by the defendant or by any person who was found in possession of infringing goods or goods implementing the infringing processes or who provides services used in infringing activities or was reported to take part to the production, manufacturing, or distribution of such products, the implementation of such processes, or the supply of such services ('Right of information'). The communication of documents or information shall be ordered if there is no legitimate hindrance (Article L. 615-5-2).

595. The plaintiff may request that the customs administration withholds the suspect goods; an ex officio withholding is also possible (Article L. 614-32–L. 614-39, created by the Act No. 2014-315 of 11 March 2014). The conditions are here similar to those applicable to trademarks (*see infra*, paragraph 846).

3. Comparisons Between the Protected and the Infringing Techniques

596. The patent is infringed when the technique worked by the defendant is similar to the protected one in its essential elements. Infringement may consist of the working of an invention technically equivalent to the one covered by the patent.[356]

B. The Defendant's Arguments

597. The defendant may question either the existence of the infringement and/or the efficacy of the plaintiff's patent right.

598. The defendant may show that his working of the invention is not infringing the plaintiff's patent because the technique is different.[357] When the patent covers a process for the obtaining of a product, the tribunal may order the defendant to show that the process he used to obtain an identical product is different from the patented one. Where the defendant fails to provide such proof, any identical product manufactured without the consent of the owner of the patent shall be presumed to have been manufactured by the patented process in the following two cases: (a) the product manufactured using the patented process is new; (b) there is a strong probability that the identical product has been manufactured using the patented process, but the owner of the patent has been unable, in spite of reasonable effort, to establish what process has in fact been used. In the production of proof to the contrary, due regard shall be

356. Cass. com., 18 Oct. 1994: PIBD 1995, III, 3.

357. An invention the structure of which is different is nevertheless infringing if the function of the structural elements is identical: Cass. com., 13 Jun. 1995: PIBD 1995, III, 392.

had to the legitimate interests of the defendant regarding the protection of his manufacturing and trade secrets. (Article L. 615-5-1).

599. The defendant may argue that he was authorized (either by law or by the patentee) to work the patent. He may also evidence his good faith when bad faith is required to qualify an infringement (*supra*, paragraphs 462 et seq.).

600. The defendant may also argue that the patent was inefficient at the time when he worked the invention (e.g., the patent rights were expired, exhausted, or forfeited).

601. The most frequent defence consists of questioning the validity of the patent. Such an argument is highly efficient, since an invalidated patent is deemed to have never existed and, therefore, may not have been infringed.

602. The grounds for revocation of a patent are listed under Article L. 613-25:

- if its subject matter is not patentable;
- if it does not disclose the invention in a manner sufficiently clear and complete for it to be carried out by a person skilled in the art;
- if its subject matter extends beyond the content of the patent application as filed;
- where the patent was granted on a divisional application, if its subject matter extends beyond the content of the earlier application as filed;
- if, after a limitation of the claims, the scope of protection of the patent has been increased.

A European patent for France may be declared invalid by a French court on one of the grounds listed under Article 138, §1 of the EPC 2000 (Article L. 614-12).

603. If the grounds for revocation affect only a part of the patent, the court may pronounce only a partial nullity, in the form of limitation of the claims (Article L. 613-25, §2). In case of partial revocation, the court may send the patentee back to the INPI with the duty to draft a new version of the claims (Article L. 613-27, § 3). When the patent contains several claims, the validity of the main claim entails the validity of dependant claims.[358] The contrary rule is not admitted: in case of revocation of the main claim, it is necessary to check the validity of each dependant claim.[359]

604. The final judgment of revocation is published in the National Register of Patents and as from that date produces an absolute *erga omnes* effect (Article L. 613-27, §1).

III. The Outcome of the Action

605. Upon action for infringement, a court may either issue a temporary injunction, or dismiss the action, or order sanctions for infringement.

358. Cass. com., 12 Dec. 1995: JCP ed. E 1995 II 844, note Mousseron and Hagel.
359. Paris, 25 May 1989: PIBD 1989, III, 467. – TGI Paris, 12 Mar. 2004: Propr. industr. 2004, comm. 77, obs. P. Vigand. – Cass. com., 6 May 2008: Propr. intell. October 2008, p. 473, obs. B. Warusfel. – Cass. com., 9 Jul. 2013: PIBD 2013, III, 1416. – Cass. com., 20 May 2014: PIBD 2014, III, 585.

A. Temporary Injunction (Article L. 615-3)

606. Before the court decides on the merits of the action, any person with authority to bring an action for infringement may, in preliminary proceedings on grounds of pressing urgency, request the competent civil court ('Tribunal de grande instance' of Paris) to order, under a penalty of a daily fine if necessary, against the alleged infringer or intermediaries whose services it uses, any measure aimed at preventing an infringement about to be committed against rights conferred by the title or aimed at stopping any further allegedly infringing act. The competent civil court may also order ex parte urgent measures when the circumstances require that such measures should not be taken in the presence of both parties, in particular when any delay would be likely to cause an irreparable damage to the claimant. The court, in preliminary or ex parte proceedings, may order the requested measures only if evidence, reasonably accessible to the claimant, make it likely that its rights are infringed or that such infringement is about to be committed. The court may enjoin the carrying out of the allegedly infringing acts, condition it on the furnishing of security to ensure, if necessary, the claimant's compensation or may order the seizure or the remittance to a third person of the products allegedly infringing the rights conferred by the title, to prevent their introduction or circulation in the channels of commerce. If the claimant can give reasons that circumstances are likely to compromise the payment of damages, the court shall order the sequestration of the alleged infringer's movable or immovable assets, including the freezing of the bank accounts and other assets, under the general rules of law. To determine the goods likely to be seized, the court may order the submission of banking, financial, accounting, or commercial documents or the access to relevant data. The court may also award an advance payment to the claimant when the damage suffered cannot be seriously disputed. The court, in preliminary or ex parte proceedings, may condition the implementation of the measures it has ordered on the furnishing of security by the claimant to ensure, if necessary, the claimant's compensation if the infringement proceedings are subsequently held unfounded or if the measures are void. When the measures taken to stop the infringement of rights are ordered before the commencement of proceedings on the merits, the claimant shall institute legal proceedings, either by civil action or criminal action, within a period of time set by regulation. Failing that, upon the defendant's request and without its having to justify its application, the measures ordered are void, without prejudice to the damages which may be claimed.

B. Dismissal of the Action

607. In this case, no sanction for infringement may be ordered. The plaintiff may be liable for damages towards the defendant, if he misused his right to sue. Such a liability is seldom accepted by the courts.[360] Most often, damages are refused because the plaintiff was in good faith mistaken as to the scope of his rights.[361]

360. For example, Cass. com., 19 Jan. 1993: PIBD 1993, III, 252: patent taken only in view of threatening a competitor. – Cass. com., 3 Jun. 2003 : PIBD 2003, III, 437. –Paris, 18 Oct. 2013 : PIBD 2014, III, p. 1. – Paris, 7 May 2014, No. 12/02428. – TGI Paris, 5 Nov. 2015, No. 10/10178.
361. For example, Lyon, 11 May 1984: PIBD 1988, III, 298.

608. The dismissal of the action for infringement does not exclude the plaintiff's liability for unfair competition. Such a liability must be grounded on facts distinct from those which were argued as infringing the patent.[362]

C. *Success of the Action*

609. If the action is well-grounded, civil and/or criminal sanctions may be ordered against the defendant.

1. Civil Sanctions

610. Civil sanctions may consist of an injunction, recall, or definitive removal from channels of commerce, destruction, confiscation, publicity measure, and compensation ordered by the court.

611. An injunction to discontinue the working of the infringing technique is ordered by the court, at the plaintiff's request. Most often the injunction is supplemented by civil fines (e.g., an amount of money to be paid on any further infringing product). However, when an invention which is the subject of a patent application or of a patent is worked, in order to meet the requirements of national defence, by the State or its suppliers, subcontractors, and subsidiary suppliers, without a licence having been afforded to them, the Court may order neither the discontinuance nor the interruption of the working nor the confiscation provided for in Article L. 615-3 or in Article L. 615-7-1 (Article L. 615-10, §1)

612. Article L. 615-7-1 also provides that in the case of civil liability for infringement, the court may order, at the injured party's request, the recall from the channels of commerce, the definitive removal from such channels, the destruction and the confiscation, in favour of the injured party, of the products recognized as infringing and of the materials and implements principally used in their creation or their manufacturing. The court may also order any appropriate publicity measure of the judgment, in particular its display or its publication, in whole or in part, in such newspapers or over such in-line services of communication to the public it may designate, pursuant to the conditions it specifies. All the measures mentioned are ordered at the cost of the infringer.

613. The plaintiff may claim compensation of the damage he suffered as the consequence of the infringement. Since the Act No. 2007-1544 of 29 October 2007 and its revision by the Act No. 2014-315 of 11 March 2014, Article L. 615-7 states that 'To set the damages, the court takes into account separately: 1° the negative economic consequences of the rights infringement, including the loss of profit and loss suffered by the injured party; 2° the moral prejudice caused to the latter; 3° the profits made by the infringer, including economies of intellectual investments, material and promotional economies due to the infringement.'

614. The legislator's intention was to break with the old general rules of the Civil Code about torts and especially with the traditional rule that damages are covering all the loss suffered but only such loss. Because of this old rule, the profits made by

362. Paris, 9 Apr. 1992: PIBD 1992, III, 570: scheming in order to grab the plaintiff's commercial methods.- Cass. com., 8 Oct. 2002: PIBD 2002, III, 564, such a fault may consist of parasitism.

the infringer were of no relevance, so that the infringer, even paying damages, could still have interest to infringe. Thanks to the new rule of Article L. 615-7, it is now possible to award to the injured party a sum covering all his loss (economic or moral prejudice) but also a part of or all the profits made by the infringer because of the infringement. After a short time of hesitation, French courts now frequently use this possibility in order to repair and discourage intellectual property rights infringement.

615. The judges may also, if required by the injured party, use another method of evaluation of the indemnity to be paid by the infringer: it consists of a lump sum superior to the royalties amount which the infringer would have to pay to receive the rightholder's authorization. Article L. 615-7, §2 states 'The court, however, shall, as an alternative and upon request of the injured party, award as damages a lump sum. This sum is higher than the amount of royalties or fees which would have been due if the infringer had requested authorization to use the right which it has prejudiced. This sum is not exclusive of compensation for the moral prejudice caused to the injured party.'[363]

616. The basis on which the compensation is computed consists of the whole ensemble of infringing objects. It is evaluated taking into account the number and the market value of these objects. This ensemble also includes necessary accessories sold together with the infringing products.[364]

617. When the patentee worked the infringed patent (himself or through a licensee), the lost profits consist of the profits (after tax) which the patentee could have made in absence of infringement.[365]

618. When, on the contrary, the patent holder does not work the patent, lost profits are usually equal to the price the infringer should have paid to legally exploit the invention.

619. The loss suffered by the patentee consists usually of the damage exceeding the missed benefits, e.g., the depreciation of the patented product.

2. Criminal Sanctions

620. Criminal sanctions of infringement, which were suppressed by the Act of 13 July 1978, were reintroduced by the Act of 26 January 1990, strengthened by the Act of 5 February 1994, by the Act of 9 March 2004, by the Act of 29 October 2007 and again by the Act No. 2016-731 of 3 June 2016 (Article L. 615-14).

621. The person who knowingly infringed a patent may be sentenced to three years of imprisonment and a fine of EUR 300,000. Where the offence was committed by an organized criminal group or when the facts relate to goods dangerous for the health, the safety of man or animal, the penalties will be increased to a seven-year imprisonment and a fine of EUR 750,000. In case of relapse, or if the infringer is or was linked by contract (e.g., former employee) to the plaintiff, the sanctions are doubled.

363. Cass. com., 1 Mar. 1994: Bull. civ. IV, No. 84; D. 1996, som., p. 20, obs. Mousseron and Schmidt; RTD com. 1994, 495, obs. Azéma.

364. The so-called commercial ensemble: Cass. com., 23 May 1995: PIBD 1995, III, 341.- Cass. com., 23 May 1995: PIBD 1995, III, 341.

365. Paris, 28 Feb. 1989: Ann. propr. Ind. 1990, 133.- Paris, 18 Nov. 1997: PIBD 1998, III, 189.

Moreover, the tribunal may deprive the infringer from the right to vote and to be elected in professional elections (Article L. 615-14-1).

622. Natural persons liable for the offence provided for in Article L. 615-14 may also be ordered, at their cost, to remove from the channels of commerce the articles held infringing and any item which was used or intended for committing the offence (Article L. 615-14-2, §1). The court may order the destruction at the cost of the convicted person or the remittance to the injured party of the articles or items removed from the channels of commerce or confiscated, without prejudice to all damages (Article L. 615-14-2, §2). It may also order, at the cost of the convicted person, the display of the judgment or the dissemination of the judgment ordering the decision, pursuant to the conditions set out under Article 131-35 of the Penal Code (Article L. 615-14-2, §3).

623. According to Article L. 615-14-3, legal persons incurring criminal liability pursuant to the conditions set out under Article 121-2 of the Penal Code for the offence defined in Article L. 615-14 of this Code, incur the following: (1) a fine, pursuant to the conditions set out under Article 131-38 of the Penal Code; (2) the penalties set out under Article 131-39 of that Code (*see supra,* paragraph 106). The legal persons incurring criminal liability may also be ordered, at their cost, to remove from the channels of commerce the articles held infringing and any other item which was used or intended for committing the offence. The court may order the destruction at the cost of the convicted person or the remittance to the injured party of the articles or items removed from the channel of commerce or confiscated, without prejudice to the damages.

Chapter 10. Relation to Other Intellectual Property Rights

624. A risk of overlapping exists between the patent protection and the protection by the registration of designs and models, when such creations involve both technical and aesthetic elements. The solution of such conflicts is provided for in Article L. 511-8, 1° (*see infra*, paragraph 954).

Part III. Utility Models

625. Some legislations provide for a protection of utility models, in the sense of 'petty patents', designed to cover inventions whose merit and/or technical importance are lower than those required for patent protection. Such is the case for instance, as for the German 'Gebrauchmüster'.

626. Such titles are unknown in French law. The 'certificate of utility' ('certificat d'utilité') is subject to the ordinary rules of patentability, but the duration of the protection is shorter than the patent one.

Chapter 1. Sources and Legislation Relating to 'Certificates of Utility'

§1. Substantive Conditions of Protection

627. The possessor of a technical invention has the choice between a patent and a certificate of utility. The substantial conditions required are identical for both. From this point of view, French law does not provide for any specific rule as for the certificates of utility.

§2. Formal Conditions of Protection

628. At the time of the filing of the application, the applicant must chose the title of protection (*see supra*, paragraph 403). Certificates of utility are excluded for medicine. If he chooses a patent, he may convert his patent application into an application for a utility certificate at any time until the grant of the title (Article L. 612-15). The contrary transformation is impossible.

629. The search procedure (Article L. 612-14) does not apply as for certificates of utility (Article L. 611-2, §2). The remaining aspects of the grant procedure are identical for patents and certificates of utility.

Chapter 2. The Protection of Utility Models

630. The scope of protection is identical to patent rights. The duration is the only difference: the certificate of utility protects the invention during six years from the filing date (Article L. 611-2, 2°). When bringing an action for infringement, the owner must produce a search report (Article L. 615-6), since certificates of utility are granted without an automatic search procedure.

Part IV. Trademarks

631. A trademark consists of a sign placed on a product or accompanying a service and designed to show the industrial or commercial origin of these goods or services. In French law, the trademark is not a warranty of quality: a producer may sell under the same mark products of different quality. Frauds on quality are sanctioned under consumer protection rules, but not under industrial property law. A trademark may be a reference to the quality only in an indirect way, since the public sometimes associates the mark with the reputation of the product or service. This phenomenon is amplified for well-known marks (e.g., *Swatch, IBM, Sofitel*, *Dior*, etc.).

632. In 2015, the INPI received 91,898 applications for registration under the national procedure.

Chapter 1. Sources: Legislation

633. The modern French trademark law dates back to the Act of 23 June 1857, which remained in force for over one century, until the statute of 31 December 1964, modified by those of 23 June 1965, and 30 June 1975. This last statute was abrogated by the Act of 4 January 1991. As for the other intellectual property rights, all the applicable texts are today collected in the Intellectual Property Code: Articles L. 711-1–L. 717-7 and Articles R. 712-1–R. 718-4 are devoted to trademarks.

634. To these national sources, the EU rules as well as the international conventions ratified by France must be added.

635. The EU trademark[366] granted by the European Union Intellectual Property Office (EUIPO) in Alicante, Spain, automatically covers France and is subject to the provisions of the EC Regulation No. 207/2009.

636. France ratified the Madrid Agreement of 14 April 1891 on the international registration of trademarks (as revised in Stockholm on 14 July 1967, entered into force on 12 August 1975), and its Protocol signed at Madrid on 28 June 1989 (in force since 7 November 1997); the Nice Agreement of 15 June 1957 on the international classification of products and services in view of the registration of trademarks (as amended in Geneva on 13 May 1977, entered into force on 22 April 1980).

366. EC Regulation No. 207/2009 of 26 Feb. 2009 on the Community trademark (codified version) (OJEC, No. L. 78, 24 Mar. 2009), which replaces EC Regulation No. 40/94 of 20 Dec. 1993 of the Council on the Community trademark (OJEC, No. L. 11, 14 Jan. 1994).

Chapter 2. Subject Matter of Protection

637. Article L. 711-1, §1 defines the mark in the following terms: 'A trade, commerce or service mark is a sign capable of a graphic representation which serves to distinguish goods or services of a natural or legal person.'

638. Article L. 711-3 lists categories of signs which may not serve as marks. Finally, the 'collective trademarks' are a specific category, subject to some special rules.

§1. Signs Which May Not Serve as Trademarks

639. Article L. 711-3 lists four categories of signs which may not be protected as trademarks in France:

- Signs excluded under Article *6ter* of the Paris Convention of 1883 for the Protection of Industrial Property. This text lists the following signs: armorial bearings, flags, and other official emblems of Member States of the Paris Convention; signs and official hallmarks of control and warranty used by these States as well as any imitation thereof.
- Signs listed under Article 23, §2 of the TRIPs Agreement: signs which contain or consist of a geographical indication identifying wines or spirits may not be registered as trademarks for wines or spirits not having this origin.
- Signs liable to mislead the public, particularly as regards the nature, quality, or geographical origin of the goods or services. The deceiving character is evaluated by comparing the sign with the products or services to which it is applied: a mark may be deceiving for some goods, not for others. For example, the following marks were invalidated as deceiving: 'Ritzlinger' referring to wines, which may be confused with Riesling, a famous appellation of origin of wines from the Alsace region;[367] 'Evian' applied to syrups, when the consumer may believe that this beverage contains Evian mineral water;[368] 'Tele Europe Satellite 1 ', which may imply an official European control and warranty of quality,[369] etc. On the contrary, 'Ceramiflex' for a product which is not made out of ceramics;[370] 'Miel Epil' for a depilatory cream without honey,[371] etc. were not held as deceiving.
- Signs contrary to public order and morality or whose use is prohibited by law. It has been decided that the French part of an international trademark registration (Madrid Agreement of 1891) should be evaluated according to the French notion of public order, and not to the one of the country of origin.[372] The interpretation of the notion of public order and morality comes under the discretionary power

367. Cass. com., 3 May 1984: Ann. propr. Ind. 1984, 22.
368. Cass. com., 17 Jan. 1984: Ann. propr. Ind. 1985, 23.
369. Paris, 25 Jan. 1989: Ann. propr. Ind. 1990, 155.
370. Paris, 23 Sep. 1991: PIBD 1992, III, 40.
371. Cass. com., 27 Nov. 1963: Ann. propr. Ind. 1964, 136.
372. Paris, 22 Apr. 1986: Ann. propr. Ind. 1987, 31.

of lower judges.[373] Public order includes mandatory rules of the economic legislation and consumer protection.[374] The compliance with public order is to be evaluated as for the sign itself, not the product or service designed by the sign.[375] For instance, the trademark 'Vins de femme' ('Womens' Wines') which is contrary to the French and EU vines and spirit regulations was held contrary to public order.[376] On the contrary, the trademark '*Opium*' registered for a perfume is not contrary to public order.[377]

640. Article L. 711-3, b) mentions signs whose use is prohibited by law. Specific French statutes forbid such use in several cases:

- French and foreign decorations, such as the Legion of Honour (Circ. 23 June 1979).
- The Olympic emblem and motto.[378]
- The name of a plant variety mentioned on its title of protection (Article L. 623-15, §6, IP Code).
- Foreign terms may not be used as trademarks by French public legal persons or persons in charge of a mission of public service 'when an appropriate term exists in the French language'.[379]

§2. Signs Which May Serve as Trademarks

641. After providing for a definition of the trademark, Article L. 711-1 gives examples of three categories of signs which may serve as marks: denominations, audible signs, and figurative signs.

I. Denominations

642. Verbal marks constitute 80% of registered French marks. Any word may serve as a mark; Article L. 711-1 cites the following examples: words, combinations of words, surnames and geographical names, pseudonyms, letters, numerals, acronyms.

A. Current Words

643. A word in its current use may be registered as a trademark; it does not have to be new or original. It is enough that the meaning of the word is arbitrary when

373. Cass. com., 28 Jun. 1976: Bull. civ. IV, No. 217.
374. Paris, 15 Feb. 1990: PIBD 1990, III, 489.
375. Lyon, 27 Jun. 1984: Ann. propr. Ind. 1985, 149; PIBD 1985, III, 39.
376. Paris, 5 May 1988: Ann. propr. Ind. 1989, 257.
377. Paris, 7 May 1979: Ann. propr. Ind. 1979, 306, obs. Chavanne; it was argued that this mark encouraged consumption of drugs.
378. Article L. 141-5 of the French Sport Code.
379. Act No. 94-665 of 4 Aug. 1994, JORF 5 Aug. 1994, pp. 11393–11394, Art. 14.

applied to the product or service it designates.[380] A mark may consist of one or several words ('Culotte Petit Bateau', 'Savon Le Chat', etc.).

B. *Fantasy Words*

644. A mark may consist of fantasy words,[381] known or intended (Végétaline, Bichoco), slogans ('Omo lave plus blanc'), French or foreign terms ('*Breakfast*' to designate biscuits).

C. *Letters, Numerals, Acronyms*

645. French courts held valid numerous of such trademarks: *Nr 5* and *Nr 9* for perfumes by Chanel,[382] Pastis 51 for an aperitif,[383] etc. An acronym consists of a succession of initials of a complex name (*IBM, SVP*), etc.

D. *Surnames and Pseudonyms*

646. A personal name may be registered as such: it may be trademark owner's name or a third person's name (with his consent[384]).

1. The Trademark Owner's Name

647. A natural person may register his name or first name[385] or pseudonym.[386] A legal person may register its corporate name (*IBM*, Galeries Lafayette).

648. Conflicts may arise with homonyms. Article L. 713-6, a) provides rules for solution of such conflicts. The homonym may use his name as a corporate name, trade name, or shop sign, if he began such a use prior to the registration of this name as a trademark by a third person; he may also use in good faith his personal name.[387] However, if such a use violates the trademark rights, the owner may request that the homonym stops or limits the use of his name.

649. In fact the trademark owner may suffer a loss when the public is likely to confuse his products or services with the firm using the homonym. The conflict is

380. Paris, 27 Nov. 1991: PIBD 1992, III, 201.
381. Cass. com., 4 Oct. 1988: PIBD 1989, III, 113 'Cotonelle'. – TGI Paris, 13 Jan. 1986: PIBD 1986, III, 273, 'Biotherm'. – Paris, 1 Jun. 2005: D. 2005, p. 2467, note J. Passa; RTD com. 2005, p. 715, obs. J. Azéma, Cass. com., 10 Jul. 2007: PIBD 2007, III, 562, 'Nutri-rich'.
382. Cass. com., 16 May 1984: Ann. propr. Ind. 1984, 27.
383. Cass. com., 7 Oct. 1980: PIBD 1981, III, 7.
384. The use of the pseudonym of a third person, without his consent, is prohibited: Cass. civ. 1, 19 Feb. 1975, 'Lova Moor'. – Paris, 10 Jan. 2003: Propr. industr., 2013, comm. 60. – Cass. com., 25 Apr. 2006: PIBD 2006, III, 471.
385. Paris, 1 Jun. 1970: Ann. propr. Ind. 1891, 84: '*Bettina*' for textiles.
386. Cass. civ., 23 Feb. 1965: Ann. propr. Ind. 1967, 333.
387. Paris, 11 Oct. 1995: PIBD 1996, III, 122; the homonym is the effective manager of the corporation which uses his name.

frequently solved by ordering a limitation or precision to be brought to the use of the homonym, such as the addition of the first name.[388]

2. A Third Person's Name

650. A person may authorize another party to register his name as a trademark.[389] The transferor may no longer then use his name for commercial purposes in the same economic area.[390] Lacking such an authorization, the only question is to know whether the third person's name may be considered as available to be registered as trademark (*see infra* paragraphs 694 et seq.).

E. Geographical Names

651. A geographical name (country, province, region, or town), even well-known, may serve as trademark, if it is arbitrary when applied to goods or services it designates (e.g., 'Mont-Blanc' is a valid mark for desserts). Such a name must comply with the general rules of validity of trademarks: it must be vacant, not deceiving and distinguishing (*see infra,* paragraph 661). Third parties may continue to use the registered name in its ordinary function, to indicate an address or a location.[391]

II. Audible Signs

652. Article L. 711-1, b) cites 'audible signs, such as: sounds, musical sentences'. The application for registration of trademarks must include a graphic representation of such audible signs.

III. Figurative Signs

653. Article L. 711-1, c) cites as figurative signs which may serve as trademarks: 'figurative signs such as: drawings, labels, seals, selvages, reliefs, holograms, logos, synthesized images; shapes, especially those of the product or its packaging, or those characterizing a service: arrangements, combinations or shades of color'.

654. A trademark may consist of various flat shapes, either figurative (the shell of 'Shell'; effigy of Napoleon, etc.), or not (the red circle of 'Elf'). They may be placed on the goods as labels, seals, etc. Colours may serve as trademarks. They must be registered either as specific combinations of colours,[392] or as an individual colour, but

388. Cass. com., 9 Nov. 1987: Ann. propr. Ind. 1988, 159, case Leclerc. – Cass. com., 13 Jun. 1995: PIBD 1995, III, 398, Max Poilane case.
389. Cass. com., 12 Mar. 1985 and 25 Feb. 1990: Ann. propr. Ind. 1985, 3 and 1990, 3, notes by P. Mathély.
390. Paris, 7 Nov. 1979: Ann. propr. Ind. 1950, 183.
391. Cass. com., 17 May 1982: Ann. propr. Ind. 1983, 87; Baccarat.
392. Paris, 3 Mar. 1971: D. 1971, jur., p. 368. – Cass. com., 7 Dec. 1993: PIBD 1994, III, 179.

in a specific shape or[393] a specific shade.[394] A colour as such may not be a valid trademark.[395]

655. A product or a service may be identified by a plastic shape either independent or inherent to the marked object. The first category may be illustrated by the Tiger of Esso or the Bibendum of Michelin, or also by the packaging of a product if it is not usual or banal.[396] The shape characteristic of the product itself may be registered,[397] unless this shape gives to the product its essential value (Article L. 711-2, c) *see infra* paragraph 673).

§3. Collective Trademarks

656. The collective trademarks belong to a legal person who generally lets it to be used by its members under certain conditions of use. The listing for registration should include a 'regulation of use' of the trademark which defines the conditions of use and is a condition of validity of the collective trademark.[398]

657. Two categories of collective trademarks should be distinguished: 'ordinary' and 'certification'.

I. 'Ordinary Collective Trademarks'

658. Under Article L. 715-1, they may be used by any person who enforces the 'regulation of use' established by the owner. As for the rest, they are subject to the ordinary rules of trademark law.[399]

II. 'Collective Trademarks of Certification'

659. Under Article L. 715-1, they are applied to goods or services which present, especially as to their nature, properties or qualities, the characters listed in its 'regulation of use'. Such trademarks may be owned only by legal persons who are neither producers, nor importers or distributors of such products or services (Article L. 715-2, 1°). This trademark may be used by any person other than the owner, who complies with the regulation of use (Article L. 715-2, 3°).

393. Paris, 26 May 1910: Ann. propr. Ind. 1911, 5.
394. Paris, 1 Jul. 1952: Ann. propr. Ind. 1952, 161, note Dusolier.
395. Paris, 4 Feb. 1988: RTD com. 1988, obs. Chavanne; 'pale blue'.
396. Paris, 28 Oct. 1986: Ann. propr. Ind. 1988, 91.
397. Paris, 28 May 1962: Ann. propr. Ind. 1962, 196; the shape of a wafer.
398. A trademark may not be treated as a collective one if it was not registered as such and is not completed by a 'regulation of use': Aix-en-Provence, 24 Oct. 1974: Ann. propr. Ind. 1978, 48. Cass. com., 28 Jun. 1976: eod. loc.; RTD com. 1977, 737, obs. Chavanne and Azéma.- Cass. com., 29 Jun. 1999: PIBD 1999, III, 478.
399. TGI Bordeaux, 6 Sep. 1993: PIBD 1993, III, 718.

660. The collective trademark of certification may not be transferred, or pledged, or subject to any measure of enforcement. However, in case of termination of the legal person who owns it, the collective mark may be transferred to another legal person (Article L. 715-2, 4°).

Chapter 3. Conditions of Protection of Trademarks

661. In order to serve as a valid trademark, a sign must be distinguishing and vacant.

§1. The Sign Must Be Distinguishing

662. A sign is distinguishing when it is capable to distinguish products or services to which it is applied. The distinguishing character is evaluated in relation to goods or services at stake.[400] This character is not to be confused with originality or novelty: a known sign may be distinguishing in relation to certain goods or services.

663. The law provides for criteria of the distinguishing character and for the date of its evaluation.

I. Criteria of the Distinguishing Character

664. Article L. 711-2, §2 gives only negative criteria of the distinguishing character of a trademark: the sign must not consist of the common designation of the goods, or be descriptive, or consist of the shape of the product itself.

A. The Sign Must Not Consist of the Common Designation of the Object

665. The common denomination of a product or a service must be left accessible to all the producers or merchants as a normal way to designate their production. A sign is the common designation of an object when it is generic, necessary, or usual (Article L. 711-2, §2).

1. Generic or Necessary Signs

666. A sign is necessary when its use is dictated by the nature or the function of the object. For instance, the words 'Banquette-lit' (Box-bed') are the necessary designation of such type of bed and may not be registered as trademark for this specific piece of furniture.[401]

667. A sign is generic when it designates the category, kind, or type to which the object belongs. For instance, the words '*Ticket Restaurant*' designating tickets, vouchers, or tokens used to pay for restaurants services, are generic and usual.[402] But the words 'Pages jaunes' ('Yellow Pages') are neither necessary nor generic to designate

---

400. Cass. com., 4 Oct. 2011: PIBD 2011, III, 661. – Cass. com., 7 Jun. 2011: Propr. industr. 2011, comm. 73. – Cass. com., 11 Mar. 2003: JCP E 2003, 1434, No. 2. – Cass. com., 13 Mar. 2001: PIBD 2001, III, 309.

401. Paris, 26 Apr. 1956: Ann. propr. Ind. 1957, 190.

402. Paris, 9 Jul. 1980: PIBD 1981, III, 241.

telephone books;[403] the word 'Neurones' is not generic to identify computers and electronic systems.[404]

2. Usual Signs

668. A sign is usual when it is generally and currently used by the public to designate a given object.[405] For instance, the word 'Château' ('Castle'), generally used in French wine-growing regions for designation of best vineyards, is not a distinctive trademark for wines.[406] On the contrary '*Digital*' is not usual to designate computer software.[407]

669. The usual meaning of a word is evaluated either in the common French language, or in the professional language when the products or the services are offered to a professional public. For instance, the words 'Cardio Fitness' are used by sportsmen and may not serve as a distinguishing trademark for a method of cardio-training.[408]

670. Neologisms may be distinguishing trademarks, if they are remote enough from the initial word. For instance, 'Triscuit' is a valid trademark for foodstuffs, whereas 'Otomatic' is not distinguishing for mechanical devices. Foreign words are treated as neologisms; they are not distinguishing if the word is currently used and understood in France (e.g., '*Management*'), or if it is understood in its French translation (e.g., '*Supermint*' to designate products with mint).

671. A word which is generic or usual may become distinguishing when associated with another one.[409]

672. Terms from everyday language may be distinctive if they are arbitrary in relation to the goods or services to which they are applied. For instance, the words 'Hippo' and 'Hippopotamus' are distinguishing of restaurants where hippopotamus meat is not served.[410]

B. The Sign Must Not Consist of the Necessary or Essential Shape of the Product

673. Under Article L. 711-2, c), are devoid of distinguishing character: 'The signs consisting exclusively of the shape dictated by the nature or the function of the product, or which gives its substantial value to the product.' For instance, the shape of a sports shoe designed to protect the Achille's heel[411] is not distinguishing, or the shape necessary to obtain a technical result which was protected by an expired patent.[412]

---

403. Paris, 27 May 1992: D. 1992, I.R., p. 240.
404. Cass. com., 30 Jun. 1998: PIBD 1998, III, 434.
405. Cass. com., 18 Oct. 1994: PIBD 1995, III, 39.
406. Paris, 5 Jun. 1991: PIBD 1991, III, 690.
407. TGI Paris, 13 Jan. 1993: PIBD 1993, III, 364.
408. TGI Paris, 28 Oct. 1988: PIBD 1989, III, 145.
409. Cass. com., 7 Dec. 1983: Bull. civ. IV, No. 342.
410. Paris, 9 Mar. 1987: Ann. propr. Ind. 1988, 261.
411. TGI Paris, 30 Apr. 1987: PIBD 1987, III, 450, Adidas case. – Cass. com., 3 Jan. 1996: RTD com. 1997, 248, obs. Azéma. Paris, 7 Feb. 1996: PIBD 1996, III, 345.
412. Cass. com., 19 Nov. 1991: PIBD 1992, III, 226.

II. Date of Evaluation of the Distinguishing Character

674. As all the conditions of validity of a trademark, the distinguishing character is to be evidenced at the date of application for registration. However, according to Article L. 711-2, §3 (which enforces Article 6*quinquies*, c) of the Paris Convention of 1883), a trademark may become distinguishing following the use which was made of it. This rule does not apply to trademarks which consist of the necessary or substantial shape of the product (*see supra,* paragraph 649). For instance, the words 'Camping Gaz', which were not distinguishing of this product (gas for camping) at the date of application for registration, became distinguishing later, as a consequence of a long use.[413] But a long use may not validate a mark which is void for another reason than the lack of distinguishing character.[414]

§2. The Sign Must Be Vacant

675. The sign chosen as trademark must not have been earlier appropriated by a third person. Article L. 711-4 lists eight examples of conflicts between a trademark and an earlier exclusive right.

I. Conflict with an Earlier Trademark (Article L. 711-4 a)

676. A sign is unavailable for registration as trademark if it was earlier appropriated by a third person as trademark for the same or similar goods or services. Exceptionally, well-known trademarks occupy an even wider area of activity.

677. A sign is unavailable to serve as a trademark when it was earlier appropriated as trademark for the same or similar goods or services on the French territory. Such an earlier trademark may have been registered under French law (or appropriated by use under the Act of 1857 and later registered under the Act of 1964), or under the Madrid Agreement of 1891 on the International Registration of Marks; it may also consist of the Community trademark, which automatically covers France. But the same sign may be registered for other products or services. In order 'to evaluate' similarity of goods and services, the courts take into account their use and image.[415]

678. As a consequence of the principle of territoriality of trademarks, a sign is appropriated only for the territory of the state which granted the right: it is free abroad. Only the Community trademark is an exception, where the protected territory is the one of the EU.

679. An extended protection of well-known trademarks is provided for by Article 6*bis* of the Paris Convention of 1883 (text of 1967), which only mentions 'a mark

413. Paris, 23 Jun. 1981: D. 1982, jur., p. 484, note Rebove; RTD com. 1983, 77, obs. Chavanne and Azéma.
414. Paris, 7 Nov. 1994: PIBD 1995, III, 69.
415. Cass. com., 13 Oct. 1992: PIBD 1993, III, 93; 'Visa' may not be registered for credit cards and advertising. -Versailles, 16 Apr. 1992: PIBD 1992, III, 395; 'A fond la forme' may not designate a fitness institute and sports goods.

considered by the competent authority of the country of registration or use to be well known in that country as being already the mark of a person entitled to the benefits of this Convention'. The TRIPS Agreement (Article 16.2) provides for more precise criterias of notoriety: 'determining whether a trademark is well-known, Members shall take account of the knowledge of the trademark in the relevant sector of the public, including knowledge in the Member concerned which has been obtained as a result of the promotion of the trademark'.

680. Such well-known marks are subject to the principle of specialty,[416] but their scope of protection is wider than that of the ordinary trademarks, because they are exposed to an increased risk of imitation and parasitism. Consequently, a well-known mark may make the sign unavailable to third persons even as for other goods and services. The scope of this extended protection is defined in a more precise way by the TRIPS Agreement (Article 16.3). The protection may apply to goods or services which are not similar to those in respect of which a trademark is registered, provided that use of that trademark in relation to those goods or services would indicate a connection between those goods or services and the owner of the registered trademark and provided that the interests of the owner of the registered trademark are likely to be damaged by such.

681. Some examples of conflicts solved by the French courts may be cited: 'Waterman', well-known for pens, may not be registered for razors;[417] and 'Château Yquem' well-known for wines may forbid 'Yquem' for watches.[418] But the extended protection does not apply if the goods or services are too remote: 'Chanel', well-known for luxury goods, may not forbid 'Chanel' for alcoholic beverages;[419] and '*Coca Cola*' may not block '*Coca*' for perfumes.[420] Sometimes, the courts order a delimitation of the respective trademarks: 'Mazda' well-known for electric products, may be registered for cars as '*Mazda Automobiles*'.[421]

682. A mark notorious in France is protected even if it was not registered with the French INPI.[422]

II. Conflict with the Name or Style of a Company (Article L. 711-4 b)

683. A sign is unavailable for registration as trademark when it was earlier the name or style of a company and where there is a risk of confusion in the public mind.[423] To determine the risk of confusion, the geographical scope of the earlier sign must be taken into account.

416. Cass. com., 7 Mar. 1995: PIBD 1995, III, 305, 'Asterix' case.
417. Trib. Civ. Seine, 5 Jan. 1940: Ann. propr. Ind. 1940-1948, 209.
418. TGI Paris, 5 Jun. 1991: PIBD 1991, III, 691.
419. Cass. com., 23 Jan. 1990: RD. propr. intell. 1990, No. 27, p. 96.
420. Cass. com., 4 Jun. 1991: PIBD 1991, III, 646.
421. Paris, 19 Oct. 1970: RIPIA 1971, 188, note Dusolier.
422. Paris, 29 Oct. 1987: PIBD 1988, III, 216, 'Bulgari' case.- Cass. com., 21 Mar. 2000: JCP ed. E 2000, p. 582, 'La Tour d'Argent'.
423. Cass. com., 9 Oct. 2007: PIBD 2007, III, 701. – Cass. com., 19 Nov. 2002: PIBD 2003, III, 100.

III. Conflict with a Geographical Name (Article L. 711-4 d)

684. A geographical name protected as a designation of origin is collectively appropriated by the producers located in the delimited area. It may be used only to designate products coming from this area and having specific characters.

685. A producer entitled to use the geographical name may register this name as trademark, if he adds some specific elements (such as: Chateau or Domaine, for wines) in order to distinguish his products from the others coming from the same area.

686. The same word may not serve as a designation of origin and a trademark for the same product, even when the geographical area is owned by only one person.[424]

687. A third party may not register a protected geographical name (Article L. 711-4, d) for a product which is not entitled to be identified by this geographical name.[425] Foreign designations of origin are treated in the same way as the French ones.[426]

688. The courts extended the scope of protection of famous designations of origin, which may not serve as trademarks even for goods which are not similar. In a well-advertised case, the Paris court nullified the trademark 'Champagne' registered by the Yves Saint Laurent Corporation for a perfume.[427] Moreover, a trademark may be invalidated even if it does not reproduce a protected geographical name, but is likely to cause confusion as to the geographical origin of the product (Article L. 711-3).

IV. Conflict with Trade Names or Shop Signs (Article L. 711-4 c)

689. A trade name is the name under which a person identifies his business activity to the public; a shop sign identifies a sales point. Such names are not registered, they are only protected against unfair competition, which implies the evidence of an unfair behaviour.

690. Article L. 711-4, c) prohibits the registration of signs which harm an earlier trade name or shop sign 'known on the whole national territory'.[428] Commercial signs which are known only by the local public may be registered as trademarks by a third party.[429] The owner of the earlier local sign will be still allowed to use it after the registration; he does not infringe the trademark.[430]

691. The trade name or a shop sign are also subject to the principle of speciality: they may be opposed to a trademark only as far as the same or similar goods or services

424. Cass. com., 1 Dec. 1987: Bull. civ. IV, p. 192, 'Romanée Conti'.
425. Cass. com., 26 Oct. 1993: PIBD 1994, III, 59; RTD com. 1994, 269, obs. Chavanne and Azéma.
426. Cass. com., 29 Mar. 1994: PIBD 1994, III, 381.
427. Paris, 15 Dec. 1993: D. 1994, jur., p. 145, note Le Tourneau; RTD com. 1994, 269, obs. Chavanne; JCP 1994 II 22229, note Pollaud-Dulian.-Paris, 12 Sep. 2001: PIBD 2002, III, 57, 'Bain de Champagne' and 'Royal Bain de Champagne' are void.
428. Paris, 15 Oct. 1997: PIBD 1997, III, 646. – Cass. com., 13 Dec. 1988: PIBD 1989, III, 259.
429. Paris, 12 May 1982: Ann. propr. Ind. 1983, 261.
430. Cass. com., 22 Mar. 1988: Ann. propr. Ind. 1989, 143.

are concerned,[431] and only if both signs are likely to cause confusion.[432] Domaine names on the Internet are treated in the same way as the traditional trade names.[433]

V. Conflict with a Right on a Design or Model (Article L. 711-4, f)

692. The shape registered as a design or model may not be later registered as trademark by a third person. The earlier registration must, however, have been published before the filing date of the trademark.[434]

VI. Conflict with Copyright (Article L. 711-4, e)

693. The registration as trademark of a copyrighted work amounts to an infringement of copyright when it reproduces its original elements. The copyrighted work is appropriated for all the goods and services.[435] For instance, a trademark which reproduces the original characteristics of a drawing by Fujita is an infringement of copyright and must be nullified;[436] the original title of a song ('Retiens la nuit') may not be a valid trademark of perfumes.[437] An original shape is protected by copyright even if it is not registered as design and model and, therefore, may not be registered as trademark.[438]

VII. Conflict with Personal Rights (Article L. 711-4, g and h)

694. According to this provision, a trademark may not harm a third person's 'personal right' ('droit de la personnalité'), such as the name, pseudonym or image, or a public territorial collectivity's name, image or reputation. A pseudonym under which a person is known is treated as a family name.[439] However, a person may forbid the registration of his name only upon evidence that its commercial use is likely to harm his personal rights. In practice, he must show a likelihood of confusion prejudicial to his interests. For instance, the commercial use of the name Boissy d'Anglas harms the historical value of the name;[440] a likelihood of confusion exists when the plaintiff's name is known in the region where he does business and where he is the only one to

431. Cass. com., 27 May 1986: D. 1986, jur., p. 526, note Durrande.-Paris, 16 Jun. 2000: PIBD 2000, III, 577.
432. Paris, 18 Sep. 1998: PIBD 1999, III, 11.
433. Paris, 18 Oct. 2000: D. 2001, jur., p. 1379, note Loiseau. – Versailles, 22 Nov. 2001 : Comm. com. électr. 2002, comm. 56, obs. Ch. Caron. – Versailles, 27 Feb. 2003: PIBD 2003, III, 245.
434. TGI Paris, 26 Mar. 1986: JCP ed. E, 1988 II 15149.
435. Rouen, 20 Jan. 1994: PIBD 1994, III, 239.- Cass. com., 25 Jan. 2000: PIBD 2000, III, 254.
436. Paris, 15 May 1990: Ann. propr. Ind. 1991, 131.
437. TGI Paris, 22 Feb. 1990: PIBD 1990, III, 525.
438. Paris, 27 May 1981: Ann. propr. Ind. 1981, 76.
439. Paris, 17 Dec. 1980: Ann. propr. Ind. 1981, 76.
440. Cass. com., 19 Jun. 1961: Ann. propr. Ind. 1962, 236.

use it.[441] On the contrary, the holder of a commonplace family name may not complain about the registration of this name as trademark by a third party.[442] A nobiliary title is protected as a family name.[443]

695. First names do not identify a person and may not be opposed to their registration as trademarks.[444]

696. A legal person is identified by its corporate name and may oppose its registration as a trademark if there is a likelihood of confusion.[445]

697. Finally, under Article L. 711-4, h) a 'territorial collectivity' (village, town, group of towns, etc.) may prohibit the registration of its name as trademark. Any such territorial collectivity may request the National Institute of Industrial Property (INPI) to be alerted in the event of the filing of an application for registration of a trademark containing its name or containing the name of a place located in its geographical territory (Article L. 712-2-1).

698. The defendant may argue that he was authorized by the holder of the name or his predecessor to use it for commercial purposes, which may include the registration of the name as trademark.[446]

441. Cass. com., 15 Oct. 1994: PIBD 1995, III, 88, 'Lord Astor'.
442. Cass. civ., 26 May 1970: Ann. propr. Ind. 1970, 98, the name Dop.
443. Paris, 21 Mar. 1973: Ann. propr. Ind. 1974, 154, case Marquis de Noailles.
444. Cass. com., 26 Apr. 1988: Ann. propr. Ind. 1988, 163.
445. Paris, 18 Apr. 1989: PIBD 1989, III, 627; the corporate name 'Resocom' may not be a valid trademark in a similar area of business.-Paris, 18 Sep. 1998: D. Aff. 1998, p. 2021, obs. B.P.
446. Paris, 14 Mar. 1995: PIBD 1995, III, 324: Duc de Praslin and the trademark 'Praslines du Duc de Praslin'.

Chapter 4. Formalities

699. Under the Act of 1857, ownership of a trademark was acquired through the use of the sign; the Act of 1964 introduced registration and allowed earlier trademarks to be registered. Finally, the Act of 4 January 1991 (Article L. 712-1) states: 'The ownership of the trademark is acquired by registration.' By exception, well-known trademarks (*see supra* paragraph 682) are protected in France even without registration.

700. Registration consists of the entry of the trademark into the National Register of Trademarks by the INPI, after an application was filed by the interested person. The material conditions of the registration procedure are regulated under Article L. 712-2–L. 712-14 and Article R. 712-1–R. 712-28.

§1. Filing of Applications

701. The application for registration may be made by one or several natural or legal persons, able or not to use the trademark (a holding corporation may own trademarks). When the application is filed by several persons, a common representative must be appointed.

702. The application may be filed either personally, or through a representative. Representation is compulsory when the applicant has no domicile or head office in a Member State of the EU or of the EEA (Article R. 712-2). The representation is subject to conditions of Article L. 422-4 and L. 422-5 (*see supra*, paragraph 406).

703. The application is filed either directly with the INPI. It may also be made by registered mail with acknowledgement of receipt, or any other means of teletransmission (fax) defined by decision of the Director General of the INPI (Article R. 712-1, §2). An online application is possible and now very usual.

704. The application must contain: a request for registration of a sign as trademark, identification of the applicant, a graphic representation of the proposed sign, a list of goods and services in respect of which the registration is requested and the corresponding classes, and the identification of an earlier foreign application if a priority right is claimed. Each application may concern only one trademark (Article R. 712-3).

705. It must also include the following supplementary documents: receipt of payment of filing fees, the power of representative if any, justification of prior use of the sign when its distinguishing character is grounded on such a use, and when the applicant is a foreigner who has no domicile or establishment in France, the justification that he duly applied for registration in the country of his domicile or establishment and that this country grants reciprocal protection to French trademarks (under reservation of international conventions, Article L. 712-11) (Article R. 712-3). If a priority right is claimed (according to Article 4 of the Paris Convention or according to Article L. 712-12 which grants a priority right to any foreign application on condition that the foreign country in question grants equivalent priority right to French trademarks), a proper justification should be provided within three months from the filing date. Where this obligation is not complied with, the priority shall be deemed not to have been claimed (Article R. 712-4).

706. A date and number of filing are granted by the INPI upon reception of a correct application.

§2. Processing of Applications

I. Examination

707. The INPI examines whether the application satisfies the formal requirements laid down by the legislation and that the sign may serve as trademark in accordance with Article L. 711-1, L. 711-2 and L. 711-3. However, the INPI does not search for the existence of prior rights likely to conflict with the proposed trademark. Such prior rights may only be sanctioned through the opposition procedure (*see infra,* paragraph 711).

708. When the application does not satisfy the examined conditions, the INPI invites the applicant to remedy the deficiencies or discuss the INPI's objections within the prescribed period. If the deficiencies are not remedied within this period or arguments are unable to remove the objections, the application is refused (Article R. 712-11). Notification of deficiencies may include a proposal of regularization by the INPI; if the applicant does not contest this proposal within the prescribed period, it is deemed accepted. No regularization may amount to an extension of the scope of the application (Article R. 712-11, 3°).

709. The applicant who did not comply with the requirements within the prescribed period may appeal for restoration of his rights to the Director General of the INPI (Article L. 712-10). He must bring proof of a legitimate excuse which prevented him from complying with the deadline. The formal conditions of the appeal are listed under Article R. 712-12. In the other cases of refusal, an appeal may be lodged before the competent 'Cour d'Appel' (Article R. 411-19).

II. Publication

710. All receivable applications are published in the 'Bulletin officiel de la propriété industrielle' (BOPI) within six weeks from their reception by the INPI, unless it emerges that their presentation does not satisfy the technical requirements necessary for reproduction or that their publication would be such as to be prejudicial to public order or morality (Article R. 712-8). The publication mentions the option offered to third persons to formulate either observations or oppositions against the registration within two months.

III. Observations and Oppositions by Third Parties

A. Observations

711. Written observations by third parties are communicated to the applicant by the INPI. They are disregarded if they obviously are without relation to the legislative provisions (Article R. 712-9). Even well grounded, observations do not allow the INPI to refuse the application.

B. Oppositions

712. Within a period of two months following the publication of the trademark application, notice of opposition to the registration may be given (Article L. 712-4):

- by the owner of an earlier trademark registered or filed, or having an earlier priority date;
- by the owner of an earlier well-known trademark;
- by the director of the National Institute of Origin and Quality (INAO), where there is a risk of damage to the name, image, or reputation of an appellation of origin or of an geographical indication;
- by the holder of an exclusive right to use the trademark (e.g., exclusive licensee), unless a contrary clause is provided for in the agreement;
- by a 'territorial collectivity';
- by a geographical indication defence and management body.

713. Opposition must be expressed in writing and specify the arguments whereby the trademark application should be refused. An opposition fee must be paid.

714. The opposition is deemed refused if it has not been processed within eight months from the publication of the application (Article L. 712-4, §2). This period may be suspended when the opposition is grounded on an earlier application for registration of a trademark, when an action for invalidity, forfeiture, or vindication of ownership were brought, and upon the parties' agreement (up to six months).

715. The INPI decides upon the opposition according to a contradictory proceeding where the parties may exchange their arguments (Article L. 712-5).

716. If the examination of the opposition reveals that the trademark may not be registered, the application shall be refused, in respect of all the goods or services for which it was made, or in respect of only some of them. Otherwise the opposition is rejected.

717. The applicant may request that the trademark be registered in spite of the opposition, if this registration is necessary to the protection of the trademark abroad (Article L. 712-8) (under the Madrid Agreement, the international application must be grounded on an earlier national registration).

IV. Registration

718. If the application was not withdrawn or refused during the proceedings, the trademark is registered by entry of the sign into the National Register of Trademarks under its filing date.

719. The date of publication of the registration in the BOPI makes the right effective against third parties. A certificate is delivered to the applicant (Article R. 712-23).

Chapter 5. Scope of Exclusive Rights

720. According to Article L. 713-1, 'Registration of the trademark confers to the holder a right of ownership on this trademark for the specified goods and services.' The use of a trademark to identify goods or services is optional, except in some cases provided by law (e.g., for medicine, playing cards, or oil products). The owner may use the trademark himself or through a licensee and may prohibit any unauthorized use by third persons (under the exceptions listed by the IP Code: *see infra*, paragraphs 792 et seq.).

721. The Code defines the scope of the trademark protection by reference to specific prohibitions: 'The violation of the prohibitions listed under Article L. 713-2, L. 713-3 and L. 713-4 amounts to an infringement of the trademark rights' (Article L. 716-1).

722. Some of the acts listed under these articles are prohibited to unauthorized third persons, even when they do not imply a likelihood of confusion with the marked goods or services; some other acts are forbidden only if such a likelihood of confusion exists. In any case, good faith is not material.[447]

§1. Infringement Without Likelihood of Confusion

723. Article L. 713-2 prohibits the following unauthorized acts: reproduction, use, affixing of a trademark, use of a reproduced trademark for products or services identical to those listed in the registration, suppression, or modification of lawfully affixed trademarks.

I. Reproduction

724. The trademark right is infringed through the reproduction of the characteristic elements of the sign, independently from its use.[448] Consequently, the filing for registration of the same sign is an infringement of an earlier trademark.[449] A denigrating reproduction, even with laudable intentions is also an infringement.[450]

725. A trademark which consists of a shape is also protected against reproduction of the corresponding word.[451]

726. For a long time, an almost identical copy was treated as reproduction: for instance, the trademark *'Kendo'* registered for clothes is a reproduction of the earlier

447. Cass. com., 26 Jun. 1973: D. 1974, jur., p. 558, note Foulon-Pigagnol.
448. Cass. com., 23 Nov. 1993: RDPI 1994, No. 51, p. 64.- Cass. com., 5 Nov. 2002: PIBD 2003, III, 44.
449. Paris, 18 Feb. 1975: PIBD 1975, III, 376.
450. Paris, 28 Jan. 1992: JCP ed. E, 1992 pan. 335: the denigration of a cigarette trademark on posters during an anti-tobacco campaign is an illicit reproduction.
451. Paris, 17 Apr. 1974: PIBD 1974, III, 335; the trademark which consists of the emblem of a turtle is infringed by the word 'Turtle' for identical goods.

trademark 'Kenzo';[452] '*West Jean's*' is an infringement of '*Jean's West*' for trousers,[453] etc. So was also the case when the trademark was reproduced with subtractions or additions.

727. Partial reproduction is illegal when essential and distinctive elements of the trademark are reproduced: for instance, '*McDouglas*' is infringed by '*King Douglas*' for leather goods;[454] 'Lambert Diffusion' infringes 'Lambert Ollivier' both for clothes;[455] 'Leader Conseil' infringes *Leaders Trust International.*[456] On the contrary, '*Good Life*' is not infringed by '*Life*' which is not distinctive as such,[457] etc.

728. The original trademark is often reproduced with additions. Infringement remains in spite of such additions, unless in the new sign the earlier trademark lost its individuality and distinguishing power. For instance, 'Azur Inter Assurance' infringes 'Azur' registered for insurance services;[458] 'Afer du Rond Point' infringes 'Rond Point',[459] etc. On the contrary, 'Roche' is not infringed by 'Eau de Roche' which has its specific distinguishing power to designate perfumes;[460] 'Aigle' is not reproduced by '*American Eagle*',[461] etc.

729. These solutions evolve following the decisions of the European Court of Justice (ECJ). Asked to interpret the EC Directive No. 89/104 of 21 December 1988,[462] in order to clarify the distinction between the use of an identical sign and the use of a similar sign (where infringement requires proof of a risk of confusion), the Court ruled that an identical sign may be the one which includes differences so minimal that they are not perceived by an ordinary consumer.[463] French courts now apply this reasoning. Almost identical copies are treated as reproductions only when the differences are so minimal that they are not perceived by an ordinary consumer. And when the trademark is partially reproduced with subtractions or additions, it is treated no more as a

452. Paris, 21 Apr. 1988: Ann. propr. Ind. 1989, 268.
453. Paris, 29 Oct. 1984: Ann. propr. Ind. 1984, 194.
454. Paris, 31 Jan. 1990: Ann. propr. Ind. 1992, 26.
455. Cass. com., 16 Jun. 1998: PIBD 1998, III, 433.
456. Paris, 14 Jan. 1998: PIBD 1998, III, 252.
457. Paris, 21 Nov. 1990: Ann. propr. Ind. 1991, 101.
458. Cass. com., 27 Jun. 1995: PIBD 1995, III, 426.
459. Cass. com., 24 Jan. 1983: Bull. civ. IV, No. 30.
460. Cass. com., 2 Dec. 1974: Bull. civ. IV, No. 310.
461. Paris, 16 Jan. 1989: Ann. propr. Ind. 1990, 281.
462. First Council Directive No. 89/104/EEC of 21 Dec. 1988 to approximate the laws of the Member States relating to trademarks, OJEC, No. L. 40, 11 Feb. 1989, pp. 1–7, repealed and replaced by the EC Directive No. 2008/95 of the European Parliament and of the Council of 22 Oct. 2008 to approximate the laws of the Member States relating to trademarks (codified version), OJEC, No. L. 299, 8 Nov. 2008, pp. 25–33, repealed and replaced by the EU Directive No. 2015/2436 of the European Parliament and of the Council of 16 Dec. 2015 to approximate the laws of the Member States relating to trade marks (recast), OJEU, No. L.336, 23 Dec. 2015, pp. 1–26.
463. ECJ, 20 Mar. 2003, case C-291/00: Propr. intell., April 2003, p. 203, note Bonet.

reproduction but as an imitation (where infringement requires proof of a risk of confusion).[464]

730. In a steady line of cases, French courts did not take into consideration the means and destination of the reproduction in order to excuse infringement. Any reproduction was deemed illicit, whatever its aim; for instance, the reproduction on a decoration of a shop window,[465] in a trade name,[466] in advertisements,[467] on postcards,[468] in a cartoon,[469] etc. However, the evaluation of the infringement should take into consideration the essential function of the trademark as defined by the ECJ.[470] Thus, third parties should be free to use the sign for purposes other than the designation of products or services.[471] Recent cases accepted that the trademark be reproduced in a humorous way, under condition 'it does not dissimulate a mercantile or negative motivation'.[472]

731. Infringement may also consist of the reproduction of the trademark to identify non-authentic goods;[473] in the reference to a trademark by asserting that products are compatible with those of the infringer's.[474]

II. Use

732. Most often, the illicit trademark is used by the person who reproduced it: reproduction and use are, however, distinct acts of infringement. The courts consider as infringing any act of commercial competition carried out with an infringing trademark. For instance, a mere oral reference to a trademark amounts to an infringement by use, even when the user did not affix the mark on his own goods.[475]

---

464. For example, Paris, 15 Dec. 2000: PIBD 2001, III, 171, '*La Poste' v. 'Post'Air'*.- Versailles, 14 Jan. 2003: PIBD 2003, III, 155. – Cass. Com., 26 Nov. 2003: No. 00-20923, Bull. civ. IV, No. 185. – Cass. com., 2 Febr. 2010: No. 09-11686, PIBD 2010, III, 166. – Paris, 20 May 2011: PIBD, III, 463.
465. Orléans, 23 Nov. 1972: Ann. propr. Ind. 1973, 353.
466. Cass. com., 8 Dec. 1975: Bull. civ. IV, No. 295.
467. Cass. crim., 11 Jul. 1978: D. 1979, I.R., p. 179.- However, a reseller of authentic products does not infringe the trademark in the normal advertisements; he benefits of an implied licence: Cass. com., 27 Oct. 1992: Ann. propr. Ind. 1992, 162.
468. Cass. crim., 11 Oct. 1989: Bull. crim., No. 351.
469. Paris, 26 Oct. 1994: PIBD 1995, III, 8.
470. ECJ, 25 Jan. 2007, case C-48/05: Propr. industr. 2007, comm. 18, note A. Folliard-Monguiral. – ECJ, 11 Sep. 2007, case C-17/06: PIBD 2007, III, 698, Propr. industr. 2007, comm. 86, note A. Folliard-Monguiral.
471. Paris, 31 Oct. 2008: PIBD 2008, III, 762.
472. *See* the case 'Guignols de l'Info' where a trademark was used in a caricatural television series: Cass. Ass. plén., 12 Jul. 2000: D. 2001, jur., p. 259, note Edelman.- Also: Paris, 26 Feb. 2003: Propr. Industr.2003, comm. 40, note Tréfigny, deciding that the sign 'E$$O' used by Greenpeace did not relate to the business life and was used in a polemic way.
473. Paris, 7 Dec. 1992: PIBD 1993, III, 865.
474. Paris, 16 May 1991: PIBD, 1991, III, 713.
475. Paris, 30 Apr. 1987: Ann. propr. Ind. 1988, 246.

733. Modern methods of marketing brought to the courts new cases of unauthorized uses of trademarks.

734. It was held, for instance, that the 'concordance charts' ('Tableaux de concordance') were infringing by using the trademarks they cited. Such 'charts' consist of lists of cross references between ordinary products and other (usually well-known) trademarked goods (e.g., 'The perfume No. 1 on the chart is the same as "Shalimar" by Guerlain').[476]

735. Another form of illicit use consists of the co-called Appeal trademark ('Marque d'appel') whereby a renowned trademark is used to promote not only authentic products, but also other similar competing goods.[477]

736. Marketing of authentic goods by unauthorized (parallel) dealers who are not members of a selective distribution network is another example of infringement by use of a trademark. Regrettably, the Commercial and the Criminal Chamber of the French Supreme Court hold opposite solutions on this problem. Whereas the Criminal Chamber never accepted to apply criminal sanctions of infringement by use (*see infra,* paragraph 858) to parallel distribution,[478] the Commercial Chamber holds such a distributor to be liable for civil damages.[479]

737. The most recent case of infringement consists of the use of the trademark on Internet, either on a third person's website, or as a domain name to identify same or similar goods or services. The ordinary rules of trademark infringement apply to such disputes.[480]

738. This extensive understanding of the notion of usage of the trademark finds a limit when the usage seems to be complying with the ordinary trade practices. Therefore, there is no infringement when the sign is used not as a trademark with a distinguishing function, but as a mere information,[481] or in its ordinary banal meaning.[482]

739. A steady line of cases holds that infringement by use is independent from a likelihood of confusion with the authentic trademark.[483]

---

476. Cass. com., 2 Feb. 1988: Ann. propr. Ind. 1989, 43, note Mathély. Cass. crim., 20 Mar. 1989: D. 1989, I.R., p. 160.
477. Cass. com., 9 Feb. 1992: Bull. civ. IV, No. 56. Cass. com., 23 Feb. 1993: JCP ed. E, 1993 pan. 525. Cass. com., 30 Jan. 2002: Bull. civ. IV, No. 28. Paris, 19 Mar. 2008: Propr. industr. 2009, comm. 12.
478. Cass. crim., 5 Oct. 1987: Bull. crim., No. 335. Cass. crim., 16 Jun. 1993: Bull. crim., No. 216.
479. Cass. com., 23 Feb. 1993: RDPI 1993, No. 49, p. 81: D. 1994, jur., p. 398, note Fort-Cardon.
480. TGI Bordeaux, 22 Jul. 1996: Gaz. Pal. 1997, 1, jur., p. 245.-Paris, 13 Oct. 1999: PIBD 2000, III, 424.- 19 Oct. 2001: PIBD 2002, III, 359.- Paris, référés, 4 Dec. 1998: JCP ed. E 1999, p. 955, No. 23, obs. Vivant and Le Stanc. However, the mere registration of a domain name is not an infringement: Versailles, 22 Nov. 2001: CCE April 2002, comm. No. 56, obs. Caron.
481. TGI Paris, 22 Feb. 1995: PIBD 1995, III, 257.-Paris, 1 Jul. 1998: PIBD 1998, III, 486.
482. Paris, 25 Apr. 1994: Ann. propr. Ind. 1994, 166: the trademark 'Louisiana' is not infringed by the reference to 'an atmosphere of Louisiana'.
483. Cass. com., 7 Jun. 1988: Ann. propr. Ind. 1988, 161.

III. Affixing

740. Affixing consists of placing the mark on non-authentic products. Most often, the cases deal with the filling of bottles or containers bearing a trademark with different content.[484] Infringement by affixing may also consist of assembling a new object with used spare parts bearing a trademark.[485]

IV. Suppression or Modification

741. The trademark owner may decide to affix it or not on the goods or services he produces or sells. When an authentic product has been marketed under the trademark, it is illicit for an unauthorized person to suppress or modify such a trademark.[486] Suppression is, however, legal when it was necessary to escape sanctions on other grounds, such as illicit use of a trademark.[487]

§2. Infringement with Likelihood of Confusion

742. The unauthorized use of a sign is forbidden in two series of cases, under condition it generates a likelihood of confusion with the authentic trademark.

743. Reproduction, use, affixing of a trademark, as well as, the use of a reproduced trademark for products or services similar to those listed in the registration (Article L. 713-3, a), and imitation of a trademark and use of an imitated trademark for goods or services identical or similar to those listed in the registration (Article L. 713-3, b).

744. These provisions allow the protection of a trademark outside of the classes for which it was registered and against imitations.

I. Use for Similar Goods or Services

745. According to the courts, two goods or services are similar if the public may attribute them to the same origin, in consideration of their nature and destination. For instance, a trademark registered for ships is protected also for sail-boards,[488] and 'Joker' registered for communication services is protected also for the telematic access code '3615 Joker'.[489] On the contrary, were not held as similar, for instance, hotel and restaurant services on the one hand, and marketing of pastries on the other hand.[490]

---

484. Cass. crim., 11 Mar. 1964: RTD com. 1964, 319, obs. Roubier and Chavanne, gaz station containers. Cass. com., 10 Feb. 1998: PIBD 1998, III, 251, motor oil containers.
485. Paris, 28 Jan. 1972: Ann. propr. Ind. 1972, 177.
486. Cass. com., 6 May 1991: Bull. civ. IV, No. 156.
487. Lyon, 13 Jul. 1976: D. 1977, jur., p. 17, note Chavanne.
488. Paris, 7 May 1988: Ann. propr. Ind. 1989, 230.
489. Paris, 16 Feb. 1995: PIBD 1995, III, 2118.
490. Paris, 16 Apr. 1992: Ann. propr. Ind. 1992, 279.- Cass. com., 23 Mar. 1999: PIBD 1999, III, 239, sweets and coffee are not similar.

746. Similarity is not to be evaluated on the date of registration, but on the day of the action for infringement.[491] Similarity may exist between products and services.[492]

II. Use of an Imitated Trademark

747. Article L. 713-3, b) allows the protection of the trademark against imitations, which consist of an approximate reproduction. Imitation is evaluated in consideration of its likeliness with the authentic trademark;[493] it is illicit when it reproduces the distinguishing characters of the trademark, in spite of other differences.

748. Similarities between trademarks may be numerous: visual and phonetic;[494] or only phonetic, when the clients may not make a visual comparison;[495] or only visual.[496] Moreover, French courts hold as imitating trademarks which give to the public 'a general impression of analogy',[497] likelihood may be simply 'intellectual'.[498]

III. Condition of Likelihood of Confusion

749. The above-mentioned uses of a trademark are sanctioned only if they create a likelihood of confusion, which is evaluated following the jurisprudence of the ECJ, by taking the place of an average consumer who does not have both signs in view and must, therefore, resort to his memory.[499] It is not necessary to evidence an effective confusion; it is enough to show a 'risk' of confusion.[500] The confusion may be total, when the consumer believes he buys a product or a service bearing the authentic trademark; or it may consist of the risk of association, when the consumer makes a relationship between them. The courts make a balance sheet between similarities and differences of the conflicting signs. For instance, there is no likelihood of confusion when the imitating trademark, although including part of another one, consists of an 'all indivisible' sign which has a specific meaning.[501]

---

491. Paris, 3 Feb. 1994: Ann. propr. Ind. 1994, 21.
492. Cass. com., 6 Apr. 1993: PIBD 1993, III, 485; restaurant services are similar to culinary products.
493. Cass. com., 25 Mar. 2014: PIBD 2014, III, 411.
494. Paris, 18 Sep. 1991: Ann. propr. Ind. 1992, 286: 'Joker' and 'Poker'.
495. Paris, 17 Mar. 1981: Ann. propr. Ind. 1981, 132; 'Chairman' and 'Sherman'.
496. Paris, 5 Mar. 1975: Ann. propr. Ind. 1975, 247.
497. Paris, 30 Oct. 1971: Ann. propr. Ind. 1972, 57; 'Safari Infernal' and 'Safari du Diable'.
498. Paris, 4 Mar. 1959: D. 1960, jur., p. 26, note Desbois; 'La vache qui rit', is imitated by 'La vache sérieuse' ('Laughing Cow' and 'Serious Cow').
499. Paris, 9 Jun. 1994: PIBD 1994, III, 480. Paris, 6 May 1998: PIBD 1998, III, 371. – Paris, 24 Sep. 2003: PIBD 2004, III, 106. – Cass. com., 26 Nov. 2003: PIBD 2004, III, 129.
500. Paris, 9 Nov. 1993: PIBD 1994, III, 152.-Paris, 29 May 2002: JCP ed. E 2002 II 1648.
501. Cass. com., 30 Jun. 1998: PIBD 1998, III, 462.

IV. Protection of Well-Known Trademarks

750. Well-known trademarks as well as trademarks enjoying repute benefit of an extended protection. The use of such a trademark may be prohibited even for products or services which are not similar to those listed in the registration, 'if it is likely to harm the rights of the owner, or if it is an unjustified exploitation of the trademark' (Article L. 713-5). Such a harm may consist, for instance, of the dilution of the attractive power of the trademark.

751. Moreover, the owner of the well-known trademark may bring action for revocation of a mark registered by a third party in another area of activity (Article L. 714-4).

Chapter 6. Ownership and Transfer

§1. Ownership

752. If the registration was requested in fraud of a third person's rights, or in violation of a legal or contractual obligation, the person who considers to have a right on the trademark may claim its ownership in courts. Unless the applicant for registration acted in bad faith, the action for recovery of ownership is to be brought within five years from the publication of the filing for registration (Article L. 712-6). Fraud is evidenced by the knowledge by the applicant, at the time of registration, of the earlier use of the sign by a third party.[502]

§2. Transfer

753. As any exclusive right, the trademark right is economically interesting only when it is used. Instead of using his right himself (or in spite of using it), the owner may prefer to authorize third persons to do so. French law does not provide for any expropriation or compulsory licence of the trademark rights.

754. The law only states that trademark rights 'are transferable totally or partially' and may be licensed or pledged (Article L. 714-1). This limited provision is interpreted extensively: trademark rights may be transferred by any legal means, inter vivos, or post mortem. Such transfers are subject to the general rules of contract law or the law of successions.

755. Two most important contracts will be studied here: assignment and licence of trademark rights.

I. Assignment of Trademark

756. Assignment is a contract whereby the owner of a trademark transfers his rights to an assignee in exchange for the payment of a price. The Intellectual Property Code provides for some punctual rules; as for the rest, assignment of trademark right is subject to the law of sales (Articles 1582–1685, Civil Code).

502. Cass. com., 12 Jul. 1976: Bull. civ. IV, No. 236. For instance, a court ordered the transfer to the SEAT corporation of a trademark registered by the CASTOR corporation, with which it was engaged in business relations, and which had knowledge of the use of the sign by SEAT for the promotion of its goods: Cass. com., 13 Feb. 1996: PIBD 1996, III, 279.-Paris, 30 Sep. 2002: PIBD 2002, III, 573.

A. *Conditions of Assignment*

757. Whereas the substantial conditions are mainly borrowed from the contract of sale, the formal conditions are specific to trademarks.

1. Substantial Conditions

758. The assignee must be the owner of the trademark. In case of joint ownership, unanimous consent is required.

759. Transfer of an international trademark registration should be made to an assignee who is national of one Member State of the Madrid Agreement of 1891 (Article 9 of the Madrid Agreement). However, it was decided that the French trademark resulting from such an international registration may be assigned to a non-national.[503]

760. The object of the assignment should consist of a valid trademark. As the right takes effect from the filing date, it may be assigned before registration (under condition precedent that the registration will follow). The assignment may be total or partial, when only some elements of the right are transferred, or if the use of the sign is authorized only for some of the goods or services listed in the trademark registration.

761. The transfer of a French trademark does not imply the transfer of parallel trademarks registered abroad (and vice versa, because of the principle of territorial independence of industrial property rights). It does not imply either, unless a contrary provision is included in the contract, the transfer of the right of priority.

762. Following the EU Directive No. 2015/2436 of 16 December 2015 on the harmonization of trademark laws,[504] Article L. 714-1, §1, states that trademarks may be transferred independently from the business where they are used. On the contrary, transfer of the business implies transfer of trademarks, unless a contrary clause is made.[505]

763. The assignment made with the sole aim to acquire a means of blocking a competitor's activity can be invalidated for fraud.[506]

764. The assignment of a French trademark transfers the rights for the whole French territory (Article L. 714-1, §1).

503. Paris, 8 May 1963: Ann. propr. Ind. 1963, 193.
504. First Council Directive No. 89/104/EEC of 21 Dec. 1988 to approximate the laws of the Member States relating to trademarks, OJEC, No. L. 40, 11 Feb. 1989, pp. 1–7, repealed and replaced by the EC Directive No. 2008/95 of the European Parliament and of the Council of 22 Oct. 2008 to approximate the laws of the Member States relating to trademarks (codified version), OJEC, No. L. 299, 8 Nov. 2008, pp. 25–33, repealed and replaced by the EU Directive No. 2015/2436 of the European Parliament and of the Council of 16 Dec. 2015 to approximate the laws of the Member States relating to trademarks (recast), OJEU, No. L.336, 23 Dec. 2015, pp. 1–26.
505. Cass. com., 24 Mar. 1980: Bull. civ. IV, No. 14.
506. Paris, 11 Feb. 1982: Ann. propr. Ind. 1983, 256: purchase of the trademark 'Yval' in view of opposing it to 'Yvoal'.

2. Formal Conditions

765. Signature of a written contract is a condition of validity of the assignment (Article L. 714-1, §4). The transfer is effective against third parties after its entry into the 'Registre National des Marques' (Article L. 714-7).

766. Moreover, when the transfer is made between a party domiciled in France and another person domiciled abroad, the contract should be notified to the Ministry in charge of International Commerce (Article R. 624-1–R. 624-7; *see supra,* paragraph 496).

B. Effects of the Assignment

767. Being a sale of the trademark, the contract of assignment operates a transfer of the right of ownership and creates obligations for the parties.

768. The transfer of ownership is effective between the parties as from the signature of the contract. It is effective against third persons as from the date of its entry into the National Register of Trademarks.[507]

769. The parties' obligations may be defined by reference to those which exist in the assignment of patent rights (*see supra*, paragraphs 490 et seq.).

770. The transferor must deliver the trademark to the assignee, which implies the remittance of the title and the authorization to use it.

771. He must also warranty the assignee against hidden defects of the trademark right and against eviction (*see supra*, paragraphs 490 et seq. the content of these obligations in the assignment of patents).

772. The assignee's main obligation consists of the payment of the price. Such price must be determined, or at least determinable by reference to objective elements allowing its computation for the sale to be valid.

II. Licence

773. The licence is a contract whereby the licensor authorizes the licensee to use the trademark in exchange for payment of a price. This contract may take the form of an 'agreement for coexistence', whereby the owners of virtually conflicting trademarks agree to define their respective areas of exploitation (Article L. 714-1, §3).

774. A licence may be concluded as an isolated contract, or as part of another broader agreement. For instance, franchising contracts usually include licence of the franchisor's trademarks to the franchisee.

775. Article L. 714-1, §2 authorizes the conclusion of trademark licences, but does not provide for any substantial rules. Such contracts are to be treated as a variety of contracts for rental and subject to the pertinent rules of the Civil Code (Articles 1708 et seq.) as for their conditions and effects.

---

507. Cass. com., 24 May 1994: JCP ed. E, 1994 pan. p. 992: the assignee may sue infringers as from the date of registration of the assignment in the National Register.

A. Conditions of the Licence

1. Substantial Conditions

776. The licensor is usually the owner of the trademark right. In case of joint ownership, the rules applicable to patent licences should serve as a model (*see supra*, paragraphs 514 et seq.). Licence may also be granted by the usufructor of the trademark, or by a licensee (as a sub-licence), with the main licensor's consent.

777. The object of the licence should consist of a valid trademark, or a filing for registration (under condition precedent that the registration follows). When the trademark is invalidated, the licence becomes voidable for lack of object (nullity is retroactive).

778. The licence may be global, when the licensee is authorized to use the trademark for all the goods and services for which it was registered, and without restriction as to the conditions of such a use. But authorization may also be partial, for some goods or services, or for a part of a complex trademark. The licensor may not authorize the use of his trademark for goods or services other than those listed in the registration, even if they are similar.[508] The licensee who uses the trademark out of the contractual limits may be sued by the licensor for infringement (Article L. 714-1, §3).[509]

779. The duration of the licence is agreed by the parties. The duration may be indeterminate, since the trademark right is indefinitely renewable (*see infra*, paragraph 801). In such a case, each party may terminate the contract at any time, upon notice given to the other party, according to the general rules of contract law.

780. After the termination of the contract (for any reason), measures should be taken in order to prevent the licensee from keeping to use the trademark.

781. The licence may be terminated by anticipation, in case of nullity of the trademark. The licence may also be terminated for the future, in case of forfeiture of the owner's rights (*see infra,* paragraph 804).

2. Formal Conditions

782. Although no statutory provision requires a written document, such a document is necessary in order to enter the contract into the National Register of Trademarks. This registration is the starting point of the contract's efficacy against third persons (Article L. 714-7).

B. Effects of the Licence

783. Unlike an assignment, the licence does not entail the transfer of the right of ownership on the trademark, but only creates obligations for the parties. Globally, the content and the legal treatment of these obligations are modelled on the patent licence (*see supra*, paragraphs 514 et seq.).

508. Cass. com., 24 Oct. 1984: D. 1986, I.R., p. 89, obs. Burst.
509. Paris, 29 Oct. 1992: PIBD 1993, III, 132; RTD com. 1993, 312, obs. Chavanne.

1. The Licensor's Obligations

784. The licensor's obligations consist of the classical obligations of a renter: he should deliver the authorization to use, and warranty against hidden defects and against eviction. Other obligations may be added by the parties in compliance with public order and the competition law.

a. Warranty of Hidden Defects

785. The object of this obligation is to warranty the validity of the licensed trademark. When the trademark is nullified upon action brought by a third person, the licensor should indemnify the licensee for the loss following the termination of the exclusive right. Clauses limiting or eliminating such warranty may be included in the contract, but are valid only if the licensor acted in good faith, i.e., thought at the time of conclusion of the licence that his trademark was valid.

786. The validity of the so-called non-contestation clauses, whereby the licensee undertakes the obligation not to challenge the validity of the trademark, must be checked towards French and eventually EU competition law.

b. Warranty of Eviction (or of Peaceful Enjoyment)

787. The licensor should warranty the peaceful enjoyment of the trademark by the licensee. Consequently, he should not behave in a way troublesome to the licensee, and should protect him against trouble coming from third persons.

788. Personal eviction by the licensor could consist, for instance, of not renewing the registration, or of using the trademark himself in case of an exclusive licence, unless contrary clauses are provided.[510]

789. Eviction by third parties may consist either of legal or of material troubles. Legal troubles may be illustrated by an action for infringement brought by third persons against the licensee.[511] Material troubles consist mainly of infringements of the licensed trademark by third persons. In such cases, the licensor should bring action against the infringer.[512] The licensee may act by himself, under limited conditions (*see infra*, paragraph 817).

c. Other Obligations

790. Any other obligation may be provided by contract, under condition it complies with public order and competition law. The most frequent provisions are: exclusivity of the licence whereby the licensor undertakes the duty not to grant licences on the same trademark (or part of it) to third parties, obligation to assist the licensee and to communicate to him a know-how,[513] the obligation to register the trademark abroad, etc.

---

510. Cass. com., 10 Jan. 1995: Bull. civ. IV, No. 12; RTD com. 1996, 269, obs. Azéma.
511. Cass. com., 5 Oct. 1993: JCP ed. E, 1993 pan. p. 1316.
512. Paris, 26 Jun. 1970: Ann. propr. Ind. 1970, 213.
513. Paris, 7 Jun. 1960: Ann. propr. Ind. 1963, 245.

2. The Licensee's Obligations

791. The licensee's main obligation consists of the payment of the licence price. The problems are similar to those of the patent licence (*see supra*, paragraph 526), except for the duration of this obligation, since the trademark right may last for an indeterminate time, as long as the trademark is renewed. Moreover, the licensee may be bound by other obligations provided by contract. The most frequent examples are the following:

- obligation to affix the trademark on the products manufactured or sold by the licensee;
- obligation to maintain the reputation (the image) of the trademark;
- obligation to buy products or raw materials from the licensor;
- obligation not to export the trademarked products.

In all these cases, the validity of the obligation must be checked against the rules of the applicable competition law.

Chapter 7. Exceptions and Limitations

792. According to Article L. 713-6 of the I.P. Code, the owner of a trademark may not prohibit the use of the same or a similar sign by a third person in the three following cases. And another case must be added.

§1. The Use by the Owner of an Earlier Right

793. A third person may use the same sign as a corporate name, a trade name, or shop sign, when such a use was either prior to the registration of the trademark, or is made by a person who in good faith uses his family name. This rule deals with the case of persons who are not able to oppose their prior right as a ground for nullification of the trademark, for instance, because of the strictly local scope of their goodwill (*see supra,* paragraph 690). They may nevertheless continue to use the sign after its registration by a third person without risk of sanction for unauthorized use. However, if such a use harms the rights of the trademark owner, he may require that it be limited or prohibited (Article L. 713-6, §2).[514]

§2. The Use as a Necessary Reference

794. Third persons may use the protected sign in order to identify the destination of a product or a service.

795. This rule applies to sales of goods such as accessories or spare parts, under condition there is no confusion as to their origin. This exception allows third parties to use the trademark as a technical reference. However, Article L. 713-6, §2 applies here to allow the owner to set aside the exception (*see supra*, paragraph 793).

§3. The Use as a Geographical Indication

796. A third person may use the same sign as a geographical indication (defined in Article L. 721-2, *see infra* paragraphs 867 et seq.), except where the mark, given its reputation and duration of use, is the exclusive origin of reputation or knowledge by the consumer for the product for which a geographical indication is requested. However, if such a use harms the rights of the trademark owner, he may require that it be limited or prohibited (Article L. 713-6, §2)

§4. The Use in 'Comparative Advertising'

797. A trademark may be used by a competitor in a 'comparative advertisement' campaign, which compares competing products or services by identifying them by

514. Cass. com., 17 Oct. 1995: Bull. civ. IV, No. 243.

their trademark (e.g., 'OMO' washes better than 'ARIEL'). Such advertising is strictly regulated under the Act of 18 January 1992 (Article L. 121-8–L. 121-11, Consumer Code. The ordinance No. 2001-741 of 23 August 2001 implemented into French law the EC Directive No. 97/55 of 6 October 1997 concerning misleading advertising so as to include comparative advertising[515]). The mention of a trademark is authorized only if the whole campaign complies with the legal conditions. Otherwise, it may be sanctioned as an illegal reproduction of the trademark (e.g., Versailles, 15 November 2001: JCP ed. E 2002, p. 342).

515. EC Directive No. 97/55 of European Parliament and of the Council of 6 Oct. 1997 amending Directive 84/450/EEC concerning misleading advertising so as to include comparative advertising, OJEC, No. L. 290, 23 Oct. 1997, pp. 18–23.

Chapter 8. Use Requirements

798. The owner of a trademark who does not use it for an uninterrupted period of five years, may be forfeited of his rights under Article L. 714-5 (*see infra*, paragraph 805).

Chapter 9. Duration of Protection

799. The duration of the exclusive right on a trademark is defined by the date of its entering into force and the date of its extinguishment.

§1. Date of Entry into Force

800. The exclusive right starts as from the date of filing for registration (Article L. 712-1), but takes effect against third parties only from the date of publication of the registration (Article L. 716-2, §1). Meanwhile, the right arising from filing may be effective against a third party (probable infringer) to whom it was notified (Article L. 716-2, §2).

§2. Date of Extinguishment

I. Normal Date of Extinguishment

801. The exclusive right is effective during ten years from the filing date, but may be kept in force indefinitely, by renewals done every ten years (Article L. 712-1). In other terms, as long as the trademark remains attractive, it may be maintained. The renewal consists in a mere written declaration, which should be made within the last six months prior to the expiration of the previous period of ten years. However, the declaration may still be filed or the fees may be paid within an additional six-month to be counted as of the day after the last day of the month of expiry of the protection with a supplementary fee (Article R. 712-24). If the declaration does not satisfy these requirements, a time limit shall be given to the holder in order to regularize (Article R. 712-24, §4 and R. 712-11). Application for renewal may not contain any modification of the trademark or an extension of the list of products or services for which it is registered (Article L. 712-9). It is not subject to the examination or the opposition procedure (Article L. 712-9, §2).

II. Anticipated Date of Extinguishment

802. An anticipated termination of the right may take place by renunciation, forfeiture, exhaustion, or judicial nullification of the trademark.

803. Renunciation to the right may be done at any time by the owner of the trademark. It may be total or partial, when, for instance, only a part of a complex mark is abandoned (Article L. 714-2). Formally, it requires a written request for radiation from the National Register of Trademarks, addressed to the Director General of the INPI. The request shall be accompanied by the proof of the payment of the prescribed fee (Article R. 714-1).

804. Forfeiture of the trademark rights, which sanctions two types of behaviours by the owner is a second case of anticipated termination.

805. Judicial forfeiture sanctions non-use of the trademark by its owner during an uninterrupted period of five years.[516] It may be requested from the competent first instance court ('Tribunal de grande instance'), upon action by any interested person (e.g., a competitor or distributor of competing goods or services) (Article L. 714-5, §3). The forfeiture may be claimed as a principal action or as an action for defence. The plaintiff does not have to bring evidence of non-use of the trademark; on the contrary 'The burden of proof of exploitation belongs to the owner of the trademark' (Article L. 714-5, §5). In order to escape forfeiture of his rights, the owner must show either a serious use, or equitable grounds for non-use of the trademark (Article L. 714-5, §1).[517] Shall be assimilated to such a serious use: (a) Use made with the consent of the owner of the mark, or in the case of collective marks, in compliance with the regulations; (b) Use of the mark in a modified form which does not alter its distinctive nature;[518] (c) Affixing of the mark on goods or their packaging exclusively for export (Article L. 714-5, §2). As for the equitable grounds for non-use of the trademark, it is not required that they amount to a force majeure. Obstacles such as difficulties to buy raw materials,[519] or an administrative refusal of the authorization necessary to market the product,[520] or the fact that the marketing of the product under the trademark was likely to create a confusion in the consumers' minds between two products of different origin,[521] etc. may serve as a 'legitimate excuse' for non-exploitation of the trademark. On the contrary, strictly commercial reasons do not amount to such an excuse.[522] Genuine use of the mark begun or resumed after the five-year period referred to in the first paragraph of Article L. 714-5 shall not constitute an obstacle to the forfeiture if it has been undertaken during the three months prior to the request for revocation and after the owner has gained knowledge of the possibility of such a request[523] (Article L. 714-5, §4).

806. When the action for forfeiture is well-grounded, the owner loses his right as from the date of expiration of the five years period (Article L. 714-5, §6). It shall have absolute effect, i.e., everybody shall freely use the sign and not only the plaintiff who brought the action. The forfeiture may be partial, i.e., it may concern only a part of the goods or services referred to in the registration.

807. Forfeiture also sanctions the owner who lets his trademark degenerate (most often a judicial decision is, however, necessary to check the conditions of the

516. As for the application of this rule in time, *see* an advisory opinion by the Cour de cassation: 2 May 1994: PIBD 1994, III, 270. Cass. com., 3 Jan. 1996: JCP ed. E, 1996 II 865, note Reboul and Storck.
517. Paris, 5 Jun. 1998: PIBD 1998, III, 465.
518. Cass. com., 20 Jun. 2006: PIBD 2006, III, 610. – Cass. com., 15 Sep. 2015: Propr. industr. 2015, comm. 74.
519. TGI Paris, 29 Jun. 1987: PIBD 1987, III, 513.
520. Cass. com., 18 May 1993: Bull. civ. IV, No. 197; RTD com. 1993, 658, obs. Chavanne. – Orléans, 13 Febr. 2003: Propr. industr. 2004, comm. 3.
521. Cass. Chambre mixte, 6 Jul. 1984: JCP ed. E, 1985 II 14449, concl. Sadon.
522. Cass. com., 3 May 1981: Bull. civ. IV, No. 119.
523. Cass. com., 9 Jun. 2009: PIBD 2009, III, 1273. – TGI Paris, 16 Apr. 2010: PIBD 2010, III, 593. – Cass. com., 19 Mar. 2013: PIBD 2013, III, 1193.

forfeiture). Such is the case: (a) when the trademark became the usual designation in commerce of the product or service, losing its distinctive character (e.g., Bikini applied to bathing suits, Frigidaire applied to refrigerator[524]), or (b) when the trademark became likely to deceive the public, especially as to the nature, quality, or geographical origin of the product or service[525] (Article L. 714-6).

808. In such cases, forfeiture is not automatic; the plaintiff must show that the degeneration of the trademark is the consequence of its owner's behaviour, who did not try to prevent it.[526]

809. Exhaustion of the trademark rights is the most recent cause of partial extinguishment.

810. Following the decisions of the ECJ, the French legislator introduced the notion of exhaustion of trademark rights (Article L. 713-4). The rightholder may no longer forbid the use of his trademark for products which were marketed in the EU, or in the EEA under this mark with his consent.

811. A third party may claim the benefit of the exhaustion of the trademark rights only upon showing that the use of the trademark was authorized by its owner within the EU and that this consent is still effective.[527] Absent such a consent, the exclusive right is not exhausted and may be enforced by its holder. For instance, the trademark owner may forbid importation to France of identical products from third countries, as the French courts follow the EU case law and do not recognize international exhaustion,[528] or the manufacturing of labels picturing the trademark, intended to be affixed on authentic products, but which were not marketed in the EEA with the owner's consent,[529] or marketing of the goods by a former licensee after the end of the licence.[530]

812. Moreover, according to Article L. 713-4, §2, the rightholder may forbid any new act of marketing if he offers legitimate grounds, such as modification or alteration of the goods after their authorized sale.

813. Finally, when international or intracommunity commerce is concerned, the case law of the ECJ must be taken into account in this matter.

814. Nullification of the trademark is another case of anticipated extinction of rights; it is studied together with the action for infringement (*see infra,* paragraph 837).

524. Riom, 31 Oct. 1958: Ann. propr. ind. 1959, 135.
525. Paris, 15 Dec. 2004: PIBD 2005, III, 142.
526. Paris, 14 Nov. 1995: PIBD 1996, III, 68; the owner let the public use the sign as the usual designation of the goods.-Paris, 19 Oct. 2001: Propr. intell., Mar. 2001, p. 94, Pina Colada has degenerated. – Cass. com., 18 May 2010: PIBD 2010, III, 487, 'La Pierrade' has not degenerated because of its owner's behaviour.
527. Paris, 29 Oct. 1992: PIBD 1993, III, 132.- Cass. com., 9 Apr. 2002: JCP ed. E 2002, p. 869; Propr. industr. 2002, comm. 51, p. 23, note Schmidt-Szalewski, the consent may be implicit.
528. Cass. com., 2 Dec. 1997: Bull. civ. IV, No. 320; D. 1998, jur., p. 604, note Agostini.-Paris, 8 Feb. 2002: JCP ed. E 2002, p. 1164, note Boespflug, Greffe and Barthélémy.
529. Paris, 24 Nov. 1993: PIBD 1994, III, 147.
530. Paris, 29 Oct. 1992: JCP 1993 IV 493.

Chapter 10. Infringement and Remedies

815. Facing the recent growth in infringement of trademarks, the French legislator increased the sanctions and organized prevention in this matter.

§1. Preliminary Proceedings

816. Any person with authority to bring an action for infringement may, in preliminary proceedings on grounds of pressing urgency, request the competent civil court ('Tribunal de grande instance') to order, under a penalty of a daily fine if necessary, against the alleged infringer or intermediaries whose services it uses, any measure aimed at preventing an infringement about to be committed against rights conferred by the trademark right or aimed at stopping any further allegedly infringing act. The competent civil court may also order ex parte urgent measures when the circumstances require that such measures should not be taken in the presence of both parties, in particular when any delay would be likely to cause an irreparable damage to the claimant. The court, in preliminary or ex parte proceedings, may order the requested measures only if evidence, reasonably accessible to the claimant, makes it likely that its rights are infringed or that such infringement is about to be committed. The court may enjoin the carrying out of the allegedly infringing acts, condition it on the furnishing of security to ensure, if necessary, the claimant's compensation or may order the seizure or the remittance to a third person of the products allegedly infringing the trademark rights, to prevent their introduction or circulation in the channels of commerce. If the claimant can give reasons that circumstances are likely to compromise the payment of damages, the court shall order the sequestration of the alleged infringer's movable or immovable assets, including the freezing of the bank accounts and other assets, under the general rules of law. To determine the goods likely to be seized, the court may order the submission of banking, financial, accounting, or commercial documents or the access to relevant data. The court may also award an advance payment to the claimant when the damage suffered cannot be seriously disputed. The court, in preliminary or ex parte proceedings may condition the implementation of the measures it has ordered on the furnishing of security by the claimant to ensure, if necessary, the claimant's compensation if the infringement proceedings are subsequently held unfounded or if the measures are void. When the measures taken to stop the infringement of rights are ordered before the commencement of proceedings on the merits, the claimant shall institute legal proceedings, either by civil action or criminal action, within a period of time set by regulation. Failing that, upon the defendant's request and without its having to justify its application, the measures ordered are void, without prejudice to the damages which may be claimed (Article L. 716-6).

§2. The Starting of the Action for Infringement

817. The action is usually brought by the trademark owner. The assignee may act as from the date of the entry of the assignment into the National Register of Trademarks.[531] The exclusive licensee may bring an action after the publication of his licence in the Register and, unless otherwise laid down in the contract, if after formal notice the owner does not exercise such right (Article L. 716-5, §1).

818. Any party to a licence contract may intervene in the action brought by the other party, in order to claim compensation of his own loss caused by the infringement (Article L. 716-5, §2).

819. The defendant is any person using the trademark without its owner's authorization. It may be the ex-licensee or the licensee using the trademark out of the limits set by the contract.[532] If the criticized behaviour took place on the Internet, the action for infringement may be brought also against the technical intermediaries, according to the provisions of the Act of 1 August 2000 relating to the freedom of communications.

820. The criminal action is brought against the infringer and his accomplices. A legal person may be held liable for a criminal offence in the conditions of Article 121-2 of the Penal Code (Article L. 716-11-2). In the other cases, the criminal action is directed against the corporate directors who are personally liable. However, since 31 December 2005, any criminal offence entails the criminal liability of the legal person which committed it (Act No. 2004-204, 9 March 2004, Article 54).

821. The action may be brought as from the date of the publication of the registration of the trademark and in order to obtain sanction of subsequent acts of infringement. Exceptionally, the applicant for registration may sue an infringer after notifying him the certified copy of his application. In such a case, the tribunal suspends its decision until the publication of the registration of the trademark (Article L. 716-2).

822. The action is subject to a five years' time limitation (Article L. 716-5, §3). And any proceedings for infringement by a later registered mark of which use has been tolerated for five years shall not be admissible unless the registration was applied for in bad faith. However, non-admissibility shall be limited to those goods and services for which use has been tolerated (Article L. 716-5, §4).

823. Civil actions and claims relating to trademarks, even when they also address a related issue of unfair competition, are exclusively brought before the 'tribunaux de grande instance' determined by regulation (Article L. 716-3). These 'tribunaux de grande instance' are the ten cited in Article D. 211-6-1 of the Judicial Organisation Code. The criminal action is within the jurisdiction of the criminal court ('tribunal correctionnel' which is the criminal formation of the 'tribunal de grande instance').

824. Arbitration is allowed in the conditions of Articles 2059 and 2060 of the Civil Code (the matter should not relate to a question of public order) (Article L. 716-4). The problems are the same as for patents (*see supra*, paragraph 584).

531. Cass. com., 24 May 1994: JCP ed. E, 1994 pan. p. 992.

532. Versailles, 7 Jul. 1986: Ann. propr. Ind. 1990, 304. Paris, 29 Oct. 1992: RTD com. 1993, 312, obs. Chavanne.

§3. THE DEVELOPMENT OF THE ACTION FOR INFRINGEMENT

825. The court follows its ordinary procedural rules. The outcome of the action is determined by the parties' arguments.

I. The Plaintiff's Arguments

826. The plaintiff has the burden of proof of the infringement. The means of such evidence are facilitated by the existence of the 'counterfeit seizure'.

827. In a civil action, infringement consists of any violation of the trademark owner's right, such as defined in Article L. 713-2 and L. 713-3 (Article L. 716-1). It is not necessary to evidence the defendant's bad faith. It may be necessary to bring evidence of a likelihood of confusion between the protected trademark and the allegedly infringing sign.

828. In a criminal action, some acts of infringement may be sanctioned only upon proof of bad faith. Such is the case for the acts listed under Article L. 716-9 and L. 716-10. Article L. 716-9 sanctions any person, who, for the purpose of selling, supplying, offering for sale, or lending goods under an infringing mark: (a) imports, under any customs regime, exports, re-exports, or tranships goods presented under an infringing mark, (b) reproduces industrially goods presented under an infringing mark, or (c) gives instructions or orders to commit the acts provided for at (a) and (b). Article L. 716-10 sanctions any person who: (a) holds without legitimate reason, imports under all customs procedures, or exports goods presented under a infringing mark; (b) offers for sale or sells goods presented under an infringing mark; (c) reproduces, imitates, uses, affixes, removes, modifies a mark, a collective mark or a collective mark of certification in violation of the rights conferred by its registration, and of prohibitions which rise from this; (d) delivers knowingly a product or provides a service other than that which is required of him under a registered mark. The infringement, under the conditions provided for at (d), shall not be considered constituted if a pharmacist exercises the faculty of substitution provided for under Article L. 5125-23 of the Public Health Code.

829. It was decided that there is no infringement by the use of a trademark when the products sold outside of a selective distribution network were put into commerce in the EU by the trademark's owner or with his consent.[533]

830. In a criminal action, infringement may be evidenced by the means of proof specific to the criminal procedure (e.g., searches and seizures). For instance, Article L. 716-8-9 states that 'Officers of the judicial police may, as soon as offences under Article L. 716-9 and L. 716-10 have been reported, effect the seizure of goods unlawfully manufactured, imported, stocked, placed on sale, delivered or supplied, and of any material and equipment specially installed for the purposes of such unlawful acts.'

831. In a civil action, it may be evidenced by all the means accepted by the civil procedure (e.g., witnesses, presumptions, writings, etc.). However, the trademark owner may use the specific procedure of 'counterfeit-seizure', organized by Article L. 716-7. Even if the counterfeit-seizure is very common in practice, it is not a

533. Cass. crim., 16 Jun. 1993: Bull. crim., No. 216.

compulsory procedure. That is the reason why the Act No. 2014-315 of 11 March 2014 added Article L. 716-7-1 A to precise that a court may order, on its own initiative or at the request of any person having quality, all legally admissible investigative measures, even if a counterfeit-seizure has not previously been ordered. The rules are similar to those applicable to the 'counterfeit-seizure' in patent matters (*see supra*, paragraph 579). The seizure should be previously authorized by the President of the competent 'Tribunal de grande instance', who defines its conditions and scope and may order warranties to be given by the plaintiff. The seizure is executed by a bailiff who may be assisted by an expert and a police officer if necessary. He may proceed in any place with either the detailed description, with or without taking samples, or the effective seizure of the allegedly infringing products or services as well as any related document, according to what was authorized by the president. The order may authorize the effective seizure of any document relating to the allegedly infringing goods or services, even in the absence of the latter. The court shall also order, for the same evidential purposes, the detailed description or effective seizure of equipment and tools used to manufacture or distribute the goods or to provide the allegedly infringing services. The bailiff drafts a report which must be delivered to the defendant. An irregular seizure may be declared invalid and the plaintiff sentenced to pay damages to the defendant.

832. The seizure must be followed by the introduction of the action for infringement – either a civil or criminal action – within twenty working days or thirty-one civil days if this time limit is longer, as from the date of the report of seizure. If not, the entire seizure, including the description, shall be void upon the defendant's request, without its having to motivate its request and without prejudice to the damages which may be claimed. A void seizure may not be used as evidence during the proceedings.

833. And since the Act No. 2007-1544 of 29 October 2007, if so required, the court hearing civil proceedings relating to trademark, shall order, under penalty of a daily fine if necessary, in order to determine the origin and the distribution networks of the infringing goods which prejudice the claimant's rights, the communication of any document or information held by the defendant or by any person who was found in possession of infringing goods or who provides services used in infringing activities or was reported to take part to the production, manufacturing, or distribution of such products, or the supply of such services ('Right of information'). The communication of documents or information shall be ordered if there is no legitimate hindrance (Article L. 716-7-1).

II. The Defendant's Arguments

834. In order to escape sanctions, the defendant may attempt to question either the existence of the plaintiff's right, or the existence of the infringement.

835. If the defendant succeeds in negating the efficacy of the trademark right, the plaintiff's action for infringement will be dismissed, since a non-existing right may not be infringed. The right may be questioned either on the ground of forfeiture, or of nullity. It may also be argued that the right is exhausted when such an argument is pertinent as to the motivation of the action (*see supra*, paragraph 809).

836. For instance, forfeiture of the trademark right may sanction its non-use during five years (*see supra*, paragraph 805). The action for infringement shall also be not admissible because of the owner's tolerance of the infringement by a later registered mark[534] (Article L. 716-5, §4). When the owner of the trademark did not sue the infringer, he may no longer do so after five years.[535] This time limitation does not apply when the defendant's trademark was registered in bad faith. The forfeiture is limited to the goods and services for which the use of the trademark was tolerated by its owner.

837. Nullity of the trademark right is the classical defence in the infringement trials. The nullity may be claimed as a principal action or as an action for defence, as long as the trademark right is in force.

838. The registered trademark right is presumed valid and may be nullified only by a court decision, upon action brought by an entitled person.[536] Any person showing an interest may bring such an action. Exceptionally, the nullity grounded on the conflict with an earlier right may be requested only by the holder of such earlier right (Article L. 714-3). However, his action is to be dismissed if the second (conflicting) trademark was registered in good faith and when he tolerated its use during five years.

839. The action may be brought as long as the trademark right is in force. However, the nullity grounded on Article L. 714-4 (damage to a well-known trademark) should be claimed within five years from the registration of the second trademark, unless this registration was made in bad faith.

840. The plaintiff in the action for nullification (who is usually also the defendant in the action for infringement) should show that the challenged trademark was registered in violation of a substantial condition of validity (the sign may not be a trademark, the sign is illicit, it is not distinguishing, it violates an earlier right; *see supra*, paragraph 663), or the registration was done with a fraudulent intention.[537] Nullity may not sanction the violation of a formal condition of registration.

841. The nullity may be total or partial; the exclusive right is retroactively destroyed (Article L. 714-3). The nullity does not mean that the use of the sign is prohibited, only that this sign may be freely used by anyone, since the exclusive right has disappeared. The holder of the nullified trademark may, however, still use the sign on another function; e.g., as a commercial name.

842. The judgment nullifying the trademark is published in the National Register of Trademarks.

§4. The Outcome of the Action for Infringement

843. The action for infringement may lead to temporary measures, then to definitive measures.

534. Cass. com., 7 Jan. 2014: PIBD 2014, III, 229, no forfeiture of the action for infringement directed against a company name.
535. Cass. com., 11 Feb. 2003, PIBD 2003, III, 210, tolerance implies the knowledge of the infringement.
536. Cass. com., 28 Oct. 1980: Ann. propr. Ind. 1981, 33.
537. Cass. com., 27 Jan. 1998: PIBD 1998, III, 197.

I. Temporary Measures

844. Such temporary measures may be taken either by a court, or by the customs administration.

845. The president of the tribunal may, at the plaintiff's request, issue an injunction against the defendant, ordering him to cease the use of the allegedly infringing trademark, or authorizing its continuation, upon constitution of warranties (Article L. 716-6, *see supra* paragraph 816). The conditions and consequences of such an injunction are modelled on the patent law (*see supra*, paragraph 594).

846. Under Article L. 716-8, the customs administration may withhold in the course of its inspections the allegedly infringing goods upon the written request of the holder of a trademark or the exclusive licensee. The request shall be accompanied by proof of his right. The withholding measure shall be notified without delay to the plaintiff (with information on the nature, the actual or estimated quantity, and images of the goods) and the party in possession of the goods. The Public Prosecutor shall be informed without delay by the customs service of the withholding measure that they have taken.

847. The withholding measure shall be lifted as of right where the plaintiff fails, within ten working days (on duly motivated request of the plaintiff that period of ten working days shall be prorogated by a new period of a maximum of ten working days), or three workings days if the withheld goods are perishable, following notification of the withholding of the goods, to prove to the customs service – either that precautionary measures have been taken – or that he has instituted proceedings before the civil court or the criminal court and has provided the necessary guarantees to cover his liability in the event of the infringement claim being eventually considered unfounded (Article L. 716-8, §4). During the withholding period, the holder of the trademark or his exclusive licensee may inspect the goods withheld, upon his request or upon the customs administration's request. On the occasion of the control of the goods withheld, the customs administration may take samples which may be transferred, upon request, to the holder of the trademark or the exclusive licensee for the sole purpose of analysis and to facilitate his civil or criminal action (Article L. 716-8-3).

848. For the purpose of the institution of the legal proceedings referred to in the foregoing paragraph, the plaintiff may require the customs administration to communicate the names and addresses of the sender, the importer and the consignee of the goods withheld, or of the holder thereof, images of the goods, and also the quantity, origin, and destination thereof, notwithstanding the provisions of Article 59*bis* of the Customs Code concerning the professional secrecy to which officials of the customs administration are bound (Article L. 716-8, §6).

849. Under some precise conditions, the withheld goods may be destroyed under control of the customs administration (Article L. 716-8-4 and L. 716-8-5).

850. The French customs administration cannot withhold: (a) goods that have European status, which are legally produced or released for free circulation in a Member State of the EU and intended, having entered by the French territory as defined in the first article of Customs Code, to be released in the market of another Member State of the EU, to be legally commercialized; (b) goods that have European status, which are legally produced or released for free circulation in a Member State of the EU, where they have been placed under the transit regime and destined, after their transit on the French territory, to be exported towards a non-Member State of the EU.

851. The French customs may also, without any request (ex officio, excluded for perishable goods), withhold in the course of its inspections goods capable to prejudice to a registered trademark or an exclusive licensee. This withholding measure shall be immediately notified to the holder of the trademark or the exclusive licensee with indication of the nature and the actual or estimated quantity of goods, and communication of images of the goods, notwithstanding the provisions of Article 59*bis* of the Customs Code. The Public Prosecutor is also informed of the withholding measure. The withholding measure shall be lifted as of right where the holder or his exclusive licensee does not, within four working days following notification of the withholding of the goods, submits the withholding written request according to Article L. 716-8, its acceptation by the customs administration opening the ten working days withholding period(Article L. 716-8-1).

II. Definitive Measures

852. If the action for infringement is dismissed, no sanctions may be ordered on this basis. Most often, an accessory action for unfair competition is brought, which may succeed independently from the main one.[538] If an infringement of the plaintiff's trademark is evidenced, sanctions are always at least the civil ones, and may also be criminal, when the plaintiff chose this type of procedure.

A. Civil Sanctions of Infringement

1. Injunction

853. The injunction orders the plaintiff to cease the use of the infringing trademark under the sanction of civil fines defined by the court. The prohibition applies to the reproduction and use of the trademark, but does not affect the marketing of the products themselves. The court must specify the uses to which the injunction applies.[539]

2. Recall, Removal, Confiscation, Destruction, or Publicity Measures

854. Article L. 716-15 provides that in the case of civil liability for infringement, the court may order, at the injured party's request, the recall from the channels of commerce, the definitive removal from such channels, the destruction and the confiscation, in favour of the injured party, of the products recognized as infringing, and of the

538. Sometimes, the owner of a trademark prefers to act only on the basis of unfair competition: e.g., Cass. com., 19 May 1998: PIBD 1998, III, 408; the use of the trademark as 'marque d'appel' and the sale of marked products outside a selective distribution network amounted to acts of unfair competition.- Cass. com., 22 Oct. 2002, *Metro v. Cartier*: JCP ed. E 2003, p. 563, note Mainguy, the copy of a 'famous marked product' may amount to an unfair competition act even in absence of infringement (the right was expired).

539. Cass. com., 30 Jun. 1998: PIBD 1998, III, 464.

materials and implements principally used in their creation or their manufacturing. The court may also order any appropriate publicity measure of the judgment, in particular its display, or its publication, in whole or in part, in such newspapers or over such in-line services of communication to the public it may designate, pursuant to the conditions it specifies. All the measures mentioned are ordered at the cost of the infringer.

3. Damages

855. Since the Act No. 2007-1544 of 29 October 2007 and its revision by the Act No. 2014-315 of 11 March 2014, Article L. 331-1-3 states that 'To set the damages, the court takes into account separately: 1° the negative economic consequences of the rights infringement, including the loss of profit and loss suffered by the injured party; 2° the moral prejudice caused to the latter; 3° the profits made by the infringer, including economies of intellectual investments, material and promotional economies due to the infringement.' The legislator's intention was to break with the old general rules of the Civil Code about torts and especially with the traditional rule that damages are covering all the loss suffered but only such loss. Because of this old rule, the profits made by the infringer were of no relevance, so that the infringer, even paying damages, could still have interest to infringe. Thanks to the new rule of Article L. 716-14, it is now possible to award to the injured party a sum covering all his loss (economic or moral prejudice) but also a part of or all the profits made by the infringer because of the infringement. After a short time of hesitation, French courts now frequently use this possibility in order to repair and discourage intellectual property rights infringement.

856. The judges may also, if required by the injured party, use another method of evaluation of the indemnity to be paid by the infringer: it consists of a lump sum superior to the royalties amount which the infringer would have to pay to receive the rightholder's authorization. Article L. 716-14, §2 states 'The court, however, shall, as an alternative and upon request of the injured party, award as damages a lump sum. This sum is higher than the amount of royalties or fees which would have been due if the infringer had requested authorization to use the right which it has prejudiced. This sum is not exclusive of compensation for the moral prejudice caused to the injured party.'

857. The loss consists mainly of: the violation of the exclusive right itself, the loss of profits which would have been made in absence of infringement,[540] the depreciation of the value of the trademark,[541] the costs of litigation, etc. Only the acts realized by the defendant in France are taken into account.[542] Independently from the damages following the infringement, the plaintiff may claim damages for unfair competition if he may evidence a wrongdoing distinct from the infringement itself.[543]

540. Cass. com., 14 Feb. 1984: D. 1985, I.R., p. 86, obs. Burst.

541. Cass. com., 19 Feb. 1991: Ann. propr. Ind. 1991, 11. – Cass. com., 3 Jun. 1998: PIBD 1998, III, 484, depreciation of the luxurious image of the trademark.

542. Paris, 24 Jun. 1998: PIBD 1998, III, 488.

543. Versailles, 10 Mar. 1995: PIBD 1995, III, 307; dismissal of the action for infringement, but damages granted for parasitism and disparagement. Cass. civ. 2, 2 Apr. 1997: Bull. civ. II, No. 113; use of the trademark in a satirical television show.

B. *Criminal Sanctions of Infringement*

858. The criminal sanctions of trademark infringement were increased by the Act of 5 February 1994 then again by the Act of 9 March 2004. They consist presently of a three years imprisonment and a fine of EUR 300,000 (Article L. 716-10) or of five years imprisonment and a fine of EUR 500,000 where it is committed by an organized gang or on an online public communication network, or in cases foreseen under Article L. 716-9, of four years imprisonment and EUR 400,000 fine, or of seven years imprisonment and a fine EUR 750,000 where it is committed by an organized gang or on an online public communication network, or when the facts relate to goods dangerous for the health, the safety of man or animal. In case of relapse, these sanctions are doubled, as well as when the infringer is or was linked by contract with the plaintiff (e.g., former licensee or employee) (Article L. 716-12, §1). The offender may also be deprived from the right to vote and to be elected in professional elections during a maximum of five years (Article L. 716-12, §2). Criminal sanctions imply evidence of acts made knowingly.

859. Legal persons may be declared penally liable in accordance with Article 121-2 of the Penal Code. According to Article L. 716-11-2, the infringement committed by a legal person shall be punishable by a fine whose maximum amount shall be five times that which is applicable to natural persons by the law sanctioning the offence (Article 131-38 Penal Code) and the penalties listed in Article 131-39 of the Penal Code (*see supra,* paragraph 106). The legal persons incurring criminal liability may also be ordered, at their cost, to remove from the channels of commerce the articles held infringing and any other item which was used or intended for committing the offence. The courts may also order the destruction, at the expense of the infringer, or the delivery up to the injured party of the goods removed from the channels of commerce or seized, without prejudice to the damages which may be claimed.

860. Natural persons penally liable may be further obliged, at their own costs, to remove from the channels of commerce the goods found to be infringing and all things which were used or intended to infringe the trademark right. The courts may also order the destruction, at the expense of the infringer, or the delivery up to the injured party of the goods removed from the channels of commerce or seized, without prejudice to the damages which may be claimed. The courts may also order the dissemination of the information concerning the decision, including displaying and publishing, at the expense of the infringer (Article L. 716-13) without, however, the costs of such publication exceeding the maximum amount of the fine incurred (Article 131-35, Penal Code).

C. *Customs Sanctions of Infringement*

861. Importation or exportation of goods bearing an infringing trademark is the criminal offence of smuggling (combination of Article L. 716-9, an IPC with Article 38, §4, Customs Code). Absent the proof of their regular origin, the goods arguably infringing are presumed to be smuggled (Articles 215, 215*bis* and 419, Customs Code). Sanctions of Article 414 of the Customs Code apply: up to three years imprisonment, confiscation of fraudulent goods and of vehicles used to transport the goods, and fine comprised between one and two times the value of the goods.

Chapter 11. Relation to Other Intellectual Property Rights

§1. Trademarks and Patents

862. Both rights relate to a different subject matter. The patent is a temporary exclusive right on an invention; the trademark is a distinguishing sign of goods and services listed in the registration: whereas the patent right is limited to twenty years, the trademark right may be indefinitely renewed.

863. A product may be protected by a patent as for its technical aspects and may be sold under a trademark, belonging to the same owner (or used under licence). After the termination of the patent right, all the competitors will be able to manufacture and sell the product, but only the owner of the trademark will retain the right to sell it under this trademark, a situation which gives to him an interesting commercial advantage.

§2. Trademarks, Designs, and Models and Copyright

864. The trademark may consist of a sign which is an artistic creation, protected as such either by copyright, or as a registered design, or model. Cumulation of the three types of protection is possible. The creator of the sign may apply for registration of this sign as a trademark in his own name. A third party may not register this sign as a trademark without the copyright holder's consent (*see supra*, paragraph 693).

§3. Trademarks and Trade Names

865. The function of a trademark is to identify products or services; the role of a trade name is to identify a business, e.g., on letterheads, on catalogues, etc. Both may, however, play the same role, e.g., the trade name may be affixed on products in order to identify them, playing the role of a trademark. This explains why the affixing on manufactured goods of a false name of a producer, or a false trade name may be deceiving of the consumers' interests.

866. When the trademark and the trade name belong to different persons, conflicts may arise. An earlier trade name may prevent a valid registration by a third person as a trademark only if it is able to ruin the distinguishing character of such a trademark (*see supra*, paragraph 690). An earlier trademark may not be lawfully used by a third person as a trade name without the trademark owner's consent.[544]

544. Paris, 2 Oct. 1986: Ann. propr. Ind. 1987, p. 164.

§4. Trademarks and Geographical Names

867. A geographical name may be protected as a geographical indication, i.e., as a French appellation of origin ('appellation d'origine') or indication of origin ('indication de provenance') or as a EU geographical indication ('Protected Designation of Origin' and 'Protected Geographical Indication'[545]) which are protected against infringement by Articles 722-1 et seq. of the French IP Code).

868. Article L. 721-1 of the IP Code sends back to Article L. 115-1 of the Consumer Code for the definition of the appellation of origin: 'An appellation of origin consists of the name of a country, a region or a town, used to identify a product originating therefrom, and the quality and characters of which are related to the geographical environment, including natural and human factors.' Appellations of origin are collectively owned by all the producers of the given geographical area. The protection of an appellation of origin is in principle acquired through a lasting and loyal use; no registration is required (e.g., 'poteries de Vallauris', 'dentelle du Puy'). However, as for agricultural, food, forestry, and marine products, the geographical name may be protected as a 'controlled appellation of origin' ('appellation d'origine contrôlée' AOC) which, on proposal of INAO, is recognized by a decree (Articles L. 641-5 et seq. of the French Rural Code; e.g., 'Epoisses', 'Pomme du Limousin', 'Camembert de Normandie', 'Champagne', 'Crémant de Bourgogne'). Since the Ordinance No. 2015-1246 of 7 October 2015, a 'controlled appellation of origin' must also be registered as a Protected Designation of Origin, which is a EU geographical indication (if not, the product loses its 'controlled appellation of origin', Article L. 641-10 of the French Rural Code). The products covered by a 'controlled appellation of origin' and a Protected Designation of Origin shall only mention the latter; there is an exception for wines which shall mention the 'controlled appellation of origin'. And, as for industrial and craft products, the Act No. 2014-344 of 17 March 2014 has created a new type of appellation of origin, called 'geographical indication protecting industrial and craft products' (Article L. 721-2–L. 721-10). The operators (producers, transformers…) of the given geographical area shall gather in a 'defense and management body', prepare a 'regulation of use' of the geographical indication and file an application with the INPI. The INPI will examine the application and decide if the said geographical indication shall be registered and protected.

869. An indication of origin is also a geographical name but it simply refers to the place where the product has been produced or cultivated. The product may be

545. Regulation EC No. 110/2008 of the European Parliament and of the Council of 15 Jan. 2008, on the definition, description, presentation, labelling, and the protection of geographical indications of spirit drinks, OJEU, No. 39, 13 Feb. 2008, pp. 16 et seq.; Regulation EU No. 1151/2012 of the European Parliament and of the Council of 21 Nov. 2012 on quality schemes for agricultural products and foodstuffs, OJEU, No. 343, 14 Dec. 2012, pp. 1 et seq.; Regulation EU No. 1308/2013 of the European Parliament and of the Council of 17 Dec. 2013 establishing a common organisation of the markets in agricultural products, OJEU, No. 347, 20 Dec. 2013, pp. 671 et seq.; Regulation EU No. 251/2014 of the European Parliament and of the Council of 26 Feb. 2014 on the definition, description, presentation, labelling, and the protection of geographical indications of aromatised wine products, OJEU, No. 84, 20 Mar. 2014, pp. 14 et seq.

known for some special quality or characters but these quality or characters are not due to this geographical location. The French protection of an indication of origin is in principle acquired through a lasting and loyal use; no registration is required. An indication of origin shall also be protected in France, as in all the EU, as a registered 'Protected Geographical Indication.'

870. The geographical name protected as a geographical indication may not be registered as a trademark either by a producer entitled to use the geographical indication,[546] or by a third person: such a mark is deceptive.[547] However, a producer entitled to use the geographical indication may include it in a complex trademark including additional distinguishing signs.[548] The geographical indication or any other name referring to it may not be affixed on a similar product (Article L. 115-5, Consumer Code). Such a use may even be prohibited as for totally different goods, 'when it is likely to weaken or exploit the notoriety of the appellation of origin' (Article L. 115-5, Consumer Code). For instance, the trademark 'Champagne' registered for a perfume was invalidated as fraudulently exploiting the famous appellation of origin of Champagne wines.[549]

546. Paris, 22 Apr. 1986: PIBD 1986, III, 314.
547. Angers, 17 Feb. 1992: RDPI 1992, No. 43, p. 22.
548. Cass. com., 8 May 1973: PIBD 1974, III, 44.
549. Paris, 15 Dec. 1993: D. 1994, jur., p. 145, note Le Tourneau.

Part V. Trade Names

871. The trade name is an appellation used by a merchant (physical or legal person) in the exploitation of his business. In other words, it is the name under which the business is known to the clients. For this reason, the trade name is mentioned on all the documents and papers addressed to the public: letterheads, advertisements, etc. But the trade name may also be used to identify a sales point, such as a shop or a store: it becomes then a shop sign (which may of course be different from the trade name). Less frequently, the trade name may be affixed on products or services provided by the merchant: it plays then the role of a trademark.

Chapter 1. Sources: Legislation

872. The trade name is not considered in French law as the object of an intellectual property right. It is not protected by the action for infringement and no administrative procedure of registration is organized. Therefore, no provision of the Intellectual Property Code deals with the protection of trade names. Litigation is treated in terms of liability in torts, under Articles 1240 and 1241 of the Civil Code (old Articles 1382 and 1383), as a specific case of unfair competition.

Chapter 2. The Protection of Trade Names

§1. Acquisition

873. The trade name under which a business is worked should be mentioned in the Register of Commerce and Corporations. But its legal protection starts only with its public use. Any public use is effective, such as: advertisements, mailing, catalogues, etc.; it is not necessary that the business opens effectively.[550] The protection ceases by non-use, either when the trade name is given up, or when the business is closed. On the contrary, when the merchant moves his business to another place, he may keep the same trade name. Consequently, the landlord who leased the premises to the merchant may not use the same trade name after the merchant's departure.[551]

§2. Transfer

874. In case of assignment of the goodwill, the trade name is transferred automatically, unless a contrary provision is included in the contract.[552] Consequently, the buyer of the business may use the seller's trade name, under condition he does not create confusion with the seller's business (he should add, e.g., 'successor of..'). The seller, on the contrary, may no longer use this trade name unless it is also his personal name. In this latter case he will be able to use his name for commercial purposes, under condition he adds an element in order to avoid confusion with the buyer's business (e.g., his first name). The trade name may be sold as such independently from the business, if it is notorious enough to have an economic value.

§3. Protection

875. Since the trade name is not an intellectual property right, it is not protected by an action for infringement, but for unfair competition. Whereas the first one requires only evidence of violation of an exclusive right, the second one implies evidence of a wrongdoing, in compliance with the rules of civil liability in torts. The holder of a trade name may bring such an action with chances of success against anyone who uses the same or similar name in conditions implying a likelihood of confusion with his business. No wrongful intention is required.[553] On the contrary, such an action is dismissed when there is no evidence of likelihood of confusion.[554] The existence of

550. Paris, 26 Oct. 1957: Ann. propr. Ind. 1958, 43.
551. Paris, 3 Jul. 1996: D. Aff. 1996, No. 37 p. 1187.
552. Cass. req., 3 Feb. 1909: DP 1910, 411. Paris, 3 Jul. 1996, *supra.*
553. Cass. com., April 1958: D. 1959, jur., p. 87, note Derrida. Cass. com., 8 Oct. 1981: Bull. civ. IV, No. 342.
554. Cass. civ. 3, 17 Dec. 1964: Bull. civ. III, No. 573.

such a risk of confusion requires that both businesses be competing in the same geographical and commercial area.

876. First, a trade name is protected only in the geographical area where it is known to the public (city, region, or country). Therefore, the same name may be lawfully used by a third person outside of this geographical area.[555] Some well-known trade names are protected on the whole French territory.[556]

877. Second, the likelihood of confusion implies that both names are used in the same business area. Identical trade names may be used in totally distinct activities.[557] However, French courts accept to protect extensively well-known trade names, even out of the limits of their business activity.[558]

878. The trade name used by a merchant may not be lawfully registered as a trademark by a third party for identical or similar goods or services (*see supra*, paragraph 866).

555. Cass. com., 8 Jan. 1964: D. 1964, jur., p. 186; protection only in a given district of a city; the name is free for use in the rest of the city.
556. Aix-en-Provence, 23 Apr. 1980: Bull. Aix, 1980, 40, No. 2; a night club in the South of France may not use the name 'Crazy' which implies a confusion with 'Crazy Horse' located in Paris.
557. Cass. com., 8 Jun. 1955: D. 1956, som., p. 52.
558. Paris, 27 Nov. 1959: RIPIA 1960, p. 33, 'Ritz' case. – Cass. com., 2 Nov. 1966: Gaz. pal. 1967,1, jur., p. 45; 'Maxim's'.

Part VI. Industrial Designs

879. The so-called industrial designs and models are useful objects including an aesthetic aspect. They may consist either of two-dimensional shapes (designs), or three-dimensional ones (models). Such 'industrial design' or 'applied art' plays an increasing role in the marketing of products or services, as the consumers become more attentive to the aesthetics of the goods they purchase.

880. The Article L. 511-1, §1 of the French I.P. Code gives the following definition of designs and models: 'May be protected as a design or model the appearance of a product, or part of a product, especially characterized by its lines, outlines, its colour, its shape, its texture or its materials. These characteristics may be those of the product itself or of its decoration.'

881. In 2014, 63,249 designs and models were registered in France.

Chapter 1. Sources: Legislation

882. Book Five of the Intellectual Property Code organizes a specific regime of protection of registered designs and models (Articles L. 511-1–L. 522-2). The EC Directive No. 98/71 of the European Parliament and the Council of the EU of 13 October 1998 on the legal protection of designs and models[559] was introduced into the French law by the Ordinance No. 2001-670 of 25 July 2001 and modified the above-mentioned articles of the IP Code. It orders the Member States to cumulate the protection by registration with protection by copyright, under conditions and scope they determine in their national law (Directive, Article 17). Article L. 513-2 states that this specific protection may be claimed without prejudice to copyright (Books One and Three of the Code). This provision means that a design or a model may be protected either only by copyright without any formality, or by both copyright and the specific rules of Book Five, if it was registered. However, cumulation is never automatic; it is up to the creator of the design or model who wishes to enforce his rights, to choose either system or to use them both.

883. This possibility of cumulation, has been a long time rule specific to French law, as it is the application of the theory of the 'unity of the art' elaborated by the famous jurist Eugène Pouillet. He considered that any original form should be copyrightable, whatever its destination (useful or aesthetic) or its merit.

884. The creator may have an interest in claiming protection under both systems: e.g., when the registration is void or expired, copyright may still be used, since it does not require any registration and its duration is longer (the counterfeit-seizure procedure is easier to enforce for copyright). As for foreign works, they may benefit in France of the double protection by registration and copyright only if they may claim such a double protection under the law of their country of origin.[560]

885. France also ratified the main international agreements relating to designs and models: The Hague Agreement of 6 November 1925 on the international registration of industrial designs and models, entered into force in France on 20 October 1930,[561] and the Locarno Agreement of 8 October 1968 creating an international classification of the industrial designs and models, entered into force in France on 13 September 1975.

559. EC Directive No. 98/71 of the European Parliament and of the Council of 13 Oct. 1998 on the legal protection of designs, OJEC, No. L. 289, 28 Oct. 1998, pp. 28–35.

560. Paris, 14 Mar. 1991: JCP 1991 II 21780, note Ginsburg. 25 Sep. 1996: RIPIA 1997, p. 243. 10 Dec. 1997: RIPIA 1998, p. 87, applying Art. 2-7 of the Berne Convention.- Cass. civ. 1, 5 Mar. 2002: Propr. intell. 2002, No. 5, p. 56, obs. A. Lucas.

561. Last modified by the Geneva Act of 2 Jul. 1999, entered into force in France on 18 Mar. 2007.

Chapter 2. Conditions of Protection

886. Following the provisions of the EC Directive, French law separated the definition from the criteria of protection. The design or model to be protected under the registration system (Book Five of the Code) should consist of a shape which is independent from its function, is visible, new, and individual.

§1. The Shape Should Be Independent from Its Function

887. The patent protection is excluded as for purely aesthetic items (Article L. 611-10, §2b). When the shape plays not only an aesthetic, but also a functional role, this situation raises the question of choice between patents and specific protection by registration.

888. Under the regime prior to the ordinance of 2001, this problem was dealt with under Article L. 511-3, §2, of the IP Code, which stated: 'But if the same object may be considered both as a new design or model and as a patentable invention and if the elements constituting the novelty of the design or model are inseparable from those of the invention, such an object may be protected only under provisions of Book 4' (on patents). Consequently, when the shape was inseparable from its function, it could be protected only by a patent and its registration as a design or model should be nullified. This complicated rule gave way to an abundant and subtle case law.

889. It was held that the 'inseparable' character of the shape and of the utilitarian function is to be evaluated in relation to the shape the protection of which is claimed. When the shape is dictated exclusively by a 'functional necessity', or seeks a precise functional aim, it is to be protected under patent law, and may not be validly registered as a design or model.[562] For instance, the registration of the model of a stackable chair, the shape of which was necessary to make it stackable was invalidated.[563] Such a 'functional form' is not copyrightable either.[564]

890. On the contrary, the shape could be registered as a model even if it offered utilitarian advantages, when these advantages were separable from the shape; most often it was checked whether the advantages could be obtained by different shapes.[565] When the shape was separable from its utilitarian function, both protections could be cumulated: the functional elements could be covered by a patent (if they fulfil the conditions of patentability), whereas the aesthetic elements registered as a design or model.[566]

---

562. Cass. com., 27 Feb. 1987: D. 1987, I.R., p. 167. *See also*: F. Greffe, note in JCP ed. E, 1998 Chron., p. 1492 and references cited. – Cass. com., 21 Oct. 1997: PIBD 1998, III, 21.
563. Paris, 29 Sep. 1994: PIBD 1995, III, 16. – Cass. com., 22 Jan. 1973: D. 1973, jur., p. 217, note X.L., where the model registered for a tile was invalidated because the tile was protectable only by a patent since its form was necessary to produce a technical effect of tightness.
564. Cass. com., 29 May 1981: Dossiers Brevets 1981, 1, 4.
565. Cass. com., 21 Mar. 1995: PIBD 1995, III, 313; RIDA, October 1995, 281; model of a coat. – Cass. com., 7 Apr. 1998: PIBD 1998, III, 388, model of a jacket.
566. Paris, 23 Jun. 1995: PIBD 1995, III, 475.

891. The new Article L. 511-8 provides for a much simpler rule: 'May not be protected: 1° The shape the characteristics of which are exclusively imposed by the technical function of the product.'

892. The new Article L. 511-8, 2°, supplements the provision, by excluding the protection of shapes necessary to allow the assembling of products and their functioning (interconnexion models). This provision is to be explained by the necessity to allow free competition for the manufacturing of spare parts or the connexion of products of various origins. The EC Directive brought an 'exception to the exception': are protectable elements allowing the connexion of parts of a 'modulable ensemble' (Article L. 511-8, last §). This relates to connexions of interchangeable elements in an unitary ensemble (e.g., kids building kits, stackable furniture, scaffolding, etc.).

§2. The Shape Should Be Visible

893. This condition is implied from the terms of Article L. 511-1, which mentions 'the appearance'. Moreover, the new Article L. 511-5 requires that 'the component part, once it has been incorporated in the complex product, remains visible during normal use of the latter by the end user, excluding maintenance, servicing or repair work'. Under the former system, French courts already took in consideration a similar requirement.[567] For instance, it was held that a sofa bed only characterized by its internal elements could not be protected as a model,[568] nor was protectable the shape of a lamp socked not visible and thus unable to attract consumers.[569] As another consequence, it was not possible to validly register an idea,[570] a type or style of shapes.[571] Only the concrete shape, embodying the idea or style was protectable. These solutions should remain under the new system[572] following the introduction of the EC Directive.

§3. The Shape Should Be New

894. Under the former system, novelty was required under Article L. 511-3 ('Provisions of the present Book apply to any new design, any new plastic shape …'), which, however, did not provide for a definition. The new Article L. 511-3 states: 'A design or model shall be considered to be new if, on the date of the filing of the application for registration or on the date of priority claimed, no identical design or model has been disclosed.' Novelty, proper to industrial property rights, is to be

567. TGI Paris, 19 Oct. 2005: PIBD 2006, III, 68, still according to the former system.
568. Trib. Civ. Mulhouse, 2 Apr. 1954: JCP ed. CI, 1954 I 53665.
569. Lyon, 12 Sep. 1996: PIBD 1996, III, 500.
570. Paris, 7 Oct. 1982: PIBD 1983, III, 15: the idea of inclusion of a cloth into a transparent plastic matter to create jewels may not be protected.
571. Paris, 12 Jun. 1891: Ann. propr. Ind. 1892,100: the protection of a sweets box taking the shape of a book does not extend to all the boxes of this type.
572. Cass. com., 9 Mar. 2010: PIBD 2010, III, 289.

distinguished from originality, proper to copyright law.[573] Novelty consists of a material difference between the creation and the prior art, whereas originality consists of the expression of the creator's personality.

895. Novelty is a condition of protection of registered designs and models (Book Five of the Code), whereas originality is a condition of protection by copyright (Books One and Three). However, due to the cumulative application of both systems, the French courts required originality even as for registered designs and models, when copyright was not claimed. The new provision should put an end to this critical case law, since the notion of novelty is treated in a purely objective way.

896. The definition of the disclosure is borrowed from the patent law: 'A design or model shall be deemed to have been disclosed if it has been made available to the public through publication, use, or by any other means' (Article L. 511-6). Thus, in order to destroy novelty of a registered design or model, it is necessary to show the existence of identical shapes accessible to the public prior to the date of registration.[574] Novelty is, as in patent law, an absolute novelty: the design or model must not have been accessible to the public at any time and in any place.[575] The disclosure may even result from a prior registered design or model owned by the applicant himself.[576]

897. However, the new Article L. 511-6 provides for three exceptions to the rule of absolute novelty: The first exception relates to the case where a design or model could not be reasonably known 'according to the normal course of business in the sector concerned, by professionals operating in the European Community, before the date of filing of an application for registration or before the date of priority claimed'.

898. Secondly, the novelty of a design or model is not ruined by disclosures made within twelve months before the application or the priority date, by the creator himself, his successors in right, or third parties acting on the basis of information or acts done by the above persons.[577] As a transitory provision, a creator is protected against his own disclosures[578] or the ones resulting from an abuse by a third party, whatever their date, if prior to 1 October 2001.

899. Finally, novelty is not destroyed by a disclosure made within twelve months prior to the application or the priority date as the result of an abuse towards the creator or his successor in title. The same transitory rule applies as above.

900. In the state of prior art, it should be checked if 'no identical design or model has been disclosed' (Article L. 511-3). As under the former system, novelty may be destroyed only by a 'whole' anteriority ('antériorité de toutes pièces'), i.e., a shape consisting of the same material elements, combined in the same way.[579] The

573. Cass. civ. 1, 11 Feb. 1997: Gaz. Pal., 2, som., p. 249. – Cass. com., 26 Febr. 2008: PIBD 2008, III, 291.
574. Cass. com., 14 Oct. 1975: Ann. propr. Ind. 1976, 107.
575. Paris, 19 Jun. 1985: Ann. propr. Ind. 1986, 185; a Roman mug destroys the novelty of a modern identical model.
576. Cass. com., 27 May 1997: PIBD 1997, III, 474.
577. Cass. com., 15 Mar. 2011: No. 10-30419.
578. Cass. com., 19 Dec. 1989: Bull. civ. 1989, IV, No. 319.
579. Cass. com., 21 Mar. 1995: PIBD 1995, III, 313. -Paris, 20 Sep. 1995: PIBD 1996, III, 24. – Paris, 14 May 2008 and 26 Mar. 2008: Propr. intell. 2008, No. 29, p. 443, obs. P. de Candé. – Cass. com., 24 Jun. 2014: Propr. intell. 2014, No. 53, p. 429, obs. P. de Candé.

same Article brings a precision: 'Designs or models shall be deemed to be identical if their features differ only in immaterial details.'

§4. The Shape Should Be Individual

901. According to the EC Directive of 13 October 1998 (Articles 4 and 5), the condition of 'individual character' (translated in French as 'caractère propre') was introduced into French law (Article L. 511-4). This condition is to be evaluated by considering the 'global impression' of the work on an informed observer[580] (the directive spoke about the 'user'), and taking into account 'the degree of liberty enjoyed by the creator in the elaboration of the design or model'. This condition differs from the one of originality formerly required by the French courts:[581] it should be evaluated towards the feeling suggested by the object. An impression of 'déjà vu' (already seen) excludes the individual character within the meaning of the statute.

902. As for the 'degree of liberty enjoyed by the creator', the court could rely on former cases, where protection was refused when the aspect of the shape was fortuitous or resulted from technical constraints.[582] It could further require proof of a 'personal effort' by the creator;[583] or a 'creative effort'.[584] This condition of individual character will be especially useful in the evaluation of validity of designs or models when some of their elements are not new; in such cases, the combination of the various elements should be original. Such is especially the reasoning as for copies of known shapes,[585] scale models,[586] and reproductions of natural objects.[587]

903. Both conditions of novelty and individual character are specifically difficult to enforce as for complex products, consisting of multiple elements which may be replaced (Article L. 511-5, last §). Isolated elements may be protected as such, if they fulfil the above conditions. Such would be the case, for instance, for elements of a car body. However, it remains to check if they are visible during a normal use (*see supra*, paragraph 893).

580. TGI Paris, 15 Febr. 2002: JCP E 2003, 1291, No. 20. – Douai, 11 Mar. 2004: D. 2005, pan. 1711. – Paris, 11 Jan. 2013: PIBD 2013, III, 999.
581. Cass. com., 10 Febr. 2015: PIBD 2015, III, 333. – Paris, 18 Nov. 2011: Propr. industr. 2012, comm. 27, obs. J.P. Gasnier. – Paris, 14 May 2008 and 26 Mar. 2008: Propr. intell. 2008, No. 29, p. 443.
582. Paris, 23 Jun. 1970: D. 1972, jur., p. 66.
583. Paris, 13 Oct. 1994: PIBD 1995, III, 46.
584. Paris, 8 Feb. 1995, 3, 295; is void the model of stockings when their aspect resulted of technical constraints.
585. Rouen, 16 Nov. 1904: Ann. propr. Ind. 1905, 213.
586. Paris, 28 Jun. 1984: PIBD 1984, III, 287: a scale model of an ancient tapestry is protectable when it implies adaptations which make it original.
587. Paris, 20 Oct. 1995: PIBD 1996, III, 54; a design of birds is protectable when original.

Chapter 3. Formalities

904. The protection under the specific rules of Book Five of the Code is based on the registration of the design or model (Article L. 511-9 and Articles R. 512-1 et seq.). The applicant may choose between two systems: the ordinary or the simplified registration.

§1. The Ordinary Registration

905. Application for registration should be filed either directly with the INPI. The filing may also result from a mailing to the INPI by registered letter with advice of delivery or by a message using any type of remote transmission (fax) according to the conditions defined by Director General of the Institute to guarantee, in particular, the safety of mailing. In such cases, the date of submission of the documents shall be the date of receipt at the INPI. The Director General of the INPI may require a filing by an electronic means where this simplifies the examination and publication of the patent application. (Article R. 512-1). An online filing is also possible and now very usual. The applicant may be the creator or his successor in title (Article L. 511-9). If the applicant does not have his domicile or head office in a Member State of the EU or in a State party to the agreement on the EEA, a representative, which has his domicile or head office in a Member State of the EU or in a State party to the agreement on the EEA, must be appointed (Article R. 512-2). The application includes (R. 512-3): (1) a request for registration; (2) a graphic or photographic reproduction of the designs or models; (3) proof of payment of filing fees; (4) power of the representative, if any, unless he has the capacity of 'conseil en propriété industrielle' ('industrial property counsel') or of 'avocat' (attorney). To be admissible, the application must comprise an identification of the applicant and a reproduction of the design or designs concerned (Article L. 512-2).

906. The INPI grants a filing date to the regular application: it may refuse a formally irregular application as well as the one contrary to public order or morality (Article L. 512-2, §3).[588] The INPI does not verify the substantial conditions of protection. The quality of creator is not verified by the INPI. The applicant for registration is, failing proof to the contrary, considered to be the beneficiary of this protection (Article L. 511-9). The application is published in the 'Bulletin officiel de la propriété industrielle' (BOPI), according to Article R. 512-10. However, some applicants may wish to keep their application secret in order not to make it immediately known to the competitors (especially in the fashion industry). It is possible to request the postponement of the publication up to three years from the filing date (Article R. 512-10). The applicant may renounce at any time to such a postponement and request publication: he must do so before introducing an action for infringement (about 10% of applications are unpublished).

588. Paris, 3 Apr. 1998: PIBD 1998, III, 389, refusal of an application for a model of game banknotes likely to be confused with authentic ones.

§2. The Simplified Registration (Article L. 512-2)

907. The applicant may prefer this type of registration, which may include up to one hundred designs and models in a simplified presentation. The application fees are lower than for the ordinary registration. The publication is automatically postponed up to three years, but the applicant may renounce the postponement for the whole application or a part of it. The applicant must renounce the secret six months prior to the expiration of the three years period and make the application comply with the ordinary formalities, under the sanction of forfeiture of rights by the INPI (Article R. 512-11). Article L. 512-2 states that this type of application is open to industries which frequently renew the shape and decoration of their products. However, no list of such industries is provided: it is up to the Director General of the INPI to decide whether an application is receivable in the simplified form.

Chapter 4. Ownership and Transfer

§1. Ownership

908. The word 'creator' should be understood in the meaning of 'author' as in copyright law. From this point of view, both systems have the same area of application. It should, therefore, be referred to copyright as for the definition of the creator of a design or a model (*see supra* paragraphs 127 et seq.).

909. If the registration was requested in fraud of a third person's rights, or in violation of a legal or contractual obligation, the person who considers to have a right on the design or model may claim its ownership in courts. If the applicant for registration acted in good faith, the action for recovery of ownership is to be brought within five years from the publication of the registration; if he acted in bad faith, the action for recovery of ownership may be brought until five years after the expiry of the protection of the design or model (Article L. 511-10).

§2. Transfer

910. Book Five of the IP Code contains no provision relating to contracts on registered designs and models. It only states that the rights may be transferred or licensed (Article L. 513-2) and that any act modifying or transferring the rights on a design or model produces effects against third parties only from the date of its entry to the National Register of Designs and Models. However, before its entry to the National Register, an act already produces effects against third parties who have acquired rights after the date of this act but who were aware of this act before the acquisition of those rights. The licensee, party to a licence agreement not registered on the national or international register of designs, is entitled to intervene in infringement proceedings brought by the owner of the design in order to obtain compensation for its own damage (Article L. 513-3).

911. Because of the cumulation of the rules specific to registration with those applying to copyright (*see supra*, paragraphs 866 et seq), the contracts relating to designs or models (whether registered or not) are concluded under the rules of copyright; it should be thus referred to these rules for drafting, interpretation and enforcement of such contracts (*see supra* paragraphs 148 et seq.).

912. However, these rules are sometimes set aside by the courts as for assignments of rights on designs and models. First, it is held that the requirement of a written document (Article L. 131-2) does not concern the works of applied art, but only assignment of rights of representation and publishing. The second paragraph of this article states that 'In all other cases, the provisions of Articles 13591362 of the Civil Code apply.' In other words, as against third parties, the assignment may be evidenced by all means.[589] Second, the provisions of the Article L. 131-4 mandating a proportional

589. Cass. com., 10 Jun. 1997: JCP ed. E, 1998 Chron., p. 1495, note Greffe.

remuneration of the author do not apply to the assignment of rights on designs and models: such assignments may be done in consideration of a lump sum.[590]

913. There are no compulsory licences of designs and models.

590. Cass. soc., 22 Jan. 1981: Ann. propr. Ind. 1981, 4; Paris, 3 Apr. 1990: Ann. propr. Ind. 1992, p. 88.

Chapter 5. Scope of Exclusive Rights

§1. General Rules

914. According to Article L. 513-2, 'the registration of a design or model confers upon its holder a right of ownership'. The following Article L. 513-4–L. 513-8 list the content and scope of such rights: 'Are prohibited, without the owner's consent, the production, the offer, the marketing, the import, the export, the transhipment, the use, or the possession in view of one of these aims, of a product incorporating the design or model.' The scope of the protection conferred by a design right shall include any design, which does not produce on the informed observer a different overall impression (Article L. 513-5).

915. The principle of 'the unity of the art' allows the owner to claim such protection either in cumulation or separately from his copyright (Article L. 513-2; *see supra*, paragraphs 882 et seq). Only the rules specific to the registered designs and models will be explained in the present chapter (as for the scope of copyright: *see supra,* paragraphs 162 et seq).

916. According to The Hague Agreement of 1925 (Article 7), the international publication entitles to the protection on the French territory without any further formality.[591]

§2. The Exclusive Right to Use

917. The most frequent case of infringement consists of a reproduction of the design or model. It may be either a slavish copy or an approximate one. A protected shape is counterfeit when its essential elements are reproduced.[592] The change in the size does not exclude infringement when the shape is totally reproduced.[593]

918. The infringement is judged after the similarities between the protected shape and the shape arguably infringing.[594] However, the similarities should concern the protected elements of the design or model.[595]

919. The means of reproduction are not important: e.g., an unauthorized photography of the protected model;[596] a reproduction of a protected bottle of perfume on a tee shirt;[597] an unauthorized reproduction of jewels in an advertising campaign,[598]

591. Paris, 23 Jan. 1995: PIBD 1995, III, 231.
592. Cass. com., 16 Mar. 1992: PIBD 1992, III, 474.
593. Cass. Ass. plén., 5 Nov. 1993: Gaz. Pal. 1993, I.R., p. 301.
594. Cass. com., 19 Feb. 1996: PIBD 1996, III, 321.
595. Paris, 26 Feb. 1997: PIBD 1997, III, 313: there is no infringement when the similarities concern only the general style of a model, and not its specific characteristics.
596. Paris, 17 Mar. 1971: Gaz. Pal. 1972, 1, jur., p. 94.
597. Paris, 19 Mar. 1992: PIBD 1992, III, 444.
598. TGI Paris, 2 Jun. 1992: PIBD 1992, III, 671.

etc. The poor quality and low price of the reproduced object do not excuse infringement.[599] The reproduction of an unauthorized reproduction is a new act of infringement.[600]

920. Likelihood of confusion between both shapes is not a condition of the infringement,[601] although it may be an indicia of infringement.[602]

§3. The Exclusive Right to Offer to Sell

921. An unauthorized offer to sell a counterfeit design or model is another case of infringement.[603] Even intermediaries between producers and supermarkets, who only list selected products participate in the marketing of such products and are infringers if the products are unauthorized reproductions of protected shapes.[604] It was even decided that a professional jeweller who repairs a counterfeit model of ring by replacing some of its elements participates in the infringement.[605] However, the courts tend to be more lenient with resellers and sanction them only under particular circumstances where such professionals could not reasonably ignore the existence of the exclusive rights (e.g., Lyon, 15 May 2004: JCP ed. E 2004, No. 974, p. 1052, note Greffe).

§4. The Exclusive Right to Import

922. Importation to France, even in transit, of counterfeit designs or models amounts to an infringement.[606] It is, however, necessary to take into account the possible exhaustion of rights (Article L. 513-8 'The rights conferred by the registration of a design or model shall not extend to acts covering a product comprising this design or model, when this product has been put on the market in the European Community or in the European Economic Area by the owner of the design or model or with his consent').

599. Cass. crim., 29 Oct. 1964: JCP ed. CI, 1965 II 75893.
600. Cass. crim., 18 May 1938: Gaz. Pal. 1938, 2, jur., p. 311.
601. Cass. com., 30 Nov. 1966: Bull. civ. III, No. 460.
602. Paris, 30 Jan. 1998: JCP ed. E, 1998 Chron. p. 1496, note Greffe, who cites numerous cases of the lower courts.
603. Paris, 12 Jul. 1972: JCP 1973 II 17290. Paris, 10 Mar. 1994: PIBD 1994, III, 362.
604. Cass. com., 27 Feb. 1996: RJDA 1996, No. 717. -16 Dec. 1997: PIBD 1998, III, 180; an exclusive distributor may be sued.
605. Paris, 10 Jan. 1996: PIBD 1996, III, 201.
606. Paris, 23 Jan. 1995: PIBD 1995, III, 231.

Chapter 6. Limitation of the Scope of Protection

923. When the rightholder claims protection under copyright, all the limitations specific to this system may be applied (private use, citation, etc.: *see supra*, paragraph 223). The Article L. 513-6 and L. 513-7 provide for limitations and exceptions borrowed from the EC Directive. Third parties are authorized to use a registered design or model in the private scope and for non-commercial purposes; for experimental purposes; to reproduce it in view of illustration or teaching, under condition to mention the registration and the owner's name and as far as such acts are not incompatible with loyal business practices and do not unduly damage the normal working of the design or model. Article L. 513-7 authorizes the use of protected shapes on board or for the repair of foreign ships or aircrafts in transit ('The rights conferred by the registration of a design or model shall not be exercised: (a) Concerning the equipment on ships and aircraft registered in another country when these temporarily enter French territory; (b) When spare parts and accessories are imported into France for the repair of these ships or aircraft or during the repair').

924. The exhaustion of the industrial property right may be opposed to the rightholder. Consequently, the importation to France and working on the French territory are not an infringement after the product was marketed within the EEA with the rightholder's consent (Article L. 513-8).

Chapter 7. Duration of Protection

925. According to Article L. 513-1, § 1, a registered design or model is protected during five years from the filing date. The protection may be extended upon written request of the rightholder for supplementary periods of five years up to a maximum of twenty-five years. Transitory rules are set forth under Article L. 513-1, § 2: the shapes registered before 1 October 2001 are protected for twenty-five years from the application or from the renewal if it took place before that date.

926. Enforcement of the protection is not subject to the effective use or exploitation of the right; there is no forfeiture similar to the one of trademarks.

Chapter 8. Infringement and Remedies

927. Violation of the exclusive right on a registered design and model is sanctioned through the action for infringement which was not changed under the new law.

§1. Starting of the Action for Infringement

928. Any person with authority to bring an action for infringement may, in preliminary proceedings on grounds of pressing urgency, request the competent civil court ('Tribunal de grande instance') to order, under a penalty of a daily fine if necessary, against the alleged infringer or intermediaries whose services it uses, any measure aimed at preventing an infringement about to be committed against rights conferred by the trademark right or aimed at stopping any further allegedly infringing act. The competent civil court may also order ex parte urgent measures when the circumstances require that such measures should not be taken in the presence of both parties, in particular when any delay would be likely to cause an irreparable damage to the claimant. The court, in preliminary or ex parte proceedings, may order the requested measures only if evidence, reasonably accessible to the claimant, make it likely that its rights are infringed or that such infringement is about to be committed. The court may enjoin the carrying out of the allegedly infringing acts, condition it on the furnishing of security to ensure, if necessary, the claimant's compensation or may order the seizure or the remittance to a third person of the products allegedly infringing the trademark rights, to prevent their introduction or circulation in the channels of commerce. If the claimant can give reasons that circumstances are likely to compromise the payment of damages, the court shall order the sequestration of the alleged infringer's movable or immovable assets, including the freezing of the bank accounts and other assets, under the general rules of law. To determine the goods likely to be seized, the court may order the submission of banking, financial, accounting, or commercial documents or the access to relevant data. The court may also award an advance payment to the claimant when the damage suffered cannot be seriously disputed. The court, in preliminary or ex parte proceedings, may condition the implementation of the measures it has ordered on the furnishing of security by the claimant to ensure, if necessary, the claimant's compensation if the infringement proceedings are subsequently held unfounded or if the measures are void. When the measures taken to stop the infringement of rights are ordered before the commencement of proceedings on the merits, the claimant shall institute legal proceedings, either by civil action or criminal action or by filing a complaint with the public prosecutor, within a period of time set by regulation (twenty working days or thirty-one civil days if this time limit is longer, as from the day on which the order is given, Article R. 521-1). Failing that, upon the defendant's request and without its having to justify its application, the measures ordered are void, without prejudice to the damages which may be claimed (Article L. 521-6).

929. The action for infringement may be brought by the owner of the registered design or model.[607] The exclusive licensee may bring an action after the publication

607. Cass. com., 12 Jul. 1993: PIBD 1993, III, 686.

of his licence in the Register and, unless otherwise laid down in the contract, if after formal notice the owner does not exercise such right. Any licensee shall be entitled to take part in the infringement proceedings instituted by the rightholder in order to obtain compensation for an injury he has personally sustained (Article L. 521-2). A legal person does not have to evidence that it is the author of the design or model: the exploitation of such a work lets presume (rebuttable presumption) that the plaintiff is vested as against third persons with intellectual property rights.[608] The distributor of the protected objects[609] may not sue the infringers. The criminal action may also be brought by the public prosecutor, who seldom does.

930. Jurisdiction is determined according to Article L. 521-3-1. Civil actions and requests relating to design or model, including when they also address a related issue of unfair competition, shall exclusively be brought before a restricted number (10) of 'Tribunaux de grande instance': Bordeaux, Lille, Lyon, Marseille, Nanterre, Nancy, Paris, Rennes, Strasbourg, Fort-de-France. Arbitration is allowed in the conditions of Articles 2059 and 2060 of the Civil Code (the matter should not relate to a question of public order).

931. The action may be introduced as from the date of publication of the registration. The unauthorized acts done by third parties after the filing date but prior to the publication of the registration of the design or model are not considered as infringing acts. However, those acts are illicit if they follow the notification to the infringer of a certified copy of the application (Article L. 521-1, §§2 and 3).

932. The civil action should be brought within five years, computed from each illicit act (Article L. 521-3). The criminal action is terminated after three years.

§2. Development of the Action for Infringement

933. The court follows its ordinary proceedings and decides after the examination of the plaintiff's and the defendant's arguments. According to Article L. 521-3-1, 'civil actions and claims relating to designs and models, even when they also address a related issue of unfair competition, are exclusively brought before the "tribunaux de grande instance" determined by regulation'. These "tribunaux de grande instance" are the ten "tribunaux de grande instance" listed in Article D. 211-6-1 of the Judicial Organisation Code. Arbitration is allowed in the conditions of Articles 2059 and 2060 of the Civil Code (the matter should not relate to a question of public order) (Article L. 521-3-1, §2).

I. The Plaintiff's Arguments

934. The plaintiff should bring evidence of a violation of the rights flowing from the registration of a design or model. If he also looks for sanction of infringement of his copyright in this design or model, he should show the existence of such an

608. Cass. civ. 1, 9 Jan. 1996: JCP 1996 IV 496. – Cass. com., 7 Apr. 1998: JCP ed. E, 1998, Chron., p. 1493, obs. Greffe. – Cass. civ. 1, 1 Oct. 1998: JCP ed. E, 1998, pan. p. 1859.
609. Paris, 23 May 1995: PIBD 1995, III, 402.

infringement. Existence of an infringement is independent from the benefits made by the defendant and from the loss suffered by the plaintiff.[610]

935. Evidence of the infringement may be brought by any means of proof accepted under the rules of civil or criminal procedure.

936. As for the other intellectual property rights, the legislator facilitates such evidence, by organizing a specific procedure of counterfeit-seizure (Article L. 521-4). The rules are similar to those applicable to the 'counterfeit-seizure' in patent matters (*see supra*, paragraph 590). The seizure should be previously authorized by the President of the competent 'Tribunal de grande instance', who defines its conditions and scope and may order warranties to be given by the plaintiff. The seizure is executed by a bailiff who may be assisted by an expert and a police officer if necessary. He may proceed in any place with either the detailed description, with or without taking samples, or the effective seizure of the allegedly infringing goods as well as any related document, according to what was authorized by the president. The order may authorize the effective seizure of any document relating to the allegedly infringing goods, even in the absence of the latter. The court shall also order, for the same evidential purposes, the detailed description or effective seizure of equipment and tools used to manufacture or distribute the allegedly infringing goods. The bailiff drafts a report which must be delivered to the defendant. An irregular seizure may be declared invalid and the plaintiff sentenced to pay damages to the defendant.

937. The seizure must be followed by the introduction of the action for infringement – either a civil or criminal action – within twenty working days or thirty-one civil days if this time limit is longer, as from the day on which the seizure is realized. If not, the entire seizure, including the description, shall be void upon the defendant's request, without its having to motivate its request and without prejudice to the damages which may be claimed. A void seizure may not be used as evidence during the proceedings. An abusive exercise of the counterfeit-seizure may entail the plaintiff's liability in torts.[611]

938. And since the Act No. 2007-1544 of 29 October 2007, if so required, the court hearing civil proceedings relating to designs or models, shall order, under penalty of a daily fine if necessary, in order to determine the origin and the distribution networks of the infringing goods which prejudice the claimant's rights, the communication of any document or information held by the defendant or by any person who was found in possession of infringing goods or who provides services used in infringing activities or was reported to take part to the production, manufacturing, or distribution of such products, or the supply of such services ('Right of information'). The communication of documents or information shall be ordered if there is no legitimate hindrance (Article L. 521-5).

939. In a criminal action, infringement may be evidenced by the means of proof specific to the criminal procedure (e.g., searches and seizures). For instance, Article L. 521-9 states that 'Officers of the judicial police may, as soon as offenses under Article L. 521-10, §1 have been reported, effect the seizure of goods unlawfully

---

610. Paris, 16 Nov. 1936: Gaz. Pal. 1936, 2, jur., p. 855; an offer to sell is an infringement even when no products were sold.

611. Cass. com., 27 Jan. 1998: JCP ed. E, 1998 Chron. p. 1495, note Greffe; multiple seizures of a non-protectable model entailing a decrease in sales.

manufactured, imported, stocked, placed on sale, delivered or supplied, and of any material and equipment specially installed for the purposes of such unlawful acts.'

940. The plaintiff may request that the customs administration withholds the suspect goods; an ex officio withholding is also possible (Article L. 521-14–L. 521-19, revised by the Act No. 2014-315 of 11 March 2014). The conditions are here similar to those applicable to trademarks (*see supra*, paragraph 846).

II. The Defendant's Arguments

941. The defendant may discuss the materiality of the infringement, by showing that the products he manufactures, sells, or imports do not reproduce the essential elements of the registered design or model belonging to the plaintiff.

942. Proof of good faith, in the meaning of ignorance of the existence of an exclusive right, in spite of taking reasonable measures will excuse the defendant's acts of exploitation.

943. Professionals should check, before manufacturing or selling, the legal status of the products, and, therefore, they are presumed acting in bad faith.[612] However, a professional may be excused if he made an excusable mistake.[613] Such proof may excuse the defendant from criminal sanctions but not necessarily from civil ones. Since the civil action is an action in torts, the defendant should evidence that he did not commit any wrongdoing, having made the reasonable verifications.[614] Some lower courts tend today not to presume the bad faith when the professional is a mere reseller. Such a professional is held liable only under specific circumstances showing his bad faith, such as a wide advertisement for the model made by the rightholder,[615] or the existence of a specialized department within the buyer's firm.[616] Nevertheless, the *Cour d'Appel* of Paris held liable for infringement an importer of jewels, who acted as a wholesaler buying on catalogues. The court noted that such a professional could not escape the presumption of bad faith 'whereas he has necessarily the duty to seek information by all the other professionals and undertake any diligence in order to learn whether he may lawfully and without risk to harm others, sell the disputed model'.[617]

944. Lawfulness of the exploitation may be another line of defence. The plaintiff may show that his use of the registered design or model was lawful, either because it was authorized by the rightholder (licence), or because the latter's right was ineffective (nullity, exhaustion, non-renewal).

612. Paris, 7 Jul. 1994: PIBD 1994, III, 550.
613. Paris, 1 May 1975: RTD com. 1977, 503, obs. Desbois.- Cass. com., 10 May 1994: PIBD 1994, III, 436.
614. Cass. com., 10 May 1994: D. 1996, jur., p. 521, note Greffe; PIBD 1994, III, 436.
615. Paris, 8 Nov. 1978: JCP 1979 II 19221.
616. Paris, 15 Jun. 1981: PIBD 1982, III, 10.
617. Paris, 17 Sep. 1997: JCP ed. E, 1998 Chron. p. 1494, note Greffe.

§3. Outcome of the Action for Infringement

I. Dismissal of the Action

945. In such a case no sanction for infringement may be ordered against the plaintiff. However, most frequently, the action for infringement is supplemented by the action for unfair competition. The latter may succeed even when the former is dismissed. Such is the case, especially in presence of a likelihood of confusion, even if there is no infringement. Since both actions stay on distinct legal grounds, it is not possible to imply the absence of unfair competition from the absence of infringement.[618]

II. Success of the Action

A. Success of the Criminal Action

946. The wilful infringement of a registered design or model is sanctioned by three years of imprisonment and a fine of EUR 300,000 or by seven years' imprisonment and a fine of EUR 750,000 where it is committed by an organized gang or on an online public communication network or when the facts relate to goods dangerous for the health, the safety of man or animal. (Article L. 521-10, §1). In case of relapse, or when the infringer is or was linked by contract (e.g., ex-licensee) with the plaintiff, these sanctions are doubled (Article L. 521-13, §1).

947. Legal persons may be declared penally liable in accordance with Article 121-2 of the Penal Code. According to Article L. 521-12, the infringement committed by a legal person shall be punishable by a fine whose maximum amount shall be five times that which is applicable to natural persons by the law sanctioning the offence (Article 131-38 Penal Code) and the penalties listed in Article 131-39 of the Penal Code (*see supra,* paragraph 106). The courts may also order the destruction, at the expense of the infringer, or the delivery up to the injured party of the goods removed from the channels of commerce or seized, without prejudice to the damages which may be claimed.

948. Several supplementary sanctions may be applied:

- The infringer may be deprived for a period not exceeding five years of the right to elect and to be elected in professional elections (Article 521-13, §2).
- The court may order the total or partial, permanent or temporary (for a period not exceeding five years) closure of the establishment that has served for the commission of the offence. Temporary closure may not be a cause of either termination or suspension of employment contracts, or of any monetary consequence prejudicial to the employees concerned. And in case of a permanent closure, the rights of the employees are protected according to Article L. 122-14-4 and L. 122-14-5 of the Labour Code (Article L. 521-10, §§2 and 3).

618. Cass. com., 14 Nov. 1995: PIBD 1996, III, 75.

- The natural persons penally liable may be further obliged, at their own costs, to remove from the channels of commerce the goods found to be infringing and all things which were used or intended to infringe the trademark right. The courts may also order the destruction, at the expense of the infringer, or the delivery up to the injured party of the goods removed from the channels of commerce or seized, without prejudice to the damages which may be claimed. The courts may also order the dissemination of the information concerning the decision, including displaying and publishing, at the expense of the infringer (Article L. 521-11) without, however, the costs of such publication exceeding the maximum amount of the fine incurred (Article 131-35, Penal Code).
- The legal persons incurring criminal liability may also be ordered, at their cost, to remove from the channels of commerce the articles held infringing and any other item which was used or intended for committing the offence. The courts may also order the destruction, at the expense of the infringer, or the delivery up to the injured party of the goods removed from the channels of commerce or seized, without prejudice to the damages which may be claimed (Article L. 521-12, §§3 and 4).

B. Success of the Civil Action

949. The plaintiff may claim compensation of the damage he suffered as the consequence of the infringement. Since the Act No. 2007-1544 of 29 October 2007, revised by the Act No. 2014-315 of 11 March 2014, Article L. 521-7 states that 'To set the damages, the court takes into account separately: 1° the negative economic consequences of the rights infringement, including the loss of profit and loss suffered by the injured party; 2° the moral prejudice caused to the latter; 3° the profits made by the infringer, including economies of intellectual investments, material and promotional economies due to the infringement.' The legislator's intention was to break with the old general rules of the Civil Code about torts and especially with the traditional rule that damages are covering all the loss suffered but only such loss. Because of this old rule, the profits made by the infringer were of no relevance, so that the infringer, even paying damages, could still have interest to infringe. Thanks to the new rule of Article L. 521-7, it is now possible to award to the injured party a sum covering all his loss (economic or moral prejudice) but also a part of or all the profits made by the infringer because of the infringement. After a short time of hesitation, French courts now frequently use this possibility in order to repair and discourage intellectual property rights infringement.

950. The judges may also use another method of evaluation of the indemnity to be paid by the infringer: it consists of an amount equivalent to the royalty, which the infringer would have to pay to receive the rightholder's authorization. Article L. 521-7, §2 states 'The court, however, shall, as an alternative and upon request, award a lump sum. This sum is higher than the amount of royalties or fees which would have been due if the infringer had requested authorization to use the right which it has prejudiced. This sum is not exclusive of compensation for the moral prejudice caused to the injured party.'

951. Article L. 521-8 provides that in the case of civil liability for infringement, the court may order, at the injured party's request, the recall from the channels of commerce, the definitive removal from such channels, the destruction and the confiscation, in favour of the injured party, of the products recognized as infringing and of the materials and implements principally used in their creation or their manufacturing. The court may also order any appropriate publicity measure of the judgment, in particular its display or its publication, in whole or in part, in such newspapers or over such in-line services of communication to the public it may designate, pursuant to the conditions it specifies. All the measures mentioned are ordered at the cost of the infringer.

952. The courts may also issue an injunction ordering the infringer to cease the unlawful acts. Usually this injunction is supplemented by a private fine to be paid upon each new act of infringement. Such private fines are set at a high level in order to dissuade from further continuation of the infringement.[619]

619. For example, Paris, 18 Jan. 1995: PIBD 1995, III, 227.

Chapter 9. Relation to Other Intellectual Property Rights

953. Relations may exist between registered designs and patents *(see supra,* paragraph 888*)*, trademarks, and copyright. To some extent, unfair completion rules may also apply.

§1. Relations with Patents

954. Designs and models sometimes raise the question of choice between patents and specific protection by registration. Under Article L. 611-10, §2 b), aesthetic creations are not patentable as such. But sometimes the form plays not only an aesthetic but also a functional role.

955. Before the introduction of the EC Directive in 2001, Article L. 511-3, §2 stated: 'But if the same object may be considered both as a new design or model and as a patentable invention and if the elements constituting the novelty of the design or model are inseparable from those of the invention, such an object may be protected only under provisions of Book VI (patents).'

956. French courts held that the 'inseparable' character of the shape and of the utilitarian function was to be evaluated in relation to the shape the protection of which was claimed. When the shape was dictated exclusively by a 'functional necessity' or sought a precise functional aim, it was protected under a patent. When the shape was separable from its utilitarian function, both protections could be claimed: aesthetic elements could be registered as a design or model, whereas functional characteristics could be protected by a patent (if patentable).

957. Since 2002, this problem is dealt with under the new Article L. 511-8, which excludes the protection of characteristics exclusively imposed by the product's technical function. It does no longer refer to the notion of 'separability' of the shape and its useful function, as did the former Article L. 511-3. In the interpretation of this provision, it is necessary to consider the decision by the ECJ, stating that a purely functional shape is excluded from the protection as trademark, 'even when other shapes would be able to produce a similar technical result' (ECJ, 18 June 2002, aff. C-299/99, *Konninklijke Philips Electronics NV v. Remington Consumer Products*). Although relating to trademarks, this solution is also pertinent as for designs and models.

958. Article L. 511-8, 2° supplements the above provision, by excluding the protection of characteristics necessary to allow the assembly of products and their functioning (parts of interconnection). The EC Directive has brought an 'exception to the exception': are protectable the elements which allow to connect interchangeable parts of a modular ensemble (Article L. 511-8, last §). This rule would apply, for example, to construction games, stackable furniture, etc.

§2. Relations with Copyright

959. A shape registered as design or model may also be protected by copyright under the usual condition of originality. The creator or his successor in title may claim either of these rights, or claim them in cumulation (*see supra*, paragraph 866).

§3. Relations with Trademarks

960. A shape registered as a design or model may also be registered as a trademark by the same person. It may be registered as a trademark by another person, but only with the authorization of the owner of the prior registration (*see supra*, paragraph 692).

961. As for other industrial property rights, an infringer of a right on a registered design or model may be also liable for unfair competition, if he is engaged in an unfair behaviour distinct from the acts of infringement. Such may be the case, for instance, when the infringing goods were marketed in a way creating a risk of confusion in the eyes of the consumers.

Part VII. Plant Variety Protection

Chapter 1. Sources: Legislation

962. Plant varieties are excluded from patent protection (Articles L. 623-2 and L. 611-19, 2°), in as much as they benefit from a specific protection, the 'plant variety certificate' ('certificat d'obtention végétale' or COV). This specific system of protection was first organized by the Act No. 70-489 of 11 June 1970, which was in turn codified in 1992 in the French Intellectual Property Code (Article L. 623-1–L. 623-35, IP Code). The first general reform of this system occurred through the Act No. 2011-1843 of 8 December 2011, entered into force on 11 December 2011. This reform aimed to improve and modernize the French 'plant variety certificate' in order to permit the French ratification of the last version (1991) of the Paris Convention of 2 December 1961 on the Protection of Plant Varieties (UPOV).[620] This reform was also largely influenced by the existing Community plant variety rights, organized by the Regulation No. 2100/94 of the Council of 27 July 1994,[621] which can be seen both as a model or a competitor for the French 'plant variety certificate'.

620. On 27 Apr. 2012, the French Republic deposited its instrument of ratification of the Paris Convention (version of 1991); the latter then entered into force, with respect to the French Republic, on 27 May 2012; *See also*: Decree No. 2012-865, 5 Jul. 2012 publishing the Paris Convention (version of 1991) in France: JORF, 10 Jul. 2012.
621. Council Regulation (EC) No. 2100/94 of 27 Jul. 1994 on Community plant variety rights, OJEC, No. L. 227, 1 Sep. 1994, pp. 1–30.

Chapter 2. Subject Matter of Protection

963. Article L. 623-1 and L. 623-2 of the Intellectual Property Code defines the subject matter of protection. It is a 'plant variety' which is precisely defined by Article L. 623-1 as 'a plant grouping within a single botanical taxon of the lowest known rank, which grouping can be – defined by the expression of the characteristics resulting from a given genotype or combination of genotypes, – distinguished from any other plant grouping by the expression of at least one of the said characteristics and – considered as a unit with regard to its suitability for being propagated unchanged'. This definition is directly drawn from Article 1 vi of the Paris Convention of 1991 and is consequently identical to Article 5 of EC Regulation No. 2100/94 (since this regulation was inspired by the Paris Convention of 1991). Since the Decree No. 95-1407 of 28 December 1995 (JORF 4 January 1996), Article R. 623-55 of the Intellectual Property Code states that the COV may protect 'any variety belonging to a species of the vegetable kingdom'. In other words, the protection may benefit any plant variety, all plant genera, and species of the vegetable kingdom, without any restriction. The only remaining difficulty is then to delimit the vegetable kingdom. From a scientific point of view, it seems that the vegetable kingdom must be distinguished from the animal kingdom, bacteria, and fungoid organisms, so that it limits to land plants and seaweeds. However, despite they are fungoid organisms, mushrooms may benefit from the COV protection as certain mushrooms (pleurotus) were registered, since the Decree No. 87-573 of 22 July 1987, among the species to be protected. Furthermore, several varieties of pleurotus are at the moment protected by Community plant variety rights. On the contrary, plant microorganisms, despite the fact that they belong to vegetable kingdom, may not be protected by COV since they are already protected by patents and have a too high mutation rate to be considered as stable (*see infra* paragraphs 972 et seq.).

Chapter 3. Conditions of Protection

964. The protectable plant variety should satisfy the conditions of novelty, distinctness, uniformity, and stability (Article L. 623-2). However, it should be first underlined that Article L. 623-2 is misleading as it provides that the subject matter of protection is 'a new created plant variety'. The protection seems then to be reserved to man-made varieties and excluded for varieties which were pre-existent in the nature and discovered by man. This is a legislative error. The French legislator, adopting the Act No. 2011-1843 of 8 December 2011, thought he could modify the existing law (which granted protection for any object belonging to the vegetable kingdom, either man-made, or pre-existent in the nature) and reserve protection only to man-made varieties. In his mind, only these man-made varieties deserve protection as their creation suppose work and investments (and not the varieties only discovered in the nature). The problem is that this idea is both false (a variety discovered in the nature also supposes work and investments, especially to develop the variety and make it stable) and directly violating the French international obligations as Article 1 iv) of the Paris Convention 1991 (and already Article 1 iv) of the Paris Convention 1978) provides that the protected 'breeder' is 'the person who bred, *or discovered and developed*, a variety' (*see also* Article 11 of EC Regulation No. 2100/94). As France is first compelled to satisfy its international obligations and as an international convention is superior to an ordinary French statute, this problematic wording ('created') must be ignored. The protection under a COV may be granted for any object belonging to the vegetable kingdom, either man-made, or pre-existent in the nature.

§1. Novelty

965. A plant variety is new if it is not already known by the public. French law requires an 'absolute novelty': the plant variety must not have been accessible to the public at any time, place, and by any means prior to the filing date of the application for a COV (or, possibly, to the priority date of the first application in one of the Contracting Parties of the UPOV Convention or in one of the Member States of the EU).

966. According to Article L. 623-5, I, a variety is not considered as new when propagating or harvested material of the variety has been sold or otherwise disposed of to others, by or with the consent of the breeder, for purposes of exploitation of the variety: (i) in the territory of France or of EEA more than one year before the filing date; or (ii) in another territory earlier than four years or, in the case of trees or of vines, more than six years before the said date.

967. On the contrary, the following disclosures do not affect the novelty (Article L. 623-5, II):

– disposal of the variety's material to an official or officially empowered authority for administrative purposes;

- disposal of to others for experimental purposes, on condition that the breeder had not expressly prohibited the commercial exploitation of the disposed variety material;
- disposal of to others for the purposes of displaying the variety at an officially recognized exhibition, on condition that the breeder had not expressly prohibit the commercial exploitation of the disposed variety material.

§2. Distinctness

968. If beforehand Article L. 623-1, 1°, gave some indications about the appreciation of the distinctness of a variety (it had to differ from the already known varieties by at least one precise, important and little varying character, or by a combination of characters), since the Act No. 2011-1843 of 8 December 2011, Article L. 623-2, 1° now simply states that the variety must be clearly distinguishable from any other variety whose existence is a matter of common knowledge at the time when protection is applied for.

969. It is no legislative error or forgetting. It is on the contrary a deliberate and reasonable reflux of law. By remaining silent on the criteria of distinctness, the legislator implicitly recognizes, on this point, the primacy of scientific experts (agronomists, botanists), which already listed the characters relevant for each plant species and developed techniques for calculating the 'varietal distance' (especially in the 'Test Guidelines' established by the UPOV as recommendations to the national authorities competent for granting plant breeders' rights, *see* http://www.upov.org/en/publications/tg_rom/tg_index_latin.html). In this context, efforts to formulate abstract and general criteria for the distinctness are useless and may tomorrow be thwarted by the development of knowledge and techniques. It is, therefore, more reasonable for the legislator to remain silent on this issue.

970. The distinctness is evaluated by comparing the proposed variety with any other variety whose existence is a matter of common knowledge at the time when protection is applied for (or priority date). Article 6 of the Paris Convention 1978 already stated that 'common knowledge' could be established by reference to cultivation, marketing, entry in an official register of varieties already made or in progress, presence in a reference collection or precise description in a publication. It was pointed out (*see* UPOV, *The Notion of Breeder and Common Knowledge*, C [Extr.] / 19/2 Rev. 9 August 2002), that among these facts, some, such as the addition of a variety to a reference collection, would not necessarily be known to the public. The variety of common knowledge is not only a variety in which the public has actual knowledge, it is rather a variety whose existence could be easily known to the public at the filing date, in respect of various events such as its cultivation, its marketing, its entry in a register, its presence in a reference collection, its precise description in a publication, etc. And it was clearly a non-exhaustive list of examples of how a variety could become a matter of common knowledge ('knowledge may be established by various factors such as…', Article 6 a Paris Conv. 1978). Any other circumstances, proved with sufficient certainty, sufficient to establish that the public, regardless of the country (*see* UPOV, C [Extr.] / 19/2 Rev: 'It is a worldwide test'), was able to take cognizance of the existence of the variety could also be retained (for instance, it would be possible to refer to the common knowledge of botanists since UPOV invited to consider 'not only knowledge that exists in documented form, but also the knowledge of relevant communities around the world', UPOV C [Extr.] / 19/2 Rev). It may also be noted that a variety, as defined in Article L. 623-1 (and Article 1, vi, Conv. UPOV (1978)) does not necessarily need to fully meet the requirements for the granting of a breeder's right and is not necessarily a variety protectable by COV. Consequently, the varieties of common knowledge in order to assess the distinctness of the candidate variety are all varieties of common knowledge, not only protected varieties, but also non-protectable or unprotected varieties. The Paris Convention 1991 still establishes the distinctness of the candidate variety by comparison with varieties whose existence is a matter of common knowledge at the time when protection is applied for (or priority date). Article 7 of the Paris Convention 1991 states that 'in particular, the filing of an application for the granting of a breeder's right or for the entering of another variety in an official register of varieties, in any country, shall be deemed to render that other variety a matter of common knowledge from the date of the application, provided that the application leads to the granting of a breeder's right or to the entering of the said other variety in the official register of varieties, as the case may be'. This indication is very important. It must be added to the list of varieties of common knowledge, the varieties whose application has just been filed, provided that it leads to the granting of a COV. It is obviously a legal fiction ('shall be deemed to render that other variety a matter of common knowledge') because a variety whose application for protection has only recently been filed will often not be known to the public.

§3. Uniformity

971. The new plant variety should be sufficiently uniform in its relevant characteristics, subject to the variation that may be expected from the particular features of its propagation (Article L. 623-2, 2°). Its means that the various existing single plants of a same variety must present the same identifying and distinctive characteristics which define the plant variety. The uniformity is a prerequisite for meaningful exploitation of a variety, which would be impossible if the various existing single plants had different characters. Only a sufficient and not an absolute uniformity is required ('sufficiently uniform'). It appears inevitable that, given the particular features of its propagation as expressly contemplated by Article L. 623-2, 2°, like Article 8 of the UPOV Convention (cross-fertilization ensures less uniformity than vegetative propagation), or other causes of any kind (accidental mixing, spontaneous mutation…), some single plants present some diverging characteristics. There is, therefore, an acceptable level of variation. But, apart from these very few variations, the single plants are similar to the common characteristics that define the variety.

§4. Stability

972. The new plant variety should remain stable, i.e., its relevant characteristics remain unchanged after repeated propagation or, in the case of a particular cycle of propagation, at the end of each such cycle (Article L. 623-2, 3°). Whatever the number of reproduction or multiplication, the specific characteristics of the variety must be present in all the single plants. The single plants obtained after successive cycles of propagation must have the same characteristics as the plant of origin. Stability, therefore, needs to be studied for several years. But again, the requirement of stability cannot be absolute because of the unstable nature of living matter, causing frequent degeneration (faster or slower depending on whether the plants are self-pollinating or cross-pollinating, sexed, or asexual). One can reasonably just require a sufficient stability: only essential characters must remain consistent, that is to say similar and not strictly identical.

Chapter 4. Formalities

973. The application for grant of a protection is filed with the 'Instance nationale des obtentions végétales' (National authority for Plant Varieties) replacing the former 'Comité de la protection des obtentions végétales' (Committee for the Protection of Plant Varieties). Article L. 412-1 of the Intellectual Property Code states that the INOV is a public interest group gathering the French State and the 'Institut national de la recherche agronomique' (National Institute of Agronomic Research, INRA). The INOV includes a 'responsible' who is in charge of its missions and is appointed by the Minister of Agriculture. He acts independently of any superior authority. The INOV is physically installed in the 'Groupe d'étude et de contrôle des variétés et des semences' (Varieties and seeds study and control Group – GEVES) in Beaucouzé near Angers. Article L. 412-1 gives two missions to INOV, one administrative, the other advisory. Its basic administrative task is to make the French system of COV work. It must 'enforce laws and regulations for the protection of plant varieties and, in particular, grant the COV'. And this is the 'responsible' who makes decisions regarding the grant, refusal or, maintaining of the COV. The INOV is responsible for receiving, recording, and processing applications relating to COV (it shall retain the applications for a period of ten years after the extinction of the rights attached to the corresponding COV, Article R. 623-30). As already seen, some of the conditions of protection (homogeneity and stability) imply that cultivation experiments are carried out by experts. This is GEVES, hosting the INOV, or an equivalent official service (usually selected within the EU) that performs these cultivations and technical examinations. And the INOV grants the COV if the candidate variety meets the legal requirements. It also keeps the national register of COV's applications and of COV (Article R. 623-38), which record all important informations, and publishes the 'Bulletin officiel de la protection des obtentions végétales' to inform the public. If necessary, the INOV may cancel a breeder's right under the conditions provided by law. In the accomplishment of its mission, INOV is in a similar position to the INPI. Its decisions, constituting civil rights, may be appealed before the 'Cour d'appel' of Paris (Article L. 623-31, §2). Article L. 412-1, 2°, also gives an advisory mission to INOV: it shall help the French State for the development of national legislation and international agreements relating to plant varieties. If INOV does not have an independent regulatory authority, it can propose to the Minister of Agriculture some provisions for law enforcement and, more generally, make any suggestions for the implementation of the Plant Varieties protection. As such, the INOV is also involved in certain working groups, including those of UPOV.

974. The right to the title belongs to the first applicant, whether a physical or a legal person. If the applicant is not the creator of the plant variety, the creator's name must be mentioned (Article R. 623-16, §3). If the plant variety is the creation of a team, the application and the COV may be the object of a joint ownership ruled *mutatis mutandis* by the provisions of Article L. 613-29 (Article L. 623-24, §1). The Act No. 2011-1843 of 8 December 2011 has finally remedied the former legislative gap about plant varieties made by employees. A new paragraph 3 of Article L. 623-24 adopts the solution, supported by some authors, of an application *mutatis mutandis* of Article L.

611-7 of the Intellectual Property Code, relating to employee inventions. Except if the employee has more favourable contractual clauses (Article L. 611-7, §1), it is necessary to distinguish three categories of plant varieties: 1° 'mission plant varieties', that is to say, the varieties created or discovered and developed by an employee in the execution either of tasks related to creation or discovery corresponding to his functions, or of studies or research explicitly entrusted to him by the employer. The difference between the two cases should be that, in the first case, the desired plant variety is clearly defined (e.g., the mission entrusted to the employee is to create or discover and develop a rose whose blue color should be the strongest possible), while in the second case, it is rather a mission of research in a plant area that is entrusted to the employee, without a specific desired plant variety (e.g., the employee's mission is to conduct research in the field of Solanaceae in order to create or discover and develop any possible plant variety). The right to the COV then belongs to the employer. The employee is entitled to an 'additional remuneration' (in addition to his salary) whose characteristics are determined by collective agreements, company agreements, and individual employment contracts. However, if the employer is not subject to a collective agreement, any dispute relating to the additional compensation is subject to conciliation before a conciliation commission or to judicial resolution before the 'tribunal de grande instance'; 2° 'attributable plant varieties': these are varieties created or discovered and developed by an employee during the execution of its functions or in the field of activity of the company or by reason of knowledge or use of technologies or specific means of the company or of data acquired by the company. In other words, the employment contract did not give the employee a mission to create or discover a desired plan variety, or to make studies or researches in some vegetal area, but nevertheless gave him the opportunity or knowledge to create or discover a plant variety. In this case, in principle, the right to the COV belongs to the employee, but the employer may, at its request, be given (by sending a communication to the employee specifying the nature and extent of rights that the employer wants), in whole or in part, property, or enjoyment of the COV's rights on the plant variety. In return, the employee will be entitled to a 'fair price' which, failing agreement between the parties, is determined by the conciliation commission or the 'tribunal de grande instance'. To determine that fair price, the commission or court takes into account the initial contributions of the employer's and employee and the commercial interest of the plant variety; 3° 'unattributable plant varieties': plant varieties that are not the result of a work's mission and do not directly concern the employer are and remain the only property of the employee. As for certain officials or public servants who have taken part to the creation of a plant variety in 'the execution either of tasks comprising an inventive mission corresponding to his attributions, or of studies or research explicitly entrusted to him', a decree No. 96-858 of 2 October 1996 provides that the right to the title shall belong to the public person on behalf of whom he carries out those tasks, studies, or research if the public person decides to exploit the variety. But the official or public servant will receive a bonus, which is a part of the benefits made by his public employer because of the exploitation of the plant variety. This bonus is due annually until the death of the official or public servant who cannot assign or renounce his right. As for the plant varieties created neither in the execution of tasks comprising an inventive mission corresponding to his attributions, nor in the execution of studies or research explicitly entrusted to him, the right to the title belongs to the official or public servant and his public employer has no right over it.

975. The application consists of a file including a request, a description of the manner whereby the plant variety was obtained or discovered, a description of the plant variety mentioning the characters which allow to distinguish it from the varieties whose existence is a matter of common knowledge, the denomination (*see infra,* paragraph 1018) proposed by the applicant for the plant variety, the indication of the countries where an application was already filed for this plant variety, and the authorization for the INOV to exchange with such States any information as to the results of the examination of the proposed plant variety (Article R. 623-4).

976. A sample of the plant variety should be deposited (Article L. 623-3) and permanently kept in a collection of cultures (Article L. 623-15).

977. Article L. 623-6, §2, provides, according to the Paris Convention, for a priority right of twelve months.

978. Following the application, the Ministry in charge of National Defence may inspect the deposited plant varieties (Article L. 623-8). This preliminary examination should be conducted very quickly, the application is to be submitted to the INOV within fifteen days from the date of receipt (Article R. 623-43). The varieties interesting National Defence (it seems to have no practical application) should be kept secret until an authorization to disclose and exploit is granted by the Ministry (Article L. 623-9), under criminal sanctions (Article L. 623-35). If the plant variety is kept secret more than five months, the owner of the application is entitled to an indemnity (Article L. 623-10 and L. 623-11) to compensate the damage he suffers.

979. The examination then begins with the publication of the application in the 'Bulletin officiel de la protection des obtentions végétales.' This publication shall mention the date of filing, the name and address of the applicant, and of the breeder (if he is not the applicant), indicate the genus (or species) to which the variety belongs and its summary characteristics, the proposed denomination, or the provisional reference breeder. As of this publication, any person may examine the application as it is in the register of COV's applications (Article R. 623-16) and any person who has an interest has a period of two months to present observations to the INOV on the plant variety or its denomination (Article R. 623-17). The INOV notifies the observations to the applicant and shall indicate the period within which he must answer (Article R. 623-20). The INOV examines the application and checks whether the legal conditions of protection are fulfilled. The examination, or 'DUS Test' (Distinctness, Uniformity, Stability), is based mainly on growing tests, carried out by the authority competent for granting plant breeders' rights or by separate institutions, such as public research institutes, acting on behalf of that authority or, in some cases, on the basis of growing tests already carried out by the breeder or authorities of another UPOV Contracting State (Article L. 623-12). Once completed the various measures of examination decided by the INOV, a report summarizing its findings is established and notified to the applicant. The applicant then has two months to submit his observations and to have access, if desired, to the entire investigation file by the secretariat of the INOV (Article R. 623-24, §1). Similarly, any person who submitted observations is informed of the conclusions of the report and may ask the INOV to allow him to read the full file, and can present new observations in the same two-month period (Article R. 623-24, §2).

At the end of that period of two months, the INOV may decide either to reject the application or order a further investigation or grant the COV (Article R. 623-25). Its decision must be substantiated (Article L. 623-7 required it in case of rejection, Article R. 623-25 for any decision). It shall be notified to the applicant and, if applicable, to the authors of observations. The decision to grant or refuse the COV's protection may be appealed before the 'Cour d'appel' of Paris (Articles R. 412-15 et seq.) within one month after receipt of the notification. The COV granted by the INOV mentions the name of the applicant and of the breeder (if he is not the applicant). If by some unlikely chance, the plant variety has different denominations in different UPOV Contracting States, the COV must mention those different denominations. It also includes the information relating to the date of filing of the application, of the grant, of the various publicity measures and, where appropriate, references regarding priorities (Article R. 623-26, §2). A description of the new variety is attached to the certificate (Article L. 623-15). The certificate is registered on the National Register of COV (Article R. 623-27). The various mentions appearing in the register are listed in Article R. 623-40. The grant of COV is published in the 'Bulletin officiel' within three months of its notification to the owner (Article R. 623-28). As from this publication, any person may, at the headquarters of INOV, have access to the COV, obtain extracts of the register, consult the documents of the application or examination, and receive all information about the plant variety (Article R. 623-29). If the COV has effect as from the date of the application (Article L. 623-7), it has effect vis-à-vis third parties only as from the date of its publication (Article L. 623-15, §4). The Act No. 2011-1843 of 8 December 2011 introduced a new provision specific to the nullity of the COV (Article L. 623-23-1). The COV can be declared void by a court if: (1) it has been granted to a person who was not entitled to it, unless it is transferred to the person who is so entitled, or; (2) the variety did not meet the conditions set out in Article L. 623-2, that is to say the conditions of novelty, distinctness, uniformity, and stability, at the time of the grant of the breeder's right.

980. Appropriate fees are to be paid by the applicant at various stages of the proceedings.

981. Foreigners may have access to the protection of the COV. Pursuant to Article L. 623-6 §1, the nationals of an UPOV Contracting Party or an EU Member State as well as persons having their domicile, registered office, or establishment within the territory of such an UPOV Contracting Party or EU Member State, may also have access to the protection of the French COV, under the conditions listed in Article R. 623-55: Any foreigner who is a national of a State party to the International Convention for the Protection of New Varieties of Plants of 2 December 1961, amended by the supplementary Act of 10 November, 1972, or who has his domicile, registered office, or establishment in one of those States may obtain a new plant certificate for varieties belonging to the genera or species subject to the same protection by that State and mentioned in the list appended to that Convention or in a supplementary list drawn up for the implementation of the provisions of that Convention. Any foreigner who is a national of a State party to the International Convention for the Protection of New Varieties of Plants as defined in the revised text of 23 October 1978 or of 19 March 1991 (Cyprus, Greece, Luxembourg, and Malta, which are no members of the UPOV Convention indirectly benefit from the ratification of the UPOV Convention of 1991 by the EC in 2005), or who has his domicile, registered office, or establishment in one of those States may obtain a new plant certificate under the same conditions as French nationals for any plant variety belonging to the vegetable kingdom. Foreigners who are not nationals of one of the States referred to above or who do not have their domicile, registered office, or establishment therein may obtain new plant variety certificates provided that French nationals are accorded reciprocal protection by the State of which the foreigner is a national or in which he has his domicile, registered office, or establishment (Article L. 623-6, §4). Orders of the Minister of Foreign Affairs and of the Minister of Agriculture issued on the proposal of the Committee for the Protection of New Plant Varieties, shall fix the list of States whose legislation satisfies the condition of reciprocity. Such orders may include a restrictive list of the plant species for which the condition of reciprocity is satisfied (Article R. 623-55).

Chapter 5. Scope of Exclusive Rights

982. The certificate of protection confers to its holder the exclusive right to produce, reproduce, condition for the purpose of propagation, to use, to offer, to offer for sale, to sell, or other market on the French territory, to export from the French territory, to import into the French territory, to make the transshipment on the French territory, or to stock on the French territory for any of these previous purposes all any element for the reproduction or vegetative propagation of the variety (Article L. 623-4, I and V added by the Act No. 2014-315 of 11 March 2014). The COV's right also covers all these acts in respect of harvested material, including entire plants and parts of plants, obtained through the unauthorized (not fortuitous or accidental) use of propagating material of the protected variety, unless the breeder has had reasonable opportunity to exercise his right in relation to the said propagating material (Article L. 623-4, II, 1°). The breeder's right also covers all these acts in respect of products made directly from harvested material of the protected variety falling within the provisions of Article L. 623-4, II, 1°, through the unauthorized use of the said harvested material, unless the breeder has had reasonable opportunity to exercise his right in relation to the said harvested material (Article L. 623-4, II, 2°). The exclusive right shall also apply in relation to varieties which are not clearly distinguishable from the protected variety, to varieties whose production requires the repeated use of the protected variety, to varieties which are essentially derived from the protected variety, where the protected variety is not itself an essentially derived variety (Article L. 623-4, III). A variety shall be deemed to be essentially derived from another variety, referred to as 'the initial variety' when: (a) it is predominantly derived from the initial variety, or from a variety that is itself predominantly derived from the initial variety; (b) it is distinct from the initial variety; and (c) except for the differences which result from the act of derivation, it conforms essentially to the initial variety in the expression of the characteristics that results from the genotype or combination of genotypes of the initial variety (Article L. 623-4, IV).

Chapter 6. Ownership and Transfer

§1. Contractual Transfers

983. The holder of a certificate of protection may conclude any contract relating to his exclusive right. The Code sends back to the provisions relating to patents (Article L. 623-24, §1). In order to be effective against third parties, such contracts should be entered into the National Register of Certificates of Plant Varieties (Article L. 623-14 and R. 623-40).

§2. Authoritative Transfers

984. The French State may, at any time, by decree, expropriate totally or partially the rightholder in the interest of National Defence. An indemnity is either agreed between the parties, or decided by the 'Tribunal de grande instance' (Article L. 623-22).

985. When a plant variety is necessary for the life of humans or animals, or interests public health, it may be subject to a regime of ex officio licence by a decree (a decree in *Conseil d'Etat* or a joint decree of the Minister of Agriculture and the Minister Responsible for Public Health, Article L. 623-17). Consequently, any person 'offering appropriate technical and professional guarantees' may request a licence from the Ministry of Agriculture (Article L. 623-18, §2). Such a licence is non-exclusive, its conditions are set by decree and the royalties are to be either agreed by the parties, or to be determined by the 'Tribunal de Grande Instance' (Article L. 623-18, §4). The licence shall take effect on the date of notification of the order to the parties (Article L. 623-18, §3).

986. When a plant variety interests the national defence, the French State may at any time obtain an ex officio licence to exploit a plant variety being the subject matter of an application for a certificate or of a new plant variety certificate, whether such exploitation is to be made by the State itself or on its behalf (Article L. 623-20). Such a licence is ordered by a decree of the Ministry of Agriculture upon request from the Ministry of Defence. The decree shall fix the terms of the licence, to the exclusion of those relating to royalties arising from its use. The licence shall take effect on the date of the request for the ex officio licence. In the absence of an amicable settlement, the amount of royalties shall be fixed by the 'Tribunal de Grande Instance'.

987. Where the holder of the patent of a biotechnological invention cannot exploit it without infringing a prior plant variety right, he may apply for the grant of licence for exploitation of the variety protected by the plant production right, inasmuch as this invention constitutes with regard to the plant variety an important technical progress and is of considerable economic interest. The applicant must show that he could not obtain from the holder of the COV a licence for exploitation and that he is in a position to exploit the variety in an effective and serious way (Article L. 623-22-1).

988. The request for licence shall be brought before the 'Tribunal de grande instance'. The licence is non-exclusive. The court shall determine, in particular, its duration, its field of application and the amount of the royalties to which it gives rise. These conditions may be modified by a court decision, at the request of the holder of the right or the licence. The rights attached to this licence may be transmitted only together with the business or the part of the business or goodwill to which they are attached. Where such a licence is granted on application brought before the court, the holder of the COV shall be granted a cross-licence to use the protected invention under equitable conditions. If the holder of a licence does not satisfy the conditions to which this licence was granted, the holder of the plant variety certificate and, if necessary, the other licensees may obtain by court decision the withdrawal of such licence (Article L. 623-22-2).

989. A reciprocal compulsory licence has been introduced in Article L. 613-15-1 for the holder of a plant variety right. 'Where a breeder cannot acquire or exploit a plant variety right without infringing a prior patent, it may request the license of this patent inasmuch as the license is necessary for the exploitation of the plant variety to be protected and in so far as the variety constitutes with regard to the invention asserted in this patent an important technical advance and is of considerable economic interest.'

990. The application for a compulsory licence shall be made to the 'Tribunal de grande instance' of Paris; it must be accompanied by evidence establishing that the applicant has been unable to obtain a licence from the owner of the patent and that it is in a position to exploit the invention in an effective and serious manner.

991. The compulsory licence shall be granted on fixed terms, particularly in respect of its duration, its field of application and the amount of the royalties to be paid in consideration thereof. Those terms may be amended by court decision following a request by the owner or the licensee. Where such a licence is granted, on application brought before the court, the holder of the patent will be entitled, under equitable conditions, to a cross-licence to use the protected variety. In case of non-performance of his obligations by the licensee, the court may decide to terminate the compulsory licence (Article L. 613-14).

992. Any public or private legal person may obtain a compulsory licence if it shows that: it fails to obtain a licence, within one year from the date of its request to the holder of the COV; it is able to exploit the variety in a serious and effective manner; and the licence is of public interest, having regard in particular to the severe insufficiency of supply of the agricultural market concerned by this variety (Article L. 623-22-3, §§1–5). This new case of compulsory licence (introduced by Act No. 2011-1843 of 8 December 2011) accompanies the introduction of the concept of 'variety essentially derived' as the compulsory licence may in particular be useful for the holder of an essentially derived variety who could not obtain from the holder of the COV on the initial variety the authorization necessary for the exploitation of his own variety (Article L. 623-22-3, §6). And, in return, the owner of the COV on the initial variety can get, under the same conditions, a licence on the COV protecting the essentially derived variety (Article L. 623-22-3, §7). This compulsory licence is non-exclusive. The court determines its duration, scope, and the amount of royalties. These conditions may be modified by the court at the request of the owner or licensee. If the compulsory licensee does not meet the conditions under which the licence was granted, the holder of the COV and, where appropriate, other licensees may obtain from the court the withdrawal of the licence (Article L. 623-22-3 §§ 7-9). The rights attached to a compulsory licence may be assigned or transferred only together with the business, the company or the part of the company to which it belongs. The sale or transfer, to be valid, is subject to court approval (Article L. 623-22-4).

Chapter 7. Limitations of the Scope of Protection

993. A third person may, without the rightholder's consent, use the protected plant variety for the purpose of breeding other varieties' (Article L. 623-4-1, I, 3°). Consequently, improvements of a plant variety which are sufficient to constitute a new plant variety (clearly distinct and not an essentially derived variety from the initial variety) are not legally dependant from the initial variety and may be obtained and worked without the initial right holder's consent. It should be noted that a similar limitation exists in patent law (Article L. 613-5-3). A breeder may freely use a plant material protected by patent in order to create or discover and develop other plant varieties.

994. Since the Act No. 2011-1843 of 8 December 2011, the breeder's right shall not extend to acts done for experimental purposes (Article L. 623-4-1, I, 2°).

995. No 'personal possession right' analogous to the one recognized in patent matters is admitted for plant varieties. If the 'Cour d'appel' of Paris admitted the principle of such a personal possession right,[622] the courts have no power to create such an exception. And if a personal possession right is expressly organized by a legal provision in patent law, there is no equivalent legal provision for plant variety rights.

996. The breeder's right shall not extend to acts concerning any material of his protected variety, of any variety essentially derived from his protected variety or of any variety which is not clearly distinguishable from his protected variety, which has been sold or otherwise marketed by the breeder or with his consent, unless such acts involve further propagation of the variety in question or involve an export of material of the variety, which enables the propagation of the variety, into a country which does not protect varieties of the plant genus or species to which the variety belongs, except where the exported material is for final consumption purposes (Article L. 623-4-1, II). The problem is that the exhaustion provided under this new Article L. 623-4-1, II, does not require that the sale or marketing happened on a certain territory. Therefore, the French legislator introduced not the national exhaustion (provided under Article 16 §1 of the UPOV Convention 1991: 'the territory of the Contracting Party'), nor the European exhaustion (provided under Article 16 §3: 'the territories of the Member States of the Organization'), but an international exhaustion, going well beyond what is imposed or proposed by the UPOV Convention 1991.

997. A farmer who has legally acquired the material of a protected variety and who cultivates it on his own holding, may save all or part of his harvested material for re-cultivation on his own holding in the next season ('farm saved seed'). Without this exception, the practice of farm saved seed would be an infringement, since the farmer reproduces the protected variety. This exception applies only to varieties of certain species, those listed in Article 14 of EC Regulation No. 2100/94, eventually completed by certain species listed in a decree (Article L. 623-24-1). There is no quantitative restriction of the level of the farmer's holding to the extent necessary for the requirements of the holding. Small farmers (farmers who do not grow plants on an area bigger than the area which would be needed to produce 92 tonnes of cereals or 185 tonnes of potatoes per harvest) are not required to pay any remuneration to the

622. Paris, 19 Jun. 1986: RDPI 1987, No. 7, p. 63.

holder. Big farmers are required to pay an equitable remuneration to the holder, which shall be sensibly lower than the amount charged for the licensed production of propagating material of the same variety in the same area (amount which has to be determined by individual contracts, collective agreements, or by a decree in *Conseil d'Etat*, Article L. 623-24-3). Suppliers of processing services (in order to separate the seeds of good quality which will be used to reseed fields and the seeds of bad quality and their waste which will be consumed or used for the animal feed) must ensure the traceability of the products issued from the protected plant varieties. Otherwise, the seeds are regarded as marketed and infringing (Article L. 623-24-4). It should be noted that the 'farm saved seed' exception exists also in patent law: a farmer who has legally acquired seeds protected by a patent and who cultivates it on his own holding, may save all or part of his harvested material for re-cultivation on his own holding in the next season (Article L. 613-5-1) under the same conditions.

998. The breeder's right shall not extend to acts done privately and for non-professional or non-commercial purposes (Article L. 623-4-1, I, 1°). The benefit of this exception is subject to two cumulative conditions. The first condition, the requirement of a 'private' framework means that the act can only benefit the person who does it or his family. The second condition, the requirement of a 'non-professional or non-commercial' purpose means that the committed act must not participate in a regular and lucrative activity.

Chapter 8. Duration of Protection

999. The exclusive right has a duration of twenty-five years from the grant of the certificate (Article L. 623-13). For forest, fruit, or ornamental trees, for the vine as well as for graiminaceae and perennial leguminous fodders, potatoes, and endogamous lines used for the production of hybrid varieties, the protection period shall be thirty years.

1000. Before the expiration of its normal duration the right may be terminated following a decision of forfeiture by the Committee. Such a forfeiture of rights may sanction one of the following behaviours (Article L. 623-23):

- lack of payment of annual fees;
- non-conservation of elements of reproduction or vegetative multiplication of the plant variety, with morphological and physiological characteristics defined in the COV, in a permanent culture;
- owner's refusal to submit to inspections in view to verify the measures undertaken for the conservation of the plant variety.

1001. In the first case of forfeiture, the owner may appeal against the decision within six months if he offers a legitimate excuse. The appeal is made with the INOV. In the second and third cases, the owner may remedy the situation which motivated the forfeiture within two months. The breeder shall be formally requested to put an end to the situation in a notification addressed to him by the INOV. If, on expiration of a period of two months from receipt of the notification, the formal request has not been complied with, the INOV shall declare the breeder's rights to be forfeited. The decision of the INOV shall be notified to the owner of the new plant variety certificate. It shall be entered in the National Register of New Plant Variety Certificates and published in the Official Bulletin of the Committee for the Protection of New Plant Varieties (Article R. 623-37).

1002. The exclusive right may also be terminated prematurely if the holder(s) or an agent with a special power surrenders it by sending to the INOV a written declaration to such effect. If a pledge or a licence were entered in the National Register of COV, the declaration must be accompanied by the consent of the holders of these rights. It takes effect on the date of its registration in the national register (Article R. 623-36) after payment of the radiation fee.

Chapter 9. Infringement and Remedies

1003. Any intentional violation of the exclusive rights (as defined in Article L. 623-4) on a plant variety is an infringement which entails the infringer's civil and criminal liability (Article L. 623-25–L. 623-30). Since the Act No. 2011-1843 of 8 December 2011, the incorrect (non-intentional) or abusive (intentional, committed with bad faith) use of the denomination of the variety protected by a COV is also considered as an infringement of the exclusive right on the plant variety (Article L. 623-25, §1) but it entails only the infringer's civil liability. Only the acts committed after the publication of the COV's grant may be regarded as an infringement. Acts committed before that date may only be treated as an infringement if they have been committed by someone which had previously been notified a copy of the application by the applicant (Article L. 623-26; the court must suspend the proceedings until the grant of the COV) and the publication of the application is to be regarded as such a notification (Article L. 623-14).

1004. Before the court decides on the merits of the action, any person with authority to bring an action for infringement may, in preliminary proceedings on grounds of pressing urgency, request the competent civil court (one of the ten 'Tribunaux de grande instance' listed in Article D. 211-5 of the Judicial Organisation Code) to order, under a penalty of a daily fine if necessary, against the alleged infringer or intermediaries whose services it uses, any measure aimed at preventing an infringement about to be committed against rights conferred by the title or aimed at stopping any further allegedly infringing act. The competent civil court may also order ex parte urgent measures when the circumstances require that such measures should not be taken in the presence of both parties, in particular when any delay would be likely to cause an irreparable damage to the claimant. The court, in preliminary or ex parte proceedings, may order the requested measures only if evidence, reasonably accessible to the claimant, make it likely that its rights are infringed or that such infringement is about to be committed. The court may enjoin the carrying out of the allegedly infringing acts, condition it on the furnishing of security to ensure, if necessary, the claimant's compensation or may order the seizure or the remittance to a third person of the products allegedly infringing the rights conferred by the title, to prevent their introduction or circulation in the channels of commerce. If the claimant can give reasons that circumstances are likely to compromise the payment of damages, the court shall order the sequestration of the alleged infringer's movable or immovable assets, including the freezing of the bank accounts and other assets, under the general rules of law. To determine the goods likely to be seized, the court may order the submission of banking, financial, accounting, or commercial documents or the access to relevant data. The court may also award an advance payment to the claimant when the damage suffered cannot be seriously disputed. The court, in preliminary or ex parte proceedings, may condition the implementation of the measures it has ordered on the furnishing of security by the claimant to ensure, if necessary, the claimant's compensation if the infringement proceedings are subsequently held unfounded or if the measures are void. When the measures taken to stop the infringement of rights are ordered before the commencement of proceedings on the merits, the claimant shall institute legal proceedings, either by civil action or criminal action, within a period of time set by regulation. Failing that, upon the defendant's request and without its having to justify its application, the measures ordered are void, without prejudice to the damages which may be claimed (Article L. 623-27).

1005. The owner of a plant variety certificate may request that the customs administration withholds the suspect goods; an ex officio withholding is also possible (Article L. 623-36–L. 623-44, created by the Act No. 2014-315 of 11 March 2014). The conditions are here similar to those applicable to trademarks (*see supra*, paragraph 846).

1006. Civil actions and claims relating to plant varieties, even when they also address a related issue of unfair competition, are exclusively brought before the 'tribunaux de grande instance' and, more precisely one of the ten courts which have jurisdiction in patent matters (Article L. 623-31). Arbitration is allowed in the conditions of Articles 2059 and 2060 of the Civil Code (the matter should not relate to a question of public order) (Article L. 623-31, §3). The action may be brought within five years from each infringing act (Article L. 623-29). A specific counterfeit-seizure procedure is organized (Article L. 623-27-1) in order to facilitate the evidence of infringement. It is modelled on the patent's 'saisie-contrefaçon' (*see supra*, paragraphs 590 et seq.). Even if the counterfeit-seizure is very common in practice, it is not a compulsory procedure. That is the reason why the Act No. 2014-315 of 11 March 2014 added Article L. 623-27-1-1 to precise that a court may order, on its own initiative or at the request of any person having quality, all legally admissible investigative measures, even if a counterfeit-seizure has not previously been ordered. And since the Act No. 2007-1544 of 29 October 2007, if so required, the court hearing civil proceedings relating to a plant variety certificate, shall order, under penalty of a daily fine if necessary, in order to determine the origin and the distribution networks of the infringing goods which prejudice the claimant's rights, the communication of any document or information held by the defendant or by any person who was found in possession of infringing goods or who provides services used in infringing activities or was reported to take part to the production, manufacturing, or distribution of such products or the supply of such services ('Right of information'). The communication of documents or information shall be ordered if there is no legitimate hindrance (Article L. 623-27-2).

1007. The plaintiff may claim compensation of the damage he suffered as the consequence of the infringement. Since the Act No. 2007-1544 of 29 October 2007 and its revision by the Act No. 2014-315 of 11 March 2014, Article L. 623-28 states that 'To set the damages, the court takes into account separately: 1° the negative economic consequences of the rights infringement, including the loss of profit and loss suffered by the injured party; 2° the moral prejudice caused to the latter; 3° the profits made by the infringer, including economies of intellectual investments, material and promotional economies due to the infringement.'

1008. The legislator's intention was to break with the old general rules of the Civil Code about torts and especially with the traditional rule that damages are covering all the loss suffered but only such loss. Because of this old rule, the profits made by the infringer were of no relevance, so that the infringer, even paying damages, could still have interest to infringe. Thanks to the new rule of Article L. 623-28, it is now possible to award to the injured party a sum covering all his loss (economic or moral prejudice) but also a part of or all the profits made by the infringer because of the infringement. After a short time of hesitation, French courts now frequently use this possibility in order to repair and discourage intellectual property rights infringement.

1009. The judges may also, if required by the injured party, use another method of evaluation of the indemnity to be paid by the infringer: it consists of a lump sum superior to the royalties amount which the infringer would have to pay to receive the rightholder's authorization. Article L. 623-28, §2 states 'The court, however, shall, as an alternative and upon request of the injured party, award as damages a lump sum. This sum is higher than the amount of royalties or fees which would have been due if the infringer had requested authorization to use the right which it has prejudiced. This sum is not exclusive of compensation for the moral prejudice caused to the injured party.'

1010. Article L. 623-28-1 also provides that in the case of civil liability for infringement, the court may order, at the injured party's request, the recall from the channels of commerce, the definitive removal from such channels, the destruction and the confiscation, in favour of the injured party, of the products recognized as infringing and of the materials and implements principally used in their creation or their manufacturing. The court may also order any appropriate publicity measure of the judgment, in particular its display or its publication, in whole or in part, in such newspapers or over such in-line services of communication to the public it may designate, pursuant to the conditions it specifies. All the measures mentioned are ordered at the cost of the infringer.

1011. Article L. 623-30 provides that if a variety being the subject matter of an application for a certificate or of a new plant variety certificate is exploited for the purpose of national defence by the State or by its contractors, subcontractors, and subsidiary suppliers, without a licence for exploitation having been granted, the court hearing the case shall have no authority to order either the discontinuance or the interruption of exploitation, or the confiscation provided for in Article L. 623-28. If an official appraisal or a description, with or without effective seizure, is ordered by the presiding judge of the court hearing the case, the appointed law official shall refrain from proceeding with the seizure, the description and any investigation into the business if the contract for research or reproduction or propagation has a defence security classification. The same shall apply where research or reproduction or propagation is carried out in a military establishment. The presiding judge of the court hearing the case may, if so requested by the entitled person, order an official appraisal, which shall be carried out only by persons approved by the Minister Responsible for Defence and in the presence of his representatives. The provisions of Article L. 623-26 shall not apply to applications for a new plant variety certificate the subject matter of which is being exploited under the conditions set forth in Article L. 623-30 so long as such applications are subject to the prohibitions provided for in Article L. 623-9 and L. 623-10. The person engaged in such exploitation shall incur, ipso jure, the liability referred to in Article L. 623-30.

1012. The criminal action for infringement (except for incorrect or abusive use of the denomination of the protected variety) may be brought either by the rightholder or the public prosecutor upon complaint by the victim (Article L. 623-33, §1). The criminal court has exclusive jurisdiction, but must suspend the proceedings until the civil court renders a final decision admitting the existence of the infringement (Article L. 623-33, §2).

1013. The exercise of the criminal action is limited to three years from each illicit act. The introduction of the civil action suspends the prescription of the criminal action (Article L. 623-29, §2).

1014. Any infringement made knowingly is sanctioned by a fine of EUR 10,000 (Article L. 623-32). In case of relapse within a period of five years, or if it was committed by an organized gang or online on a public communication network, an imprisonment of six months may also be ordered.

1015. Natural persons liable for the offence provided for in Article L. 623-32 may also be ordered, at their cost, to remove from the channels of commerce the articles held infringing and any item which was used or intended for committing the offence (Article L. 623-32-1, §1). The court may order the destruction at the cost of the convicted person or the remittance to the injured party of the articles or items removed from the channels of commerce or confiscated, without prejudice to all damages (Article L. 623-32-1, §2). It may also order, at the cost of the convicted person, the display of the judgment or the dissemination of the judgment ordering the decision, pursuant to the conditions set out under Article 131-35 of the Penal Code (Article L. 623-32-1, §3).

1016. According to Article L. 623-32-2, legal persons incurring criminal liability pursuant to the conditions set out under Article 121-2 of the Penal Code for the offence defined in Article L. 623-32 of this Code, incur the following: (1) a fine, pursuant to the conditions set out under Article 131-38 of the Penal Code; (2) the penalties set out under Article 131-39 of that Code (*see supra,* paragraph 106). The legal persons incurring criminal liability may also be ordered, at their cost, to remove from the channels of commerce the articles held infringing and any other item which was used or intended for committing the offence. The court may order the destruction at the cost of the convicted person or the remittance to the injured party of the articles or items removed from the channel of commerce or confiscated, without prejudice to the damages.

Chapter 10. Relation to Other Intellectual Property Rights

§1. Relations to Patents

1017. French patent law (Article L. 611-19, I-2° IPC) excludes from patentability the plant varieties as defined in Article 5 of EC Regulation No. 2100/94 ('a plant grouping within a single botanical taxon of the lowest known rank, which grouping, irrespective of whether the conditions for the grant of a plant variety right are fully met, can be – defined by the expression of the characteristics resulting from a given genotype or combination of genotypes, – distinguished from any other plant grouping by the expression of at least one of the said characteristics and – considered as a unit with regard to its suitability for being propagated unchanged'). Plant varieties may not be protected by a patent, but by a plant variety right ('certificat d'obtention végétale'). Consequently, when a patent claims a product, it must be verified if this product is a plant variety or not. In the first case, the protection by patent is excluded and only the COV's protection is available (provided that all the legal conditions for a COV are satisfied). In the second case, the protection by COV is excluded and the patent protection is available. Surely, a COV may only protect products (any material of a plant variety) and no processes. But if a patent covers a process, such a patent is also covering the products directly obtained by the process (Article L. 613-2, §2). There is consequently a possible indirect conflict between a patent covering a process (and consequently the products obtained by this process) and a COV, if the process aims at creating a plant product. Of course, there is no risk of conflict if a patent covers a process which transforms a plant product but not its genotype, since the COV may only cover plants with a new genotype. The products obtained through such a process may only be covered by a patent. There is also no risk of conflict at all with an essentially biological process, i.e., which consists entirely of natural phenomena such as crossing or selection, since it is excluded from patentability (Article L. 611-19, I-3). The products obtained through such an essentially biological process may only be covered by a COV. There is also no risk of conflict with microbiological processes since these processes and their products are patentable (Article L. 611-19, III) and, consequently, excluded from the COV protection. And, finally, for all the other processes (non-microbiological) which concern plants and may produce plants with a new genotype, the possible conflict between patent and COV is solved by the following principle: such a process shall be patentable if its technical feasibility is not confined to a particular plant variety (Article L. 611-19 II); on the contrary, if its technical feasibility is confined to a particular plant variety, only the COV protection may be available (for the plant products and not the process itself).

§2. Relations to Trademarks

1018. The denomination must enable the variety to be identified and distinguished from any other variety, and shall not give rise to any risk of confusion with another variety of the same or a closely related botanical species, in France or in States party to the Paris Convention of 2 December 1961 (Article L. 623-15, §1 and R. 623-6, §1). It should not involve a likelihood of confusion as to the origin, characteristics, value of the variety, or the person of the breeder (Article R. 623-6). It shall not be contrary to public policy or morality (Article R. 623-6). Where a variety has already been the subject of an application for protection in another State of the International Union for the Protection of New Varieties of Plants and if a denomination has been accepted by that State, it shall be mandatory to use that denomination in France for designating the variety in question, unless it has been the subject of observations found to be justified or the INOV has found it to be unsuitable in the French territory or the denomination does not meet the requirements of the first paragraph of Article R. 623-6.

Use of the denomination entered in the certificate shall be mandatory, as from the date of publication of the certificate, for any commercial transaction, even after expiry of the duration of the certificate (Article L. 623-15, §5). When the same denomination was registered as a trademark by the creator of the plant variety, either in France or in one of the Member States of the Paris Convention of 1961, for identical or similar products, or is likely to create confusion with another trademark which he uses, the creator should underwrite an obligation to renounce such marks as from the date of grant of the certificate of protection of the plant variety (Article R. 623-6, §2). Such a renunciation does not affect the validity of the trademark itself (Article R. 623-6, §4).

1019. The denomination may not be registered as a trademark in any Member State of the Paris Convention of 1961. Such a registration may, however, be made in a conservatory manner, under condition that proof of renunciation to such a registration be brought prior to the grant of the certificate of protection of the plant variety (Article L. 623-15, §6). This provision does not preclude the addition of a trademark to the plant denomination (Article L. 623-15, §7).

1020. It is possible that a denomination coexists with a trademark if the two signs are different. In such a case, Article R. 623-58 only provides that:

> Any person who desires at the time of any act of assignment, concession or commercialization of the varieties referred to in the foregoing Articles, to avail himself of the possibility offered under Article L. 623-15 of adding a trademark to the variety denomination, whether he is the owner of the mark or other lawful user thereof, shall take the necessary precautions, especially in correspondence, in advertisements, in the preparation of trade catalogues, and on packaging or labels, to ensure that this denomination is sufficiently visible in its context so as to prevent any likelihood of confusion in the mind of the purchaser as to the variety's identity.

Part VIII. Chip Protection

Chapter 1. Sources: Legislation

1021. The protection of semiconductor chips was organized by the Act No. 87-890 of 4 November 1987, implementing the EC Directive No. 87/54 of 16 December 1986.[623] It was implemented into the IP Code under the Article L. 622-1–L. 622-8. It must be noted that this protection has no more practical application (chip's protection is, in practice, ensured by patents).

1022. On the international side, under the TRIPs Agreement (Articles 35–38), the members should protect semiconductor chips according to the WIPO Treaty signed in Washington on 26 May 1986.

623. EEC Council Directive No. 87/54 of 16 Dec. 1986 on the legal protection of topographies of semiconductor products, OJEC, No. L. 24 of 27 Jan. 1987, pp. 36–40.

Chapter 2. Subject Matter of Protection

1023. The protectable subject matter consists of 'the final or intermediate topography of a semi-conductor product implying an intellectual effort of the creator' (Article L. 622-1, §1). A 'semi-conductor' is the final or an intermediate form of any product: (i) consisting of a body of material which includes a layer of semiconducting material; (ii) having one or more other layers composed of conducting, insulating, or semiconducting material, the layers being arranged in accordance with a predetermined three-dimensional pattern; and (iii) intended to perform, exclusively or together with other functions, an electronic function. 'Topography of a semi-conductor' means a series of related images, however fixed or encoded; (i) representing the three-dimensional pattern of the layers of which a semiconductor product is composed; and (ii) in which series, each image has the pattern or part of the pattern of a surface of the semiconductor product at any stage of its manufacture.

Chapter 3. Conditions of Protection

1024. The protectable topography should imply an intellectual effort of the creator and should not be banal (Article L. 622-1, §1).

Chapter 4. Formalities

1025. The protection is subject to the registration of the chip with the INPI (Article L. 622-1, §1):

- if the topography is worked, the registration must be applied for within two years after the first commercial use;
- if it is not worked, within fifteen years from the first fixation or encoding.

1026. The irregular application may be refused by the Director General of the INPI; the regular one is registered in a specific section of the National Register of Patents (Article L. 622-4 and R. 622-6). The registration is mentioned in the 'Bulletin officiel de la propriété industrielle' (BOPI).

Chapter 5. Ownership and Transfer

§1. Ownership

1027. The right to the protection belongs to the creator or his successor in title (Article L. 622-3). No specific rules are provided as for the employees' creations. Therefore, the rules of ownership relating to copyrightable works should apply (*see supra*, paragraphs 127 et seq).

1028. Protection on the French territory is granted to:

- creators who are citizens of a Member State of the World Trade Organization, or who have either their habitual residence or a real and effective industrial or commercial establishment in such country, and their successors in title;
- persons meeting the aforesaid conditions of nationality, residence, or establishment, who in a Member State engage in the first commercial exploitation anywhere in the world of a non-protected topography, for which exploitation they have received exclusive authorization from the entitled person for the whole of the EC or the EEA;
- other persons, under condition of reciprocity.

Where a registration has been done in violation of the rights of the creator or of his successor in title, the injured party may claim ownership thereof. Actions claiming ownership shall be barred after five years following publication of the registration (Article L. 622-3, §2).

§2. Transfer

1029. The rules applicable to contracts on patents apply to semiconductor chips (Article L. 622-7, §1, sending back to Article L. 613-8 and L. 613-9 relating to patents).

1030. The compulsory licence for the needs of National Defence is also applicable to chips (Articles L. 613-19 and L. 615-10).

Chapter 6. Scope of Exclusive Rights

1031. The registration entails the exclusive right to reproduce the topography, to use in commerce or to possess, make the transhipment, use, export, or import in view of such a use in commerce such a reproduction or any semiconductor product which incorporates it (Article L. 622-5, §1).

Chapter 7. Limitations of the Scope of Protection

1032. The protection does not cover (Article L. 622-5, §2):

- the reproduction for the purpose of teaching, evaluation, or analysis;
- the creation, on the basis of such an analysis or evaluation, of a distinct topography which is protectable;
- the good faith buyer, who may continue to use the chip for commerce, in exchange for a reasonable royalty;
- the exhaustion of rights applies under the normal conditions (*see supra* paragraphs 575 et seq.).

Chapter 8. Duration of Protection

1033. The title of protection is granted for ten years from the date of application or from the first commercial use if it is earlier (Article L. 622-6, §1).

1034. If the registered chip is not used in commerce, the registration lapses fifteen years after the date of first fixation or encoding (Article L. 622-6, §2).

Chapter 9. Infringement and Remedies

1035. Most of the rules of procedure applicable to patents apply also to chips (Article L. 622-7 sending back to Article L. 615-2, L. 615-3, L. 615-5, L. 615-5-1-1, L. 615-5-2, L. 615-7, L. 615-7-1, L. 615-8, L. 615-10 and L. 615-17; Article L. 622-8 sending back to Article L. 614-32–L. 614-39).

1036. The person entitled to bring an action for infringement is in principle the rightholder. A licensee may act only when the following conditions are fulfilled:

- the licence is exclusive;
- the licence agreement does not provide for a clause whereby the licensee may not bring such action;
- the licensee has unsuccessfully summoned the rightholder to act against the infringer;
- the licence was entered into the National Registry of Patents.

1037. The holder of a compulsory licence may bring an infringement action if, after a formal notice, the rightholder does not institute such proceedings (Article L. 615-2).

1038. Before the court decides on the merits of the action, any person with authority to bring an action for infringement may, in preliminary proceedings on grounds of pressing urgency, request the competent civil court ('Tribunal de grande instance') to order, under a penalty of a daily fine if necessary, against the alleged infringer or intermediaries whose services it uses, any measure aimed at preventing an infringement about to be committed against rights conferred by the title or aimed at stopping any further allegedly infringing act. The competent civil court may also order ex parte urgent measures when the circumstances require that such measures should not be taken in the presence of both parties, in particular when any delay would be likely to cause an irreparable damage to the claimant. The court, in preliminary or ex parte proceedings, may order the requested measures only if evidence, reasonably accessible to the claimant, make it likely that its rights are infringed or that such infringement is about to be committed. The court may enjoin the carrying out of the allegedly infringing acts, condition it on the furnishing of security to ensure, if necessary, the claimant's compensation or may order the seizure or the remittance to a third person of the products allegedly infringing the rights conferred by the title, to prevent their introduction or circulation in the channels of commerce. If the claimant can give reasons that circumstances are likely to compromise the payment of damages, the court shall order the sequestration of the alleged infringer's movable or immovable assets, including the freezing of the bank accounts and other assets, under the general rules of law. To determine the goods likely to be seized, the court may order the submission of banking, financial, accounting, or commercial documents or the access to relevant data. The court may also award an advance payment to the claimant when the damage suffered cannot be seriously disputed. The court, in preliminary or ex parte proceedings, may condition the implementation of the measures it has ordered on the furnishing of security by the claimant to ensure, if necessary, the claimant's compensation if the infringement proceedings are subsequently held unfounded or if the measures are void. When the measures taken to stop the infringement of rights are ordered before the commencement of proceedings on the merits, the claimant shall institute legal proceedings, either by civil action or criminal action, within a period of time set by regulation. Failing that, upon the defendant's request and without its having to justify its application, the measures ordered are void, without prejudice to the damages which may be claimed (Article L. 615-3).

1039. The plaintiff may request that the customs administration withholds the suspect goods; an ex officio withholding is also possible (Article L. 622-8 created by the Act No. 2014-315 of 11 March 2014 and sending back to Article L. 614-32–L. 614-39). The conditions are here similar to those applicable to trademarks (*see supra*, paragraph 846).

1040. The law organizes a specific procedure of counterfeit-seizure ('saisie-contrefaçon') designed to facilitate the proof of infringement (Articles L. 615-5 and R. 615-2 et seq.). The plaintiff must first request the authorization to seize from the President of the 'Tribunal de grande instance'. The judge may not refuse the authorization, but only define its scope and order the payment of a warranty. The judge may condition the implementation of the measures it ordered to the furnishing by the claimant of security to ensure, if necessary, the defendant's compensation if the infringement action is subsequently held unfounded or the seizure is cancelled (L. 615-5, §4).

1041. The seizure is executed by a bailiff who may be assisted by an expert and a police officer if necessary. He may proceed in any place with either the detailed description, with or without taking samples, or the effective seizure of the allegedly infringing articles as well as any related document, according to what was authorized by the president. The order may authorize the effective seizure of any document relating to the allegedly infringing goods, even in the absence of the latter. The court shall also order, for the same evidential purposes, the detailed description or effective seizure of equipment and tools used to manufacture or distribute the allegedly infringing goods. The bailiff drafts a report which must be delivered to the defendant. An irregular seizure may be declared invalid and the plaintiff sentenced to pay damages to the defendant.

1042. The seizure must be followed by the introduction of the action for infringement – either a civil or criminal action – within twenty working days or thirty-one civil days if this time limit is longer, as from the date of the report of seizure. If not, the entire seizure, including the description, shall be void upon the defendant's request, without its having to motivate its request and without prejudice to the damages which may be claimed. A void seizure may not be used as evidence during the proceedings.

1043. Since the Act No. 2007-1544 of 29 October 2007, if so required, the court hearing civil proceedings relating to patent, shall order, under penalty of a daily fine if necessary, in order to determine the origin and the distribution networks of the infringing goods which prejudice the claimant's rights, the communication of any document or information held by the defendant or by any person who was found in possession of infringing goods or who provides services used in infringing activities or was reported to take part to the production, manufacturing, or distribution of such products, or the supply of such services ('Right of information'). The communication of documents or information shall be ordered if there is no legitimate hindrance (Article L. 615-5-2).

1044. There are no criminal sanctions but only civil sanctions of the infringement against chip protection (Article L. 622-5, §4). The action may be brought within five years from each illicit act of exploitation of the protected topography (Article L. 615-8).

1045. The plaintiff may claim compensation of the damage he suffered as the consequence of the infringement. Since the Act No. 2007-1544 of 29 October 2007 and its revision by the Act No. 2014-315 of 11 March 2014, Article L. 615-7 states that 'To set the damages, the court takes into account separately: 1° the negative economic consequences of the rights infringement, including the loss of profit and loss suffered by the injured party; 2° the moral prejudice caused to the latter; 3° the profits made by the infringer, including economies of intellectual investments, material and promotional economies due to the infringement.'

1046. The legislator's intention was to break with the old general rules of the Civil Code about torts and especially with the traditional rule that damages are covering all the loss suffered but only such loss. Because of this old rule, the profits made by the infringer were of no relevance, so that the infringer, even paying damages, could still have interest to infringe. Thanks to the new rule of Article L. 615-7, it is now possible to award to the injured party a sum covering all his loss (economic or moral prejudice) but also a part of or all the profits made by the infringer because of the infringement. After a short time of hesitation, French courts now frequently use this possibility in order to repair and discourage intellectual property rights infringement.

1047. The judges may also, if required by the injured party, use another method of evaluation of the indemnity to be paid by the infringer: it consists of a lump sum superior to the royalties amount which the infringer would have to pay to receive the rightholder's authorization. Article L. 615-7, §2 states 'The court, however, shall, as an alternative and upon request of the injured party, award as damages a lump sum. This sum is higher than the amount of royalties or fees which would have been due if the infringer had requested authorization to use the right which it has prejudiced. This sum is not exclusive of compensation for the moral prejudice caused to the injured party.'

1048. Article L. 615-7-1 also provides that in the case of civil liability for infringement, the court may order, at the injured party's request, the recall from the channels of commerce, the definitive removal from such channels, the destruction and the confiscation, in favour of the injured party, of the products recognized as infringing, and of the materials and implements principally used in their creation or their manufacturing. The court may also order any appropriate publicity measure of the judgment, in particular its display or its publication, in whole or in part, in such newspapers or over such in-line services of communication to the public it may designate, pursuant to the conditions it specifies. All the measures mentioned are ordered at the cost of the infringer.

1049. Since the Decree No. 2008-624 of 27 June 2008, jurisdiction for civil actions belongs exclusively to the First Instance Court ('Tribunal de grande instance') of Paris (Article D. 631-2). Jurisdiction for criminal actions belongs to the criminal Court of First Instance ('Tribunal correctionnel') designated under the ordinary rules of procedure. Actions for unfair competition connected to the action for infringement are brought in the same court (Article L. 615-17).

1050. Article L. 615-17 §2 states that the above rules of jurisdiction do not exclude arbitration. However, semiconductor chips matters may be arbitrated following the conditions of Articles 2059 and 2060 of the Civil Code, which prohibit arbitration in matters interesting public order. It is thought that infringement affects only private interests and is, therefore, arbitrable.

Chapter 10. Relation to Other Intellectual Property Rights

1051. The protection organized under Article L. 622-1 forms a sui generis system which excludes per se the application of patent law, except when the legislator himself sends back to the rules of patents (e.g., Article L. 622-7, as for the decisions taken by the Director General of the INPI, the assignment of rights and the litigation).

1052. Nothing prohibits the application of copyright law to semiconductor chips: such an application could be grounded on the theory of 'unity of art', applied in the area of industrial designs (*see supra*, paragraphs 882 et seq).

Part IX. Trade Secrets/Confidential Information

Chapter 1. Sources: Legislation

1053. Trade secrets and confidential information are not defined by any legislative provision. Both notions are included in the broader term of know-how (savoir-faire) of which trade secrets are a specific example. Today the definition should take into account the provisions of Article 39 of the TRIPs Agreement relating to the 'Protection of Undiclosed Information'.

1054. The know-how consists of an ensemble of technical information, transmissible, not immediately accessible to the public. It constitutes an immaterial asset, and should be distinguished from the material support in which it may be incorporated. Such technical information may relate to any area of activity: although the expression is traditionally used in relation to processes of manufacturing, the tendency today is to extend it to other sectors, such as commercial or social management. In any case, the know-how consists of information able to be used in practice, and not only of a theoretical knowledge.

1055. The information constituting the know-how must be able to be communicated to third persons; it is, therefore, to be distinguished from mere personal aptitudes and professional competence.

1056. Such technical transmissible knowledge should not be immediately accessible to the public. This does not imply that the know-how consists of a patentable subject matter: the know-how may sometimes be patentable, most often it is not and it is always unpatented (otherwise, it would be a mere chapter of patent law). Therefore, the notions of patent law do not apply to know-how. It is thus, not necessary that the know-how consists of information which is new or implies an inventive step; the economic value of the know-how comes from its usefulness for the beneficiary, not from any exclusive right. This explains that a person may accept to pay an amount of money in exchange for communication of such information. The French Supreme Court aptly summarized these characteristics, when it held valid a contract for communication of know-how, although the information was known by several persons: 'The court of appeals has exactly decided that by revealing to an industrial firm processes or tricks yet ignored by the receiver, and which the latter could have discovered by himself only after long and costly research and tests, the communicant delivered a valuable advantage, in consideration of which he may claim the payment of a price.'[624]

624. Cass. com., 13 Jul. 1966: JCP 1967 II 15131, note Durand.

1057. It follows that a know-how has an economic value when its immediate communication allows the receiver to save time and/or money. Such may be the case even when the information is not absolutely new; its degree of diffusion may only influence the price which the receiver will accept to pay for it.

Chapter 2. The Protection

1058. The possessor of a know-how usually seeks to protect this knowledge against misappropriation. He may obtain an exclusive right by applying for a patent; most often, however, either the information is not patentable, or its possessor does not wish to disclose it during a patent application procedure. He might also prevail himself of a copyright on the formal expression of the information, if it is original; the practical interest of such a protection is, however, limited, since it does not cover the technical elements.

1059. Absent a patent or a copyright, know-how as such is not considered as object of an intellectual property right; consequently, its possessor may not bring an action for infringement against third persons who use this know-how without his authorization.

1060. The mere act of making a technical invention does not imply the existence of an exclusive right for the benefit of the inventor; such a right may be obtained only upon filing for the grant of patent.[625] Nor does the intention to keep the information secret imply an exclusive right: 'such a secret is only protected against fraud on the part of the firm's employees or its competitors, under condition of evidence of a wrongdoing'.[626]

1061. The reservation of the know-how is, therefore, the factual consequence of its secret character: as long as the secret is kept, third persons may not access the information and, therefore, may not use it. The legal rules only sanction the usurpation of the secret against the will of the possessor of the know-how. Such an usurpation may entail either the criminal or/and civil liability of the usurper.

§1. Criminal Liability for Usurpation of Know-How

1062. The possessor of a know-how may use the classical incriminations of theft (if documents were stolen);[627] breach of faith (which implies the existence of a contract between the victim and the offender); or the new incriminations relating to the violation of computer software (Article 323-1, New Penal Code).

1063. A specific incrimination is provided as for 'the disclosure of secret of manufacture' by Article L. 1227-1 of the Labour Code, to which Article L. 621-1 of the IP Code sends back.

1064. Article L. 1227-1 states: 'The fact, for any director or employee of a firm where he is employed, to disclose or attempt to disclose a secret of manufacture is punished by two years' imprisonment and EUR 30,000 fine.'

1065. The tribunal may also order, as a supplementary sanction, for a duration of at most five years, the prohibition to exercise the civil and family rights provided for by Article 131-26 of the Penal Code.

625. Trib. Civ. Seine, 8 Feb. 1962: JCP 1962 II 12854, note J.M. Mousseron: 'This exclusive right may be obtained only by a patent application.'
626. Paris, 3 Jul. 1975: PIBD 1976, III, 219; Gaz. Pal., 21 Jan. 1976, note Calvo and Morelle.
627. Cass. crim., 29 Apr. 1986: JCP 1987 II 20788, note Croze. -12 Jan. 1989: Bull. crim., No. 14.

1066. According to the courts, a secret of manufacture consists of any process of manufacture implying a practical interest, used by an industrialist and kept secret by him against his competitors.[628] The offence is realized when such a secret is disclosed by one of the persons listed in the legal provision, even if it is not used by the beneficiary of the disclosure.[629] Violation of secret of manufacture is an intentional offence: the employee must have acted with the intention to harm his employer.[630]

§2. Civil Liability for Disclosure of Know-How

1067. In cumulation with, or most often independently from the criminal liability, the usurper of a secret information may be liable either in torts or in contracts towards the possessor.

1068. Although the use of an unpatented technique is free, the user may be liable in torts either if he subtracted the information against its possessor's will, or if he used it in a way likely to create confusion.

1069. Violation of a secret implies the existence of an intention to keep the information confidential; there is no usurpation and no liability when the possessor of a technical information did not undertake any steps or measures in order to keep its information secret,[631] so that any person could access it.

1070. Such a secret may be protected either by factual means (locking of the doors of the laboratories, controlling the entrance to industrial premises, etc.), or by creating an obligation of confidentiality for the persons able to access the information.

1071. The usurpation may be the consequence of industrial spying, or various acts of scheming, for instance by the founders of a new corporation in order to learn the know-how of a competitor,[632] especially the massive leading astray of a competitor's employees in order to benefit from their competence and know-how.[633] More generally, such disclosure and/or use may constitute acts of unfair competition.[634]

§3. Liability in Contracts

1072. The contractual obligation to keep the information secret may be accessory of another contract, in the performance of which a person may learn another person's

628. Cass. crim., 15 Apr. 1982: PIBD 1982, III, 207.
629. Cass. crim., 20 Jun. 1973: Ann. propr. Ind. 1975, 85.
630. Cass. crim., 20 Jun. 1973: Bull. crim., No. 289. -Lyon, 19 Dec. 1968: RTD com. 1970, p. 114, obs. Chavanne.
631. Paris, 10 Apr. 1962: Ann. propr. Ind. 1962, 210.
632. Paris, 9 Apr. 1992: PIBD 1992, III, 570.
633. Paris, 29 Sep. 1994: D. 1995, som., p. 210, obs. Serra.
634. For example, Rouen, 13 Jan. 1981: PIBD 1981, III, 62, the contractor who communicates to another sub-contractor plans and designs of his client is liable for unfair competition. – Cass. com., 3 Oct. 1978: D. 1980, jur., p. 55, note Schmidt-Szalewski, exploitation of information communicated during failed pre-contractual negotiations. *See also*: Paris, 27 Sep. 2000: D. 2001, som., p. 1309, obs. Auguet.

know-how, such as a contract for employment, franchising,[635] or a preliminary agreement entered into during the negotiation of another contract.

1073. The communication of a know-how may be the object (main or incidental) of an onerous contract[636] creating an obligation to keep the knowledge secret. It may supplement a patent assignment or licence, since the patent does not necessarily disclose the best mode of use, nor the practical know-how which may be useful in the working of the invention. Such 'mixed contracts' are frequent, and associate the rules of patents and those applicable to know-how. For instance, the royalty to be paid by the licensee may be payable even after the expiration of the patent, if such a royalty also covers the communication of know-how.[637] They are also subject to the rules of competition law, either national[638] and/or EC.

1074. In French law, contracts for communication of know-how are not qualified as 'license' or 'assignment', since there is no exclusive right on unpatented information (*see supra*, paragraphs 1053 et seq): such contracts are subject to the rules of contracts for services.

1075. The disclosure of the secret information in violation of such a contractual obligation of confidentiality entails the liability in contracts: the violator must indemnify the possessor of the know-how according to the rules of contract law.

635. Colmar, 9 Jun. 1982: D. 1982, jur., p. 553, note Burst.
636. Cass. com., 13 Jul. 1966, cited *supra.*
637. Paris, 22 May 1990: Ann. propr. Ind. 1990, 52.
638. For example, a decision by the French Commission technique des ententes of 8 Nov. 1974: J.O. Doc. Adm. 1975, 1216.

Selected Bibliography

Intellectual Property

Alleaume, C. *Propriété intellectuelle.* Montchrestien 2010.

Bergé, J.S. *La protection internationale et européenne du droit de la propriété intellectuelle,* Larcier, coll. 'Manuels', 2015.

Binctin, N. *Droit de la propriété intellectuelle.* LGDJ 2016.

Bruguière, J.M. *Droit des propriétés intellectuelles.* Ellipses, 2nd ed. 2011.

Bruguière, J.M. (dir.). *La propriété intellectuelle entre autres droits*, coll. *Thèmes et commentaires*, série *La propriété intellectuelle autrement.* Dalloz 2009.

Bruguière, J.M. (dir.). *L'articulation des droits de propriété intellectuelle*, coll. *Thèmes et commentaires*, série *La propriété intellectuelle autrement.* Dalloz 2011.

Bruguière, J.M. (dir.). *La propriété intellectuelle dans les droits du marché et de la rivalité concurrentielle.* Dalloz 2016.

Bruguière, J.M., N. Mallet-Poujol & A. Robin (dir.). *Propriété intellectuelle et droit commun.* PUAM 2007.

Marcellin, Y. *Le droit français de la propriété intellectuelle.* CEDAT 1998.

Marino, L. *Droit de la propriété intellectuelle.* PUF 2013.

Vivant, M. (dir.). *Les grands arrêts de la propriété intellectuelle.* Dalloz 2e éd. 2015.

Vivant, M. (dir). *Propriété intellectuelle et mondialisation*, coll. *Thèmes et commentaires*, Dalloz 2004.

Vivant, M. (dir.). *Droit et économie de la propriété intellectuelle.* LGDJ 2014.

Mélanges

Mélanges Daniel Bastian, LITEC, 1974.

Mélanges Georges Bonet, LITEC, 2010.

Mélanges André Bretton et Fernand Derrida, Dalloz, 1991.

Mélanges Jean-Jacques Burst, LITEC, 1997.

Mélanges Henry Cabrillac, LITEC, 1968.

Mélanges Michel Cabrillac, LITEC, 1999.

Mélanges Claude Champaud, Dalloz, 1997.

Mélanges Albert Chavanne, Paris, LITEC, 1990.

Mélanges André Colomer, Paris, LITEC, 1993.

Mélanges Jean Derruppé, Paris, GLN Joly and LITEC, 1991.

Mélanges Henri Desbois, Paris, Dalloz, 1974.

Mélanges Jacques Flour, Répertoire du notariat Defrénois, 1979.

Mélanges Jean Foyer, Paris, PUF, 1997.

Mélanges André Françon, Paris, Dalloz, 1995.

Mélanges Yves Guyon, Paris, Dalloz, 2003.

Etudes Pierre Kayser, Presses univ. Aix-en-Provence, 1979.

Mélanges Xavier Linant de Bellefonds, LITEC, 2007.

Mélanges André Lucas, LexisNexis 2014.

Mélanges Paul Mathély, Paris, LITEC, 1990.

Mélanges Marcel Plaisant, Paris, Sirey, 1960.

Mélanges Paul Roubier, Paris, Dalloz, 1961.

Mélanges Jerry Sainte-Rose, Bruylant, 2012.

Mélanges Joanna Schmidt-Szalewski, LexisNexis, coll. du CEIPI, 2014.

Encyclopaedias

Dalloz. *Répertoire Droit commercial, varii auctores* (*see* specific bibliographies).

Dalloz. *Répertoire Droit civil, varii auctores* (*see* specific bibliographies).

Dalloz. *Répertoire Droit international*, '*Contrefaçon*', by E. Treppoz, '*Propriété intellectuelle (OMC)*', by P. Arhel; and *varii auctores* (*see* specific bibliographies).

Dalloz. *Répertoire, Droit communautaire*, '*Propriété intellectuelle*', by J. Azéma; and *varii auctores* (*see* specific bibliographies).

Juris-Classeur. *Commercial, Marques – Dessins et modèles, varii auctores* (*see* specific bibliographies).

Juris-Classeur. *Commercial, Brevets, varii auctores* (*see* specific bibliographies).

Juris-Classeur. *Propriété littéraire et artistique*, *varii auctores* (*see* specific bibliographies).

Lamy. *Droit commercial.* Industrial property, by J. Azéma (annual re-edition).

Specialized Reviews

Revue internationale du droit d'auteur (RIDA), since 1953.

Selected Bibliography

Les annales de la propriété industrielle et artistique (Ann. propr. Ind), since 1855.

Propriété industrielle, Bulletin documentaire (PIBD, edited by the INPI).

Dossiers brevets (published by the CDE, Faculty of Law, University of Montpellier).

La propriété industrielle et droit d'auteur. Industrial Property and Copyright (Propr. ind., published by WIPO, Geneva).

Cahiers du droit d'auteur.

Legipresse.

European Intellectual Property Review (EIPR).

Revue du droit de la propriété intellectuelle (RDPI).

Revue du droit de la propriété industrielle (Rev. dr. propr. Ind).

Revue internationale de la propriété industrielle et artistique (RIPIA).

Propriétés intellectuelles (Propr. Intell., edited by the IRPI), since 2001.

Propriété industrielle (Propr. industr., edited by LexisNexis), since 2002.

Revue Lamy Droit de l'immatériel (RLDI).

Communication – commerce électronique (Com. com. électr., edited by LexisNexis).

Symposia

Blaizot-Hazard, C. (dir.), *Les droits de propriété intellectuelle sur les inventions et créations des chercheurs salariés*, Paris 5 December 2000, organized by the Académie des sciences and the Académie des sciences morales et politiques; with the collaboration of the Institut de recherche en propriété intellectuelle Henri-Desbois (IRPI); Paris Londres New York: Ed. Tec & Doc, 2001.

Nourissat, C. & E. Treppoz (dir.), *Droit international privé et propriété intellectuelle – Nouveau cadre, Nouvelles stratégies*, Lyon 4 June 2009, Université Lyon 3 Jean Moulin, Lamy coll. Axe Droit, 2010.

Publications of the Institut de Recherche en Propriété Intellectuelle Henri Desbois (IRPI) (http://www.irpi.fr/publications/?ref_arbo=32).

Publications of the Centre d'études internationales de la propriété intellectuelle (Strasbourg) (http://www.ceipi.edu/uploads/media/Collection_CEIPI_04.pdf).

Articles

Binctin, N. 'La loi renforçant la lutte contre la contrefaçon'. *JCP E* 2014, act. 270.

Buffet Delmas d'Autane, X & J. Fabre 'Nouveauté, clarification, carences et incertitudes du dispositif de lutte contre la contrefaçon tel que renforcé par la loi n° 2014-315 du 11 mars 2014'. *Propr. industr.* 2014, étude 12.

Galloux, J.C. 'La loi 2014-315 du 11 mars 2014 renforçant la lutte contre la contrefaçon: vers la saturation ?'. Propr. intell. 2014, p. 242.

Galloux, J.C. 'Les lois n° 2014-315 renforçant la lutte contre la contrefaçon et n° 2014-344 du 17 mars 2014 relative à la consommation'. *RTD com.* 2014, p. 579.

Part I. Copyright and Neighbouring Rights

Treatises and Manuals

Bertrand, A. *Droit d'auteur*. Paris, Dalloz, coll. Dalloz Action 3rd ed. 2011–2012.

Caron, C. *Droit d'auteur et droits voisins*. Paris, LITEC, 4th ed. 2015.

Chatelain, F. *Œuvres d'art en droit français*. Paris, Berger-Levrault, 2nd ed. 1990.

Colombet, C. *Les grands principes du droit d'auteur et des droits voisins dans le monde*. Paris, LITEC, 2nd ed. 1992.

Colombet, S. *Propriété littéraire et artistique*. Paris, Dalloz, coll. Précis Dalloz, 9th ed. 1999.

Derieux, E. *Droit de la communication*. Paris, Victoires, Legipresse, 3rd ed. 2011.

Desbois, H. *Le droit d'auteur en France*. Paris, Dalloz, 3rd ed. 1978.

Dumas, R. *Propriété littéraire et artistique*. Paris, PUF, coll. Thémis, 1987.

Edelman, B. *Droits d'auteur, droits voisins, droit d'auteur et marché*. Paris, Dalloz, 1993.

Françon, A. *Le droit d'auteur (Aspects internationaux et comparatifs)*. Cours à l'Université McGill, Montreal, ed. Y. Blais, 1993.

Françon, A. *Cours de propriété littéraire, artistique et industrielle*. Paris, LITEC-Les Cours de Droit, 2001.

Gautier, P.-Y. *Propriété littéraire et artistique*. Paris, PUF, coll. Droit fondamental, 10th ed. 2017.

Greffe, P., F. Greffe, P.-B. Greffe, & M. Lévy. *La publicité et la loi*. Paris, LITEC, 11th ed. 2009.

Hassler, Th. & Y.H. Nédélec. *Guide pratique des contrats de l'audiovisuel*. Paris, LITEC, 1992.

Le Tarnec, A. *Manuel de le propriété littéraire et artistique*. Paris, Dalloz, 2nd ed. 1966.

Selected Bibliography

Linant de Bellefonds, X. *Droits d'auteur et droits voisins*. Paris, Dalloz, Coll. Cours Dalloz Série Droit privé, 2nd ed. 2004.

Linant de Bellefonds, X. & C. Caron. *Droit d'auteur et droits voisins*. Paris, Delmas, 1996.

Lucas, A. *Droit d'auteur et numérique*. Paris, LITEC, 1998.

Lucas, A. *Propriété littéraire et artistique*. Paris, Dalloz, coll. Connaissance du Droit, 5th ed. 2015.

Lucas, A., H.-J. Lucas & A. Lucas-Schloetter. *Traité de la propriété littéraire et artistique*. Paris, LITEC, 4th ed. 2012.

Olagnier, P. *Le droit d'auteur*. Paris, LGDJ, 1934.

Plaisant, R. *Propriété littéraire et artistique*. Paris, Delmas, 1985.

Pollaud-Dulian, F. *Le droit d'auteur*. Paris, Economica, 2nd ed. 2014.

Pouillet, E. *Traité théorique et pratique de la propriété littéraire et artistique et du droit de représentation*. Paris, Imprimerie et Librairie Générale de Jurisprudence, 3rd ed. by G. Maillard and C. Claro, 1908.

Savatier, R. *Le droit de l'art et des lettres*. Paris, LGDJ, 1953.

Sirinelli, P. *Propriété littéraire et artistique*. Paris, Dalloz, coll. Mémentos Dalloz, 3rd ed. 2016.

Steward, S.M. *International Copyright and Neighboring Rights*. London, Butterworth, 2nd ed. 1989.

Vivant, M. & J.-M. Bruguière. *Droit d'auteur et droits voisins*. Paris, Dalloz, coll. Précis Dalloz, 3rd ed. 2015.

Monographs

Azzi, T. Recherche sur la loi applicable aux droits voisins du droit d'auteur en droit international privé. LGDJ, 2005.

Bergé, J.S. *La protection internationale et communautaire du droit d'auteur. Essai d'une analyse conflictuelle*. Paris, LGDJ, 1996.

Blaizot-Hazard, C. *Les droits de propriété intellectuelle des personnes publiques*. Paris, LGDJ, 1992.

Bochurberg, L. *Le droit de citation*. Paris, Masson, 1994.

Boncompain, A.J. *La Révolution de auteurs, Naissance de la propriété intellectuelle (1783–1815)*. Fayard 2001.

Bouche, N. *Le principe de territorialité de la propriété intellectuelle*. Paris, L'Harmattan, Coll. Logiques juridiques, 2002.

Caron, C. *Abus de droit et droit d'auteur*. Litec 1998.

Carreau, C. *Mérite et droit d'auteur*. Paris, LGDJ, 1981.

Castell, B. *Contribution à la règle de l'épuisement du droit intellectuel en droits allemand, français et communautaire*. Paris, PUF, 1989.

Cherpillod, Y. *L'objet du droit d'auteur*. Université de Lausanne, CEDIDAC, and Paris, LITEC, 1985.

Cornu, M. & N. Mallet-Poujol. *Droit, œuvres d'art et musées*. CNRS Droit, CNRS Editions 2001.

Daverat, X. *L'artiste-interprète*. Thesis, Univ. Bordeaux 1, multigr., 1990.

de Pierredon-Fawcett, L. *Le droit de suite en propriété littéraire et artistique. Etude de droit comparé*. Thesis, Univ. Paris-Sud, multigr., 1984.

Desbois, H., A. Françon & A. Kéréver. *Les conventions internationales du droit d'auteur et des droits voisins*. Paris, Dalloz, 1976.

Desjeux, X. *La convention de Rome (10-26 octobre 1961)*. Paris, LGDJ, 1966.

Desurmont, Th. *L'incidence du droit d'auteur sur la propriété corporelle des œuvres d'art*. Thesis, Univ. Paris 2, Multigr., 1974.

Dietz, A. *Le droit d'auteur dans la Communauté européenne*. Bruxelles, Commission des Communautés Européennes, 12/125/76-F, 1976.

Doutrelepont, C. *La notion de droit voisin. Analyse de droit comparé*, in *Les journées du droit d'auteur*. Collection de la Faculté de Droit de l'Université Libre de Bruxelles, Bruylant, 1989, p. 1.

Durrande, S. *La détermination du pays d'origine de l'œuvre en droit international privé*. Thesis, Univ. Paris 2, multigr., 1980.

Gaudrat, Ph. *Commercialisation des données publiques*. Paris, La Documentation française, 1992.

Gendreau, Y. *La protection des photographies en droit français, américain, britannique et canadien*. Paris, LGDJ, 1994.

Gotzen, F. *Le droit de destination de l'auteur*, Bruxelles, Larcier, 1975. *Les contrats d'exploitation des droits de l'artiste-interprète ou exécutant*, Bruxelles, Commission des Communautés Européennes, 12/47/80-F.

Graz, D. *Propriété intellectuelle et libre circulation des marchandises. Etude de l'épuisement des droits de propriété intellectuelle en droit suisse, en droit communautaire et selon l'accord de libre-échange Suisse-CEE*. Genève, Librairie Droz, 1988.

Hovasse-Banget, S. *La propriété littéraire et artistique en droit des successions*. Thesis, Univ. Rennes, multigr. 1990.

Huet, J. & H. Maisl. *Droit de l'informatique et des télécommunication*. Paris, LITEC, 1989.

Hugon, Ch. *Le régime juridique de l'œuvre audiovisuelle*. Paris, LITEC, 1993.

Huguet, A. *L'ordre public et les contrats d'exploitation du droit d'auteur*. Paris, LGDJ, 1962.

Selected Bibliography

Ilardi, A. *Propriété intellectuelle. Principes et dimension internationale.* Paris, L'Harmattan – Innoval, 2005.

Josselin-Gall, M. *Les contrats d'exploitation en droit international privé.* Paris, GLN Joly, 1995.

Laligant, O. *La divulgation des œuvres artistiques, littéraires et musicales en droit positif français.* Paris, LGDJ, 1983.

Laligant, O. *La véritable condition d'application du droit d'auteur: originalité ou création.* Aix-en-Provence, PUAM 1999.

Latreille, A. *Les mécanismes de réservation et les créations multimédias.* Thesis, Univ. Paris 11, multigr.,1995.

Leloup, J.M. *Le journal, le journaliste et le droit d'auteur.* Paris, LITEC, 1962.

Lucas, A., J. Devèze & J. Frayssinet. *Le droit de l'informatique et de l'Internet.* Paris, PUF, coll. Thémis, 2001.

Macrez, F. 'Créations informatiques: bouleversement des droits de propriété intellectuelle ? Essai sur la cohérence des droits', LexisNexis Litec, 2011.

Parent, E. *Le droit d'auteur sur les créations publicitaires.* Paris, Eyrolles, 1989.

Piotraut, J.-L. *La propriété intellectuelle en droit international et comparé.* Paris, Editions Tec & Doc, Lavoisier, 2007.

Pollaud-Dulian, F. *Le droit de destination. Le sort des exemplaires en droit d'auteur.* Paris, LGDJ, 1989.

Ravillon, L. *Les télécommunications par satellite, aspects juridiques.* Paris, LITEC, 1997.

Raynard, J. *Droit d'auteur et conflits de lois.* Paris, LITEC, 1990.

Recht, P. *Le droit d'auteur, une nouvelle forme de propriété.* Paris, LGDJ, 1969.

Schmidt, A. *Les sociétés d'auteurs, SACEM-SACD, Contrats de représentation.* Paris, LGDJ, 1971.

Sirinelli, P. *Le droit moral de l'auteur et le droit commun des contrats.* Thesis, Univ. Paris 2, multigr., 1985.

Strohmholm, S. *Le droit moral de l'auteur en droit allemand, français et scandinave.* Stockholm, P.A. Norstedt & Söners forlag, Vol. 1, 1967, Vol. 2, Tome 1, 1967, Tome 2, 1973.

Strowel, A. *Droit d'auteur et Copyright. Divergences et convergences. Etude de droit comparé.* Bruxelles, Bruylant and Paris, LGDJ, 1993.

Tafforeau, P. *Le droit voisin de l'interprète d'œuvres musicales en droit français.* Thesis, Univ. Paris 2, multigr., 1994.

Zolynski, C. *Méthodes de transposition des directives communautaires. Etude à partir de l'exemple des droits d'auteur et des droits voisins.* Paris, Dalloz, 2007.

Collective Books

Selected Bibliography

Blin, H., A. Chavanne, R. Drago & J. Boinet (J.H. Robert, dir.). *Droit de la presse*. Paris, LITEC, 2 vol. ann. updated.

Bruguière, J.M. (gen. ed.). *Droit d'auteur et culture*, coll. *Thèmes et commentaires*. série *La propriété intellectuelle autrement*, Dalloz 2007.

Cornish, W.R. (gen. ed.). *Copyright in Free and Competitive Markets*. Oxford, ESC Publishing, 1986.

de Lamberterie, I. (gen. ed.). *Le droit d'auteur aujourd'hui*. Paris, ed. CNRS, 1991.

Dommering, E.J. & P.B. Hugenholtz (gen. ed.). *Protecting Works of Fact*. The Hague, Kluwer, Information Law Series, 1, 1991.

Françon, A. & C. Goyard (gen. ed.). *Les correspondances inédites*. Paris, Economica, 1984.

Nordemann, W., K. Vinck & P.W. Hertin. *Droit d'auteur international et droits voisins dans les pays de langue allemande et les Etats membres de la Communauté européenne*. trad. J. Fournier, Bruxelles, Bruylant, 1983.

Vivant, M., N. Mallet-Poujol & J.M. Bruguière. *Quels droits pour les artistes du spectacle?*. coll. *Thèmes et commentaires*, Dalloz 2009.

Encyclopaedias

Juris-classeurs: 'Propriété littéraire et artistique', 'Droit civil, annexes', fasc. 1050 to 1975, *varii auctores* (A. Lucas, dir.); 'Europe', fasc. 1220, '*Droit européen de l'audiovisuel*' by R. Mastroianni, fasc. 1225, '*Droit des communications électroniques de l'Union européenne*' by P. Achilleas, fasc. 1770, '*Le processus d'harmonisation communautaire du droit d'auteur*' by V.-L. Bénabou; 'Droit international', fasc. 563-60, '*Propriété littéraire et artistique – Le droit commun*' by F. Pollaud-Dulian, fasc. 563-B, '*Propriété littéraire et artistique – Conventions internationales*' by A. Françon, fasc. 568-80, '*Le processus d'harmonisation communautaire du droit d'auteur*' by V.-L. Bénabou.

Répertoire Dalloz, Droit civil, '*Propriété littéraire et artistique*' by P. Gaudrat, '*Informatique – Numérique*' by A. Latreille; *Répertoire Dalloz, Droit communautaire*, '*Droit d'auteur*', by C. Castets-Renard; *Répertoire Dalloz, Droit international*, '*Informatique*', by M. Vivant, '*Internet*', by M. Vivant, '*Propriété littéraire et artistique*', by P.-Y. Gautier, *Lamy Droit des médias et de la communication* (P. Sirinelli, Ch. Gavalda, dir.), *Lamy Droit du numérique* (M. Vivant, dir.).

Articles

Bouche, N. & J. Sainte-Rose. 'Pour la protection des fragrances par le droit d'auteur'. *LPA* 2007, No. 8, p. 4.

Buydens, M. 'La protection des idées originales: Droit d'auteur, responsabilité civile ou droit de la personnalité?'. *RDPI* 1993, 61.

Corbet, J. 'Le développement technologique conduit-il à un changement de la notion d'auteur?'. *RIDA*, April 1991, 59.

Dietz, A. 'Mutation du droit d'auteur. Changement de paradigme en matière de droit d'auteur'. *RIDA*, October 1988, No. 138, p. 61.

Françon, A. 'Le droit d'auteur au-delà des frontières: une comparaison des conceptions civilistes et Common law'. *RIDA*, July 1991, No. 149, p. 19.

Ginsburg, J. 'A tale of two copyrights: literary property in Revolutionary France and America'. *RIDA*, January 1991, No. 147, p. 155.

Hepp, F. 'Le droit d'auteur, propriété incorporelle'. *RIDA*, April 1958, 161.

Kéréver, A. 'Le droit d'auteur est-il anachronique? *Dr. auteur*, 1983, 363. 'Le droit d'auteur: acquis et conditions du développement de la culture juridique européenne'. *Dr. auteur* 1990, p. 146.

Mackaay, E. 'Les droits intellectuels. Entre propriété et monopole'. *J. des économistes et des études humaines*, Vol. 1, Winter 1989-1990, p. 61.

Pollaud-Dulian, F. 'La présomption prétorienne de titularité du droit d'auteur dans l'action en contrefaçon : la jurisprudence Aréo à l'épreuve du temps'. *RTD com.* 2011, p. 45.

Uchtenhagen, U. 'L'importance économique du droit d'auteur'. *Dr. auteur*, 1989, 297.

Industrial Property

Treaties and Manuals

Azéma, J. & J.-C. Galloux. *Droit de la propriété industrielle*. Paris, Dalloz, coll. Précis Dalloz, 7th ed. 2012.

Chavanne, A. & J.J. Burst. *Droit de la propriété industrielle*. Paris, Dalloz, coll. Précis Dalloz, 5th ed. 1998.

Galloux, J.-Ch. *Droit de la propriété industrielle*. Cours Dalloz, 2nd ed. 2003.

Gaumont-Prat, H. *Droit de la propriété industrielle*. coll. Objectif Droit, Cours, 3rd ed. 2013.

Marino, L. *Droit de la propriété industrielle*. Paris, Dalloz, coll. Mémentos Dalloz, 8th ed. 2013.

Passa, J. *Droit de la propriété industrielle, tome 1, Marques et autres signes distinctifs, Dessins et modèles*. LGDJ, 2nd ed. 2010.

Passa, J. *Droit de la propriété industrielle, tome 2, Brevets d'invention, Protections voisines*. LGDJ, 1st ed. 2013.

Pierre, J.L. *Fiscalité de la recherche, de la propriété industrielle et des logiciels*. EFE, 5th ed. 2011 (distributed by LITEC).

Pollaud-Dulian, F. *La propriété industrielle*. Economica 2011.

Roubier, P. *Droit de la propriété industrielle*. Vol. 1, Paris, Sirey, 1952, Vol. 2, Sirey, 1954.

Schmidt-Szalewski, J. & J.L. Pierre. *Droit de la propriété industrielle*. Paris, LITEC, 4th ed. 2007.

Encyclopaedias

Juris-classeurs, '*Droit international*', fasc. 568-10, '*Propriété industrielle – Droit unioniste – Organisation mondiale de la propriété* intellectuelle', by J. Larrieu, fasc. 572-160, '*Condition des étrangers et conflits de lois en matière de propriété industrielle*', by N. Bouche.

Répertoire Dalloz, Droit commercial, '*Propriété industrielle (régime fiscal)*', by E. Cruvelier; *Répertoire Dalloz, Droit international*, '*Propriété industrielle*', by J. Derruppé.

Part II. Patents

Treaties and Manuals

Casalonga, A. *Traité technique et pratique des brevets d'invention,* LGDJ, 1949.

Chavanne, A. & J. Azéma. *Le nouveau régime des brevets d'invention (Commentaire de la loi du 13 juillet 1978)*. ed. Sirey, 1979.

Foyer, J. & M. Vivant. *Le droit des brevets*. Paris, PUF, coll. Thémis, 1991.

Mathély, P. *Le nouveau droit français des brevets d'invention*. Paris, Libr. Journ. Des Not. et Avocats, 2nd ed. 1992. – *Le droit européen des brevets d'invention,* Libr. Journ. Des Not. et Avocats, 1978.

Mousseron, J.M. *Traité des brevets, Vol. 1, L'obtention des brevets*. Paris, LITEC, 1984.

Mousseron, J.M. & A. Sonnier. *Le droit français nouveau des brevets d'invention,* LITEC, 1978.

Passa, J. *Droit de la propriété industrielle, tome 2, Brevets d'invention, Protections voisines*, LGDJ, 1st ed. 2013.

Phelip, B. *Brevets d'invention: France, étranger, brevet européen*. Paris, Delmas, coll. 'Ce qu'il vous faut savoir', 3rd ed. 1989.

Vivant, M. *Droit des brevets*. Dalloz, Connaissance du Droit, 2nd ed. 2005.

Wagret, J.M. *Brevets d'invention, marques et propriété industrielle*. Paris, PUF, coll. 'Que sais-je?', 2001.

Selected Bibliography

Monographs

Alderbert-Salles. *Les clauses de propriété industrielle dans les contrats*. Thesis Univ. Montpellier, multigr., 1989.

de Haas, M. *Brevet et médicament en droit français et en droit européen,* LITEC, 1981.

Dhenne, M. 'Technique et droit des brevets'. Coll. FNDE, LexisNexis, 2016.

Hubert, O. 'Aspects procéduraux de la contrefaçon de brevets d'invention'. Coll. FNDE, LexisNexis, 2017.

Le Stanc, Ch. *L'acte de contrefaçon de brevet d'invention*, LITEC, 1977.

Lucas, A. *La protection des créations industrielles abstraites*, LITEC, 1975.

Schmidt, J. *L'invention protégée après la loi du 2 janvier 1968*, LITEC, 1972.

Vivant, M. *Juge et loi du brevet*, LITEC, 1977.

Collective Books

Boucourechliev, J. & J.M. Mousseron (dir.). *Les brevets d'invention, rédaction et interprétation*, PUF, 1973.

Gasnier, J.P., & N. Bronzo (dir.). *Les nouveaux usages du brevet: entre innovation et abus*, PUAM, 2014.

Pollaud-Dulian, F. (dir). *La brevetabilité des inventions*. Litec 1997.

Remiche, B. (dir.). *Brevet, innovation et intérêt général.* Larcier 2007.

Encyclopaedias

Répertoire Dalloz, Droit commercial, '*Brevet d'invention*' by J. Schmidt-Szalewski and J.M. Mousseron; *Répertoire Dalloz, Droit communautaire*, '*Brevet*', by J. Schmidt-Szalewski,; *Répertoire Dalloz, Droit international*, '*Brevet d'invention*', by J. Derruppé.

Juris-classeur, *Commercial, Brevets* (Y. Reboul & J.-M. Mousseron, dir.), looseleaf, *varii auctores*.

Articles

Armengaud, J. & E. Berthet-Maillols. 'La loi du 27 février 2007 transposant la directive 2004/32/CEE ou le coup de pouce donné aux génériques'. *Propr. intell.* 2007, p. 146.

Selected Bibliography

Azéma, J. 'La brevetabilité de la seconde application thérapeutique'. *JCP* 1989 I 3382.

Bronzo, N. 'Le droit moral de l'inventeur'. Propr. industr. 2013, étude 5.

Chavanne, A. & J. Azéma. 'Copropriété de brevets', *RTD com.*, 1981, 419.

Foyer, J. 'Les mirages de la priorité interne'. *JCP* 1992 I 3590.

Françon, A. 'La nullité du brevet'. *RIDC*, 1981, 575.

Galloux, J.C. 'Vers la brevetabilité des animaux-chimères en droit français'. *JCP* 1990 I 3430. – 'La brevetabilité des éléments et produits du corps humain ou les obscurités d'une loi grand public', *JCP* 1995 I 3872.

Goutorbe, F. 'Comparaison et analyse des contraintes relatives à la défense nationale dans les principaux pays européens'. *Propr. industr.* 2007, p. 14 ; *Propr. industr.* 2010, p. 18.

Gutman, E. 'Le brevet, l'éthique : au piège du langage ?'. *Propr. intell.* 2003, p. 348.

Gutman, E. 'Les substances d'origine naturelle : de la découverte à l'invention brevetable. *Propr. intell.* 2005, p. 392.

Le Stanc, Ch. 'Les malfaisants lutins de la forêt des brevets : à propos des patent trolls'. *Propr. industr.* 2008, étude 3.

Le Stanc, Ch. 'L'abus dans l'exercice du droit de brevet : les 'patent trolls''. *Propr. industr.* 2010, dossier 8.

Liotard, I. 'Les brevets sur les méthodes commerciales : état des lieux et perspectives économiques. *Propr. intell.* 2014, p. 615.

May, B. & M. Liens. 'Le caractère technique et l'éléphant'. *Propr. industr.* 2011, étude 5.

Mousseron, J.M. 'Contrefaçon et recours de l'utilisateur industriel'. *Rev. dr. Aff. Int.*, No. 5, 1991, p. 715. – 'Les inventions de salariés', *RTD com.*, 1980, 185.

Pérot-Morel, M.A. 'L'incidence, sur le droit français, de la Convention de Strasbourg unifiant certaines règles des brevets d'invention'. *JCP* 1965 I 1905.

Pollaud-Dulian, F. 'L'adieu au brevet et le retour à la Nature des séquences d'ADN'. *D.* 2013, p. 2594.

Py, E. 'Droit des brevets : la modification des revendications après la délivrance du brevet en droit français'. *Propr. industr.* 2013, étude 3.

Roux-Vaillard, S. & L. Lemercier. 'Limitation de brevets en France : trois ans après'. *Propr. industr.* 2012, étude 2.

Salvage-Gerest, P. 'Le gage des brevets d'invention'. *JCP* ed. CI, 1978 II 12781.

Schmidt-Szalewski, J. 'La distinction entre l'action en contrefaçon et l'action en concurrence déloyale dans la jurisprudence'. *RTD com.*, 1994; 455; – 'L'adaptation du droit des brevets aux nouvelles technologies', *Propr. Industr.* 2002, chron. 3.

Schmitt, Ph. 'La limitation du brevet devant l'INPI'. *Propr. industr.* 2012, étude 5.

Stenger, J.P. 'Le régime de l'antériorité tenant dans une demande de brevet antérieure non encore publiée'. *RD propr. intell.* 159/2004, p. 41.

Véron, P. & I. Romet 'Brevets : limiter pour consolider ?'. *Propr. industr.* 2009, étude 23.

Vivant, M. 'Brevetabilité de la seconde application thérapeutique'. *JCP* ed. E, 1989 II 15541.

Vivant, M. & M. Bruguière. 'Réinventer l'invention?'. *Propr. Ind.* 2003, No. 8, p. 286.

Warusfel, B. 'Pour un veritable examen au fond des demandes de brevet français'. *Propr. intell.* 2012, No. 43, p. 273.

Part III. Utility Models

Pérot-Morel, M.A. 'L'ambiguïté du concept de modèle d'utilité'. in Mélanges Franceschelli, Milano, Giuffrè, 1983, p. 425.

Part IV. Trademarks

Treatises and Manuals

Bazire, Y. 'Les fonctons de la marque. Essai sur la cohérence du régime juridique d'un signe distinctif'. Paris, Litec, coll. CEIPI, 2015.

Bertrand, A. *Le droit des marques, des signes distinctifs et des noms de domaine: droit français, droit communautaire et droit international.* Paris, CEDAT 2002.

Bertrand, A. *Droit des marques.* Paris, Dalloz Action 2014–2015.

Dreyfus, N. & B. Thomas. *Marques, dessins et modèles.* Encycl. Delmas, 2002.

Mathély, P. *Le nouveau droit français des marques.* Paris, ed. Journal des Notaires et des Avocats, 1994.

Passa, J. *Droit de la propriété industrielle, tome 1, Marques et autres signes distinctifs, Dessins et modèles.* LGDJ, 2nd ed. 2010.

Saint-Gal, Y. *Protection et défense des marques de fabrique et concurrence déloyale: droit français et droits étrangers.* Delmas, 5th ed. 1982, updated 1991.

Schmidt-Szalewski, J. *Le droit des marques.* Dalloz, Connaissance du Droit, 1997.

Encyclopaedias

Répertoire Dalloz, Droit commercial, 'Marques de fabrique, de commerce ou de service' by J. Schmidt-Szalewski; *Répertoire Dalloz, Droit communautaire, 'Marque'* byR. Kovar; *Répertoire Dalloz, Droit international, 'Marque'*, by J. Derruppé.

Juris-classeur, *Commercial, Marques – Dessins et modèles* (G. Bonet, dir.), looseleaf *varii auctores*; Juris-classeur, *Droit international*, fasc. 563-40, '*Marque communautaire*', by M. Luby.

Articles

Arhel, P. 'Les marques notoires. Protection à l'épreuve du droit de la concurrence'. *JCP* ed. E, 1993 I 214.

Bonet, G. 'La marque constituée par un nom géographique en droit français'. *JCP* ed. E, 1990 II 15931.

Bonet, G. 'La très prochaine réforme du droit des marques dans l'Union européenne, communautarisation du droit national de marque'. *Propr. intell.* Jan. 2015, No. 54, p. 4.

Bouche, N. 'La déchéance de la marque devenue déceptive'. *RJDA*, March 2002, p. 183.

Chavanne, A. 'Modèles et marques de fabrique'. in Mélanges Henri Desbois, p. 119. 'Fraude et dépôts attributifs en matière de marques', in Mélanges Bastian, 475.

Durrande, S. 'Du bâtonnet glacé à l' "Esquimau", ou les avatars des marques devenues la désignation usuelle d'un produit'. *D.* 1991, chr. p. 234.

Folliard-Monguiral, A. 'Le caractère distinctif acquis par l'usage'. *Propr. industr.* 2004, chron. p. 9.

Foulon Pigagnol, I. 'Les conflits entre marques de fabrique et autres signes distinctifs'. *D.* 1978, chr. p. 159.

Foyer, J. 'Le terme du renouvellement en matière de marques'. *JCP* ed. E, 1993 I 301.

Françon, A. 'La prohibition des marques descriptives en droit français'. *RIPIA*, 1973, p. 270; – 'L'épuisement du droit de marque'. *JCP* 1990 I 3428.

Le Tallec, G. 'La primauté des appellations d'origine contrôlées sur les marques'. in Mélanges Paul Mathély, p. 249.

Mathély, P. 'Marques collectives et marques de certification'. in Mélanges Albert Chavanne, p. 241; – 'La recevabilité de l'action en déchéance de marques sous l'empire de la loi de 1991', *Ann. propr. Ind.* 1994, 3 and 1995, 3.

Nussenbaum, M. 'L'évaluation du préjudice de marque. Le cas particulier de l'atteinte à l'image de marque'. *JCP* ed. E, 1993 I 303.

Pérot-Morel, M.A. 'L'opposabilité des antériorités en matière de marques'. *RTD com.*, 1971, 247; – 'L'usage du nom patronymique d'autrui à titre de marque', in Mélanges Henri Desbois, Dalloz, 1974, p. 181; – 'La dégénérescence des marques par excès de notoriété', in Mélanges Bastian, p. 49; – 'La marque emblématique', in Mélanges Albert Chavanne, LITEC, 1990, p. 259.

Pollaud-Dulian, F. 'L'usage du nom patronymique comme nom commercial'. *JCP* 1992 I 3618; – 'La déchéance pour défaut d'exploitation des marques et le droit transitoire'. *JCP* ed. E, 1995 I 470. – 'Marques de renommée. Histoire de la dénaturation d'un concept'. *Propr. intell.* 2001, n°1, p. 43.

Requéna, G. 'L'évolution récente de la jurisprudence française en matière d'appréciation de la contrefaçon de marque'. *D.* 2001, p. 3602.

Reboul, Y. 'La distribution sélective et la contrefaçon de marque'. *Cah. Dr. entrep.*, Suppl. *JCP* ed. E, 1988, No. 2, p. 35.

Part V. Trade Names

Encyclopaedias

Répertoire Dalloz. *Droit commercial, V° Nom commercial* by Collin & Ghestin; *Droit pénal*, eod. V°, by A. Chavanne and J. Azéma.

Articles

Pollaud-Dulian, F. 'L'usage du nom patronymique comme nom commercial'. *JCP* 1992 I 3618.

Part VI. Industrial Designs and Models

Treatises and Manuals

Bertrand, A. *Marques et brevets. Dessins et modèles*. Paris, Delmas, 1995.

Cohen, D. *Le droit des dessins et modèles*. Paris, Economica, 3rd ed. 2009.

Dreyfus, N. & B. Thomas. *Marques, dessins et modèles*. Encycl. Delmas, 2002.

Françon, A. & M.A. Pérot-Morel (dir.). *Les dessins et modèles en question: le droit et la pratique*. Etude du Centre de Recherche sur le droit des affaires de la Chambre de Commerce et d'Industrie de Paris (CREDA), LITEC, 1986.

Greffe, F. & P. Greffe. *Traité des dessins et modèles, France, Union Européenne, Suisse, USA, Amérique Latine*. Paris, LITEC, 9th ed. 2014.

Lalanne-Gobet, C. & P. de Candé. *Dessins et modèles de l'entreprise*. Paris, Delmas, coll. 'Ce qu'il vous faut savoir', 2nd ed. 1998.

Passa, J. *Droit de la propriété industrielle, tome 1, Marques et autres signes distinctifs, Dessins et modèles*. LGDJ, 2nd ed. 2010.Pérot-Morel, M.-A. *Les principes de protection des dessins et modèles dans les pays du marché Commun*. Paris, ed. Mouton, 1968.

Perret, F. *L'autonomie du régime de protection des dessins et modèles*. Geneva, Librairie de l'Université, 1974.

Pouillet, E. *Traité théorique et pratique des dessins et modèles*. 5th ed. by Taillefer and C. Claro, Paris, Marchal and Godde, 1911.

Encyclopaedias

Répertoire Dalloz, Droit commercial, 'Dessins et modèles' by J. Passa; *Répertoire Dalloz, Droit communautaire, 'Dessins et modèles'* by G. Bonet; *Répertoire Dalloz, Droit international, 'Dessins et modèles'*, by J. Derruppé.

Juris-classeur. *Commercial, Marques – Dessins et modèles* (G. Bonet, dir.), looseleaf, *varii auctores*.

Articles

Beier, F.K. 'L'industrial design entre deux chaises?' in *Etudes en l'honneur de Antoine Braun*, Bruxelles, Larcier, 1994.

Binctin, N. 'L'apparence en droit des dessins et modèles : le critère du caractère individuel'. *Propr. industr*. 2013, étude 7.

Cohen Jehoram, H. 'La protection des dessins et modèles entre la législation sur le droit d'auteur et celle sur les dessins et modèles'. *Dr. d'auteur*, 1983, 313.

de Candé, P. 'La protection en France des dessins et modèles déposés depuis l'ordonnance n. 2001-670 du 25 juillet 2001', *Propr. intell.* 2002, No. 3, p. 16.

Gaubiac, Y. 'La théorie de l'unité de l'art'. *RIDA*, 1982, 2.

Greffe, F. 'L'ordonnance du 25 juillet 2001: une harmonisation limitée et inutile'. *JCP* ed. E, 2001 I, p. 1900.

Humblot, 'Nouveauté, caractère propre: un fauteuil pour deux. Regard critique sur les critères "objectifs" de la protection des dessins et modèles'. *JCP* ed. E, 2003, I, p. 902.

Kamina, P. 'Le nouveau droit des dessins et modèles'. *D.* 2001, chr., p. 3258. – 'Propos dissidents sur l'arrêt Philips Electronics et le critère de la multiplicité des formes'. *Propr. industr*. 2003, comm. 82.

Piatti, M.C. 'Autonomisation du droit français des dessins et modèles'. *Propr. industr.* 2004, chron. 4.

Pérot-Morel, M.A. 'Les difficultés d'application de l'article 2 alinéa 2 de la loi du 14 juillet 1909'. *JCP* 1966 I 2045; – 'L'application respective du régime de protection des dessins et modèles et des inventions brevetables', *RTD com.*, 1976, 23; – 'Les limites de l'autonomie de la volonté dans les contrats relatifs aux dessins et modèles industriels', in Mélanges André Françon, Dalloz, 1995, p. 337 ; – 'A propos du maintien de l'unité de l'art dans le nouveau droit des dessins et modèles'. Propr. industr. 2005, chron. 9.

Raynard, J. 'Du nouveau droit français des dessins et modèles: de l'influence de l'ordonnance du 25 juillet 2001 sur le principe de l'unité de l'art'. *Propr. Industr.* 2002, chron. 2; – 'A propos de l'application dans le temps de l'ordonnance du 25 juillet 2001 réformant le droit français des dessins et modèles', *Propr. Industr.* 2003, chron. 6.

Reichman, J.H. 'La protection des dessins et modèles et les nouvelles technologies: l'expérience des Etats-Unis dans une perspective transnationale'. *Propr. Ind.*, 1991, p. 220.

Rodhain, C. Dépôt de modèle simplifié. Loi du 5 février 1994'. *JCP* ed. E, 1995 I 449; – 'Contrefaçon, réparation, indemnisation', *Gaz. Pal.*, 1980, 2, doct., p. 470.

Schmidt-Szalewski, J. 'La distinction entre l'action en contrefaçon et l'action en concurrence déloyale dans la jurisprudence'. *RTD com.*, 1994, 455.

Part VII. Plant Variety Protection

Treatises and Manuals

Bergmans, B. *La protection des inventions biologiques*. Bruxelles, Larcier, 1992.

Clavier, J.-P. *Les catégories de la propriété intellectuelle à l'épreuve des créations génétiques*. Paris, L'Harmattan, 1998.

Hermitte, M.A. (dir.). *La protection de la création végétale. Le critère de nouveauté*. LITEC, 1985. – *Le droit du génie génétique végétal*, LITEC, 1987.

Passa, J. *Droit de la propriété industrielle, tome 2, Brevets d'invention, Protections voisines*. LGDJ, 1st ed. 2013.

Würtenberger, G. et al. *European Community Plant Variety Protection.* New York: Oxford University Press, 2006.

Monographs

Bouvet, T. *La protection juridique de l'innovation végétale*, Thesis Univ. Versailles Saint-Quentin-en-Yvelines, multigr., 2000.

Collective Books

Institut de Recherche en Propriété Intellectuelle Henri Desbois (IRPI), 'Les inventions biotechnologiques', Litec 1999.

Encyclopaedias

Répertoire Dalloz, Droit commercial, 'Obtentions végétales', by N. Bouche; *Répertoire Dalloz, Droit communautaire, 'Obtentions végétales'*, by C. Grynfogel.

Articles

'De la protection des nouveautés végétales'. *Propr. ind.* 1932. p. 58.

Beier, F.K. & J. Straus. 'Le génie génétique et la propriété industrielle'. *Propr. ind.* 1986. p. 490.

Bonet, G. 'Pratique et abus en matière de créations variétales'. *RDPI* 1997, No. 82, p. 11.

Bouche, N. 'Variété essentiellement dérivée – Entre ombre et lumière', *Propr. industr.*, 2011, étude 2.

Bouche, N. 'La réforme du droit français des obtentions végétales. Loi n° 2011-1843 du 8 décembre 2011', Propr. industr., 2012, étude 13.

Bouche, N. 'Les premiers décrets d'application de la loi n° 2011-1843 du 8 décembre 2011 relative aux certificats d'obtention végétale', Propr. industr. 2014, étude 21*.

Bouche, N. 'Obtentions de salariés, de fonctionnaires ou d'agents publics', Propr. industr., mai 2015, étude 11.

Buffet Delmas d'Autane, X. & A. Doat. 'La protection des plantes: entre brevet et certificate d'obtention végétale'. *Propr. industr.* 2004, chron. 8.

Bustin, N. & M.-J. Guiard. 'Rapport sur la conference diplomatique de révision de la Convention internationale pour la protection des obtentions végétales'. *PIBD* 1991, II 91.

Caron, C. 'La loi n°2004-1338 du 8 décembre 2004 relative à la protection des inventions biotechnologiques'. *JCP* ed. G 2005, Aperçu rapide, No. 42, p. 297.

Chavanne, A. 'La protection des inventions végétales'. *D.* 1954, chr., p. 95.

de Coustin, A. 'A quelle exigence une variété végétale doit-elle satisfaire pour être protégeable?'. *Rev. dr. propr. Ind.* 1986, p. 13.

Delpech, H. 'La loi du 11 juin 1970 relative à la protection des obtentions végétales'. *JCP* ed. CI, 1970 I 89461.

Deniniolle, S. 'Une étude de cas: le droit des obtentions végétales à l'épreuve de la pratique'. *JCP* ed. E, 1987 II 15014.

Edelman, B. 'Le droit et le vivant'. *La Recherche*, July–August 1989, p. 966.

Galloux, J.-C. 'La protection juridique de la matière biologique en droit français'. *RIDC* 2-1998, p. 491.

Laclavière, B. 'La Convention de Paris, du 2 décembre 1961, pour la protection des obtentions végétales et l'Union internationale pour la protection des obtentions végétales'. *Propr. ind.* 1965, p. 232.

Le Buanec, B. 'Protection des variétés végétales: le fond du problème'. *Biofutur*, March 1990, p. 41.

Passa, J. 'La protection par brevet des semences génétiquement modifiées'. *Propr. industr*. 2005, étude 13.

Piatti, M.-C. & A. Jouffray. 'Plant Variety in National and International Law'. *EIPR* 1984, No. 10, p. 283 and No. 11, p. 311.

Royon, R. 'Le régime de la protection des obtentions végétales'. *Ann. propr. Ind.*, 1972, 1.

Straus, J. 'Le principe de la 'dépendance' dans le droit des brevets et le droit de l'obtenteur'. *Propr. ind.* December 1987, p. 473.

Designations of Origin or Geographical Indications

Encyclopaedias

Répertoire Dalloz, Droit commercial, '*Appellations d'origine et indications de provenance*', by N. Olszak; *Répertoire Dalloz, Droit communautaire*, '*Appellations d'origine*', by F. Pollaud-Dulian; *Répertoire Dalloz, Droit international*, '*Appellations et indications* d'origine', by J. Derruppé Juris-classeur, *Commercial, Marques – Dessins et modèles* (G. Bonet, dir.), looseleaf, *varii auctores*.

Part VIII. Chip Protection

Bonneau, G. 'La loi du 4 novembre 1987 relative à la protection de topographies des produits semi-conducteurs. Une nouvelle philosophie de la propriété intellectuelle'. *Gaz. Pal.* 1991, 1, doct., p. 15.

Combaldieu, J.C. 'La protection des circuits intégrés en France'. *Propr. Ind.*, 1988, 283.

Ferry, N. & D. Hurstel. 'La protection juridique des semi-conducteurs'. *JCP* ed. E, 1986 II 14800.

Part IX. Trade Secrets/Confidential Information

Selected Bibliography

Burst, J.J. *Breveté et licencié, leurs rapports juridiques dans le contrat de licence*. LITEC, 1970.

Centre Paul Roubier. *La propriété industrielle et le secret*. Symposium Lyon, 1996, LITEC, 1995.

Deleuze, J.M. *Le contrat international de licence de know-how*. Paris, Masson, 4th ed. 1988.

Fabre, R. *Le know-how: sa réservation en droit commun*. LITEC, 1976.

Gaudin, J.H. *Stratégie et négociation des transferts de techniques*. Paris, ed. Moniteur, 1993.

Jehl, J. *Le commerce international de la technologie. Approche juridique*. LITEC, 1985.

Lapousterle, J. 'Les secrets d'affaires à l'épreuve de l'harmonisation européenne'. *D.* 2014, p. 682.

Magnin, F. *Le Know-how et la propriété industrielle*. LITEC, 1974.

Mousseron, J.M. *Rép. Com. Dalloz, V° Savoir-faire*'; – 'Problèmes juridiques du know-how', in *Cahiers de Droit de l'entreprise*, JCP ed. CI, No. 1/1972, p. 1; – 'Secret et contrat' in *Mélanges Foyer*, PUF 1997, p. 257.

Passa, J. *Droit de la propriété industrielle, tome 2, Brevets d'invention, Protections voisines*. LGDJ, 1st ed. 2013.

Reboul, Y. *Les contrats de recherche*. LITEC, 1978.

Encyclopaedias

Répertoire Dalloz, Droit commercial, '*Savoir-faire*', by J. Schmidt-Szalewski.

Index

The numbers here refer to paragraph numbers.

Action for declaration of non-infringement, 578
Action for infringement
- copyright, 314
- designs and models, 927
- patents, 581
- trademarks, 815

Adaptations, 48, 52, 85, 122, 139, 199, 206, 208, 214, 425
Aesthetic creations, 361, 887
Animal varieties, 369
Annual fees, 429, 448, 569, 1000
Antitrust, 534, 538, 540, 790
Arbitration, 584, 824, 1050
Architecture, 54, 56, 182, 205
Art works, 54
Assignment
- chip protection, 1029
- copyright, 148, 220, 223, 224, 249, 272
- designs and models, 910
- neighbouring rights, 275, 288, 296
- patents, 493
- plant varieties, 983
- trademarks, 660, 753
- tradenames, 874

Audiovisual communication firms, 275, 291
Audiovisual works, 61, 124, 133, 148, 169, 180, 196–198, 251, 277–279, 281
Author, 127

Bad faith, 300, 301, 310, 313, 454, 462, 532, 599, 752, 822, 827–828, 836, 839, 909, 943, 1003
Berne Convention, 43, 232, 255, 468
Biotechnologies, 368, 987

Certificate of utility *see* Utility models
Civil servants, 146, 478, 488
Collecting societies, 159, 219, 231, 270, 277, 288, 303, 314, 320, 333
Collective works, 69, 127, 141, 201, 251
Comparative advertisement, 797
Composite works, 139, 199
Compulsory licences, 433, 545, 582, 753, 913, 989, 992, 1030, 1037
Computer software, 66, 127, 144, 157, 227, 241, 321, 323, 324, 331, 332, 333, 335, 341–342, 363, 414, 668, 1062
Conferences, 50
Confidential information, 376, 1053
Confiscation
- chip protection, 1048
- copyright, 314
- databases, 107, 345
- designs and models, 951
- neighbouring rights, 345
- patents, 610–612
- plant varieties, 1010–1011
- trademarks, 854, 861

Conflicts of laws, 527
Conglomerates, 519
Copies, 57, 72, 77, 78, 86, 115, 216, 221, 224, 227, 241, 242, 260, 299, 321, 902
Copyright, 35, 42
Counterfeit-seizure
- chip protection, 1035, 1040–1042
- copyright, 320
- databases, 88, 323
- designs and models, 936
- neighbouring rights, 262
- patents, 465, 590
- plant varieties, 1006
- software, 323
- trademarks, 831

Criminal liability
legal persons, 106, 336–337, 623, 859, 947, 948, 1016
natural persons, 105, 336, 337, 622, 859, 860, 948, 1015
Criminal sanctions
chip protection, 1044
copyright, 306, 327, 333, 335
designs and models, 946
neighbouring rights, 261
patents, 620
plant varieties, 978, 1014
producer's sui generis right, 104
trademarks, 858
Customs, 325, 595, 828, 846, 861, 940, 1005, 1039

Databases, 35, 42, 48, 82, 99, 116, 120, 139, 163, 227, 241, 319, 321, 323, 324, 345
Designs and models
conditions, 886
duration, 925
formalities, 904
infringement, 927
limitation, 923
ownership, 908
provisional measures, 928
scope, 914
Destination, 44, 73, 117, 221, 299, 328, 348, 460, 730, 745, 794, 848, 883
Disclosure, 168–169, 188, 376–391, 412, 414, 415, 443, 896–899, 967, 1060, 1063, 1066–1067, 1071, 1075
Discovery, 360, 368, 974
Distinctness, 968
Distinguishing force, 651, 662, 705, 728, 840, 866
Documentary search, 441
Droit moral, 35, 76, 120, 137, 146, 165–202, 250, 272–274, 285, 306, 312, 320, 499
Droit de suite, 35, 215, 249, 297, 305
Double patenting, 378
Duration
certificate of utility, 630
chip protection, 1033
copyright, 249
designs and models, 925
neighbouring rights, 260
patents, 565
plant varieties, 999
producer's sui generis right, 98
trademarks, 799

Employees inventions, 478
Equivalence, 400, 596
European Patent, 355, 379, 389, 574, 585, 602
Examination
patents, 432
plant varieties, 979
trademarks, 707
Exhaustion
chip protection, 1032
copyright, 223
designs and models, 922, 924
patents, 575
plant varieties, 996
software, 75
trademarks, 809
Expropriation, 433, 546, 753, 984

Family circle, 210, 243, 260
Family names, 646, 694, 793
Farm saved seed, 997
Fees, 429, 569, 801, 1000
Forfeiture
designs and models, 907, 926
patents, 570
plant varieties, 1000
trademarks, 781, 798, 804, 836
Fraud, 18, 302, 309, 631, 752, 763, 840, 909, 1060

Geographical names, 651, 684, 867
Good faith, 301, 544, 599, 607, 648, 722, 785, 793, 838, 909, 942, 1032
Grant of patent, 448

Homonym, 648

Imitation, 680, 743, 747
Industrial application, 402
Industrial designs, 879

Index

Infringement
  chip protection, 1031, 1035
  copyright, 103, 297
  damages, 343, 613, 855, 949, 1007, 1045
  designs and models, 927
  neighbouring rights, 261
  patents, 452, 577
  plant varieties, 1003
  software, 78
  trademarks, 723, 815
Injunction, 606, 610, 845, 853, 952
Invalidity
  designs and models, 944
  patents, 601
  trademarks, 837
Invention, 358
Inventive step, 394
Inventor, 466

Joint ownership (patents), 470
Joint works, 130, 195, 251

Know-how, 124, 352, 498, 538, 790, 1053

Licence
  chip protection, 1029, 1035
  copyright, 148, 162
  designs and models, 910, 929
  neighbouring rights, 269, 287, 317
  patents, 433, 472, 493, 514, 547, 582, 583
  plant varieties, 985–992
  trademarks, 712, 720, 773, 817
Likelihood of confusion, 65, 174, 696, 722, 749, 827, 875, 877, 920, 945, 1018
Literary works, 46

Madrid Agreement, 636, 639, 677, 717, 759
Man skilled in the art
  inventive step, 394
  novelty, 377
Manufacturing, 459
Marrakesh Convention *see* TRIPs
Medicine, 367, 370, 509, 542, 560, 568, 628, 720
Merit, 44, 125, 348, 883

Microorganisms, 369, 414, 415, 425
Moral right *see* Droit moral
Multimedia, 116, 124, 139, 204, 247, 278, 292
Munich Convention, 353, 355, 379, 402, 602
Musical works, 52

National treatment, 129, 232
Neighbouring rights, 35, 42, 129, 256
Nice Agreement, 636
Non-available books of the twentieth century, 163
Non-obviousness *see* Inventive step
Novelty
  designs and models, 894, 906, 955
  patents, 373, 388, 392, 435, 441
  plant varieties, 965

Oppositions, 712
Ordre public *see* Public order
Originality, 35, 52, 62–63, 67, 117, 119, 207, 264, 392, 662, 894–894, 901, 959
Orphan works, 127, 163
Outer space, 371
Ownership
  chip protection, 1027
  copyright, 68, 127
  designs and models, 908
  patents, 466
  plant varieties, 974
  trademarks, 699, 752

Paris Convention on industrial property, 40, 387, 389, 639, 674, 679
Patent claims, 417
Patents
  application, 404
  duration, 565
  examination, 432
  formalities, 403
  ownership, 466
  product, 460
  process, 461
  scope, 452
Performing artists, 35, 231, 256, 257, 260, 263, 291, 295, 312
Performing right, 151, 210

Perfumes, 124, 639, 645, 688, 693, 728, 734, 870, 919
Personal rights, 694
Phonograms, 231–232, 234, 257, 260, 262, 268, 269, 270, 271, 280, 282–285, 286–289, 293, 295, 310–311, 335, 341, 342
Photocopy, 228
Photographs, 58, 216
Plagiarism, 207
Plans, 54, 362
Plant varieties, 369, 557, 640, 962
  application, 975
  compulsory license, 985–992
  distinctness, 968
  duration, 999
  examination, 978
  exclusive rights, 982
  formalities, 973
  infringement, 1003
  limitations, 993
  ownership, 974, 981, 983
  stability, 972
  transfer, 983
  uniformity, 971
Priority right, 387, 408, 412, 499, 704–705, 965, 977
Prior personal possession, 544
Prior rights
  patents, 392
  trademarks, 675, 707, 712, 797
Private use, 86, 99, 227, 923
Producer, 35, 42, 90, 116, 134, 145, 150, 197, 201–202, 211–234, 256, 257, 260, 269–271, 275, 278, 280
Producer's sui generis right, 90
Producers of phonogram and videogram, 257, 280
Publication, 116, 136, 140, 149, 153, 169, 176, 179, 222, 238, 246, 251–252, 308, 338, 345, 385, 386, 407, 425, 445–447, 469, 585, 589, 612, 710, 854, 860, 895, 906, 907, 916, 951, 970, 979, 994, 1003, 1010, 1048
Public exhibition, 386
Public lending, 75, 94, 224, 240
Public order, 19, 358, 365, 501, 513, 534, 584, 639, 710, 784, 796, 824, 906, 930, 933, 1006, 1050
Public use, 221, 236, 382, 873

Recall or removal from the channels of commerce, 345, 612, 854, 951, 1004, 1010, 1015, 1016, 1048
Registration, 37
  chip protection, 1025, 1039
  designs and models, 348, 624
  patents, 500
  trademarks, 636, 693, 699, 718
Reproduction right, 151, 204, 221, 226, 245, 298
Resale right *see Droit de suite*
Restoration of patents, 572
Rights-management information, 342
Right of destination, 221
Right of information, 319, 594, 833, 938, 1006, 1043

Safeguard copies, 242
Second therapeutic application, 370
Seizure, 102, 169, 337, 345, 606, 816, 830, 928, 939, 1004, 1038
Semiconductor chips, 1021
Sequestration, 318, 606, 816, 928, 1004, 1038
Shop sign, 648, 689, 793, 871
Software *see* Computer software
Sounds, 232, 260, 265, 276, 280, 281, 293, 652
Stability, 972
State of the art, 370, 373, 392, 394, 418
Statistics, 357, 632, 881, 893
Style, 57, 63, 419, 683

Technical copies, 241
Technological measures, 341
Temporary injunction
  chip protection, 1038
  copyright, 103
  designs and models, 928
  neighbouring rights, 345
  patents, 606
  plant varieties, 1004

trademarks, 816, 845
Territoriality, 453, 678
Trademarks
collective, 656
Community trademark, 635
deceptive, 870
figurative, 653
geographical, 642, 651, 684, 867–870
generic, 666
nominal, 646
prohibited, 638
well-known, 631, 676, 679–681, 699, 712, 750–751
Tradenames, 689, 793, 865, 871
Trade secrets, 1053
Translation, 48, 85, 139–140, 149, 157, 199, 206, 214
TRIPs, 40, 224, 232, 388, 550, 564, 639, 679–680, 1022, 1053

Unfair competition, 65, 316, 522, 583, 608, 689, 852, 857, 872, 875, 945, 961, 1071
Uniformity, 971
Unity of art, 126, 348, 883–884, 915, 1052
Unity of invention, 421–422, 435
Use, 732, 797
Utility models, 625–626

Videograms, 231–232, 281
Vindication, 468, 506, 714

Warranty, 503, 528, 771, 785
Washington Treaty (PCT), 356
Works made for hire, 143